BARRY TRAVIS

ALSO BY JIMMY BUFFETT

Tales from Margaritaville

Where Is Joe Merchant?

A Pirate Looks at Fifty

JIMMY BUFFETT

A Pirate Looks
at Fifty

RANDOM HOUSE

NEW YORK

All rights reserved under International and Pan-American Copyright Conventions. Published in the United States by Random House, Inc., New York, and simultaneously in Canada by Random House of Canada Limited, Toronto.

Grateful acknowledgment is made to the following for permission to reprint previously published material:

BUG MUSIC: Four lines from "Banana Republics" by Steve Goodman, Steve Burgh, and Jim Rothermel. Copyright © 1985 by Big Ears Music (ASCAP)/Red Pajamas Music (ASCAP). Administered by Bug Music. All rights reserved. Used by permission.

CORAL REEFER MUSIC: Excerpts from the following songs: "Lone Palm," copyright © 1990 by Coral Reefer Music; "You'll Never Work in Dis Bidness Again," copyright © 1986 by Coral Reefer Music/Warner/Elektra/Asylum/Mopage/Coconutley Music/Jasper-Jeeters Music/Will-Mar/Vernon Dubusque Music; "One Particular Harbour," copyright © 1983 by Coral Reefer Music; "We Are the People Our Parents Warned Us About," copyright © 1983 by Coral Reefer Music; "Jimmy Dreams," copyright © 1987 by Coral Reefer Music; "Landfall," copyright © 1977 by Coral Reefer Music; "Something So Feminine About a Mandolin," copyright © 1976 by Coral Reefer Music; "No Plane on Sunday," copyright © 1986 by Coral Reefer Music/Coconutley Music; "Off to See the Lizard," copyright © 1989 by Coral Reefer Music/Jay Oliver Music; "First Look," copyright © 1986 by Coral Reefer Music; "Creola," copyright © 1986 by Coral Reefer Music/Antisia Music, Inc.; "Strange Bird," copyright © 1989 by Coral Reefer Music/Jay Oliver Music; and "Barometer Soup," copyright © 1995 by Coral Reefer Music/Olas Music/Alsation Music/Jay Oliver Music/Little Flock Music. All excerpts reprinted by permission of Coral Reefer Music.

HUMANICS PUBLISHING GROUP: Excerpt from *The Tao of Leadership* by John Heider. Published by Humanics Publishing Group, 1482 Mecaslin Street NW, Atlanta, GA 30309. Used by permission.

MCA MUSIC PUBLISHING: Excerpt from "Nautical Wheelers," words and music by Jimmy Buffett. Copyright © 1974 by MCA-Duchess Music Corporation; excerpts from "Migration," words and music by Jimmy Buffett. Copyright © 1974 by MCA-Duchess Music Corporation; excerpts from "He Went to Paris," words and music by Jimmy Buffett. Copyright © 1973, 1974 by MCA Music Publishing, a division of Universal Studios, Inc. International copyright secured. All rights reserved. Used by permission.

LIBRARY OF CONGRESS CATALOGING-IN-PUBLICATION DATA
Buffett, Jimmy.
A pirate looks at fifty / Jimmy Buffett.
p.   cm.
ISBN 0-679-43527-1
1. Buffett, Jimmy.   2. Country musicians—United States—Biography.
3. Rock musicians—United States—Biography.
I. Title.
ML420.B874A3   1998b   782.42164'092—dc21   98-10853
[B]   CIP
                                                                             MN

Random House website address: www.randomhouse.com
Printed in the United States on acid-free paper containing a minimum of 50% recovered waste paper, of which at least 10% of the fiber content is post-consumer waste.

24689753
First Edition

"We sit together through the evening and discuss the things that each has saved for the other to hear. We talk of Pegasus—and of how he had died, quietly one night in his stall, for no reason that anyone could ever find."

BERYL MARKHAM

WEST WITH THE NIGHT

For Jane Kennedy

Acknowledgments

I would like to thank the following people for their help in making this trip into a journal: Howard Kaufman, Mort Janklow, Sunshine Smith, Nina Avramides, Mike Ramos, Suki Collins, Rodney Gnoinsky, Priscilla Higham, and Esther Gross.

The people at Random House: Deb Futter, Lee Boudreaux, Margaret Wimberger, Jack Perry, and Wanda Chappell.

But most of all, I would like to thank all the people over the years who have bought my albums and books and have enabled me to live this way. Without an audience, we artists would be a sad lot of self-entertainers. Whether you are a Parrothead or a first-timer, I truly thank you for the enthusiasm you show for my work.

For additional information, photos, and discussions, contact www.margaritaville.com

Contents

SECTION III

Time on the Bottom

SECTION IV

Leaving Florida

SECTION V

Cuba and the Cayman Islands: Latitudes and Attitudes

SECTION VI

Costa Rica: *Pura Vida*

SECTION VII

The Songline: "Mother, Mother Ocean"

SECTION VIII

Another New Year

SECTION IX

Colombia: Send Lawyers, Guns, and Money

SECTION X

The Amazon: A Second Look

SECTION XI

The Islands: The Spicy Kind of Life

Introduction:
Trouble on the Horizon

This journal started out as an attempt at a book. I signed a new book deal, and my publisher was champing at the bit to follow on the heels of the success of *Where Is Joe Merchant?* In the beginning, so was I.

My first idea was to uproot Frank Bama from his life with Trevor in Alaska and send him back down into the fictitious world for another aeronautical adventure. Hell, he had just gotten to Alaska, and he and Trevor deserved a little time together. Then came the idea to go find Tully Mars. He was last heard of sitting in a bar in Margaritaville waiting for Donna Kaye to show up with the lottery winnings, but I couldn't quite figure out where to send him next. I had the idea of finding him on the Amazon running a fireworks company and occasionally running Mr. Twain in local horse races in the jungle. Then I had him buying a ghost ship that had come from the Skeleton Coast of Africa to the coast of Colombia. Next came the idea of a novella. I got halfway through it but didn't have the feel for where I was going. I couldn't find the genuine voice of any characters, new or old. Things were heating up in my other worlds. My scheme to write a musical with Herman Wouk had come to fruition and had siphoned off most of my creative fuel, and there is just so much of that precious propellant to go around. There was trouble on the horizon. My new book stood like a crippled rocket on a launchpad waiting for help so the countdown could continue.

As a pilot I know that if you are flying from point A to point B and a big storm blocks your way, you don't just barrel on through. You either land or do a one-eighty and go back to point A. My characters and story ideas were strung out across my course like a big squall line. I decided to land and wait it out. Eventually the storm clouds would dissipate and the route would become clear again.

You can't force characters into unnatural stories or situations any more than you can force-feed canned peas and carrots to disinterested children. Unsavory legumes and watery fiction are both offensive to the palate. Things happen because they are supposed to. That's how I felt about writing at that point in my life. I wasn't ready to take on the task of a big book. I didn't know what I was going to write about, if anything at all. Then, just when I needed it the most, I got a sign.

A Christmas present appeared on my desk one afternoon. I opened it and browsed through the familiar text and suddenly it came to me in the words of Mr. Twain, "Write what you know about."

SECTION
I

Time on the Water

My Life

(In Four Hundred Words or Less)

When I was growing up in Alabama, the beginning of the new school year was a bad time. It meant the end of summer, which is my season. I packed away my shorts and T-shirts, put on socks, shoes, and my parochial-school uniform, and dragged my ass to class. To make matters worse, the first thing the nuns would make us all do on the first day back was to write about what we had done that summer. Having to recall it all while sitting in the antiseptic atmosphere of a classroom was like staring at the goodies in a bakery window with no money in your pocket. However, the bright side to the ordeal was that it reminded me of what lay ahead the next summer, and I carried those longings through the winter and spring until the last bell of the school year rang and I charged back to the beach. I don't know why the idea of trying to put fifty years of living into the same format occurred to me, but it did, and since I am way too familiar with the format, here it is. In four hundred words or less, this is what has happened from early adolescence until now.

I broke out of the grip of Catholicism and made it through adolescence without killing myself in a car. I flunked out of college. I learned to play the guitar, lived on the beach, lived in the French Quarter, finally got laid, and didn't go to Vietnam. I got back into school, started a band, got a job on Bourbon Street, graduated from college, flunked my draft physical, broke up my band, and went out on the road solo. I signed a record deal, got married, moved to Nashville, had my guitars stolen, bought a Mercedes, worked at *Billboard* magazine, put out my first album, went broke, met Jerry Jeff Walker, wrecked the Mercedes, got divorced, and moved to Key West. I sang and worked on a fishing boat, went totally crazy, did a lot of dope, met the right girl, made another record, had a hit, bought a boat, and sailed away to the Caribbean.

I started another band, worked the road, had my second and last hit, bought a house in Aspen, started spending summers in New England, got married, broke my leg three times in one year, had a baby girl, made more records, bought a bigger boat, and sailed away to St. Barts.

I got separated from the right girl, sold the boat, sold the house in Aspen, moved back to Key West, worked the road, and made more records. I rented an apartment in Paris, went to Brazil for Carnival, learned to fly, went into therapy, quit doing dope, bought my first seaplane, flew all over the Caribbean, almost got a second divorce, moved to Malibu for more therapy, and got back with the right girl.

I worked the road, moved back to Nashville, took off in an F-14 from an aircraft carrier, bought a summer home on Long Island, had another baby girl. I found the perfect seaplane and moved back to Florida. Cameron Marley joined me in the house of women. I built a home on Long Island, crashed the perfect seaplane in Nantucket, lived through it thanks to Navy training, tried to slow down a little, woke up one morning and I was looking at fifty, trying to figure out what comes next.

That might be all some of you want to hear, but for those who want to read a little more, continue on, for though I got most of it all into four hundred words, there is a lot more meat on the bone.

Time on the Water

We sailed from the port of indecision
Young and wild with oh so much to learn
The days turned into years
As we tried to fool our fears
But to the port of indecision I returned
—"UNDER THE LONE PALM"

I wasn't born in a trunk, I was born in a suitcase. But a trunk is where I've kept the scraps of my life for the past fifty years. My many attempts to begin a journal have all fizzled out after a few pages of notes. I have a considerable collection of notebooks, cocktail napkins, memo pads, legal tablets, sparsely filled binders, and mildew-spotted pages that sit in a cedar-lined steamer trunk in my basement on Long Island.

Almost five years ago, when I had the harebrained idea of doing a musical version of my friend Herman Wouk's *Don't Stop the Carnival*, Herman would send me pages of thoughts on the matter from his journal. He had kept a daily journal since 1946. To say the least, I was quite impressed. I envy those who have the discipline to keep a chronological record of events. I do not.

My plan has always been to keep adding to that mess in the trunk and, if I make it to my eighties and am still functioning in the brain-cell department, to retire to a tropical island, buy an old beach house, hire several lovely native girls as assistants, ship in a good supply of rum and red burgundy, and then spend my golden years making a complete picture out of the puzzle pieces in the old steamer trunk. That to me is the way any good romantic would look at his life: Live it first, then write it down before you go.

Any attempts at autobiography before the age of eighty seem pretty self-involved to me. There are a lot of smart middle-aged people but not many wise ones. That comes with "time on the water," as the fisherman says. So the following pages are another stab at completing a journal inspired by the trip that my wife planned for me to celebrate my fiftieth birthday, on December 25, 1996. I am glad to report that my first fifty years were, overall, a lot of goddamn fun. I just followed my instincts and kept my sense of humor. This journal narrates the trip itself as well as stories that the trip dredged up out of my past. I hope you enjoy the ride.

Questions and Answers

Now he lives in the islands
Fishes the pilin's
And drinks his Green Label each day
Writing his memoirs, losing his hearing
But he don't care what most people say
Cause through eighty-six years of perpetual motion
If he likes you, he'll smile and he'll say
Jimmy, some of it's magic, some of it's tragic
But I had a good life all the way

— "He Went to Paris"

Fifty. A mind-boggling thought for a war baby like me. Fifty is not "just another birthday." It is a reluctant milepost on the way to wherever it is we are meant to wind up. It can be approached in only two ways. First, it can be a ball of snakes that conjures up immediate thoughts of mortality and accountability. ("What have I done with my life?") Or, it can be a great excuse to reward yourself for just getting there. ("He who dies with the most toys wins.") I instinctively choose door number two.

I am not the kind of person to spend my fiftieth birthday in the self-help section of Borders bookstore looking for answers to questions that "have bothered me so," as somebody wrote once—those questions that somehow got taken off the multiple-choice quiz of life. It seems that here in America, in our presumably evolved "what about me" capitalistic culture, too many of us choose the wrong goals for the wrong reasons. Today spirituality and the search for deeper meaning are as confusing as the DNA evidence in the O. J. Simpson case. There is a labyrinth of choices, none of which seem to suit me. Granted, I have been too warped by Catholicism not to be cynical, but there are still too many men behind too many curtains for my taste. The creation, marketing, and selling of spirituality is as organized as a bingo game. By the time most of us war babies reached high school, we were pretty much derailed from the natural order of things. We were supposed to grow up, and that's where my problems started. Parents, teachers, coaches, and guidance counselors bombarded me with the same question: "What are you going to do with your life?" I didn't even want to think about that when I was fourteen. My teachers called me a daydreamer. They would write comments on my report card like, "He seems to live in a fantasy world and prefers that to paying serious attention to serious subject matters that will prepare him for life."

The life they were so hell-bent on preparing me for bored the living shit out of me. It seemed way too serious. I saw more meaning in the mysteries of the ocean and the planets than in theology or religion. I was too busy figuring out ways to skip school, go diving, and get laid. My heroes were not presidents; they were pirates. Emerging from adolescence with a healthy "lack of respect for the proper authorities," and a head full of romanticism and hero worship, I was able to come up with an answer.

Q. What are you going to do with your life?
A. Live a pretty interesting one.

I have been called a lot of things in these fifty years on the good old planet Earth, but the thing I believe I am the most is lucky. I have always looked at life as a voyage, mostly wonderful, sometimes frightening. In my family and friends I have discovered treasure more valuable than gold. I have seen and done things that I read about as a kid. I have dodged many storms and bounced across the bottom on occasion, but so far Lady Luck and the stars by which I steer have kept me off the rocks. I have paid attention when I had to and have made more right tacks than wrong ones to end up at this moment—with a thousand ports of call behind me and, I hope, a thousand more to see. My voyage was never a well-conceived plan, nor will it ever be. I have made it up as I went along.

The Fifty-Year Reality Check

A List of Things to Do by Fifty

Learn to play the guitar or the piano

Learn to cook

Play tennis

Learn another language

Surf

Read

Take flying lessons

Travel

Swim with dolphins

Start therapy

Go to New Orleans and Paris

Learn celestial navigation (or at least how to find the planets
    in your solar system)

Go to the library

Floss

Just Getting It on Paper

My writing style is a rather unrefined stream of consciousness; I don't know when to stop telling the story. I have always begun a writing project with a loose idea of a story but without actually knowing where I'm going or how I'm getting there.

I started out wanting to be a Serious Southern Writer. My mother had made me a reader and stressed the legacy of my family's Mississippi roots. William Faulkner, Walker Percy, Eudora Welty, and Flannery O'Connor were household names—Mississippians who had made people take notice. I have a feeling my mother hoped way back then that she might have had her own serious writer in the making.

Then, just as I was about to get serious about journalism, along came that "devil music," and my whole life and direction changed course. Music replaced literature, and nightclubs were more fun than libraries. Yes, that rock 'n' roll had a definite effect on what kind of writer I became. By the time I had spent a few decades on the stages of the world, I knew I might still write one day but that I would never be a Serious Writer. There was this strange stigma I associated with Serious Writers, seeing them as tortured, lonely individuals whose somber fatalistic existences were accentuated by drunkenness, isolation, and depression. Well, I knew I wasn't one of those people. I was too warped by the court-jester–like behavior that's essential to being a good stage performer. I knew that whatever I wrote, it would have a heavy layer of humor. By the time I expanded my horizons from three verses and a couple of choruses to short stories, and then prose, my sense of humor naturally came along for the ride.

Besides, I don't have the talent to compete with the Great Serious Writers. Anyway, writing is not a competition to me. Writing is fun, and I am simply a storyteller. I also really enjoy the self-discipline writing requires. It's a great challenge, like learning celestial navigation or becoming a seaplane pilot. Anyone bellying up to a bar with a few shots of tequila swimming around the bloodstream can tell a story. The challenge is to wake up the next day and carve through the hangover minefield and a million other excuses and be able to cohesively get it down on paper.

Happy Birthday to Me

During my forty-ninth year, I spent a lot of time thinking about what to give myself for my fiftieth birthday. Reaching this landmark was a shock to a lot of people, including me. What immediately came to mind was a trip around the world. Something on the scale of Mark Twain's epic adventure, which he chronicled in *Following the Equator*. I had no intention of producing a six-hundred-page book about my trip like Mr. Twain, but a journey of that proportion would certainly warrant a few words. It is no secret to Twain's fans that *Following the Equator* was not written in celebration of some milestone in his life. He did not sit down and ponder the idea of it as some grand scheme, thought out and planned to the last detail. No, he needed money and was offered a lecture tour.

Through benefit of my middle-class work ethic and thanks to the wonderful loyalty of my Parrothead faithful, I could afford to go on a trip around the world, and as I have stated from the stage on more than one occasion, "Just remember, I am spending your money foolishly."

First of all, I would need a plane. Twain went on a steamship, but I knew that was out of the question. If it were just me, I would pick up an updated copy of Ford's freighter-passage schedules, find myself a selection of tramp steamers, and connect the dots of their rum lines to circle the Earth. No, that would have to wait.

When the Buffetts travel, we resemble some kind of misguided caravan, a cross between the Clampett family moving to Beverly Hills and *Sesame Street* on tour. Besides the human contingency and BSE (baby-support equipment) and favorite foods and fishing tackle and surfboards and computers and flight bags and guitars—and the list goes on. My Citation II jet was too small for such an undertaking. No, this trip would require a unique airplane, and I just happened to have one—a Grumman Albatross that I had bought after my recent crash. One of the reasons I bought her was to travel. I had fantasies of packing up the family in the big old romantic flying boat and heading for parts unknown. However, the fantasies and affections that surrounded this big strange bird were mine and mine alone. Jane, my lovely wife of twenty years, was a veteran of some pretty wild and crazy adventures in our days together, but this airplane was not her style. She had let her lack of adoration for the plane be known after her first 147-mile flight from Palm Beach to Key West. I knew I would never get her to even consider going around the world in my Grumman Albatross at 155 knots. She had other, more logical plans for heading south, like airliners with big comfortable seats.

My next fantasy was to do it in "big iron" and have somebody give me the plane as a birthday present. Fat chance, but remember, when reality looks too ugly, just fantasize. It can't hurt. For those not familiar with the term, "big iron" means a large, fast, and very expensive private plane, like those owned by big corporations, movie companies, and the occasional lucky son of a bitch who happens to invent the pop top or computer chips. My personal favorite fantasy planes in this category are the Gulfstream G-IV and the Dassault Falcon 50. They are as close to the starship *Enterprise* as we can get without going to the Paramount set, and they cost more than the gross national product of most of the countries I wanted to visit on my circumnavigation. Jane told me that if I even thought about chartering such a thing, she wouldn't go. My wife has the looks of Catherine Deneuve and the mind of Mr. Spock. Those who know her know what I am talking about. She has always been the voice of reason in my Peter Pan existence. "Jimmy, why would you rent a G-IV? You already have a goddamn air force. You could put that money to a lot better use." Ouch—the truth. Once again she was making way too much sense. My grand scheme was listing to port. What blew it out of the water was more good advice from another source wiser than me.

Older and Wiser Voices

For whatever reason, I have always had a connection to older people. I think that it must come from my relationship with my grandfather. He was a sea captain and possessed all the attributes one would associate with that calling. Growing up, I was much closer to him than I was to my father. Like so many other patriarchs of his era, my father had come home from World War II with a purpose. His generation had saved the world from Hitler and had dropped the atom bomb on Japan—the ultimate punishment for bad behavior. They had survived the Depression and were bound and determined that their children would never have to endure the hardships they had endured. A noble sentiment indeed, but there was a problem. They wanted to provide their children these opportunities on their terms, but the winds of fate had chosen my generation to be the first one that collectively said, "Wait a minute, don't I have something to say about this?" It was the sixties, and the rest is history.

My father's ambition was for me to go to the naval academy and become a Navy officer. This was a pretty serious plan for a ten-year-old who was still playing pirate, and I wasn't much interested. He and I remained at odds about who and what I was to become through the turbulent years of adolescence and beyond, until it became apparent that I had plotted my own course.

My grandfather, on the other hand, was my Long John Silver, full of tales from the high seas and far-off worlds that ignited my imagination. My history is full of references to him and his influence on me. He was the first in a long line of older and wiser voices that have helped me along the way. The most recent of my wiser voices is a legendary flying-boat captain named Dean Franklin, who befriended me when I first started getting interested in flying boats. He had been the chief pilot for Chalk's Airlines, the flying-boat company in Miami that had gotten me launched as a seaplane pilot, and he had taught Howard Hughes to fly.

My latest visit to Dean's office was not the first time I had gone there to test out a harebrained scheme involving long-distance flying. One day I had come up with what I thought was the ultimate scam. I had bounced into Franklin Aviation and announced to Dean that I wanted to buy a Grumman Goose, completely refurbish it, fly it around the world, and make a documentary called *Jimmy Buffett's Ten Best Bars in the World*. I would fly to places I have been from Hawaii to Tahiti, through the Orient, across North Africa, back to South America, and up the Antilles. I would play in these bars, spend a few days hanging with the locals, and get it all on film. The financing for the project would have to cover the purchase of the Goose. I had spent a good twenty minutes rattling on about this wild idea with the overexuberance of the Tasmanian Devil, and when I had finished, Dean had just looked at me across his desk and laughed that now familiar laugh. He had sat framed against the collage of flying photos on his wall, then stood up and looked at a wall map. He had stared at it for about ten seconds, then began shaking his head and laughing as he turned around and said, "Jimmy, it's a long goddamn way around the world." The words stopped me in my thought process like a good pair of disc brakes. I never did buy a Goose, and flying around the world remained a dream.

On this particular day, when I walked into Dean's office, he picked up my scent like a wise old bird dog. "I guess now that you got a plane that can actually go around the world, you want to do that damn bar tour." He had read my mind, and I could tell by his tone that he still didn't think much of the idea. "Son," he said, "it's still a long goddamn way around the world. Why don't you just do the Caribbean for starters? Think of the money you'll save on fuel, and there's enough adventure in these latitudes to keep you busy." Older and wiser voices can always help you find the right path, if you are only willing to listen.

Down to the Banana Republics

Down to the banana republics
Down to the tropical sun
Go the expatriated Americans
Hoping to find some fun

— STEVE GOODMAN

With my fantasy of an around-the-world ride on the Albatross lying in pieces on the ground, I thought about other options. Europe was out of the question. Winter in Paris—are you kidding? We had already decided not to go to Aspen, where we had lived for a long time and where my first daughter was born. It had been great, but it was time to do something different and stay warm for Christmas.

Next came the idea of a trip halfway around the world to the Orient. Well, let me tell you that it is a long way halfway around the world, and then you come back. You could look at it from any direction and any angle, but the fundamental problem was that it was a fourteen-hour trip over and a fourteen-hour trip back. I pictured myself in a ticket line in Hong Kong or Singapore being crushed to death by a stampeding sea of standby passengers. And to see everything that we wanted to see, we'd have to be on a tight schedule and have it all planned out in advance. It was beginning to look like a summer tour schedule in disguise, and I didn't even get off the road until October. I was not ready to launch this kind of an expedition on Christmas Day.

Then there is the big problem of how we travel. Combine that with the distances involved and I started having flashbacks to Joe Cocker's infamous *Mad Dogs and Englishmen* tour back in the seventies. Dean's words came back to me: "Why don't you just do the Caribbean?"

And that is exactly what we decided to do. The Orient wasn't going anywhere, and so what if Hong Kong wasn't British anymore by the time I got there? We settled on Christmas at home, and then we would take off for Central and South America and the Caribbean. I could write about it, and finish a book that I had due and didn't have a clue as to how to wrap up. There would be fishing and surfing in Costa Rica, mystery in Machu Picchu, and beyond the equator the Amazon jungle and the opera house in Manaus. Those of us who liked big, noisy airplanes (boys) could go on the Albatross. Those who didn't (girls) could ride in the Citation.

And so it came to pass that in the advent of his fiftieth birthday, one James William Buffett decided to venture down to the lands of single-digit latitudes and look for a little adventure.

SECTION
II

Time in the Air

My Idea of Life Insurance

I remember quite vividly the expression on my accountant's face when I received my first big advance check from the record company. I had instructed them to make out two checks, one to my accountant and one to me. After signing the deal, I kept one check and handed my business manager the other, telling him I was on my way to buy a sailboat. He went through his obligatory duties of reminding me that he was paid to make sure that I didn't end up like too many people in the entertainment business. Legend had it that when Errol Flynn's accountant lay on his early deathbed from cashing in too many fun tickets too early, he looked up at the doctor and whispered, "Tell Errol I'm sorry." Then he died.

I explained to my accountant that I appreciated his concern but that I saw the purchase of the boat more as an insurance policy than as a frivolous luxury. To him the boat was just a big-ticket item. To me it was freedom. The rock 'n' roll business is not known for its compassion or job security, and I reasoned that a boat was a home that was paid for. A home that could accompany me anywhere in the world that I chose to go. It did not belong to a bank or to a partner. It was mine to do with what I wanted and go where I pleased. The *Euphoria I* was the first of two great boats that took me to the places I had read about as a kid, and my love of sailing has never diminished. In time it just took a temporary backseat to another kind of boat, one that flew and went to weather a lot better.

Wheels in the Well

In my small office on Long Island amid the music computer, video gear, fly-tying desk, files, backpacks, toolboxes, and the lot is a weathered old bookshelf that houses my transient collection of books. These are the ones that I can't live without, and they go back and forth with me when I migrate like the birds between Florida in the winter and Long Island in the summer. One of my best-liked books on this shelf is called *Poster Art of the Airlines*, and it contains Art Deco posters and magazine ads for the Pan American Clippers and other great flying boats that are no more. My favorite page depicts a Clipper touching down in the lagoon of Bora Bora in French Polynesia. In the foreground, a beautiful island girl lies on the beach under a palm tree with the peaks of Bali Hai in the distance. That poster can transport me, in an instant, back to those days. If there were a time machine (will Microsoft invent one by the turn of the century?), that is where I would go—to the bridge of that flying boat, approaching that very harbor.

Flying boats are like no other machines. They were created out of the same desire to explore that drove the early pathfinders from Columbus to Captain Cook. The giant Sikorsky and Boeing flying boats that took to the skies and the seas more than half a century ago created a mysterious and romantic kind of flying that can never be duplicated. The designers and engineers who brought these flying boats to life built more than airplanes. They created art. But their time was short. Runways built for World War II were the concrete stakes that pierced the heart of the giant flying boat. Wartime ingenuity saw the distinct advantage of planes that could land on runways and in the water, and amphibious airplanes were born.

The Albatross that I presently fly is a third-generation amphibian. Leroy Grumman and his designers at his plant near

Bethpage, Long Island, brought her to life with the primary mission of search-and-rescue and the incredible ability to land in the open ocean if necessary. Most flying boats, including the incredible Boeing 314's, were designed to take off and land in relatively calm water, but necessity being the mother of invention, the Grumman folks accepted the challenge and built one big, tough airplane. The need for such planes has long passed. The Albatross was flown by the Coast Guard up until 1985 and is still in the fleet of the Chilean and Greek air forces. Though their primary purpose was military, these planes possess that inherent romantic spark that still calls to a few crazy people who think taking off and landing on the ocean is about as much fun as you can have with your clothes on. It is that pure romanticism that drew me to flying boats before I ever thought about learning to actually fly one.

It happened back in 1971 when I fled to South Florida from Nashville. I was living in Key West and working weekends in Coral Gables at a coffeehouse named the Flick. It was there that I first heard about Chalk's Airlines' weekend-special seaplane flight to Bimini. For fifty bucks, I could get a round-trip ticket to the Bahamian port and a room for two nights at the Compleat Angler hotel—hangout of Adam Clayton Powell, the flamboyant black congressman from Harlem, and of course, Ernest Hemingway. For an extra twenty bucks I could stay in the room where Hemingway reportedly wrote *To Have and Have Not*. I went for the whole enchilada. I was to show up at the Chalk's terminal on Watson Island in the Port of Miami an hour before flight time and bring a passport or driver's license.

I was there two hours before the flight. The idea that I wasn't traveling in the normal fashion presented itself from the moment the cab dropped me off in front of the terminal, and my excitement only increased when I went inside. This was the way it used to be. The little white building housed the ticket office, and the walls were filled with articles and memorabilia from the airline's early days. Chalk's had been founded by the

legendary Pappy Chalk, who had been driven by his love of
flying and his love of the tropics. At that time Chalk's was not
only one of the last commercial operators of seaplanes, it was
advertised as the safest airline in the world.* There were pictures of the old man Hemingway, Errol Flynn, Marilyn Monroe, and half a dozen antique seaplanes. I no longer wanted to
be a rock star. I wanted to be a flying-boat captain.

I bought my ticket and strolled outside to watch the arrival
of the flight from Nassau. I took a seat in the shade of a Norfolk pine along the seawall and thought about the fact that I
was leaving the country from this spot. I was daydreaming
away when out of nowhere this beautiful plane touched
down in the middle of the channel, framed by the cruise-ship
dock and the skyline of Miami in the background. The plane
circled back toward the terminal and came up out of the
water onto the ramp dripping seawater like a golden retriever. The ground crew rolled out the stairs, and a few passengers exited the plane through the rear door and headed to
the tiny customs shed. I was in a movie, or I wanted it to be a
movie with me as the captain, and Marilyn Monroe coming
out of the terminal, climbing on board the plane, and saying
to me, "Take me anywhere."

My vision was shattered by the voice of the ticket agent
yelling at me that the plane was leaving. I brushed the pine
straw from the bottom of my pants and headed for the plane.
When I passed the cockpit, I saw the pilots chatting with each
other and laughing at something. I wanted to be one of those
guys someday. I climbed on board and settled into one of the
small seats under the wing. No sign of Marilyn. I was followed

---

* Chalk's remained a fatality-free airline until the spring of 1995, when
my friend and instructor John Alberto (along with the copilot) was
killed in a takeoff from Key West Harbour. There were no passengers on
board, but we lost a great pilot. This little reminiscent section is dedicated to him.

by a German tourist couple with cameras flashing and several black men, who seemed not as excited as I was. They must get to do this all the time—the lucky bastards.

The door slammed and the engines came to life. A few minutes later the plane taxied slowly toward the ramp. The brakes squeaked, and the plane lurched gently as the pilot steered cautiously down the ramp toward the choppy waters of Government Cut. The sound of mechanical parts moving filled the hull of the ship, and I looked out the window to see the big black main gear tire break the surface of the water. I heard the copilot call out from the flight deck, "Wheels in well." At that moment it had made the amphibious transition, and it was the coolest thing I had ever felt.

Seconds later the engines roared to full power and the view of the terminal was wiped away by a sheet of salt water. For the next several seconds, all I saw was green water, but then the green branches of the tree I had been sitting under came into view, and then the traffic along Rickenbacker Causeway whizzed by. Salt water dripped from the trailing edge of the wings, and the pilot reduced the power to the engines, decreasing the noise level considerably. The plane leveled out, and in less than a minute we crossed the shoreline above Miami Beach, heading east.

The Bahamians on board were already napping, and the Germans had their Leica lenses welded to the window, testing the limits of their cameras' motor drives. We were already over the dark blue waters of the Gulf Stream, where marlin the size of submarines cruise undetected below the surface. Hell, I was in the Bermuda Triangle in an airplane, but I was far from scared. I was on an adventure. I was going to the islands. I just stared at the ocean thinking how lucky I was to be sitting there. I projected into the future and saw myself one day crossing the Gulf Stream on my own sailboat on the way to unknown encounters and adventures in what Evelyn Waugh called "a family of islands."

Before I knew it, the pilot reduced the power and we started to descend, the deep blue of the Gulf Stream giving way to turquoise. A sliver of an island appeared in the distance. The plane made a wide turn and continued its slow descent. The bottom was visible below us though the water had to be twenty feet deep, and then a hiss emanated from under my feet as the plane touched down on the surface between the island and a large bonefish flat. The pilot taxied back through an anchorage filled with sailboats and sportfishing boats, and several minutes later we were up the ramp at Bimini.

Traffic waited for us to cross the small road that dissected the ramp area, and we pulled in next to the customs shack, where a small crowd waited to greet the plane. I climbed out of that plane into another world and another time. Since that day, I have logged hundreds of hours in the Bermuda Triangle between Miami and the Bahamas. The Chalk's terminal at Watson Island has become almost a second home for my planes, and I have made that landing in Bimini dozens of times. I know the streets of the town, and the people who live and work there are now old friends. I have enough stories of Bimini alone to fill a book, but the point of this story is that it was that first experience in a seaplane that touched my soul and eventually turned me from a passenger on a flying boat into a captain.

Climbing the Aluminum Ladder

I had started flying back in college, had soloed with just five hours at English's Flying Service in Hattiesburg, Mississippi, but I had never gotten my license. I had started up and stopped again several times, but as I faced my fortieth birthday, I had to make a decision. If I was going to get my license and learn to fly a boat, I had to do it now, or I never would. I am called by many a man of impulse, and I guess that buying a seaplane before I had a license might have seemed to the casual observer a bit impulsive, but to me it made perfect sense, and on the day after my thirty-ninth birthday I was sitting in the cockpit of a brand-new Lake Renegade 250, which I promptly named *Strange Bird*.

I set up pilot school at my house in Key West with a veteran Chalk's pilot named Dick Mau to teach me to fly boats. I didn't want to just land in protected lakes up in North Florida and call myself a seaplane pilot. I wanted to learn how to fly where I would be going. Dick and I spent that winter hopping around the Caribbean until I was ready for my check ride. Once certified as a real single-engine land and sea pilot, I was flying as much as I could. I got my instrument ticket, then logged more than four hundred hours in the *Strange Bird*. We flew to Mexico, Belize, and the jungles of Central America. Then we headed south across the Caribbean Sea to the Leeward Islands. Here and there during that period, I would land at some outpost and see a Chalk's plane or a privately restored Widgeon or Goose perched like a fine piece of sculpture in some picturesque setting and the vision and promise of that first ride to Bimini would pop back into my mind. Like it or not, I was heading up the aluminum ladder toward a bigger plane.

Like most pilots, I succumbed to the need for more speed. That gratification came in the form of the souped-up turbine

Bonanza. I went faster and farther but also came very close to falling out of the sky when one day the propeller gearbox seal became dislodged and I spilled oil over the pine forests of Thomasville, Georgia, before managing to put her down in a cloud of smoke at the Thomasville airport in the middle of an air show. Most spectators thought my emergency landing was just part of the act.

I finally flew my first Grumman in February of 1993. I had fallen in love with the Widgeon on a trip to Alaska, where I flew for two weeks through the Aleutian Islands with the legendary Orin Sebert, working on background for *Where Is Joe Merchant?* Orin had more than thirty thousand hours of water time and was better known in Alaska than Mick Jagger. He told me that the Widgeon was the hot rod but a little tricky to fly, and that "if you can fly a Widgeon, you can fly anything." I knew I had to have one.

Jim Powell, my flying guru and friend, found her in Michigan, where she had just been completely rebuilt. She had started life at the Grumman factory in Bethpage, Long Island, as a patrol plane in World War II and then was sent in a crate to Pakistan, where she sat for nearly two decades until she was discovered and restored. Only trouble was that the owner never got the feel for the plane and had to put her up for sale. One trip around the patch, and I knew that for me she was the next rung in the aluminum ladder.

The Widgeon is small, fast, and maneuverable in the air, but she's difficult to land on both a runway and the water. I had heard a few horror stories about fatalities and near-fatalities in Widgeons from armchair pilots up in Alaska. I took them in stride and found myself a couple of good instructors, who checked me out thoroughly before letting me loose. It took a good many hours of cautious time with these experienced pilots before I became comfortable behind the yoke of the *Lady of the Waters.*

Her mission had gone from carrying depth charges to cradling an eight-foot surfboard, a couple of fly rods, a cooler, a bunk, and my Saint Christopher medal. I added some modern navigational toys, along with a CD player and a marine VHF radio. Still, with all these modern conveniences, my passenger list was limited to aviation nuts, fishing freaks, and a few good dogs. She was just too small and too noisy for most people, which left me the lone soul on board most of the time. I have flown from Florida to Long Island and back several times in her and never gone above five hundred feet in altitude. It is a different and wonderful view of America; life is not antlike but very visible. The solitude and responsibility of flying alone is something I cherish. I have written song and book ideas on aeronautical charts aboard the *Lady of the Waters*. And she is a better fishing tool than any secret fly or jig hidden away in the confines of my tackle box.

A Hangar Full of Memories

A year later the French came out with a rocket ship called a TBM 700. It looked like a French version of a P-51, and I had to have one. This was a very versatile airplane. She had the performance and speed of a fighter but could land in less than a thousand feet. I used to love to bring her over the hill into the narrow and windswept confines of the airfield on St. Barts and stop her halfway down the runway.

I had sold my Lake, and the TBM served me well during my bachelor period, when Jane and I were separated. It was the perfect size for my dog, a friend, my fishing junk, and flying gear. However, when Jane and I got back together, things happened fast. Our family multiplied faster than the loaves and fishes and my bachelor airplane was too small for the load. That's when the Citation came into my life.

I had bought the Widgeon by this time, and I kept it as my "fun plane" right up until the time of my crash. Then I dealt with all that trauma and eased back into the air in a classic De Havilland Beaver. It was a great plane. She had the romance of bush pilot written all over her, a radial engine, and floats that made her considerably more stable than the *Lady of the Waters.* I flew her up on Long Island for nearly a year, but on my annual run down the East Coast to Florida, there were days when I saw the cars on I-95 below going faster than I was.

As Jim Powell said, "Jimmy, your problem is, you keep running out of cubes." He meant cubic feet, and we both knew where we were headed. A few years earlier I had gone splashing around Lake Tahoe at the invitation of some flying-boat fanatics from Carson City, Nevada, who were buying, selling, and restoring a collection of old Navy and Air Force air-sea rescue Grumman Albatrosses. We did touch-and-go landings and water taxis, then shut down the engines and climbed up on the broad overhead wing and ate a picnic lunch. Afterward, I climbed into a bunk in the spacious cabin and took a nap. I knew from that day that the Albatross was the answer to my space problems and could keep me attached to my romantic view of flying. How it actually came to be sitting on the taxiway in Palm Beach is a long journey that involved not only time on the water and time in the air, but time on the bottom.

SECTION III

Time on the Bottom

Folly Chasing Death

*Only if we understand . . . can we conceive of the seemingly
paradoxical phenomenon that people who are afraid of living are
also especially frightened of death.*

— Medard Boss, *The Meaning and Content of Sexual Perversions*

One of the inescapable encumbrances of leading an interesting life is that there have to be moments when you almost lose it. There are several times in my past when there but for fortune I would be a memory. Having made it this far, though, I can't escape the gnawing fact that, most likely, I have been here more than I will be from this point on. When it comes to the basic questions of life and death, I have never considered myself a really deep thinker. It's not my nature to ponder mortality but I try to make the best out of whatever time I am supposed to have here on the good old planet. That said, death still scares the living shit out of me. But when I go, I will go kicking and screaming.

There are cults and religions that focus on death and a gazillion books written on the subject—way too much attention being paid to something that just can't be changed. My perspective on death combines the philosophies of Joseph Campbell and Forrest Gump. Campbell looks at life and death as a timeless myth in which we all must find the role that suits us. Forrest Gump, a fellow Alabamian, summed it up for me when he said that he didn't know whether life was some kind of predestined plan or whether we were just floating around like a feather on the wind, but he thought it was probably both. Anyway, I figure a few words about mortality might be in order before I take off for South America.

My façade of irreverence toward death, as well as my primal fear of it, comes from the fact that I am a child of the Mardis Gras. Though the celebration of Fat Tuesday is synonymous with New Orleans, it actually started in Mobile, Alabama, in 1842. The Mobile Mardi Gras was by most accounts a lot tamer than that of its sister city. I think that meant that the murder rate during the two weeks of celebration—and probably the arrest rate as well—was lower in Mobile. Anyway, by the time I was old enough to walk to the parade route, the foolishness had been going on for well over a hundred years, which was plenty of time for it to become permanently entrenched in the psyche of Gulf Coast children.

Parents didn't act much like parents during Mardi Gras. That's what made it such a wonderful time. My father and mother were both hardworking people, as were their friends. They were no stick-in-the-muds and had their share of good times during the normal course of the year, but at Mardi Gras they seemed to go just about as crazy as we kids did. My memories of Mardi Gras are filled with scenes from crowded hotel rooms downtown along the parade route, where my parents and their friends would rent rooms for the weekend. Bars were set up for the adults. Plates of fried chicken and bowls of potato salad were the rations of the day. For the kids, roll-away beds were lined up along the walls.

We were all genetically programmed to repeat the phrase, "Throw me something, mister" at least a million times during the weekend. I could slip eel-like into the underbelly of Mardi Gras, where we would grapple like street urchins for "throws" that older eyes could not see and larger hands could not catch. From our base camp in the hotel we roamed the streets of downtown, crisscrossing the grassy confines of old Bienville Square, the hub of the Mobile Mardi Gras. We knew the route of the parade and the points at which we could increase the spoils in our grocery bags. We gorged on candy and junk food, and when we were tired or needed real nourishment, which wasn't often, we came back to the hotel to rest.

Mardi Gras was as big as Christmas. Unlike the birth of the baby Jesus, it's one of those strange mixtures of pagan celebration and Catholic dogma that always make for lively hypocrisy. The way I understood it growing up, Mardi Gras was a time for partying, and partying at Mardi Gras took on a whole other definition. To most people, it was allowing themselves to disregard many of the rules by which they lived most of their lives. For example, you could dive like famine victims for candy, Cracker Jacks, and doubloons hurled into the streets by masked men and women from the glittering floats. To juvenile delinquents and future potential guests of the state penitentiary, celebrating the event meant hiding in the branches of the oak trees on Government Street. From that vantage point, camouflaged by Spanish moss, they would shoot construction staples from staple guns at the mounts of the parade marshals, hoping to hit one of the horses on the rump and send it stampeding through the crowd. There were also enough car wrecks, fights, carnival-ride accidents, and gypsy trickery to make Mardi Gras the world's biggest excuse for bad behavior. Also, in the heart of the then-segregated South, Mardi Gras was a time of tolerance. It was the only occasion when there were feelings of some kind of equality between the city's blacks and whites. Though segregation still had its wicked stranglehold on the South, during Mardi Gras everyone mingled freely in the streets, sharing the only thing that they could at the time— the fun of Carnival day.

For all the frolicking and carrying on, there was something spiritual about Mardi Gras. My first revelation came somewhere back in the early fifties. On Fat Tuesday the parades started at ten in the morning and went until well into the night, when the last parade of the season was presented by the oldest masking organization in Mobile—the Order of Myths, or "Double-O M's." They had the reputation for being the wildest of the revelers, and why not? Theirs was the last party, and that particular one was a bookmark of my early life.

I was standing with my parents in front of the old Sheraton Battle House Hotel when screaming police sirens signaled the approaching spectacle. The motorcycles roared by, pressing the crowd back toward the supposed safety of the curbs, but as soon as the cops were out of sight, people filled the streets again. The distant sound of the band from up the parade route ignited the crowd, and they started to move to the rhythm. The black revelers seemed mystically connected to the drums, and we white kids tried to imitate them as best we could. We weren't too successful, but we had a good time trying. A team of tired-looking, somber mules came into view, pulling the first float. If reincarnation turns out to be true, I pray I don't come back as a Mardi Gras mule.

The first float of the OOM parade came into view. It was surrounded by six sweating black men, three on each side of the street, each wearing a white bandana on his head and carrying a large gas torch with tin reflectors on it. These were the flambeaus, and their carriers gyrated to the rhythm of the band's drum section, spinning their torches so that the flames almost reached and touched the audience.

This first float was not greeted with shouts and screams. It was not an ornate moving stage filled with drunken revelers. There were only two figures on the float, which displayed the ruin of a single Greek column. A skeleton with a maniacal grin painted across his face circled the column, taunting a masker in a court jester's costume. I was sitting on my father's shoulders in order to boost my chances in the inevitable scramble for goodies. I was full of nervous energy, bouncing around on top of my father and, for that matter, on top of the world. When I saw the skeleton, I was frightened to death and let out a blood-curdling scream. He heard me, looked my way, and started to laugh. Death made no offering of candy or trinkets to me that night. All I saw was that crazed grin as he laughed in my face.

"What is it?" I cried.

"It's Folly chasing Death," my mother replied. "It's only make-believe." But I was still petrified.

Then it happened. Through my welling tears, I heard a crack that sounded like a gunshot.

While Death had been so preoccupied with scaring the living hell out of me, Folly had snuck up behind him and had given him a wallop on the butt that could be heard two blocks away. I started laughing hysterically. The crowd joined me, and soon we had Death on the run again. The parade continued, and the final hour of fun resumed. I shouted, "Throw me something, mister" a few hundred times more, then we broke camp at the hotel and headed home before the midnight hour turned us into pumpkins.

I was a half-pint kid who hadn't been beyond a 150-mile radius of where I had been born. I had seen the werewolf, Frankenstein, and the Creature from the Black Lagoon on television, and now I had stared Death in the face on the streets of my own hometown. I had survived another Mardi Gras. Next stop—Lent.

The following morning I was there with my hungover father in the packed pews of Saint Joseph's Chapel waiting for a gloomy priest to smear ashes on my forehead and utter the inevitable words: "Remember, man, that thou art dust and unto dust thou shalt return." As the priest anointed me with palm ash, I found myself giggling. I was supposed to be in a state of repentance or self-examination or whatever, but all that I could see was the vision of Folly swatting Death's ass out of my face.

Forty-five years later, I still vividly recall that first encounter with Death, and learning that Folly was the only way to deal with it. You know Death will get you in the end, but if you are smart and have a sense of humor, you can thumb your nose at it for a while.

I have been repeatedly reminded of how to approach the subject of death. In my rebellious years on the streets of New Orleans, I was introduced to the work of Lord Buckley. Though there are many of his words that are worth quoting, the most vivid to me were as follows: "Humor is the absence of terror, and terror is the absence of humor." Years later, on some unholy wall in some ungodly Third World bathroom, I found these words scribbled: "Living well is the best revenge," echoing Calvin Tompkins's famous words. It is Folly chasing Death.

Death Chasing Folly

(Thank You, Jack Andrade)

The first time I ever saw Death catch up with Folly's ass, I was eighteen years old, on the bottom of the Gulf of Mexico beneath ninety feet of water. A member of the Mobile Devilfish Skindiving Club, I was chasing giant amberjack with a speargun through the mangled remains of a torpedoed Liberty ship when the air in my scuba tank ran out. I can still clearly see the figure of my buddy spearing a big fish, about to disappear into the darkness of the wreck, when I reached out and caught him by the ankle, signaling him about my dilemma. Letting go of the big fish on the line, he "buddy-breathed" me to the surface. My ears and nose were bleeding from the rapid ascent, and I remember swimming like hell to the dive boat, worried about sharks. The man who brought me to the surface that day was Jack Andrade. I'm sure I thanked him, but our paths went separate ways and I haven't seen him in thirty-two years, so I would just like to thank him again for saving my life.

I think that if you live an interesting life, you have to come face-to-face with death on occasion, and it should scare you. There are many terms for the experience: "facing the grim reaper," "reality check," "dodging the proverbial bullet." By whatever name you call it, you'll know it when you see it.

One Small Bass

Note from Jimmy: *Before we set out on this trip, I would like to tell you about an old one. What we learn from our mistakes and misfortunes is the best knowledge, and before I go blasting off for Central America, I find myself thinking back to August 25, 1994. It began as a day of total fun, doing the things that I love to do the most—fly and fly-fish. It ended in the nightmare crash of my flying boat that would have killed me if it hadn't been for the intervention of God, Buddha, Saint Christopher, my guardian angel, my fishing buddies, luck, and the United States Navy water-survival training. This is the story of how I survived to pack for another adventure.*

Viewed from space or on a map, the Atlantic Ocean is a meandering indigo image that runs from pole to pole. It looks big, pretty, and benign from these observation points, but I assure you, it is much more than that. The Atlantic is a liquid Pandora's box containing icebergs and coral reefs, hurricanes and horse latitudes, rock-hard shorelines and soft-sand flats. The earliest trade routes on the East Coast of America were dictated by where the wind would take you and how deep the water was when you got there, up and down the contrasting latitudes and landmass that comprise the western limits of this enormous ocean.

The Atlantic is the reason Florida itself became much more than just a swamp-filled peninsula. Early in the century, for the wealthy Easterners who could afford it, jumping on a ship or a train to change latitudes on a semiannual basis was a natural way of life. Many working seamen who had the good sense not to freeze their asses off in Nantucket opted for a winter in the waters surrounding the Tropic of Cancer. There are stories in Key West of a time before electricity and refrigeration when hotel guests in the southernmost portion of the

United States were served lemonade with ice, a delicacy in those days that rivaled beluga caviar. It was not a Merlin-like piece of magic that produced the marvel of ice. It was simply the entrepreneurial spirit of some crazy sailor up in Maine who probably laughed himself silly all the way to the bank thinking that he had sold the sun-mad inhabitants of Florida frozen river water from Maine and Massachusetts.

The New York–to–Florida connection started a long time before I discovered it, but through life revealing itself as it does, I found myself doing the East Coast "bunny hop" regularly, running to or away from the sun, depending on the season. My first summer as a Long Island resident, I quickly came to realize that the kind of fishing I was used to in Florida, the Bahamas, and the Caribbean didn't exist in the Northeast. It was the same ocean but different water.

I first began to chase big fish across the shallow flats of the Florida Keys with a fly rod some twenty years ago, learning from guides and friends the unique skills required for this peculiar sport. Back then there were no bookshelves full of expert advice, no videos, no high-priced fly shops. What few fly fishermen there were were perceived by the rest of the fishing community to be a bunch of nuts paddling around with one oar out of the water, spending a lot of time and effort to find and catch fish that they often ended up letting go. Then and now, I considered that definition a badge of honor. But I can no sooner describe the emotions involved in this kind of fishing than I can describe what it feels like to land a seaplane on the smooth, clear waters of a Bahamian harbor, or taxi to a deserted beach where the footprints of previous visitors have been long ago swept away by the wind and tide.

Fly-fishing in the East was not the familiar pastime it was in the Florida Keys. First of all, there were far fewer flats to do it in, so it hadn't evolved in the region. There were a few guys who "sort of" fly-fished, but the tackle shops on the eastern end of Long Island carried more frozen bait and big lead sinkers than fly rods. There were, of course, exceptions. A fine fisherman named Lou Tabory had recently written a book on how to fly-fish the Northeast. I went out and bought it and soaked up the local knowledge about surf casting and fishing the rips, but there was still one big difference—seeing what you were catching. Never fully understood by layman or long-liner, fly-fishing's most alluring appeal is the view. The vista alone of the clear shallow flats where fish can be spotted a hundred feet away from the boat is worth the trip. Then there are the fish. You look in the places where you think they'll be eating. The payoff comes when you actually find them and cast a fly line firmly and quietly near the telltale wake or periscopelike dorsal fin. It's another payoff as you watch the fish get fooled into thinking that a glob of glue, some feathers, hair, and a sharp stainless-steel hook resembles an eight-course meal at Le Colonial in New York.

Though the coastline of eastern Long Island lent itself to all kinds of great fishing, it still was not my cup of tea, and so I sought out places where I could get close to the kind of fishing that I loved in the lower latitudes. That's when I found the perfect use for my flying boat and my flying skills. My plane could get me to where the fish were. Thus, Strange Bird Airways found a mission. To seek out other flats, to go where no fly fisherman had gone before. In the ensuing years, there were countless trips back and forth over successive summers between Sag Harbor, Nantucket and Martha's Vineyard, the Connecticut River, and up to the coast of Maine. The skies and waters of the East Coast provided me with some of the finest hours of my life, and eventually almost took it.

Same Ocean, Different Water

The *Lady of the Waters,* my first Grumman flying boat, gave me the best of both worlds. I could live with my family in Sag Harbor but commute to a variety of places less than two hours from the East Hampton airport. I was able to fly out in the early morning to Nantucket with my fly rods and surfboard. If the fish weren't biting, there could always be a wave to catch. I could choose my options and still be home by sunset for supper.

Striped bass on fly rod is what fly-fishing in these waters is all about for me. Stripers are challenging, elusive, protected by wise fish management, and delicious, if you happen to be lucky enough to snag one over thirty-six inches long, the minimum length for keepers. But according to local custom and lore, they are said to be only catchable on a fly rod at night or in the early-morning darkness when their food supply of sand eels and hatching sea worms try to use darkness to fulfill their needs at the lower end of the food chain. Night fishing did not agree with my sleeping habits or interest me at all. So I started to become more interested in the creeks, inlets, and bars of Long Island, closer to home.

After marking places that looked good on my chart while flying, I would climb into my flats skiff and explore the waters around Shelter Island and the North Fork. It didn't really matter whether I caught fish. I was just testing the instincts that had worked so well for me down South. Surely some of it would translate to these waters and I could find some fish. This to me is what fishing is all about, underlining the simple and lucid statement I heard as a kid in Mobile Bay when my dad would take me out on the water: "If you caught a fish every time you put your line in the water, they would call it catching, not fishing."

I had gone out at sunrise in my flats skiff, toward a promising spot I had seen from my plane. With its sharp bow, flush deck, and poling platform, the boat itself was an odd sight on the waters of Shelter Island and Sag Harbor. She stood out like a sore thumb among the traditional fleet of cruisers and sport-fishing boats that crowded the small marina in Deering Harbor. Many a dock stroller would come by and ask, "What do you do with this thing?" The flats skiff was not a part of the

South Fork cultural scene as it was in the Florida Keys, where it was recognized for what it was and where it would take you.

After nearly a half-dozen exploratory forays without sighting a fish or fish by-product, I was about to give up on my local expeditions and go back to full-time Nantucket fishing. But I decided to give it one last try. My destination that morning was Hallock Bay, near the end of Long Island's North Fork, between Greenport and Orient Point. I had spotted it from my plane on my route from the East Hampton airport up the Connecticut River past Essex, where I would land my plane in the fresh water after splashing around in the salt, and practice a few short-field landings and ramping at the Goodspeed Airport. From the air I could see the features of the small bay, where according to Lou Tabory's book I might find striped bass. There were several flats near the mouth of the bay. I had made an earlier trip there with my kids. They had collected shells and chased land crabs while I played the part of a hungry fish and looked for signs of places to eat.

Long Beach jutted like an outstretched index finger to the west. At the base of the first knuckle, a small tidal creek flowed out over an oval-shaped sand flat, which tapered off to a point at the bottleneck that separated Hallock Bay from Orient Bay and held the waters of the high tide back until they could squeeze through the tiny opening and catch up with the rest of the current as the moon did its magic on earthly liquids. The escaping water raced through the small entrance at a speed of around five knots, carrying with it everything that floated or couldn't swim. Once through the bottleneck, the water swirled around in semicircular patterns of rips and eddies, where the tumbling, exhausted bait fish would fall victim to the circling gulls who used the narrow stretch of Long Beach as a staging point for their sorties, or to the larger species of fish who instinctively knew a good thing when they sensed it. This was a perfect spot for striped bass.

On this morning the protected waters of Orient Harbor were as smooth as glass. There were small wisps of fog on the water, and the sky had a high gray overcast. I made a mental list of landmarks along my route in case the lurking fog decided to bed down for a while. My friend Ken at the Bayview tackle shop in Sag Harbor had told me this stretch was frequented more by clammers than by fishermen. This sounded just fine to me. While the armada of wire-liners fought for position along the drop-off between Orient Point and Plum Island called "The Gut," I would be quietly prowling my own piece of deserted ocean just a few miles away.

The entrance to Hallock Bay appeared in the distance, and I eased the throttle back until the skiff came off the step and I immersed myself in the primal sights, smells, and sounds of the morning. There was no breeze at all, and the old windmill on the shoreline to the northwest was barely visible in the fog. There were no boats in sight, and I quickly spotted the signs of the eternal tidal procession I was looking for. I positioned my boat in the full axis of the escaping tide, where I quietly slipped the small Danforth anchor overboard. I had barely cleated the anchor line off when I heard the splashing on the surface just behind me. Something big had just eaten something little in the rip. I rigged up my fly rod as fast as I could and waited for a second chance. A big swirl erupted between me and the beach, and I let a cast go, landing the fly upstream of the nervous water. I quickly began to mend my line so that my glue and feathers resembled a life-form. I made several casts and settled into the silence of the morning with only the distant foghorn from the Midway Shoal Marker near Plum Gut bellowing in the distance. Suddenly behind me I heard a big splash.

Without thinking, I lifted my line out of the water, spun 180 degrees, and dropped a cast in front of the still-visible ripples that had fanned out from the splash. I watched the clauser minnow disappear beneath the surface and began to strip slowly. I knew I was close, and then I felt the tug. The trick now was to clear the loose line at my feet and get the fish on a tight line. I was moving back on the foredeck, keeping my feet away from the rapidly moving fly line. Almost there and then, *wham*, I felt a shudder humming on the line between my thumb and index finger, and then the rod straightened. The fish was gone. "Son of a bitch," I called out to no one in particular, and then just stood there with the rod sagging in my hand watching the dark water move by. My anger was short-lived, for I had felt the bend of the rod and that unique sensation of a fish tugging on the line.

Though the sun was hidden well by the thick fog, the passage of time was visible in a lighter shade of gray and a lessening of the current over the water. As quickly as the fish had been there, they were gone, feeling whatever change in the natural process told them that it was time to move on. The fishing gods had spoken, and as I picked up the anchor and retraced the route home in my mind, I felt the uncertainty of the fog. In the stories of my youth, monsters and ghost ships lived in the fog and waited for the unfortunate mariner who became lost. This morning in Peconic Bay, my monsters were out there for sure, but they were not in masquerade. They were the real-life forms of beaches, channel markers, fish traps, and other boats piloted by disoriented helmsmen who were between me and my home port of Deering Harbor.

I called up the mental picture of my trip out, and though it took several course corrections, glances at the chart, and near-collisions with several beachheads, the rocky western point of Hay Beach finally appeared out of the fog. I was close to where I wanted to be, with plenty of water under the keel, which is all any sailor can really hope for. In my trip through the foggy reaches of Peconic Bay, I somehow kept flashing to the scene of Gepetto stranded in the belly of the whale Monstro. My family has a history of being stranded at sea, but this day I would not be. I followed the north shore of Shelter Island until the familiar form of my rented dock came into view.

I could hear my kids calling to me from the house. The voices of children may be first detected by the ear, but their pure sounds of laughter and innocence go straight to the heart.

I slid my rods into the rafters of the boathouse and stowed my backpack. My time as a fisherman was over for the day. In a few moments, I would happily trade my Sage rod and Fin-Nor wedding-cake reel for a stainless steel spatula and whisk and make the paternal transition from hard-core fly fisherman to pancake maker for Savannah Jane, Cameron Marley, and Sarah Delaney. We ate our breakfast and spent the rest of the day grooming our horses at the barn. When we were ready to head home, the fog lifted and blew slowly out to sea. The sun set that evening into the background of a clear blue sky and a light breeze from the southwest. Tomorrow would be a Nantucket kind of day, and I fell asleep imagining perfect striper fishing. It just goes to show you that you better be careful what you wish for.

The Perfect Day

I had awakened to a banner day. I slipped out of the house just after sunrise and made my way to the airport. The *Lady of the Waters* was waiting to go. There was a slight chill in the air, and the engines seemed to sense it as they fired up. I took off to the west, leveled out at five hundred feet, and flew my familiar route just off the beach. I was circling Madaket Harbor, Nantucket, in less than an hour and made a perfect landing just west of the channel markers, where I was met by my fishing buddies Joe Panterno and Tom Mlesko. We were like a bunch of kids bubbling with excitement and rambling on about the picture-perfect day. I set two anchors on the plane and jumped into the boat. Ten minutes later we were catching bass off Eel Point, and it didn't stop until well after noon, when we hauled in our lines and headed back to shore.

I had boated one fish. It was the first keeper bass I had caught in Nantucket, and we had all decided that since we had let eight others off the hook, the keeper would have to be a sacrifice. Not to the fishing gods, but to the fishing wives. I could tell that Jane did not entirely share my enthusiasm over tales and keepsake photos of the fish we released. Her idea of a good-looking bass would be grilled with a reduced lobster sauce and a side order of risotto with white truffles. My chances of being able to continue my summer excursions to Nantucket would be greatly enhanced if I showed up with a little filet for the table.

We packed Mr. Bass in ice and strapped the cooler to the rear passenger seat. Joe and Tom stood by as I prepared to take off. I did my preflight, gathered in the anchor, and cranked up the engines with my lone passenger and eventual supper aboard.

I was taught that a water takeoff in a seaplane should be approached as though it isn't going to happen, and many times that's the case. The ocean is not a runway. There are waves, boats, lobster traps, debris, and the ever-present idiotic jet-skiers who can alter your plans at any moment. I made a mental picture of my takeoff run and any potential problems. The wind was light out of the southwest, and I locked in on my imaginary runway and scanned the harbor for boat traffic. I advanced the throttles and brought the *Lady of the Waters* up on a plane, concentrated on keeping my wings level and scanning the horizon for trouble, with an occasional glance at my airspeed indicator.

My takeoff path was north of the channel markers and would put me airborne well before the shallow flats in the distance. Out of my left eye I spotted the lingering boat wake just past my left wing. I didn't like it and was about to pull the throttles when the plane took an unusual attitude. I thought I had lost an engine and responded accordingly. Rule 1: Never try to fly a Widgeon at this critical stage on one engine. The other, more important thing at the moment, however, was the fact that the plane had started an uncontrollable roll right. If I knew anything at that moment, it was that my chances of dying right then and there would be heavily increased if I hit the water upside down. Pulling the throttles back gave me a bit of control and stopped the roll. I was coming down, but at least it was kind of nose-first.

My life did not flash before my eyes; no ancestors called to me from white fog on the other side of eternity. The nose of the plane slammed into the water, and I heard the engines stop. I had braced myself for the impact, but my head still slammed against the side of the plane. I did not lose consciousness. The shatterproof windshield had lived up to its name, but the whole nose was compressed like a big accordion. I was in what pilots call "condition red." That is, maximum human survival output, when adrenaline runs everything, like in the stories you hear of people lifting cars off of trapped victims or walking out of the Andes after a plane crash and a cannibal diet. Or, for me, at that moment, kicking my way through the twisted aluminum that had only moments ago been my pride and joy, my fully restored little Grumman Widgeon flying boat, which now had the potential to become my coffin. Two seconds earlier, and I would have had the time to pull the throttles back, come off the step, and abort the takeoff. Two seconds later, and I would have been airborne on my way back to Long Island with my big fat striped bass. Reality had turned ugly in a hurry.

Hanging like a captured insect in a spiderweb from the pilot's seat of a slowly sinking seaplane with the ever-present smell of aviation fuel burning my eyes and nostrils, I had an inverted view of the world. It also presented a totally fresh perspective from which to try to answer a question that had been asked quite often of me: Why did I fly my own seaplane in the first place? I hung there upside down and went quickly through an anatomy checklist. *Five fingers on the left hand, five on the right, okay now, I have both legs and feet, this is good. No huge pain anywhere, the water is not red from some unfelt or unknown severed artery. Hmmm, the fuel pumps are still running and the mags are on. I smell gas. This is not good, time to get my ass out of here.* I pulled the seat belt holding me upside down and fell down into the cockpit. It was three-quarters filled with water, and I was badly disoriented. *Okay, now how do I get out of here? Don't panic. Can't go out the pilot's windows. Too much jagged metal. Don't want to make things worse by going through a Cuisinart on the way out. The rear door won't open until it is totally under water and the pressure is equalized. Oh, shit, that means I have to stay in here until the goddamn plane is full of water. Don't panic. Don't like that idea too much. Other options. Crawl to the rear of the plane and make it sink faster so the door will be under water. Don't panic: Remember what you learned in survival school. Wait a minute, the flight-deck windows slide forward and backward and are already under water. That's it. Don't panic. If I can find the latch on the copilot's side, I can unlatch the window, slide it back, and get out, but that means I have to go under water to find the latch. Don't panic: Remember what you learned in survival school. Don't panic and you will live. You have been here before.*

It wasn't till a few days later that I was able to figure out what really did happen. I had not lost an engine. The boat wake had buried my left float as I raced along the surface at sixty knots, then caught the left wing, which got buried in the water, then snapped free, burying the right wing and float and then launching me sideways into the air with neither the power nor the speed to keep flying.

What I had learned years earlier at the U.S. Navy flight-survival school in Norfolk, Virginia, saved my life, pure and simple. A good friend of mine, Admiral James "Red" Best, had invited me out on a Navy PR trip to the carrier U.S.S. *America*, which was involved in exercises off Key West. Red had been commander of the naval air station in Key West and an F-4 Phantom pilot in Vietnam, and he was a pretty mean harmonica player to boot. We flew out to the carrier on a COD transport plane, had lunch with the captain, and watched pilots in training doing touch-and-gos on the deck. Just before we took off, a pair of F-14 Tomcats were flung from the deck of the carrier by the steam catapult. That's the kind of plane Tom Cruise flew in *Top Gun*. I watched in total amazement, and as we flew back to Key West that evening, I said to Red, "I want to do that one day." "That's a tough ticket," Red replied, "but I'll see what I can do." All I can say is, be careful what you wish for.

The call came from Red about a year later. He was now in the Second Fleet command headquarters in Norfolk. He told me that the *America* would be conducting an extensive training exercise off Puerto Rico and then returning to Norfolk. The captain wanted to have a party on board afterward, and my name had come up. Would I be available to come out to the carrier and play a show? I told Red that if I could ride to the show in the backseat of an F-14 Tomcat, I was their boy. I got the go-ahead, but before I got my hop in the Tomcat, the Navy required that I go through water-survival school in Norfolk, something that's mandatory for all Navy pilots on a regularly scheduled basis. I agreed and immediately set to swimming a mile a day in front of my house in preparation for what I was told would be a week of water-soaked hell.

In Norfolk on a Monday morning I joined a class of naval and Marine aviators for the course. Exercise one was your basic morning swim, naval-aviator style—a half mile around a gigantic pool with seventy-five pounds of flight suit, flight boots, helmet, G-suit, and survival gear loaded onto your body. I felt like a fat turtle, but I managed to cough and dog-paddle my way through. That was just the warm-up. The next three days were filled with all kinds of simulated life-threatening scenarios that I'm sure were produced for a reason. Several times along the way, I tried to reason with the Navy: I was only going out for one leisurely day in a TA-4 Skyhawk and didn't really require the whole training program. I was told that if I wanted to fly an F-14, I had better get my ass back in the water. I was dragged around in a parachute, launched from an ejection seat, spun on a G machine until every ounce of blood left my brain. I was slung to the ends of my toes, strapped, blindfolded in a sinking helicopter, rocketed to the bottom of the pool and turned upside down, then put in the sled, a cockpit that crashes headfirst into the water and turns upside down—with you in it. As I was strapped in for my ride down the rails, Red banged me on the helmet, looked straight into my eyes, and shouted, "Remember, rock star, bubbles up!"

Now I dove down into the murky waters of Madaket Harbor that filled the cockpit of my plane and searched with my hands for the window and the latches. Finally I found them and was able to unscrew them and open the window. With what little air I had left in my aching lungs, I exhaled and followed those bubbles back up to the air pocket. On the next dive, I was out the window and up on the wing as my fishing buddies—who had minutes before dropped me at the plane and waited to watch the beauty of a water takeoff—rushed toward me, having just witnessed the crash.

I was still in condition red, pumped with adrenaline. I heard the fuel pumps humming away and thought about fire. After freeing myself from the wreck, I did not want to get suddenly barbecued sitting on the wing. I swam around to the pilot's side of the plane and managed to feel my way through the window and locate the fuel-pump switches, which I turned off. Then I thought about the fish. Until just a few minutes ago, before this nightmare erupted, I had experienced one of the truly glorious fishing days of my life, catching and releasing four big striped bass. Now I found myself scrambling for release. I pushed back from the window and climbed up on the inverted wing as my fishing buddies appeared in the skiff expecting to have to drag me or my remains out of the plane. I climbed into the boat, and we immediately set to trying to salvage the plane, trying to keep her from sinking or flipping all the way over. I had no idea why I was doing what I was doing, and as I climbed up to the tail and tied the line off, the adrenaline started to leave me and I felt like I had just gone a round with Mike Tyson. Everything hurt as I swam to the boat and asked my friends to take me to the hospital.

Ambulance-chasing as a favorite late–twentieth-century pastime had unfortunately made its way to the shores of Nantucket. At the dock in Madaket I was met not by an ambulance, but by a photographer. I hurled a list of profanities at the guy as I tried to claw the camera from his hands, but I hurt too much. I sank back on the stretcher.

In the emergency room, I was the afternoon's only action. The doctors came in, poked around, asked a lot of questions, drew some conclusions. I was cut and scraped up pretty well but not seriously injured. One doctor told me that I would hurt like hell for the next few days, gave me a prescription for pain pills, and then had them wheel me down to the X-ray room for precautionary pictures. It was there, lying in the semidarkness, that I began to come out of shock and realize what had happened. It was there that I started to shake and cry. I wanted to see my wife and children. I wanted to go home.

I was released from the hospital, and Joe took me to the state troopers' office, where I had to give a statement. The press was already in hot pursuit, and the state troopers were more than helpful in speeding up the process and slipping me out the back door. Joe had arranged for a plane to pick me up at a hangar a long way from the main airport, where reporters and photographers had regrouped to ambush me. I thanked Joe for fishing me out of the water. As a good friend does, he only offered more help in terms of gathering what he could of my gear out of the plane and supervising the salvage operations. I eased myself into the copilot's seat of the chartered Navajo and sat quietly while the pilot took off and was sensitive enough not to ask questions. We climbed to our cruising altitude and headed southwest out over the ocean.

Sitting with my head pressed against the window, I thought first about my life becoming much too complicated before the plane crash. The words "too much stuff" kept flashing like a warning light on the instrument panel of my plane. I have often been referred to as "the plate spinner" when it

comes to my activities. It's a reference to the magician on the
old Ed Sullivan show who would spin china plates on the end
of long slender poles. The idea was to keep as many plates
spinning as possible. He would run back and forth across the
stage, rotating the sticks just in the nick of time to kept the
plates spinning.

I had flown this route often. It was my piece of sky and
ocean that linked together—with the help of a flying boat and
a fly rod—the many fragments that made up my life. I gazed
down at the waters of the Atlantic, from which I had just recently been plucked, and my thoughts were not of the crash.
Instead, I focused on the things that had brought me to that
place and time when all the plates had come crashing to the
deck.

The lighthouse at Montauk appeared in the distance, and
shortly afterward we touched down at the East Hampton airport, where Steve Tuma, an old friend and the mechanic who
had serviced the Widgeon, stood on the tarmac with a look of
shock painted on his face. He had spent many hours in the
hard-to-reach places of my plane, fine-tuning her and keeping
her in tip-top flying shape. It was now painfully clear to Steve
that the *Lady of the Waters* wasn't coming home. "What happened?" is all he could mutter.

I looked at him, probably mirroring his disbelief, and said,
"I really don't know."

Mike Ramos, my longtime assistant and friend, was waiting
at the airport to take me home. As we wound down Highway
114, he listened to my disjointed account of the afternoon's
events and offered his help, but there wasn't much to do. As
we sat in silence on the Shelter Island ferry, I knew I was standing in a heap of shattered plates. It was time to take a little inventory.

I had basically been on the road for twenty-five years, with
periods of shore leave. If I wasn't out on tour, my time away
from rock 'n' roll was spent on the boat, the plane, at my hunt-

ing camp in Georgia, or down-island. I had always promised myself that I would not grow old like the majority of the people I see, working their asses off until their late sixties or early seventies and then retiring and going on a cruise, wondering how they let the good things in life pass them by. That was not going to be me. I had tried to fit at least thirty-six hours into every day because you never knew when your time would be up. This approach to life had served me well, but at the same time it had almost cost me my life. I was lucky enough again to stop that catastrophe from happening.

A Strange Array of Feelings

I had made it out of the wreck in one piece and just wanted to hug my wife and kids, say that prayer to Saint Christopher, and start taking things a little slower. I walked into the house and hugged every member of my family as tight as I could and started to cry at the thought of how close I had come to never seeing them again. The prediction of the emergency-room doctor was starting to come true in regard to pain, so I took a pain pill and went to bed, anticipating that I would get worse before I got better. I went to sleep compiling a list of things to do and not to do.

The next morning I awoke feeling good, although I was sore and full of lumps, bumps, and cuts. Maybe all that dumb exercise had paid off. Had being in relatively good shape allowed me to bypass at least the physical healing process? I hopped out of bed and headed to the kitchen for breakfast.

The mental wound, however, was still fresh. I had come very close to dying, but so do a lot of other people. A strange array of feelings had been shaken loose by the crash, feelings that ranged from "Boy, I must be special to have been spared" to "Count your blessings, you dumb son of a bitch, and don't ever get in an airplane again." I had breakfast with Jane and the kids, and the crash wasn't even mentioned. Then I saw my plane upside down under water on the local New York news, and a sick feeling came over me. Shortly after that the phone started ringing off the wall. The story was now on *Headline News* every half hour. I knew I had enough to deal with with the FAA, getting the plane salvaged, and the general aftermath of the crash. I didn't feel like talking to anyone in the press about it. Anyway, I would be old news in two days. I called my mother and told her that I was okay, then I unplugged the phone and decided I needed something to distract me. I watched one of the videotapes of Bill Moyers interviewing Joseph Campbell and, as always, found comfort in Campbell's exploration of myth and mysticism. The tape was like mental Tiger Balm, taking my mind out of fastforward as I fell asleep.

Like it or not, I had to deal with fallout from the crash. You just don't flip a seaplane and swim away. This was the nineties, and there were lots of forms to fill out, plus the unfortunate reality that this would not just be an item in the Nantucket weekly paper. When I called Joe back, he had been barraged by local newscasters from Boston, and the rumors about the crash had already started flying. I thanked him again for saving my ass and then tried to put the whole thing out of my mind and went to dinner and a movie with Jane.

I got my popcorn, Cherry Coke, and Junior Mints and settled into my seat. A little escapism never hurt anybody. I should know, I've been selling it for years. The Sag Harbor art cinema was showing a Chinese film called *Eat Drink Man Woman,* by Ang Lee, about food, three sisters, and their crazy father, who was a Chinese gourmet chef. The sibling rivalry was not as interesting as the meals the old man prepared. I was watching a scene about Sunday dinner, with a baked duck in a clay container, which he smashed with a hammer. I jumped at the sound and the first flashback hit. Suddenly I was seeing the waters of Madaket Harbor coming at me rapidly. My heart was racing and I broke out into a sweat. I closed my eyes and braced myself for the impact in the theater seat. It never came. I opened my eyes, and I was back in the Sag Harbor theater. I leaned over and whispered to Jane that I had just had a flashback of my crash. She reached into my popcorn box, grabbed a handful of kernels, and said, "You better call Paul Tobias."

"Your Life Is Not a Performance"

In the hills and valleys of my life journey, one of the deep valleys I trudged through for quite a while was the valley of marriage. I come from a moderately dysfunctional background, topped off with twelve years of parochial education. Sex or anything relating to sex was not explained to me by my parents or counselors or by anybody. Like most American male war babies, I got it from the letters in *Playboy* magazine and locker-room bullshit. Now, that is not the kind of gear you want to stuff into your emotional backpack as you venture into marriage, but it was the only gear I had. It's taken a long time to figure out, first of all, that I had the wrong gear, and then an equally long time to figure out what kind of gear I needed.

Jane and I have had a wild and wonderful roller-coaster ride of a relationship, from the day I met her in the Chart Room in Key West through living together, breaking up once or twice, then getting married and having a child. We had lived in all the right places at the right time: St. Barts, Key West, Aspen, but her backpack was just as useless as mine, and so we found ourselves speeding in and out of control on a train that was about to jump the tracks. She had seen the light way before me and was working on her problems long before I had the good sense to come in from the cold. I had gone with her, and without her, to different therapists, which for a Southern man is like having a root canal and an IRS audit in the same afternoon. But I fooled myself and most therapists. I treated therapy like a performance, and I am good at that. But there was a little voice that was awakened from way down deep inside me that I didn't want to listen to but couldn't quite turn off.

The knee-jerk reaction of our faster-than-the-speed-of-light society is, of course, divorce. It's no big deal these days. What is it, half of all marriages end up in divorce? Well, I am not good at failure, and that nagged at me, along with that little voice that was getting louder by the day but still couldn't cut through the bullshit.

I was bobbing a fog on a longboard in the Pacific Ocean one morning in San Onofre, south of Laguna Beach, enjoying one of my infrequent days of West Coast surfing. Most of the people in the water are my age, and most are on longboards. I am not that good, and I have some banged-up knees and leg bones that keep me in the cruising category, which suits me just fine, but I love to ride a board on a wave. It short-circuits the thought process and allows your sense of survival to take charge. When I am surfing, nothing—I mean nothing—enters my mind other than riding the ocean on a plank. Whether I am hanging on to a surfboard with my toes, poling a flats skiff across the shallow clear water of the Exumas, sailing the Antilles on a beam reach, or landing my seaplane in some secluded, picturesque anchorage somewhere, getting off of dry land seems to help my equilibrium.

It was on that board that day where I heard the bell on the sea buoy near the Dana Point Marina clang and clang and realized that it was my wake-up call. I sat on the board in the silence of the morning, and in between the clangs, I heard that little voice speak to me clearly and unaffected by the noise of my life in motion. It simply said, "You haven't given this thing your best shot." It was the truth and I finally knew it. I was successful at most things I had undertaken in my life, most of which went against the grain, but none of it meant anything to me if I didn't at least give my marriage my best attempt. I called Jane and told her I wanted to give it one last honest shot.

I have always felt that I have a guardian angel riding on my shoulder. I am sure it is a she, and that when I really need her, she will bail my ass out. After all, I miraculously escaped death or severe injury at least a couple of times in my life. Whether it was my guardian angel, my wife's incredible store of practicality, or both, I wound up in the office of Paul Tobias in Los Angeles.

He was not like the other therapists I had seen. He had my number, he knew my act, and he called me on it every time. I hated it, but knew I had to let it happen. I trusted Paul. Hell, he was not only an amazing therapist. He was a pilot and a fly fisherman.

I was sitting on the couch in Paul's office one day. Jane sat across from me, and we were trying to put the Humpty Dumpty world of our marriage back together again. I wasn't being too helpful, still clinging to the basic notion that I didn't really need that much help. I was trying to justify some kind of pretzel logic when Paul interrupted me and said flatly, "Jimmy, your life is not a performance. Your performance is a part of your life." At first it didn't quite register, and I rambled on with some lame self-justification, and then it happened. All engines stopped. Man overboard. *Ding, ding, ding!* From the well of my soul the little voice finally screamed at me. *Get it, asshole!*

Call it a breakthrough, a revelation, or whatever, but that day changed my life, and I am pretty sure it saved my marriage. The valley is still full of sharp rocks and dangerous ledges, but at least now I know I am traveling with the right kind of gear in my backpack.

As Bill Murray sings in *Ghostbusters,* "Who you gonna call?" Paul had helped me through the most troubled time of my life. Surely a plane crash and the repercussions of that trauma would be right up his alley. I had no idea how up his alley it was.

The next day, I waited for California time to catch up to the East Coast and called Paul at home. He had seen the pictures on the news, and I wasted no time in telling him about the flashbacks and the crash itself in pilot lingo. He waited patiently for me to finish and then said, "I guess you haven't heard about me."

"What happened?" I asked.

"I had an engine failure over Big Bear Lake and had to put my plane down in the lake." I listened to his story in amazement. We shared the belief that it was our training that enabled us not to panic, combined with a lot of luck that allowed us to swim away from our respective catastrophes. Paul told me that my instincts about just getting on with my life were pretty much right. We were not terminally unique in our near-death experiences. Hell, in this age we were just two of a thousand people a day who experience the same thing. I am sure that it will be a theme on *The Oprah Winfrey Show* one day, but for now it was life throwing a hundred-mile-an-hour fastball at your head that barely missed. There was really nothing else to do but to get up, shake off the dust, and jump back into the batter's box. I was headed for California in a few weeks, and Paul and I would have lunch and go over the minute details of our near misses with the scrutiny that only two pilots could.

Tennis Anyone?

Postcrash day number two dawned and still no big hurt. I was dealing with insurance investigators, the FAA, salvaging the plane, and reassuring my concerned friends and relatives that I was indeed okay. The fog that covered the island started to burn away about midmorning. I was headed outside for a walk when my landlady, Mary Walker, called and asked if I felt like playing tennis. It would be mixed doubles, and they weren't going to be playing long. It sounded like the perfect way to get my sore and stiff tendons back into getting-on-with-my-life gear, and besides, I like playing tennis with Mary. The court became a field of battle on which we expressed our basic Hamilton versus Jefferson view of the country. (I am the Jeffersonian.) I grabbed my racket and headed down the beach toward the tennis court.

The sun was burning through the overcast, and as we warmed up on the clay court shaded by a stand of maples and live oaks it looked like it would turn out to be a glorious day. It was a perfectly manicured court, situated on a north/south line, which kept the sun out of the server's eyes. The court was bordered entirely in red and white impatiens, the green clay was freshly rolled, and the tape was as white as our required outfits. The only flaw in the picture-perfect tennis setting was a badly repaired dent in the watercooler that bore a recently applied patch of Rust-Oleum. Behind the cooler, leaning against the fence, was the smoking racket. I went over and picked it up. The face of the carbon-graphite, gut-strung racket folded in half like a flour tortilla, the victim of someone's pent-up frustrations that had no other way out than up against the watercooler. I should have taken it as a sign.

On this lovely fall morning, I felt just thankful to still be alive and actually moving around instead of being in traction in a hospital bed or worse. So it didn't matter much that during my warm-ups I wasn't exactly one with the ball. I was moving on the court with a nagging clumsiness, reminiscent of those hungover tennis-and-detox mornings of my past. But I had not done drugs for years, except for the pain pills—yeah, that was it—the pain pills I had taken the day before. They had made me feel too weird, and I had discarded them in favor of plain old Advil.

When the first game began, I took my place on the baseline and returned serve several times. Then I went to place a shot down the line and it happened. The pain started in my left ribs and then spread instantly, like the shock wave of a nuclear explosion. My body went completely out of whack as I made contact with the ball and sent it off on a ninety-degree trajectory toward the maples. I caught sight of the broken racket leaning against the cooler and felt as if I was about to break in two. I had blown a head gasket, or my voltage regulator had melted down. My normally good hand-to-eye coordination had gone south, and I knew this was not some side effect from a painkiller. I tried to play on, but I hit the ball like a two-year-old, and it ricocheted off the water-cooler. My ears started ringing, and small bubblelike spots danced in my vision. I was a mess, and I had to stop. Mary sensed that I was hurt and immediately transformed from Ed Meese to Florence Nightingale. I assured her I was okay and walked off the court and back home.

Everything that hadn't hurt since the crash was now sounding multiple alarms in the pain center of my nervous system. My heels hurt when I walked, and I was still hearing the ringing in my ears. Then came another flashback of the crash. The diagnosis of the Nantucket doctor had been right on the money, but I think it had just taken two days for my adrenal glands to stop pumping and leave me with a forty-eight-year-old body that had been slammed around inside a twisted aluminum labyrinth. I told Jane what happened as I passed through the door, then I went straight to the bedroom and collapsed on the cotton sheets, feeling about as far away from Charles Lindbergh and Jimmy Connors as one could possibly get.

One Small Bass

After my collapse on the tennis court, I spent the better part of the next two days compiling a wish list. I wished it all hadn't happened. I wished that I had seen that goddamn boat wake sooner. I wished that I didn't have to deal with the aftermath of the crash. I wished I could have punched out that asshole photographer who kept poking the lens of his camera inches away from my face as they put me in the ambulance. I wished that my big fish was not being saturated with one-hundred-octane aviation fuel and was safely resting in our freezer, and that I might possibly have a great meal out of this whole ordeal. I wished that my ribs didn't hurt.

I took my wish list with me to the kitchen, made a cup of black-currant tea, swallowed a couple of Advils, and listened to the gusts of wind rattle the windows. I switched on the Weather Channel, and the pretty woman in front of the computerized map of the States was pointing as if on cue toward the waters of Long Island Sound. She was talking about the sizable cold front that had made its way out of Canada and had sped across New England overnight and was now offshore. I grabbed my hand-held VHF radio and stepped outside to listen to the marine forecast while experiencing the elements firsthand. I shivered in the dark morning chill. The forecast was calling for winds out of the north from fifteen to twenty-five knots, with seas three to four feet in the Sound. It was not an ideal day to go fly casting, but these were extenuating circumstances. I still had not come to grips with dressing to go fishing as if you were about to scale Mount Everest, and I felt it was time.

Until the recent invention of stylish flats-fishing outfits with matching hats, glasses, and accessories, Florida Keys or Bahamian flats garb consisted of a T-shirt, cutoffs, a light foul-weather jacket, and a pair of good fishing pliers with a belt case. I had given up all thought of combining cold weather and ocean activity way back in the late seventies when I made my last trip from Newport to Bermuda on my old sailboat, *Euphoria II*. The clearest memory of that trip was the large icicles hanging from the lifelines that didn't melt until we were on the other side of the Gulf Stream. I had fished some Nantucket

nights bundled up like a Cub Scout in camp and quickly realized it wasn't for me. But today, after my brush with death, I
was going to make a fresh start. I would not bitch about the
weather to myself or to anyone else. I would try to take to
heart the words of my song "Changes in Latitudes, Changes in
Attitudes," and I was going fishing, come hell or cold water.
Reality had reared its ugly head, and shit had happened that
was not just going to go away. It was time to deal with it all,
and that meant some hydrotherapy—time on the water. It was
time to stop wishin' and go fishin'.

The ocean has always been a salve to my soul. During my
childhood on the northern shore of the Gulf of Mexico, much
of my summer vacations, free of the grasp of the Mobile
parochial school system, was spent at my grandmother's
house in Pascagoula, Mississippi. My cousin Baxter was my
best friend, and we did what most preteenage boys in the
fifties did. If we weren't building Civil War forts, we were
reenacting the Battle of New Orleans, with one side being the
British and the other the combined forces of General Andrew
Jackson and the pirate Jean Laffite. Our charges and counter-
charges up and down the muddy banks of the small bayou
that bordered the rear property of my grandparents' house inevitably would produce a corps of walking wounded. My
grandmother had patched up a lot of children and grandchildren, and we would limp to the back porch of her house for
first aid. She would nonchalantly patch us up with Bactine
and Band-Aids, then pour a bowl of hot Creole gumbo into us
for stamina and send us off to the real source of healing—the
sea. She told us that the gumbo and Bactine would help, but
that the best thing for a cut or an abrasion was to go swimming
in salt water.

We took our grandmother's advice to heart, and off we
would pedal on our old Schwinn bikes to the swimming spot
near the Coast Guard base. I remember well the apprehension
I would feel easing my skinny, prepubescent body into the

water, waiting for the sting as the salt made contact with the fresh wound. But it did work. The next day scabs would quickly form and the healing process would begin. Later down the road of life, I made the discovery that salt water was also good for the mental abrasions one inevitably acquires on land.

When you spend a lot of time on the water, you lose touch with what's happening on the land. Record deals, family problems, career decisions, all that stuff is somehow washed from your mind and you just think about the fish, the wind, the water depth, the current, the tide, the voyage. The vast ocean itself, as seen from my seaplane, often makes me stop and wonder what I'm doing going out on it in the first place. From the air, all boats look like toys bobbing in an endless sea, way too small to be out there.

I have seen my share of beaches, coves, and island harbors that instantly bring the word *paradise* to mind, and I have traveled in treacherous storms with fear and apprehension running high, hoping that I was prepared for what the sea might dish out. But there is a strange brew at work in the mind of the waterman, and imaginary lines of latitude and longitude that you occupy become your own little piece of the ocean. You are linked to it by an umbilical cord comprised of primitive instinct, inherited and acquired knowledge, and a pure passion for the sea and all the joy and terror she holds in her power. It was that sense that this morning had taken from me. I hoped it was a temporary response to the trauma of the crash. I was sinking rapidly into the quicksand of middle-age thoughts of mortality, acting way too much like too many confused people I knew.

After long concert tours, I would embark on long sailing journeys to decompress from life on the road. During my early Key West days, after a night of general misbehavior, I would swim from the beach in front of my house on Waddell Avenue down to the southernmost point and back, which gave me time and distance to get my heart and circulatory system cranked up enough to ward off the inevitable hangover until after lunch, when a nap was the next step in my recovery process. From the first day I ventured out into the mysterious world of flats fishing, I knew that time spent in this environment was good for whatever ailed you.

Now I rang up my Shelter Island fishing guru, Charlie Hergrueter. We had met at the beginning of the summer, the day I had emerged out of the fog at the Deering Harbor Marina from my Hallock Bay expedition. A lone figure was standing on the floating dock where I was maneuvering the skiff. He was tall and dressed in fishing clothes, short on style and color combination and long on comfort and warmth. "Need a hand?" he had called out, and I had tossed him the bowline and shut down the engine. I had secured the boat and climbed onto the dock. The man had held out his hand and said, "I'm Charlie. I think I'm the only other maniac on Shelter Island who would be fly-fishing on this kind of morning."

It was true, there was no one else on the dock, in the parking lot, or on the sidewalks that lined Highway 114 as it wound through the village of Deering Harbor. There were a few lights on in the houses that lined the harbors where people were slowly beginning to come to life and prepare for Sunday services. Charlie and I had already attended ours—the brotherhood of the fly rod. Over the summer, Charlie and I had spent many hours together on the water exploring the rocks, rips, and creeks around Ram Island and Coecles Harbor where we indeed had some fine days of fishing. But the big guys were still in Nantucket, and I continued my routine trips in the *Lady of the Waters*. Charlie was one of the many well-wishers who had called to inquire as to my condition after the news of my crash was splashed across the cable channels of the world. His message had been short—call when you're feeling better, and we'll go fishing.

Now we picked up our fishing time line exactly where we had left off. He gave me a quick report on fishing spots, which may have changed since the cold front had moved through. I just wanted to get out on the water, so he said he would pick me up at my dock in thirty minutes. I went back inside and dressed warmly, without uttering one cussword about the wind or weather.

The house was still quiet as I left a note on the kitchen table, then walked to the dock and eased myself into the boat. Our first stop was a familiar one not far from the house. We had no protection from the wind and the small whitecaps rolling in steadily from the north, but Charlie moved the skiff in for a look at the rocks that he could read like a book. I slipped the anchor over at his instruction, and Charlie cut the engine while we braced ourselves against the rocking caused by the waves and started to look for signs of fish. It was flat-ass cold out there, and I zipped my zippers and tightened every piece of Velcro at my neck and sleeves to keep the wind out. The water had been shaken up like salad dressing by the storm, and even in the shallow depths of the flat there was little visibility. Occasionally a patch of struggling seaweed would appear beneath the surface. I almost uttered a tirade against the weather in general but caught myself again. I was doing good here with my new lease on life. But feeding fish cannot hide themselves. Water displacement is inevitable, whether it comes from an aircraft carrier moving across the Indian Ocean at twenty knots or from a hungry fish in pursuit of a meal. Something has to move out of the way, and that is called the wake.

Not only could Charlie cast a fly line pretty well, in the real world he wielded a scalpel as a surgeon at Children's Hospital in Boston, so I took the opportunity to ask for a bit of medical advice and listed the places that hurt. Charlie told me that I wouldn't be standing on the bow of his boat with a fly rod in my hand on a day like this if I had sustained any serious injuries.

Our conversation was cut short by a noisy splash near the rocks. I spotted the well-defined wakes moving our way out of the rocks. The nervous water pushed by the approaching fish came close, and I raised my right arm to cast. The pain in my ribs was awakened at the same time that a rogue wave broadsided the boat and covered us with freezing water. I stumbled backward but was able to catch myself against the gunwale in time. The fish had been spooked by the noise from the human morons in the boat. They turned and sped away, far out of range. I made a desperate cast at them, but it fell way short. This was not a good start, and my temper was warming up.

More fish appeared at ten o'clock off the port bow—the perfect angle for wind and light. Though my first cast had seemed as strange as my tennis stroke from the previous day, I persevered. It was like everything I had learned about how to make a fly line move in these conditions had been completely erased from my memory. This time my off-beat cast didn't even make it past the rail of the boat. The wind swirled from the opposite direction at the moment I made my cast, blowing it all back into the boat and wrapping a big loop around the bow cleat at my feet. "Goddamn son-of-a-bitchin' fuckin' wind!" I screamed angrily as I tried to free the line. So much for self-control.

I bent down to loosen the knot in my fly line when I heard Charlie yell, "Look out!" Out of the corner of my eye I saw the rogue wave, but it was too late. It smacked the gunwale of the skiff and vaulted me forward. I spread my legs to try to keep my balance and heard the crunch of carbon fiber under my left foot. My three-piece Sage rod was now a four-piece, totally useless piece of shit. I was not a happy camper as I gathered my shattered rod and moved to the back of the boat.

I told Charlie to have a go at it, and I settled into the seat behind the console and attempted to get control of my temper and refuge from the wind. I watched Charlie artfully move the fly line with his rod. He offered to call it a morning and head for home. I think he was shocked when I declined. I was lost in a mental fog. It seemed like I had lost connection to the ocean, and something inside me said I couldn't go home until I found out for sure.

The wind blew increasingly strong. We sought protection and better casting conditions behind a rocky bluff called Cornelius Point, where the topography and a tall stand of sugar maples provided a lee from the howling north. Mother Nature was pitching us a shutout. I couldn't cast, I was cold, and as Oscar Hammerstein had so perfectly described in his classic song, my body was "all achin' and wracked with pain."

I was standing on the bow making lazy roll casts at nothing in particular, enjoying the calm water. Suddenly the sun peeked through a tear in the gray overcast and ripped the darkness from the surface of the water like a piece of wrapping paper. I could feel the warmth through my layers of Gore-Tex. I unzipped the heavy jacket, set my fly rod on the deck, and was attempting to climb out of my foul-weather gear when out of the corner of my eye I saw a small swirl behind one of the big boulders that stood out in the shallow water from the shore.

I cleared the clothing from the deck and started stripping out line. It would be a long cast to the rocks. The boat was pointed in the wrong direction, and I didn't have time to relay instructions to Charlie. I turned and fired to where I knew there was a fish. My cast was confident, and I felt no pain anywhere in my body. I was focused. I was back in charge of my piece of ocean. My cast unfolded perfectly in a long, decaying loop that dropped the fly inches from the boulder. I stripped the line several times and saw another swirl, then I felt the tug, set the hook, cleared the line, and started to laugh. I was back on track. It was not a long fight or an eventful one. I did not have to swing an oar at a school of predator tiger sharks as I brought the fish close to the boat. I just stood there feeling the weight of the fish on the rod and grinning like a successful shoplifter. It was only a couple of minutes until I had the fish up on the surface and next to the boat.

It wasn't a record striped bass—it wasn't even a keeper—but it was my first striper caught on a fly in Long Island Sound. I gently removed the hook from the fleshy part of the fish's mouth. This little bass was more beautiful than he could have possibly imagined. We were connected by more than the monofilament line that had brought him into my hands. I had used all my resources of modern materials and primeval stalking to fool him and catch him, and then I held him by the tail and moved him back and forth in the water so that the motion would fill his gills with water and replenish him after his morning workout. I felt the life force return to his muscular body with a powerful thrust of his tail. I let go and he was gone.

As I watched the little striper glide away from my hand to the security of the deeper, darker water, I thought back to the crash, when I was the one scrambling out of the water in search of safety. As the equatorial Africans say, "Down is up and up is down."

I didn't have to say a word to Charlie. The morning was complete, in a lot of ways. I had rediscovered my saline psyche. Two days later, I climbed back into the left seat of a De Havilland Beaver and went flying. The first water landing with my instructor was a bit shaky, but after a few more I was feeling for the water with my old skills. I had been given another shot, and I intended to learn from it and enjoy the additional time I had been afforded. There were places to go and things to do, songs to sing, old friends to visit, new stories to write. And it all began again with one small bass.

Boone's Farm Flashback

Years of traveling have taught me a lesson that seems appropriate to mention now as I am about to set out on this trip. First of all, it is more fun sharing the adventure than doing it by yourself. In the early days, I usually traveled by myself because I was too broke to take anybody along, and although I was supposed to be out there finding myself, it got pretty lonely.

In the sixties and early seventies there were a lot of hippies traversing the highways of America, Europe, and beyond, following in the wake of Jack Kerouac and Ken Kesey. It seemed more exciting to be finding yourself as a member of a band of carefree gypsies than to be shuffling along some deserted highway with your thumb stuck out, hoping for a trucker, jacked up on Benzedrine and in need of someone to talk to, to stop and give you a lift. Then there was the scene in *Easy Rider* that sent me packing. If you never saw it, or if your brain-cell damage after living through the sixties has fogged your memory, I will try to reconstruct it for you.

Peter Fonda and Dennis Hopper have just scored a big load of either heroin or cocaine (I never quite figured it out) at the Mexican border and decide to take off for New Orleans, with Steppenwolf's "Born to Be Wild" blasting above the roar of their Harleys. It wasn't exactly the kind of job placement our parents had in mind, but to me it was the coolest scene in any movie I had seen since James Dean had the switchblade fight with Dennis Hopper high above the Hollywood hills at the Griffith Planetarium in *Rebel Without a Cause*. After a hard day on the road, Peter and Dennis come upon a roadside commune somewhere in the desert and stop for the night.

The commune had everything an aspiring hippie needed. There were buses painted with flowers and peace symbols, circled like covered wagons around a rock quarry. You could almost smell the patchouli oil coming through the screen. Peter and Dennis are quickly pounced upon by a harem of hippie chicks, who get naked, give them dope, and then fuck them under the full moon while they guzzle Boone's Farm apple wine and dance to "Like a Bird." That little scene was a shot heard 'round the world to the war-baby generation. Role models for an entire generation went from presidents to gypsies. It sent millions of other inquiring young minds out onto the newly constructed interstate-highway system with their thumbs stuck out looking for a ride to somewhere, or a chance to hook up with other believers in this version of America.

I was too broke to afford a motorcycle, so in those days I just hitchhiked everywhere and fantasized about running into a lost flower child who looked like Peggy Lipton. Together we would head out to San Francisco, singing the chorus to that infamous John Phillips song, "San Francisco (Be Sure to Wear Flowers in Your Hair)." What we would do when we got there was never an issue. We didn't think much about the future; we just lived for the day, and that is the way you have to think when you decide to go a-ramblin'. There's not too much I'm certain about as we spool up for this one, but I do know that whatever plans we have made will change.

SECTION IV

Leaving Florida

Florida thrusts like a guiding thumb
To the southern islands of rumba and rum
To the mystery-cities and haunted seas
Of the Spanish Main and the Caribbees

—DON BLANDING

Blame It on
Lord Baden-Powell

I used to rule my world from a pay phone
And ships out on the sea
But now times are rough
I got too much stuff
Can't explain the likes of me
—"ONE PARTICULAR HARBOUR"

24 December 1996
Palm Beach, Florida

I am finally packed, and of course I have too much stuff. Trips are not trips to me. They have to be expeditions. I blame this all on Lord Baden-Powell, the founder of the Boy Scouts, and that unforgettable motto, "Be prepared."

In my Scout days, when we would go on weekend camping expeditions, being prepared consisted of having a backpack, a mess kit, a snake-bite kit, a poncho, some good hiking boots, a well-hidden copy of *Playboy,* and my ever-important Swiss Army knife. Even as a young child, I loved the idea of being self-contained. It's still a credo of mine. Back then my backpack held everything I needed. Later on in life, I added duct tape and dental floss to my list of survival essentials. Today, being prepared has taken on a whole new meaning, a mind-boggling selection of survival gear, and a different set of parameters.

It starts with the fact that the Albatross is the largest sea-plane Grumman ever built. It is sixty feet long, eighty feet wide, and can carry enough fuel to stay airborne for seventeen hours as well as a couple of tons of gear and ten passengers. It is a plane that has *expedition* spelled all over it. Upon my purchase of this aircraft, my lovely wife was heard to say, "I don't even want to discuss it." I have long since quit trying to justify my adult toys to Jane, and she kindly allows me my eccentricities but makes it clear that she doesn't feel required to like them or use them. As I go through the ritual of packing for a trip, Jane strolls through my room, or the garage, which is serving as staging area number two, looks at all my crap, and reminds me that she's only taking two bags. (Note to couples who might find themselves in similar situations with different ideas of what is necessary and what is fun: This kind of an understanding can only be reached after many years together and usually a good many years apart.) So now I have a plane that will literally hold tons of shit. There is only one thing for a God-fearing, red-blooded Boy Scout to do, and that is to try and fill it up. Here we go.

Flight bag. My flight bag stows right behind my pilot's seat, within arm's reach.

A pilot's flight bag is like a doctor's medicine bag or a shaman's goatskin full of potions and tricks. My flight bag contains the magic that allows me to navigate the sky, as well as a day's worth of provisions, with a little room left over for some personal things.

When I was at the Jim Hawkins stage of my life, at around ten or eleven, my grandfather showed me his sextant and told me stories of his voyages around the world. It looked like something Captain Nemo would have on the *Nautilus*, strange and magical. The knowledge to use this to "shoot the stars" and find your latitude and longitude was something a real captain had to have. Many years later, I taught myself celestial navigation. There was never any real need for it in the type of coastal sailing I started out doing, but once I went offshore into the deep ocean and the land disappeared beyond the horizon, my genetic links to my ancestry told me I had to learn this art. Being able to link my position on Earth to those of heavenly bodies with a series of imaginary lines and angles connected me to the universe.

The night sky has always been a mystery to us. Hell, heaven is supposed to be out there somewhere, along with aliens, comets, black holes, pulsars, quasars, blue novas, and, with any luck, Captain Kirk and the *Enterprise* protecting us from the Klingons. Books on astronomy and astrology fill a whole floor at Borders and have enabled aging singers and actors to find work as self-proclaimed psychics. I know there is something to the motion of the universe and the effect of gravity on the body composition of earthlings. If you don't think so, ask any doctor who works in an emergency room about how full moons affect his caseloads. Astrology is not my area of expertise. I, pardon the pun, gravitate toward navigation because it is both mysterious and explainable at the same time.

Navigation has always been somewhat arcane, dating back to the early transatlantic explorers. Only the captain and navigator knew the craft. Sextants and compasses were guarded like religious relics. It was a way of ensuring order, and although a few captains were dumped overboard here and there, the navigator was revered because he was the only one who knew how to get the crew home. It wasn't too many years after the Wright brothers soared above Kitty Hawk, North Carolina, that pilots were adapting the navigational instruments from ships into the flight panels of airplanes. Navigation for a boat is basically the same as for airplanes. The earliest pilots found their way around the skies using the same heavenly bodies.

In this century celestial navigation was not considered necessary for coastal sailing or short-hop flying. The need to rely on a sextant became even more remote with the invention of radio aids to navigation and loran stations in the thirties and forties. In the late 1960s, a science fiction writer named Arthur C. Clarke stumbled upon a concept that has revolutionized the world and the way we operate. With his amazing idea of stationary orbiting satellites, the whole world of navigation changed. The stationary satellites made possible GPS (Global Positioning System) devices. This technology often makes it very tempting to rely on the spectacular array of satellite navigational systems that are as plentiful as Gameboys. They are great when they work, and the instrument panel of my plane is full of them, but what happens if the power goes off? I want to know that I can get home, and that is what my flight bag is for, to carry the tools that can get me home when all else fails, and maybe a pack or two of peanut butter–cheese crackers to eat along the way.

As we prepare to take off for Grand Cayman and beyond tomorrow, here are the items that are in my flight bag:

Jeppesen Sanderson computer, or "Whizz Wheel"
Handheld barometer
Bottle of Advil
Trimble portable GPS computer
Tube of Bullfrog sunblock
Swiss Army watch
Brookstone thermometer
Battery-operated Garmin GPS Map 195
Pack of Rolaids
Pilot's logbook
Change of underwear, T-shirt, and fishing shorts
Eddie Bauer roll-up rain jacket
Icom handheld aircraft radio
Icom handheld VHF marine radio
Airspace reclassification card
Container of CD-ROM charts for my P.C.

2 Fischer space pens
Chart-plotter
Immigration cards
Passport
Pilot's license and medical certificates
Flashlight
AA batteries
Stash of cash ($500 in small bills)
Copy of V. S. Naipaul's *The Loss of El Dorado*
Copy of the *Pilot's Guide for the Caribbean*
2 Snickers bars
2 packs of Planters peanut butter–cheese crackers
Bottle of Evian water

Portable generator. I grew up in a hurricane zone, and from my earliest days I spent my time on and around boats. I guess that's why I have this connection to generators. When hurricanes and big thunderstorms would rumble in off the Gulf and slam into the shores of Mobile Bay, you knew the lights were going out. Our little generator brought us out of the dark until the power came back on. On board a boat, the engine and sails are the muscles that provide movement across the ocean, but the generator is the brain. It gives you vital information and provides creature comforts as well. Generators are not just machines. Every one I have ever owned had a personality that ran the gamut of human emotions, just like a teenager. It could be warm and cold, trustworthy or unreliable. Like every other part of a boat, I talked to my generator. I would compliment it, beg it, and cuss it.

A generator is about self-containment, essential to any good expedition and a damn fine attribute in general. Sailors and flyers come by self-containment because it is inherent to their craft. Before you get into the cockpit of a plane or behind the wheel of a boat heading offshore, you have to know that there is the chance that you may have to abandon ship or ditch, and you have to be able to get back home, or set up shop in the jungle, or live like Robinson Crusoe for a while.

My favorite generator story resulted in the composition of one of my songs, "Twelve Volt Man." My friend Michael Nesmith told me this story one day while we were working on one of the nine thousand screenplays for the movie version of "Margaritaville," which never did come to pass. One day while he was doing the infamous Baja California road rally, in which a group of demented and twisted humans attempt to drive pickup trucks the entire length of the Baja peninsula in Mexico, Michael broke down somewhere in the middle of the desert and needed help. He was directed by the locals to a fishing village on the coast, where, according to them, lived an old gringo who might be able to help him with his repairs.

Upon arriving at this village, he was directed to a thatched hut near the Sea of Cortez. There he found the gringo, who invited him in. The gringo told his story about how he had come south and why he hadn't gone back, and then they set out to repair the truck. When that feat was accomplished, Michael drove him back to the village and the old gringo invited him in for a drink. From a storage locker inside the hut, he produced a small generator, a five-gallon container of gas, a Sears Die-Hard battery, an old Waring blender, a bottle of tequila, a box of Holland House margarita mix, and a worn copy of *Changes in Latitudes, Changes in Attitudes*. Soon a crowd gathered on the beach. Ice arrived from one of the local fishing boats, and the old gringo fired up the generator. The music came on, the battery began to charge, the blender began to whirl, and the party began. It lasted well into the night, until all the gas in the can had been used up. When I heard the story, it confirmed an instinctive appreciation of generators as one of the best inventions of modern man.

Surfboards. I carry two. One Stewart nine-foot longboard and one Stewart eight-foot "egg" board. I know that the unfamiliar reader will associate surfing only with California or Hawaii, but for years now I have traveled the many islands of the Bahamas and Caribbean and discovered a number of isolated beaches and perfect waves for me. I am an old-fart surfer. I have a left knee full of torn cartilage and ligaments that could go at any minute, so I pick my waves accordingly. This is one of the big reasons that I decided to buy the Albatross. It's big enough to hold my surfboards, and it seemed like perfect Vulcan logic to be able to fly over the ocean until you find a spot you like, land your plane in the water, and paddle on out.

Bicycles. The surfboards only take up one whole side of the aft section of the plane's cargo area, so I had a whole other section to play with. It seemed the perfect size to strap in a couple of fold-up mountain bikes. They are amazing machines that fold up like praying Buddhist monks, only to be transformed into full-size mountain bikes with the turn of a couple of bolts. I consider my bicycles survival gear, for they give me the option to avoid taxis. It used to be that the death-wish mentality it took to drive totally with the hope of crashing into other vehicles was reserved for a few demolition-derby lunatics. (I admit that I once did drive in a demolition derby on Nantucket.) My bicycles allow me the peaceful option of traveling at a much slower rate and not trying to score a direct hit on every single pothole.

Guns. I carry a couple of guns on board. I have an old World War II military-issue .45 and a sawed-off shotgun referred to in the gun world as a "deck sweeper." Tales of hijackings and boatjackings still abound in the Caribbean, but the reality of it is that most of that activity has tapered off since the seventies. Dope smugglers don't need to steal boats. They have enough money to buy one-hundred-foot yachts like they were Kleenex and then pull the plug and send them to the bottom after they've done their dirty work. I guess the guns give me a false sense of security that would allow me to hold off attacking dope dealers or pirates who might want to steal my airplane on some remote island. I can't help it, I guess we all sometimes see ourselves as Indiana Jones. Why do you think it was such a big movie? One man with a pistol and a whip defeats Hitler's army and saves the world. Who wouldn't want that job?

Swag box. Swag is a pirate term. It means treasure, booty, and the like. The swag box on my plane is probably our most important piece of necessary gear, for it's got the goodies. Barter in the islands is still alive and well, and I love it. Since I'm a singer, and my record company doesn't have state-of-the-art distribution in the areas where I like to go, the swag box is filled with my tapes and CD's and a variety of multicolored T-shirts from the Margaritaville store. They are much more valuable than the different-colored currencies you run into. If tapes and CD's are the gold bars, then T-shirts are the silver. A CHEESEBURGER IN PARADISE T-shirt and a CD to a customs agent has an amazing effect on the amount of time one spends in a place. I have left a melodic trail through all the ports of entry that I have visited. So, if you find yourself clearing customs on some remote island in the Caribbean and hearing "Grapefruit/Juicy Fruit" coming from the blaster in the customs office, you know that I've been there before you.

Amp and mike. My favorite places to play these days are little bars on the islands where I go. It is simply back to basics. God knows, I appreciate the thousands of fans who come to hear us play in the big venues in America, but I started out as a saloon singer, and that's what I still think I am today. I occasionally get a chance to sit in in bars in the States, but the word usually gets out way ahead of me and there's a big crowd waiting. I played the beach bars of the Virgin Islands and Tortola long before I ever got famous, and there's nothing like it to me. To put it in nineties terms, it's where I can reconnect with my beach-bum roots. Most beach bars don't come equipped with sound systems, and some don't even have electricity, but in case they do, then my little Trace amp and microphone provide just the right amount of P.A. to overcome the inevitable drunk at the bar who keeps shouting "That's not him, that's not him!"

Fishing gear. If anything is necessary on an adventure, it is certainly fishing gear. Haven't you ever seen any of those disaster movies where people are sitting around in life rafts on the brink of starvation and dehydration, trying desperately to come up with a way to catch a fish? Besides, fishing is one of my sincere passions. My infatuation with saltwater fly-fishing began on the flats west of Key West more than twenty years ago. Back then, only a small percentage of fishermen did it. Today it has been cleverly marketed and the number of boats stationed out in those same flats sends me looking for more remote areas. One of the great thrills and insane justifications of having this big plane is to be able to see a flat from the air, land nearby, drop the dinghy in the water, and go fishing. Granted, it is a far cry from the inceptive intent. Yes, I would rescue the pilot, but then if he was okay and the fish were still in the area, well, that's why I always have my fishing gear on board.

Food. I have covered my obsession with carrying more than ample amounts of food on a trip in *Tales from Margaritaville* in the story about being stranded between Nantucket and Martha's Vineyard in the fog for two days with nothing to eat. Beyond the survival aspect of this idiosyncrasy of mine, it is damn near impossible to find Martinelli's apple juice, Rice Krispies snack cakes, Snickers bars, and other necessary accoutrements in the Chinese stores, bodegas, or *kitanas* of the land-low latitudes. Besides, there was a little room left behind the coolers and in front of the bicycles on the left side of the plane.

Duffel bag. Nothing really dangerous here. The original need for heavy clothing does not apply. Since the Tupac Amaru crashed the Christmas party at the Japanese Embassy in Lima, we have canceled Peru and Machu Picchu from our itinerary. No need for long underwear, wool socks, or heavy jackets. More room for extra CD's and books. See, that's my problem. Instead of being happy with less to carry, I wind up thinking of something else that I just might need. Okay, the duffel bag is stuffed to the seams and weighs fifty pounds.

Computer bag. I'm sorry. I promised myself not to be a slave to this fucking machine, but I failed. It goes everywhere with me, because it has everything in it. In simpler times I just carried one of those Chinese rice-paper journals with the yin-yang figures woven into the cloth jacket and sketches of sampans inside. It was permeated with the various scents from the head shop where it was purchased, from patchouli to paraffin, and had a little silk ribbon that served as a bookmark. It served me well before the computer entered my life, but it didn't have a word processor, or a language translator, or a tide program for the entire Atlantic Ocean, or a flight planner for the whole goddamn world, or an Internet browser, and by God, those things are essential to a traveler these days. Then you have to have an extra battery, storage for disks, CD-ROMs, and manuals, and floppy drives, and Zip drives. See, it's not easy being a writer on the road these days. My rice-paper journal has given way to my overpriced Ghurka office bag, which holds all of this shit. Besides, it weighs enough to help balance the load of the duffel bag so that I don't walk at forty-degree angles to the ground and have an out-of-whack center of gravity.

Guitar. Another piece of absolutely essential gear for any expedition is my guitar. As the ad says, "Don't leave home without it." I have lugged a good many guitars around the world but finally settled on a Martin 0-18 acoustic guitar that goes with me now wherever I travel. It is tiny and light, and the mahogany neck and fret board resist the tendency to warp brought on by changes in climate. It can be played quietly in some foreign hotel room without disturbing the nearby guests, or it can be plugged into an amp for an impromptu performance at some far-removed beach bar. Music is still the only universal language, and I have found myself in too many far-off places where my guitar was like a magic key, opening doors and igniting friendships in a way words never could have.

We were in Africa a few years back, and I remember being asked to play for the proprietor of a resort hotel after we and the other guests had been served dinner. I happily accepted the invitation but told the hotel manager that I wanted the employees of the guesthouse to be included in the audience. I sat in a circle of white and black faces under a sky full of stars on the western plains of Kenya. And I played. Savannah Jane, my daughter, joined me for the last tune of the night, and we sang Julie Gold's "From a Distance," which we had learned from our Nanci Griffith CD long before the Bette Midler version was a hit record. In that setting the words rang truer than I or the author probably ever intended them to, and that to me is the magic of music. More often than not, the writer's original ideas or inspirations are replaced by those of the listener, and the song takes on a whole new meaning. I have accumulated a huge collection of songs, but I don't think of them as my possessions. That becomes very apparent during concerts when I forget a word or a phrase and have to listen to the audience singing them to find my place. Songwriters write songs, but they really belong to the listener. I think of myself sometimes as a toymaker, who enjoys his work but who takes more pleasure from the fact that his toys live in a stranger's toy box, bringing that stranger constant joy.

The next day the paying guests of the hotel departed and went their separate ways, but the staff had become our friends. We spent the morning after breakfast laughing and trying our bad Swahili on our new friends and then we all posed together for family-style pictures next to our plane on the nearby grass strip. There were big hugs and kisses and lots of handshakes, and then we waved long good-byes from the small windows of the single-engine plane until altitude made our friends disappear into the vastness that is Africa. We had left them a new box of toys that only music could create.

Backpack. The backpack I carry these days jumped out at me from a display window in a shop next door to The Four Seasons hotel in Toronto last summer. It is a simple pack with lots of pockets, made of waterproof Gore-Tex, and it sports a ventilating system that circulates air in the large compartment. I am sure this feature was invented by someone who forgot about that banana he bought and didn't eat, the one that fermented into some gooey simple life-form. Experience is always the best teacher.

Over the last thirty years, I have spent far more time in Eddie Bauer, West Marine, Timberland, and Patagonia stores than I have in church. The old army-navy surplus stores of the fifties and sixties have evolved into gazillion-dollar businesses aimed at war babies and yuppies. I am one of the biggest victims, but I don't care. It's important to have as much fun as possible while we're here. It balances out the times when the minefield of life explodes.

I have spent nearly all of my touring and adventuring life looking for the right kind of day bag, since I have a bad propensity for losing unattached items like keys, sunglasses, money, and credit cards. I prefer the zipped-up pocket of a tote bag to the open pockets of my pants.

When I was a boy growing up in the South, men never carried bags on their shoulders, with the exception of the mailman. Shoulder bags looked like purses, and only women carried purses. As children, we were allowed backpacks for school and Scouts, but once we were into high school, the old reliable and totally functional backpack went into Mom's attic. Nobody took a backpack to high school. It just wasn't cool. We carried our books in our arms at awkward angles. Totally cumbersome and uncomfortable, but cool. I believe that part of the growing-up process is a period that starts in early adolescence and can last well into your forties, when cool rules over common sense. I suffered a bagless period through high school and college, but when I finally flunked out of school and ran away to New Orleans to be a hippie and a musician, shoulder bags were not only functional, by God, they were cool.

There has been a lot written about the good and the bad effects of the revolutionary sixties, but no one ever mentions the destigmatization of men carrying shoulder bags. Along with the emotional baggage of being a flower child, you had to carry around to the love-ins a lot of shit that just wouldn't fit in a wallet or the pockets of bell-bottom jeans. There were necessary items for the hip and infamous—rolling papers, pot, Richard Farina and Richard Brautigan paperbacks, bags of granola, extra headbands, bandanas, hash pipe, patchouli oil, fruit, and that damn Swiss Army knife. My bag of choice was a woven straw Guatemalan original that I bought at the local head shop in New Orleans. It definitely was cool, and served me well right up until the day I had some kind of a short circuit in my thinking patterns and decided that I had to get married and settle down.

This offbeat odyssey is what steered me to Nashville, Tennessee, where somehow I wound up working for *Billboard* magazine as a reporter—my only real nine-to-five job in the last thirty years. Though I worked in an office, my heart was still in New Orleans, where I had made the transition from altar boy to street musician. My one tie to my other life was my old Guatemalan shoulder bag. I dismissed the taunts of the starch-collared, briefcase-carrying soldiers of conformity who populated the building where I worked. It was only when it became obvious that my faithful Guatemalan bag could not keep up with the junk I had to carry around in my straight job that I retired it. I had tape recorders and stacks of free albums that were sent to me by the record companies to review, and then came the real killer of my straw bag—bottled water. Bottled water was the torpedo that sent many a good cheap South American shoulder bag to the Goodwill.

Of course I couldn't carry a briefcase, but what to get? I was walking home from work one day and passed a mailman. Serendipity took over; I stopped him and asked him where I could get a mailman's bag. He told me they were government-issued and not available to the public, but he just happened to have an old one at home. The next day I purchased my contraband piece of government property for twenty bucks. The day after that, at work, my new look didn't impress the briefcase bunch, but the secretaries thought it was cool.

When I ran away from Nashville to Key West, I was traveling light. I took only my guitar, a duffel bag full of clothes, and my mailbag. The tropics suited me just fine, but things soon fell victim to the hot, salty air that could rust away a car in a year. My mailbag soon took on the appearance of some giant fungus experiment and had to be thrown away. It was time to get a new bag.

One of the first people I met when I went to Key West was Tom Corcoran, who became my longtime friend. An ex-Navy officer, Tom had chosen life in the tropics over life on the high seas and invented a good number of phony-baloney jobs that have kept him afloat until this day. Back then he was making bags and hats that were the rave of Key West, and I bought one. It was great, but again, it was leather and had to be replaced often. When I ran away to St. Barts, I found a canvas version of the bag, made by LuLu Magras and sold at his store in Gustavia. LuLu's bag is still in my collection, but with no pockets and no zippers, it wasn't *the* bag I needed.

After another decade of checking out luggage stores and searching through mail-order catalogues—and purchasing a dozen or more fashionable, expensive, but not-quite-functional shoulder bags—I was beginning to think that the perfect day bag just did not exist.

And then it happened. I was home in Alabama for a visit, and I had forgotten my shoulder bag. I was headed out for a day at the Gulf and needed a bag. My mother said, "Just go down to the new mall and get one," but I don't like to go to malls. I don't know what it is about those places, but they are more frightening to me than the pictures of the Jim Jones commune in Guyana. I opted to rummage through the garage, and there I found my old Boy Scout backpack. It was badly mildewed, full of holes, and as stiff as a piece of plywood, but it was speaking to me. The solution to my problem had been there all along.

I am back to a backpack and couldn't be happier. As I sit here and see the pile of gear that's accumulating for this expedition, I know that my backpack is probably the most important item that I will carry with me. It is an extension of my gypsy soul. It is my independence and my emergency parachute. Though I have mounted this expedition and have this plane full of stuff, I know deep down inside that if it came to it, I could cram what I really need into my backpack, hit the trail, and be perfectly happy.

It's a Family Affair

24 December 1996
Palm Beach, Florida

With my packing completed, the only thing left to do is to go over the logistics. So here's the plan. Cameron and I will leave tomorrow afternoon. Randall Anderson is coming with us. Randall works for me part-time around the house. I hired him out of the Boys Club Surf Shop in Palm Beach. He is a hard worker, a surfer, and a college graduate. You don't find that combination too often. We will fly south on the Albatross. Jane and the girls will meet us in San José, Costa Rica, on the twenty-sixth. In our house, Christmas is pretty much over after noon given that I'm not religious. I did enough praying and asking for forgiveness between the ages of ten and sixteen to last me a lifetime. I guess I'm one of those casual Catholics. I still go to mass once a year at the Saint Louis Cathedral in New Orleans, which I consider my church. And I wear a medal of Saint Christopher, patron saint of travelers, and believe in guardian angels. Other than that, I get my spirituality from the ocean and the airways, Joseph Campbell and Eudora Welty.

This will be our first father-and-son trip together. Cameron Marley, who is two and a half, shares my love of airplanes, especially the Albatross. He calls it an "A-dah." On days when I'm not flying and the plane is down for maintenance, I just take him out to the airport and let him climb around and make engine noises. This is also a perfect way to separate him and his sister Sarah Delaney, who is four and a half. They are textbook sibling rivals, loving and hugging one minute, then taking cheap shots at each other when they think they're out of view of the grown-ups.

I wonder if my sisters, Laurie and Lucy, and I were the same way. My first response is of course not. Then little nerve endings seem to sizzle and I find myself feeling the hooked scar over my left eye where Laurie nailed me with a toy helicopter. Further recollections and examination find me probing the back of my head for the long calcified scar where she caught me with the broken rake handle. Just by the number of stitches alone, Cameron Marley and Sarah Delaney are way ahead of me at their age.

Savannah Jane is not coming. She is a teenager, and teenagers don't go on trips with their parents unless they are bound and gagged. We are going on a weeks-long adventure, visiting five countries, exploring the Amazon and God knows what else, but it does not interest her because we will be there. She is headed for Key West with her cousins to see Todd Snyder at the Margaritaville Club. I don't have a problem with this. First of all, the apple doesn't fall far from the tree, and there is a family history of independence. In her almost eighteen years, she has lived in New York, Malibu, Nashville, Florida, and the French West Indies. She learned her first French when asking the *pompiers* gathered at the bar in Le Select for change in francs to play the pinball machine. Marius Skatelborough and his family have baby-sat lots of boat urchins in their time, and Savannah wasn't the first. When she is older, we will have our time together, but she is a teenager now and I accept that excuse. That sounds like a model nineties kind of answer, but then I look at my little ones and a shock wave of terror rumbles through my body like an earthquake's tremor. I have to do it again, and when they are teenagers, I will be sixty. When I say my prayers tonight, I will pray that all goes well for the scientists who are working on cloning techniques.

The Holes in the Floor of Heaven

*They soared through the Milky Way counting the stars
Once around Venus, twice around Mars*
—"Chanson pour les Petits Enfants"

Somehow or other, we finally managed to get the kids to sleep, though they fought like hell to stay up and see Santa. I bored them to death teaching them some words in Spanish, and soon they were on their way to bed. It is the calm before the storm. In a few short hours it will be Christmas morning and all hell will break loose around here. I am too excited to sleep. The anticipation of Christmas morning, coupled with the excitement of turning fifty and starting the big adventure, has my head spinning. Jane and I finished assembling toys and preparing the scene for Christmas morning. Jane went to bed, but I was still wide awake. I find myself alone in my office without a creature stirring, but since we live in South Florida, I am sure there are a few mice at work around here somewhere, or a lizard or two hopping through the branches of the sea grapes. I can't help it, I still get as excited about Christmas as my children. Maybe it's the birthday thing. Since this is to be a landmark birthday, I want to stay up until my birth hour, which is just after one in the morning, to see if any bells, whistles, or internal alarm clocks sound at the moment I reach the half-century mark. If you are going to turn fifty, my suggestion is not to sleep through it or pass out. But staying up into the early hours of the morning is hard to do these days, and this comes as a bit of a shock to a former night owl like me.

I am by occupation a night creature. It started not with nightclub singing, but on the night shift at the shipyard in Mobile. During the summer before my senior year in high school,

I had worked the graveyard shift and had gotten my first taste of staying up all night. I liked it. The work wasn't hard, there were far fewer foremen around than during the day, and there was a very different feel to the industrial lighting that created giant distorted shadows out of the rigging of ships in the dry dock and the booms of the giant cranes. I slept in the afternoon, went out for a few hours, then clocked in at midnight. I was an electrician's helper then, running cable in the hold of an ancient Liberty ship that was being converted into a floating power station. The great thing about the job was that I worked only six hours but got paid for eight. When the first-shift whistle blew, I would pass the sleepy-eyed and grumbling first-shift workmen filing into the shipyard, while I was bright-eyed and bushy-tailed, heading out the gate and on my way to Dauphin Island to go surfing.

For a seventeen-year-old, this job was just too good to be true. I hadn't even come close to getting laid yet, so I needed every high-energy activity I could find to battle my hormones. Scuba diving and surfing were my passions. Since the waves in the Gulf of Mexico rarely got above three feet, except when a hurricane came roaring north, I spent more time under water than on it. I had settled into my night life and loved the odd-ball hours I was keeping.

Sure enough, only a week after I started the job, I was out at Dauphin Island to surf the two-foot chop and I stepped on a broken bottle, ripping open the bottom of my right foot and severing a couple of tendons. Next thing I knew I was coming out of the hospital on crutches. At the time I thought I had lost the best job in the world.

How I got from the shipyard to New Orleans is another story for another time, but after I secured my first job on Bourbon Street, to my delight I found that my routine was not that much different from the days of the graveyard shift. I would sleep through New Orleans's hot and humid summer mornings in the comfort of my dark and air-conditioned little apartment, which I referred to as "the bat cave." (This was way back when *Batman* was only a comic book. Long before he appeared on TV, in major motion pictures, and on the side of plastic drink cups at fast-food restaurants, Batman was the hero of the night people, a good-guy version of Dracula.)

I went to work after dark and got off at three in the morning. Then I would head to the local after-hours joints that tourists were afraid of and get lost in the culture of the night. I absolutely loved it. Staying up all night was both my rebellion and my education, and it put me on a course and into a crowd of people that were far more interesting than anything I had ever seen before. At some point in the dawn's early light, I would head home. The trick was to try and get home before seven. By then the summer heat of the city was already blistering and "regular people" were already on their way to "real jobs."

I found myself being able to feel 6:00 A.M. without ever having to look at my watch. It was as close to being a vampire as I ever came. I could just feel the hour at which I would head home, strolling alone or with a drunken group of friends through the damp, deserted streets of the French Quarter, just like Elvis in the opening of *King Creole*. If I wasn't sidetracked to one of the neighborhood hangouts, like the Seven Seas or Harry's Place, I would eventually wind up at my apartment on Ursuline Street.

At that hour of the morning, the courtyard of my building looked like a Salvador Dalí movie sequence. Time, as measured by watches and clocks, had no relevance in the building. There would be people having breakfast, people having supper. People going to and coming from their jobs, and people sitting around who had been up for days. When you're eighteen and living on your own for the first time, the one thing you don't need much of is sleep. I would join whatever activity was going on in the courtyard and listen to the stories. Eventually I would wander up the rickety stairs to my bat cave, where I would recharge my batteries for a few hours and then get up and do it again.

These days, I get up when I used to go to bed. That's when you know you're getting older. I like to think of life experiences and stories in cycles, and this surely is one. When I'm working on the road, the adrenaline rush alone keeps me up until one or two, but I am able to dull it a little with a late-night cheese-burger or a couple of slices of pizza. But I am home now, and just to stay up until my birth hour, I had to have a two-hour nap this afternoon and a double espresso after dinner.

A little before 1:00 A.M., I walk out onto the balcony and stare out over the ocean. It's a Don Blanding kind of Florida night. The ocean is calm, the sound of small waves lapping at the beach. From the safe haven of my waterfront balcony, the sky is a Christmas Eve collage. Orion's Belt stretches out above the Atlantic Ocean, the seven sisters of the Pleiades glimmer up there somewhere between midnight and infinity, and the Gemini twins seem happy and in perfect position. The new moon is invisible, and there isn't a cloud in the sky. Space, the final frontier, is the perfect backdrop to the light show overhead. The cluster of the Milky Way is clearly visible and the Christmas star easy to find. I think of an old Irish saying that was passed on to me by a fishing guide in New Zealand, on a similar night south of the equator: The stars are the holes in the floor of heaven. I think about how different one's view of the heavens can be, depending upon your location on the planet. From the deck of a rolling ship a thousand miles out in the Atlantic, I have seen these same constellations as a cosmic pinball game, as I tried to place their reflections on the tiny round mirror of my sextant.

A cruise ship moves east across the horizon, heading down-island. It is Christmas in the Caribbean. In all likeli-hood, she steers a computer course with input from several global positioning system (GPS) units, without a human hand on the wheel while the passengers sing carols. I haven't been in a tropical environment for Christmas in quite a while. We usually head for Aspen, one of my old home ports. I scan the sky hoping for a shooting star. I don't have to wait long. I wish upon the star. I wish for peace for my father, who sits in Alabama in the black hole of Alzheimer's disease, almost an angel. Then I say a little Christmas prayer. I pray to God, Buddha, Saint Christopher, Saint Jude, and my loyal guardian angels to watch over my family and me. As Billy Pilgrim said, "So it goes." I turn fifty where I was born: by the edge of the sea.

A Visit with Mr. Twain

 It's done. I walk back into my study and sit down at my desk. The espresso is still doing its thing, and I am still wide awake. What can slow the thoughts in my busy brain and allow me to get some sleep before Santa Claus arrives? What is the proper passage from the proper book with which to mark the actual passage into my fiftieth year? I scan the shelf behind me where my favorite books reside and go first to *The Tao of Leadership*, by John Heider, a little book with a lot of power. I open to a page at random like I try to do every day, and here is where I land.

#27 Beyond Techniques

An experienced traveler does not need a packaged tour to go places safely.

A good political speech does not need to make promises or antagonize the crowd.

A good mathematician does not need a computer to solve every problem.

A secure home does not have bolts and bars and locks and alarms everywhere, yet a burglar cannot get inside.

I have landed here before. It is an appropriate page for the leader of the upcoming expedition. But as calming as this little book has been to my helter-skelter sense of movement through the days, tonight it is not enough to settle me down. One page of the *Tao* cannot idle my engine, but I dare not read on. As long as I have depended on these familiar pages for advice, I have only read it one page at a time. That is the way the person who gave it to me told me it should be done, and I have not strayed from her instructions. I sit quietly for a moment and think about the passage while I stare out at the serene ocean. Instead of tranquility, the ocean speaks to me of past adventures and what lies beyond the horizon. Why do we go out there, when we know it can be dangerous? I think it is natural for some people to sit in BarcaLoungers and play it safe, while others strap themselves onto the tops of rocket ships and go out to defy gravity. It just depends on who you are and what makes you tick. I like the idea of being somewhere in the middle of those two parameters.

Today the expression "going around the world" is used with a casualness that would make Captain Cook turn over in his grave—that is, if he had one. The greatest of navigators was actually killed on the island of Maui and cut into a dozen or so pieces by the local witch doctors, who scattered his remains to the farthermost edges of the islands. The shamans' logic was that they did not want the soul of such a man to ever reconnect and come back to haunt them. Today, when you hear people talk about going around the world, it might sound like this. "Oh, you're taking a trip around the world? Are you doing the Concorde trip?" I took the QE2 to Europe once to make a record. I knew things had changed when I went looking for the skeet-shooting range at the stern of the ship and was told it had been turned into a miniature-golf course.

Following the Equator is one of a baker's dozen of books I would have to take to a desert island. I can pick it up, turn to any page, and get lost in the story. So as I sit alone in my office in the grips of a cappuccino buzz, I pull it off the bookshelf, open it up, and begin to read. I opened to the story about Twain's ship, after a six-week trip from California, arriving off the coast of Maui and being told by the missionaries who had paddled out to greet them that they could not go ashore, due to a cholera epidemic on the island. As the story goes, at this point the captain of the vessel nonchalantly announced the situation to the passengers and plotted a new course for the Orient.

I take this as a reminder that when you go off adventuring, part of the adventure is the unpredictable. That is what really separates travelers from tourists. So many Americans traveling today want to take their America with them, and many of the places they go to cater to this desire at the expense of their history and culture. It used to be that the only thing American that you could find in the boonies was Coca-Cola. Now Kentucky Fried Chicken is the caviar of the Caribbean. Taco Bells and Burger Kings permeate the lower latitudes. I remember being on St. Barts many years ago hearing a New Yorker strolling down the beach at St. Jean, yelling to her husband at the other end of the beach, "Stanley, I can't find a goddamn *New York Times* anywhere on this island." That's what I liked about St. Barts then. Unfortunately, you can find the *Times* now, at several newsstands on the island. This afternoon, we are going to light out into the territory and see what's left out there.

I am tempted to take the book with me, but it's too rare and I would hate to lose it or damage it, so it goes back up on the shelf. It is nearly 2:00 a.m. and I find myself yawning—a good sign. I am ready to attempt, as my grandfather used to say, equal strain on all body parts, which was his way of describing a nap, but something caught my eye. It is an odd

birthday gift that I had received a week earlier from a fan—
two old issues of *Life* magazine. When they arrived, I exam-
ined them wondering what the significance of such a gift
was. Now I took them down. They were big and heavy, and
the black-and-white covers were tattered. I finally understand when I look at the dates in the bottom right-hand corner. Hello, Jimmy. The first cover is dated December 23, 1946,
and features a collection of photos by Fernand Bourges of Fra
Angelico's panel episodes of the life of Christ. The other
issue is dated December 30, 1946, and has a black-and-white
photo of a famous opera star of the day on the cover. Now I
get it. The magazines span the week in 1946 in which I came
into the world. I have a pair of tiny time capsules in my hand,
and I can't wait to go inside.

The first things that catch my eye are the ads on the back covers. Baby Jesus and opera may adorn the front, but cigarettes
have the back—with this compelling slogan: MORE DOCTORS
SMOKE CAMELS THAN ANY OTHER CIGARETTE. Accompanying the
reassuring news that Camels were the choice of more than
100,000 doctors surveyed is hype about a Madison Avenue gim-
mick called the T-Zone. *T* stood for *taste* and *throat*. The Chester-
fields ad on the back of the other issue features popular singers.
There is a color-enhanced photo of Perry Como and Jo Stafford,
the Dave Matthews and Tori Amos of their time, puffing away
against a backdrop featuring the names of exciting venues
neatly arranged in an oval. Below their images is this copy: AL-
WAYS MILDER, BETTER TASTING, COOLER SMOKING. Wherever we go,
Chesterfield is on top. Tobacco companies have been at this
game a long time. As an old bonefish guide in the Bahamas once
said to me after a huge bonefish came right up to the boat chasing my fly and then swam off, "Jimmy, he didn't get big by bein'
no fool." The same thing can be said for the tobacco industry.
You have to be smart to sell poison.

I thumb through the first few pages of ads. There are ads
for Alka-Seltzer and Vitalis and Erle Stanley Gardner mystery

novels. The table of contents features the following stories of
the week:

Election Murder Shakes New York Police
Shanghai Street Vendors Riot
Grain Elevator Burns in Minneapolis
Christmas Brings Joy and Sadness to Europe's Children
Princess Elizabeth Has a Romance
Eisenhower Is Groomed for President
Astrology: It Has 3 Million Followers Who Live by the Stars
Movie of the Week: *It's a Wonderful Life*
Sports: Retriever Trials
Feature: The West Indies

I go directly to the story on the West Indies. The piece
opens predictably with a picture of a palm-lined boulevard in
Barbados, a map of the Caribbean, and this paragraph:

> Of all the overseas vacation spots favored by Americans,
> the West Indies is the first one since the war to invite tourist
> trade on anything like a prewar scale. This winter some
> 225,000 U.S. tourists will visit the West Indies—more than
> twice as many as went last winter. Most of them must travel
> by air, for only a few passenger ships have been reconverted
> to peacetime service. But the West Indies are definitely back
> on the tourists' map and are once again a lotus-eater's par-
> adise, offering an escape from gray skies, frozen radiators and
> the inflamed nose.

Some things never change. The photos that follow present
a collage of life on several different islands. First came Haiti.
There are pictures of the marketplace in Port-au-Prince and
the ruins above Cap Haitien of the palace of Henri I, the black
king of Haiti, a historical character with whom I have become
very familiar during my many trips to Haiti. In Jamaica, the

photographer captured the tranquility of the Río Cobre and the waterfalls near Ocho Rios. The section on Trinidad features the beach at Maracas Bay and a Victorian house in downtown Port of Spain. The last segment, on Cuba, includes a two-page photo of a stormy Gulf of Mexico bashing the seawall and sending towers of spray up onto the Malecon, the famous broad boulevard that parallels the Gulf Stream. I find it odd that these islands that have become such a part of my life were featured the week I was born, and prophetic enough to cover me in goose bumps. It is as if the islands had been in my cards all along.

I check out the article on astrology to see what my horoscope says.

Capricorn: December 22 to January 20—You are a patient planner [*absolutely not*], steady as a rock, conservative, but forceful [*partially true*]. You are trustworthy, reliable and good at executive jobs [*on the money*]. But you lack enthusiasm, take a fatalistic attitude toward life, and are afraid of taking risks [*You have got to be kidding*]. Stop brooding and start getting excited about your work and your family [*utter bullshit*].

So much for astrology. I picked up the other issue.
Again the ads call out to me.
There are ads for Kelvinator refrigerators, Philco hi-fis, and several new Hollywood movies. Then there is Elsie the Cow. Elsie, her husband, Elmer, and their little cow son are in a kitchen gathered around a breakfast table pouring Borden's milk on cereal and talking and acting like humans. This must be where Gary Larson went for material. It's the kind of picture I think all these "family values" advocates conjure up. I loved Elsie as a kid. I loved Borden's chocolate milk. Of course I did—there was more sugar in a glass of that stuff than in a cane field in Cuba. But now, looking at this ad, I feel used. Elsie has lost her credibility. We all knew cows live mundane

lives in barns and can't talk, but we bought it, along with
A-bomb tests, "separate but equal," housewives, *Father Knows
Best*, the Korean War, Charles Van Doren, and the list goes on.
It didn't stop until Vietnam when some brave and honest peo-
ple finally got the word out that we were being lied to. Yet, I
wouldn't want to have lived at any other time.

I get off the soapbox in my mind and thumb through the
pages. There are stories on racism in Georgia, a giant storm in
the English Channel, and Christian disunity. Hell, it sounds
like 1996. I am beginning to feel morose, when, thank God, I
see a picture of a ship that jolts my memory. I have seen this
boat before, but I can't remember where or when. Then I see
the name on the bow—*Del Norte*. As the story tells, she was the
first major U.S. liner built after World War II. The sister ship
that followed her down the way at Ingalls Shipyard in
Pascagoula, Mississippi, was the *Del Mundo*. Her captain was
named James Delaney Buffett—my grandfather. I have vivid
memories of boarding that ship at the Governor Nichols Street
pier in New Orleans to visit my grandfather when I was four
or five. I remember the incredible vision of luxury and adventure. The ships were headed for South America carrying 7,500
tons of cargo and 124 passengers. It's no secret that I thought
my grandfather was the coolest guy in the world because he
was the captain of the ship, and that is what I wanted to be
when I grew up. This great old passenger freighter has long
since gone to the scrapyard.

I let out a big yawn. The caffeine is wearing off. I thumb
through the rest of the magazine vowing to read the other stories on the ensuing trip. Then, on the second-to-last page, I see
an ad for a new movie from Liberty Films: *It's a Wonderful Life*,
directed by Frank Capra. I gaze out the French doors of my
balcony at the stars one more time. I can't agree more: So far, it
truly has been a wonderful life.

A Baker's Dozen Minus One

For those who might be interested, besides *Following the Equator,* here are the twelve other books I would take to a desert island:

The Adventures of Huckleberry Finn by Mark Twain
Treasure Island by Robert Louis Stevenson
Don't Stop the Carnival by Herman Wouk
Winds from the Carolinas by Robert Wilder
One Writer's Beginnings by Eudora Welty
The Old Man and the Sea by Ernest Hemingway
A Gift from the Sea by Anne Morrow Lindbergh
The Fables of La Fontaine by Jean de la Fontaine
West with the Night by Beryl Markham
A Collection of Poems by Pablo Neruda
The Road Less Traveled by M. Scott Peck
No One Writes to the Colonel and Other Stories by Gabriel García
   Márquez

Christmas Morning with Cecil B. DeBuffett

Cameron Marley and Sarah Delaney are tugging on the bedsheets shortly after six demanding that we get up. They have obviously sneaked a peek at the kitchen. They are wide-eyed and jabbering like macaws, alerting Jane and me to the fact that Santa did indeed come down the chimney, eat the cookies and milk we had left him, and deposit a sack around the fireplace hearth that would fill a FedEx truck. Jane and Savannah beg for a few more minutes of sleep, so I get up and take the little ones downstairs. I keep them contained in the living room as long as I possibly can. They are bouncing around like minnows that have just been plucked from the water and dropped on a beach. Mom and big sister make their appearance at the staircase. I release Sarah Delaney and Cameron from the holding area, following with video camera in hand.

Putting a state-of-the-art digital video camera with a zoom lens in the hand of a fifty-year-old man on Christmas morning is like giving a sixteen-year-old the keys to your Porsche. It just shouldn't be done. There I am, yelling a litany of parental clichés like "Look here, Cameron," "Puddy, what did you get?" "Savannah, what time did you get home last night?" We all turn into overbearing, obtrusive directors with some half-baked notion that one day we will assemble all of the footage into a meaningful chronological account of our time on Earth. I don't know about you, but I can tell you that most of the videos in my family wind up in a shoe box somewhere and surface only when some kind of cleanup is initiated around the house. At that point you might scan through the titles of the tapes; that is, if you even bothered to write down the title and date when you were filming. Then maybe you drop one in the video player and reminisce and get depressed about how quickly time is passing.

I know I've captured enough moments when I hear Savannah say through my headset, "Jesus, Christmas morning with Cecil B. DeBuffett. Dad, we're hungry. Please put the camera down and make us some pancakes." I put the camera down and carve a path through the mountains of wrapping paper and cardboard boxes to the stove, where I can put myself to better use. And do something that will really bring joy to their Christmas morning—make pancakes.

I don't know what it is about pancakes, dads, and kids. I am sure it has some hereditary link to the first pancake maker in a cave somewhere, probably France, where some inexplicable bond was created. Whoever the prehistoric father was who took a little time off from chasing saber-toothed tigers and drawing on cave walls to spend a little quality time cooking breakfast for his kids, I want to thank him. One of the great things about small children is their ability to see the world with honest little hearts. No matter what pinnacle of success you might reach in your career, children don't take that into consideration. They see you for what you are, and I don't know too many grown-ups, especially those who have attained a certain level of success, who couldn't use a little dose of humility every now and then. My kids don't give a damn about my accomplishments in the music "bidness." To them I am primarily the Pancake Man. When I'm home, our mornings have become breakfast rituals, which I start by making them pancakes and sharing time and stories before our day gets too busy. We adults think we're busy, but not compared with our kids. There's school, then play groups, swimming lessons, karate, gymnastics, and the dreaded trips to Chuck E. Cheese.

Time is really irrelevant on Christmas morning. We open presents, shoot videos, have our breakfast, open more pre-

sents, clean up, and it's barely eight-thirty. All of that anticipation, all of that overkill advertising and commercialism that
now starts as early as September, all of that insane buildup,
and it's over nearly as fast as a space-shuttle launch.

This is the first Christmas in nearly ten years that we
haven't awakened in the snow-covered mountains of Aspen. It
is eighty degrees and a beautiful beach day. I have a few hours
to kill before our big adventure begins with the departure for
the Cayman Islands. I have assembled all the toys, and the kids
are hard at work trying out everything they've gotten. Bicycles
and battery-powered plastic Jeeps have created a mini Daytona
speedway around the pool. I excuse myself from the pit crew
and head for the beach for a little time alone to reflect on how I
have actually gotten here and who I really am.

We Are the People Our Parents Warned Us About

I was supposed to have been a Jesuit priest
Or a Naval Academy grad
That was the way that my parents perceived me
Those were the plans that they had
But I couldn't fit the part
Too dumb or too smart
Ain't it funny how we all turned out
I guess we are the people our parents warned us about
—"WE ARE THE PEOPLE OUR PARENTS WARNED US ABOUT"

I get a lot of song material from bumper stickers and bathroom walls. This slogan is one of the best I ever ran across, and it made a great song. I guess I liked the idea of being my own threat so much because it meant that I had turned into something different. I always wanted to be different.

We are all products of our environment, and the child-rearing environment of the early fifties was pretty straightforward. Like most of the other war babies I know, I come from a fairly dysfunctional background. My parents worked for as far back as I can remember. I know that's where my work ethic came from. They were typical middle-class Southerners in most regards, but there were also inherited traits that set them apart.

My father was a man of simple rules, though he could be totally unpredictable. We were well-known along the Gulf Coast as a seafaring family, but when World War II broke out, my father joined the Air Corps. I guess we have a hidden flying gene in there among all that salt water. My mother was the visionary. She loved music, musicals, and anything that had to do with the arts. She had attended college for two years before the Great Depression sent her out into the workforce, where she stayed for nearly sixty years.

My father's idea of my future was hinged to the past. He saw me working on a boat. My mother taught me to dream and expand my horizons beyond family traditions and my childhood surroundings. They sure as hell did some things that I loved them for and some things that really pissed me off, but I still love them and love to go back to Alabama to visit.

Since they both worked, my two sisters and I were cared for over the years by a series of loving black women—Louise George, Ida Spavin, and Olla Mae Brazille. These women are a part of who I am today. Though they had distinctly different personalities, their influences on me are still there. They praised me when I was good and popped my ass when I was bad. They taught me to love soul food, James Brown, and Oreo cookies, but more important, they taught me not to fear or look down on their race. Their hearts were big enough to deal with injustices from slavery to segregation, raise their own families, hold down menial jobs, and still have room left to love three little white children. It was saintly behavior, and that's the way I think of them to this day.

Then there was the Catholic church, but we don't even want to begin to untangle that ball of snakes. Let's just say that I survived Catholic school in a lot better shape than other people I know.

The thing you have to remember is that our parents were once young like us, or like we think we are. It's hard enough to accept the mileposts of aging. Grandparents are real old. Parents are old, and we, of course, will stay in our twenties for at least three decades. It is almost unfathomable for us to think of our parents as young, naïve people, but they were. And without benefit of child psychologists and therapists, they were even less equipped to raise their children properly than we are. They just did it the way their parents did it, with loose interpretations of disciplinary passages from the Bible. We, the sixties generation, were going to do it all differently. We started out being the people our parents warned us about, but we turned into them, or close facsimiles, anyway, because we shared the common burden of rearing children, and children change your entire life.

The Ghosts of Christmas Past

I grew up watching *Father Knows Best* and thinking to myself that this was the way family life in America was supposed to be, but it sure wasn't what was happening at my house. There were many nights I wondered and sometimes prayed for my family and me to be as happy as the TV Andersons. Guess what, I wasn't the only kid wishing for that. While the Andersons were living out our fantasies on the boob tube, most of my generation were struggling silently in their family roles, years later requiring an entire new self-help section in bookstores. So it wasn't that much of a shock to me when Robert Young, who played the understanding Bill Anderson, and later Dr. Marcus Welby, revealed that he was a total alcoholic. It actually made me feel a lot better. It made not only the Andersons and Robert Young look more human, it made my generation aware that the solution to raising a family lay in an honest effort at addressing real hard problems, not in making up something that didn't exist.

Since that startling discovery that punctured my naïve concept of family life, I have learned a few things about raising a family. First of all, I am no expert. Parenting is a learning experience. In a way we are no more than good camp counselors to our children, guiding them through the woods. We do not own them or their thoughts. We can only influence them, in the short time we have them, by our good or bad examples. I hope that I have learned enough from the good and bad things that happened to me in my childhood to give my kids a better shot at being caring and wise children of the late twentieth century with all of its wonder and fright.

Kick the Tires and Light the Fires

Today the adventure begins. The Albatross is packed and all systems are go. The weather's perfect, and we even have a tailwind. We have permission to fly over Cuba on our direct route to the Cayman Islands, and we should be "wheels in the well" by three o'clock and having Christmas dinner in a hotel on Grand Cayman, just me and my son. No mom, no sisters, no nannies—it's just gonna be Dad and Cameron (and the pilots) flying south to the tropics. I wish that I could say that this idea of Cameron and I traveling "alone" was the well-planned idea of a thoughtful and caring father of the nineties, but I am sorry to say that it had its origins in pure sibling rivalry, to which Jane once again found a solution. In the turmoil and excitement of the holidays and the attendant chocolate overload, my kids were basically going nuts. Jane came to me in my office on Christmas Eve and in her wonderful, straightforward, no-bullshit style, said, "I can't take a three-and-a-half-hour ride with the kids. They're fighting like cats and dogs. Why don't you take Cameron with you? He loves you and that goddamn Albatross. Take Randall along. He can watch Cameron on the plane and, anyway, I don't want you surfing the Pacific alone. Cameron will be fine, just ask him." I did just that, and as matter-of-fact as any two-and-a-half-year-old can be, he just smiled and said, "That would be great, Dad."

Now this should in no way be taken as an affront to girls. Some of my best friends are girls. I love girls. I wanted my first child to be a girl, though at times I tried to make her my buddy. Savannah Jane did a great job in that role for as long as she could. She was the tomboy kid who followed me to the jungles of Central America, the beaches of Australia, and the sidewalk cafés of Paris. Then adolescence and hormonal changes turned her into a young woman.

When Sarah Delaney arrived, I was just as happy. True, they would probably turn into wild teenagers and marry guys who could never fish or tell stories as well as their father. True, they couldn't throw a curveball very well, but they were my girls and I loved them more than anything else in the world.

I was perfectly comfortable in a woman's world, or so I thought. I have two sisters and no brothers. As a child, I was very close to my mother. I was well into my thirties before my father and I, who had waged our own guerrilla warfare, luckily and finally made our peace. I now lived in what I referred to then as the International House of Women. It consisted of my wife, two daughters, two Trinidadian nannies, a Russian housekeeper, three female dogs, and a female cat. Add to that a collection of girlfriends of all the above, and there were many nights at the dinner table when I was the only man at a hen party listening to tales of PMS and agreeing with the girls that most men were pigs.

Cameron Marley came into our lives just at the right time for all of us Buffetts.

Cameron has had an attachment to airplanes from the first time he saw one. I never tried to force him to love what I love, but it's nice when it happens on its own. He is full of questions as we head through the gate at Palm Beach International. I think that even at this early age the sense of adventure has permeated his instincts. He spots the *Hemisphere Dancer* sitting on the ramp and breaks into a big grin. He sounds kind of like Tweety Bird: "Wet's go fwyin!" he shouts.

The *Hemisphere Dancer* looks majestic, sitting on the ramp with her nose pointing into the southerly breeze, as if she already knows the course we are to steer. This ship will carry a lot of dreams today. We pull up next to the rear door of the plane, and Cameron is the first one out. He races for the boarding ladder at the rear hatch and shimmies up it like a squirrel monkey and disappears inside the cabin. "Dad, dere's bicycles on dis plane, did you know that?" he calls out. I acknowledge his discovery and make the final preflight walk around the plane while pilots Pete and Alex, who will accompany Randall, Cameron, and me, load the last of our gear. She has already been thoroughly preflighted by the crew, but I want to check for any last-minute potential problems.

We humans seem to have a genetic trapping for grandiosity, and one has only to conjure up a few key words like *Titanic, Hindenburg,* and Spruce Goose to know that big things do break. Our misguided superiority complex creates an illusion of domination over our creations, but eventually they all turn around and bite us on the ass, just to remind us that we aren't as smart as we think we are. As a pilot, I know that airplanes can break: especially big ones. In my experience, flying has been 99 percent fun and adventure and 1 percent terror. I have experienced both emotions in the cockpit. You prepare for the terror by knowing your ship and how she works. You memorize emergency items and do a few vital "what if" scenarios. A little prayer to Saint Christopher doesn't hurt either. There is a certain element of risk involved in flying, but there is risk involved going to Dunkin' Donuts for breakfast, not to mention the life-threatening possibilities of standing in line at a U.S. post office. Life does not come without risks. You learn to take them, or you stay home and watch life on TV.

"Let's go, Dad," I hear Cameron call out. His face appears in the open window of the pilot's seat on the flight deck. He is ready. I am ready. It's time to kick the tires and light the fires.

If you have ever seen a 747 take off from close range, you have probably asked yourself the first question that comes to mind: How in the hell do they ever get that big son of a bitch into the air? The great thing about flying is that the essentials haven't changed since the Wright brothers got bored with building bicycles and unlocked the secret of aerodynamics. It still boils down to the basics of stick and rudder. It is the same for a 747 as it is for a Piper Cub.

As for the pilot, the person at the controls probably started out like all pilots do, clutching a model airplane gingerly between his fingers and circling the frontiers of his bedroom, making engine noises with his lips and tongue. At some point along the way, the dreams of flying are taken over by curiosity and lead to the the discovery of the reality behind the dream. Once you learn the basics of aviation—power, drag, thrust pitch, yaw—the actual feat of making a big ship fly is not as mysterious as it might look.

At first glance, the cockpit of a Grumman Albatross is frightening. An instrument panel filled with knobs, buttons, dials, switches, and levers becomes just part of the checklist. When I first bought this plane, I donned my flight coveralls and had Pete take me crawling around the engine spaces. I wanted to know how everything worked. I didn't just want to read about it or look at a picture of a system in a manual. I guess I get that from my old man. I remember seeing him in his office at the shipyard in a white shirt and tie, with lots of paperwork and drawings piled on his desk, and I remember seeing him in overalls crawling in and out of bilges and double-bottom ships. He was a lot more at home in his coveralls.

I spent one whole day with Pete up on the wings climbing on, around, and through the engine compartments, learning where the oil lines and hydraulic pumps were located, so that I knew firsthand what happened when you hit one of those switches on the instrument panel. You don't just take the wheel and point the nose at some number on the compass. If you are going to be a good captain, you need to know your ship. I now feel quite at home on this complicated flight deck, but that was not always the case. I find myself thinking back to the first time I ever sat in the pilot's seat of an Albatross.

I was heading down-island in my Lake amphibian, on my regular run from Florida to St. Barts. The trip had become very familiar but was never routine. The great fun of those solo trips was what I call the "Lindbergh factor." You are flying alone above the ocean for long distances—suspended between ocean and sky—hoping technology and navigational skills will keep you on your perch. If you fall, you have a plan: a life raft, a radio, a fishing pole, rum, and water. Hopefully, you will be plucked from the sea and live to fly again. You practice your "what if" scenario down to picking the waves on which to land. You see yourself in the life raft with your survival gear waiting for rescue. Then suddenly you see a speck of land, a voice crackles through the static of your radio, and you are back in the world of other people. The return to earth is always a celebration and an adventure. You are not in America. You are on some island in a chain of islands that has probably seen more foreign flags on its soil than the UN plaza. There is always a bar, and a grilled lobster, or a plate of cracked conch waiting, and there are the stories. These are the stories that make up my life, my songs, and now this journal. As the old song says, "I got a Caribbean soul I can barely control."

Grand Turk Island is, and always has been, a fuel stop. It lies about halfway between Miami and St. Barts. Traveling east, it is the last piece of dry land until you reach the western coast of Puerto Rico. Its geography has always been its economy. Today Grand Turk has been economically ignited by its offshore reefs and offshore corporations, but in the late seventies it was used by smugglers and treetop fliers as well as law-abiding citizens.

I landed on Grand Turk that day ten years ago for the specific purpose of having a good lunch. There were several other options in the surrounding islands, but the small Third World lunch counter at the Grand Turk International Airport put out one of the best lobster-salad sandwiches in the Caribbean. I had departed George Town, Exumas, earlier that morning to time my fuel stop with lunch. That would leave me seven hours of daylight to fly the remaining 550 miles to St. Barts. There are no night landings at the St. Barts airport, and the daytime landings are enough to scare some people out of their wits.

I was going through my landing checklist and thinking about which hot sauce I would use on my sandwich when I saw the big seaplane sitting midway down the runway in the grass just past the old wooden control tower. As I came to a halt on the runway and taxied back to the terminal, I got a close-up view of the plane. I knew from the moment I saw her how she had wound up there. Wrecked airplanes litter the islands of the Caribbean. They sit in shallow water graves on the flats of the Bahamas and beyond. They are piled up like the remnants of air battles in the mangroves and at the end of countless numbers of runways and bushes throughout the islands.

The Albatross was sitting in the cactus bushes and sand-spurs on the side of the runway, the relic of a dope deal gone bad. She was in bad shape, but she was not a wreck. The engines and propellers were still there, though there was an osprey nest resting in the port nacelle of the old radial-engine housing. The tires were flat, but the landing gear was not bent. Huge drop tanks for long-range cruising hung from the giant wing, and I'm sure that they had been put to good use. This plane could carry a lot of cargo and go a long way.

At the customs desk I went through the formalities of clearing in, and when the moment was right, I asked about the Albatross. The customs man offered little information. "She just showed up here one night. Lots of bullet holes, no fuel, and no crew." I knew that the real story would probably give a Tom Clancy novel a run for its money. I had heard some good ones in the hotel bars of the islands. I knew not to ask any more questions. The Caribbean is the land of small-sentence responses. I asked if I could take a look at the plane. "Not a problem, mon."

I guess that's one of the things that I truly love about the Caribbean. In the islands, drama is just part of life. If this plane landed under the same circumstances anywhere in South Florida, peppered with bullet holes and no one on board, it would be surrounded by every news crew from Miami to West Palm Beach. There would be battalions of federal, state, and county cops, SWAT teams in full combat gear, dogs and gun-toting DEA boys patrolling the perimeter of the quarantined crime scene. But here on Grand Turk, it was just another story. This is the land whose history is steeped in cannibal legends, slave revolts, voodoo, pirate wars, the Devil's Triangle, hurricanes, and yellow-fever epidemics. This plane on the runway was no big deal. It was just another dope plane that had dropped out of the sky.

I ate my lobster sandwich with a hot sauce from Haiti and recalculated my arrival time at St. Bart's. I could spend an hour in Grand Turk looking around the plane, and that is exactly what I did. As I approached the plane, the osprey living in the nest on the engine departed with what sounded like a pissed-off series of squawks and shrieks. I hoped it wasn't off on a recruiting mission to feathered relatives. This was just the kind of place where I could envision a reenactment of the final scenes of Hitchcock's *The Birds*.

I stepped into the cavernous fuselage. It was as big as my first apartment in college. I had gotten used to the cramped quarters of my little plane, and this much space inside an airplane just baffled me. The temperature inside was that of a toaster oven, and the plane smelled of mold and mildew. I moved toward the flight deck only to be scared stupid by a large iguana that sat motionless on the rusty forward bulkhead door. I looked out one of the dirty windows just to make sure that the sky wasn't filled with an osprey dive-bomber formation. The flight deck was bright with the rays of the afternoon sun, and I opened the escape hatches above the crew seats to let in some fresh air. I opened the windows as well, then dropped down into the pilot's seat and hung my arm out the window. There is just something cool about an airplane that you can hang your arm out of in flight. All of the flight instruments and radios were gone, but the steering yokes, throttles, and fuel-mixture handles were still on board.

She was definitely salvageable, and I had the fantasy of buying her for a penny to the dollar at some government auction on a back street in Fort Lauderdale and starting up my own sea-plane company flying to the Caribbean. But wait a minute, that would be work. Somebody once told me that if you want to make a little money in the airline business, start with a lot.

The osprey still had not returned, and the iguana seemed perfectly happy to time-travel. So there I sat, a forty-year-old man in a beat-up old dope hauler, out in the middle of nowhere playing pilot. I put my hands on the wheel, and like some kind of magic-carpet ride, my mind began to wander in the right di-rection: away from commerce and more toward fantasy.

I started making engine noises with my lips and teeth and called out commands to my imaginary copilot. I was ten years old and I was fifty. I was flying her in my bedroom, and then I was flying in the thirties, early in the era of commerical flying boats, when the captain, not the airline, ran the ship. When runways were rivers, not concrete, and flying boats descended like gods from the heavens in faraway lands. I was with Cap-tain Ralph O'Neill, flying-boat pioneer and founder of New York, Rio, Buenos Aires Airlines. We were winging our way along the Spanish Main aboard the *Havana*, one of the pre-miere Consolidated Commodores that pioneered passenger service to South America. We were bound for New York from Buenos Aires, a seven-day run that beat ship travel by two weeks. There were stops at the logistical terminals and fueling at the outposts along the way. First stop Montevideo, Uruguay, then Pôrto Alegre, Brazil, then on to Rio, where we spent the night dancing the samba at the ambassador's resi-dence. Then the next morning we splashed down at the an-cient Fortaleza, then to Belém, at the mouth of the Amazon. The steel drums welcomed us to Port of Spain. Lunch in Mara-caibo, Venezuela, then on to Barranquilla, Colombia, and Kingston, Jamaica. We arrive in the Havana harbor at sunset.

I was brought back to real time by a banging on the hull of the Albatross and shouts from the tower attendant making sure I was all right. It was then that he mentioned to me that they had found a nest of water snakes in the plane. "Poison-ous?" I asked.

"Just snakes," he answered flatly.

It was time to go, anyway, if I was to make sunset, so I left that Albatross to its bird and reptile squatters and climbed back into the tiny cockpit of my Lake. I made a short-field takeoff and initiated a sharp turn to the southeast directly above the Albatross. I spotted the osprey circling below me for his landing, and I knew that someday I would fly one of those airplanes, but the next time the engines would be real and we would be going somewhere exotic.

It has been nearly ten years since I spent the day alone in the cockpit of the beat-up Albatross on Grand Turk, but here I am about to climb aboard my own Albatross. I step back from the nose gear, look up at the giant amphibian, and pat her on the nose like one of my dogs. I am deep into some meaningful thought about yin and yang and things coming full circle when Cameron pops his head out of the window above me and shouts, "Dad, it's time to go."

"It's time to go," I repeat, and head for the ladder at the rear of the plane and climb aboard my ship. Somewhere be-tween the second or third step I make that silent and unex-plainable transformation from my earthly environment as father–husband–rock star to flying-boat captain.

Back aboard my plane, I go through the checklist and start the engines, which roar to life without hesitation. I advance the throttle and wave good-bye to the ground crew with a half-assed salute—the kind I used to see exchanged on the decks of carriers in war movies. We taxi toward the end of Runway 9 at Palm Beach International and are cleared onto the runway. At a little after three o'clock, Palm Beach Depar-ture turns us to the southwest and gives us the command to assume our own navigation.

All pilots basically start out learning to fly in their own backyard. Your hometown airport becomes as familiar to you as your favorite album. You memorize the terrain as if it were a song. Lyrics, chords, and melodies are replaced by weather, terrain, and landmarks. The airspace above the Florida Keys from Key West up to South Miami and the Tamiami Airport is my backyard in the sky. We head west out over the Everglades, staying well clear of the congested airspace that services the international airports at Miami and Fort Lauderdale. We fly directly over the Seminole reservation, and then I head for where I think Flamingo was. From seven thousand feet, the Everglades truly does look like a river of grass, but I know too well firsthand of the battle that rages below over how this land will be cared for. I have been involved in the fight to preserve the quality of life in the area that I call home, where greed is a worse epidemic than any disease transmitted by Florida's mosquito population. I see the end of the Florida peninsula appear on the horizon and catch sight of a way-too-familiar stretch of puzzling water to the east. I know that treacherous maze of winding canals well.

In the days before GPS, I once went snook fishing in Flamingo with my old friend and great fishing guide, Tommy Robinson. We had been warned by the park rangers of the relative ease with which one could become hopelessly lost in this swamp, but we just brushed off the warning. Hell, we were experienced South Florida watermen. In trying to keep up the South Florida tradition of getting the maximum amount of enjoyment out of the day's fishing, we had fired up a big old Bob Marley–sized spliff of gold bud that took my natural sense of navigation and transported it to some other region of the galaxy. We spent the entire afternoon driving around in circles, running into the same goddamn alligator about a hundred times until the setting sun forced us to sleep out in the Everglades. It was a sweltering night in the swamp, but we had to don our foul-weather gear to have any hope of retaining a blood supply. I learned that night why the Indians referred to Everglades mosquitoes as "birds with teeth" and why this stretch of water was so aptly named "Hell's Bay."

Now, as we put the Florida mainland on our tail, the silhou-
ette of the middle Florida Keys pops up. Soon I can see the gap
in the string of islands to what I know to be the Seven Mile
Bridge, west of Marathon. Though we have the latest GPS units
on board, reading out our latitude and longitude, I still do not
depend on them to navigate. They are wonderful instruments
and make life a lot easier in a cockpit or on the deck of a ship,
but I like to know my basics. I can still shoot a star sight, and I
run a pretty accurate dead-reckoning course line in the air or
on sea, and that is what I count on the most. I steer toward the
ADF needle at Marathon. When we cross it, we will pick up the
G448 air corridor, the main route from South Florida to Central
America. It goes directly over Cuba, and despite the years of
verbal and physical skirmishes between Fidel and the changing occupants of the White House and Congress, American airplanes have traveled this route on a regular basis. We pay for it
in cash, and it ain't cheap. It is one of Fidel's last sources of hard
currency. His island ferry in the sky.

Despite the existence of this little piece of air-route capitalism, the Cubans watch the traffic in the corridor very carefully,
and any deviation from the 185-degree course might bring visitors aloft, especially if you are flying in an old Navy airplane.
I instinctively check the sky for MiG's, thinking about the encounter of my famous fictional bush pilot, Frank Bama, with
the Cuban Air Force. I don't know where we get our fear of
MiG's from, but for me it came from the old cartoon *Terry and
the Pirates* and vague memories of these scary airplanes with
swept wings and open noses from the Korean War era. Then
we saw them again in the skies over Vietnam, shooting down
what we thought were our invincible fighters and sending our
pilots to the Hanoi Hilton. Wherever the fear originates, saying the word *MiG* to a pilot is like screaming "Jaws!" on the
beaches of Martha's Vineyard.

We mark our departure and time from the radio beacon at
Marathon. The shallow water of the flats that surround this
part of the Keys gives way to the deeper green of Hawk Chan-

nel. Twenty-five miles off the coast of Florida, Miami Center wishes us good evening, and we are told to contact Havana Center on our radio. I don't know what it is about talking to Havana Center. I guess it's the exotic sound of the words themselves, or the fact that most pilots never get the opportunity to talk to a Cuban controller, or maybe it's the feeling of talking to the enemy. Whatever it is, it always excites me. They, of course, are speaking perfect English, and that intimidates me, since I don't speak very much Spanish. One day I will. I'll run away to the hills of Guatemala or Costa Rica or maybe even Cuba and hole up for a couple of months where I'll *have* to learn the language. Then I will be able to talk to Radio Habana in Spanish.

I acknowledge the controller's instructions. We are cleared to enter Cuban airspace and proceed south along the corridor to Cayo del Sur on the south coast. I can't resist, I throw in a *"Muchas gracias."* No MiG's in sight. We are cruising above the Gulf Stream at ten thousand feet with a slight tailwind in clear weather, on course and on time for our arrival in Grand Cayman. Everything is as it should be, but in my mind we are about to leave the all-too-familiar and enter the Third World, which I know from experience can be all too unpredictable. Alex takes over for me on the flight deck, and I head to the aft cabin. Randall had hesitated about a quarter of a second when I asked him to come along. He had packed in less time than that and now was playing with Cameron in the rear compartment of the plane. My son is having a blast in the back, alternating his time between running his toy seaplane up and down the deck of the Albatross and staring out the windows from the bunk on the port side at the whirling propellers. Randall was just trying to keep up. If you possess the ability to love a flying machine at two, you won't lose it even if you make it to ninety-three. It is the ultimate toy.

I bring him out of his trance with the only words I know that will do it. "Hey, Cam, want a PBJ?" In a flash he is at the table, where we snack on peanut-butter-and-jelly sandwiches and wash them down with bottled designer iced tea, no doubt a fabrication of some marketing genius from Harvard Business School that has every Southern grandmother turning over in her grave. Alex calls me from the flight deck. Cameron and I climb through the hatch, and I put him up in the navigator's seat.

Ahead of us on the horizon, the dark azure waters of the Gulf Stream give way to the turquoise hue of the shallows, and then the coastline of Cuba comes into view. We gulp down the last of our sandwiches and head back to the flight deck. I change seats with Alex and then prop Cameron up in my lap. I point out over the nose of the airplane and say, "Look, son, that island is called Cuba." He stares down the line of my finger for a moment, then turns his eyes to me, looks up, smiles, and says, "Koo-ba."

SECTION V

Cuba and the Cayman Islands

Latitudes and Attitudes

The Skies over Cuba

Cuba has been a strange part of my life and my heritage for a long time. Although I have no Cuban blood, for as long as I can remember I have loved *café con leche, pecadillo,* the song "Guantanamera," and Havana. My recent Cuban adventures include my one and only trip to Havana aboard the old schooner *Western Union,* when I joined a documentary film expedition chasing the legendary Ernest Hemingway. I also had a surprise visit by a boatload of Cuban refugees who showed up early one morning at my Florida dock asking for political asylum. (I couldn't let them into the country, but I did give them coffee and a *Floridays* CD.) But the roots of my Cuban connection came from my grandfather the sailing-ship captain. He was too in love with wind and sails to give them up for more advanced methods of propulsion. He preferred the feel of a wooden deck under his feet and the romantic ports of call of the Caribbean as his landfalls.

In the years before the Great Depression and World War II, he plied the warm waters of the Caribbean as skipper of a five-masted barkentine, named the *Chicamauga,* to the various ancient Caribbean ports that dated back to precolonial days. His home port was the small fishing village of Pascagoula, Mississippi, from which timber from the abundant Gulf Coast pine forests was exported. He would discharge his cargo of lumber and load on salt and sugar for the return voyage to New Orleans.

I remember once when I was very young he showed me his weathered passport from his days as captain of the *Chicamauga.* The pages were covered with stamps. I couldn't read the faded ink, but he pronounced the names to me—names that immediately conjured up visions of romance, danger, and intrigue—Nassau, Kingston, Port-au-Prince, Santo Domingo, Fort-de-France, San Juan, Pointe-à-Pitre, Port of Spain, Caracas, Maracaibo, Barranquilla, Cartagena, and Havana. Names of places that stuck with me until I was old enough to make the voyages there myself.

Havana was his favorite. He told me that he had fallen in love with Havana the first minute he saw the port. From my grandfather's initial vision, the succeeding generations of Buffetts were filled with this strange fascination for this faraway place that we had heard so much about but had never seen.

Cuba's geography is its history and its mystery. It's as big as the 3,700 other Caribbean islands put together. Its ten million people make up one third of the total population of the West Indies. Cuba's economy is still linked to sugar, as it was in the beginning. From the earliest days of economic exploitation, this was perfectly evident to Columbus and to his successors who settled the island. Aside from the fertile land and favorable climate, the efficient production of sugar required large acreage and a large workforce. The Spanish brought slaves from Africa to work the fields. Today about half of Cuba's population are mulattoes—mixed-blood descendants of the African slaves and Europeans. As a Spanish colony for most of its modern existence, Cuba was just another island, but in recent times the island's proximity to the United States is what has really determined its fate. Most Americans' knowledge of Cuba can be summed up in a few phrases—the *Maine*, the Mafia, and the Cuban missile crisis. These are at the core of U.S.–Cuban history, tying us together, right up until today.

One of the most memorable family stories that fueled my fascination with Cuba had my father as a one-year-old aboard the old *Chicamauga* in Havana Harbor. In celebration of his son's first birthday, my grandfather raised all of his signal flags from the rigging. Messages went back and forth between the ships at anchor as to why Captain Buffett had all his flags flying. When they found out, all of the other ships in Havana Harbor raised their flags as well.

Somewhere in my adolescence, Cuba popped up again. A friend of mine and his father, from a very prominent Mobile family, were taking a sportfishing boat from Alabama to Florida and disappeared without a trace off the coast of Cuba. There were supposed radio transmissions that involved a battle with a gunboat, and sightings of the two of them being led off as spies to jail in Havana. To this day no one knows what happened, or if they do, they're not talking. But at the time, it fueled talk of rescue missions and attacks on Cuba that I was all too ready and willing to join. The Hutchins men were never found, and in the thick coastal humidity of Mobile, life moved on. I went inland for a part of my life, but I was reunited with my Cuban connection when in the early seventies I moved to Key West.

Islands on the Stream

Living in Key West in the early seventies was not like living in America. It was a hybrid culture where you were linked to the future by FedEx service, phones, and faxes, while Cuban coffee and guayabera kept alive the flavor of the ethnic past. You could not live in Key West without being exposed to Cuban culture. Key West was Cuban before there were refugees. Geography had linked the two islands together like Siamese twins when the glaciers of the Ice Age melted and left them on opposite sides of the Gulf Stream. In the colonial days, the children of Cuba's rich and poor alike came to Key West to learn English, and before the revolution, ferryboats ran daily. It was as easy to go to Cuba as it was to go from Cape Cod to Nantucket. After the revolution, even the political barrier of opposing ideologies could not totally eradicate the cultural umbilical cord. If anything, it actually enriched the relationship with a sense of loss and mystery.

The stories of the old days have long been a source of entertainment and inspiration for me. The years of prerevolutionary Cuba were some of the wildest times on the planet Earth, with Key West having a few sideshows of its own.

First there were the conchs, descendants of the original Bahamian settlers who came in search of sponges, grouper, and conch. Like the mollusk for which they are named, conchs were hard-pressed to disattach themselves from the safety of their protective shells. They were born in Key West and would die in Key West. Up until the mass migrations of mainland wackos in the late sixties and seventies, they were the political and economic power on the island. They ran the place to suit themselves and their needs, and the rest of the world could go to hell.

There were the drug smugglers, who looked at their cargo as only the most current commodity in the island's longstanding evolutionary attachment to contraband. Key West started as a pirate town, and these boys were just carrying on the legacy. They were rich and liked to show it. In the early days, they used to unload their boats at the dockside in broad daylight, and nobody much cared. That all changed when the product went from pot to cocaine and Ronald Reagan became president.

The Navy came to Key West in 1820 to chase pirates away. So far, they haven't succeeded, but they knew a good thing when they saw it and gobbled up most of the good land in the name of national defense. They've been there ever since. Duty in Key West was a cushy assignment, as exemplified by a sign in the front yard of the prime piece of waterfront property that housed the commander of the naval air station. It read, FLY NAVY AND YOU COULD LIVE HERE.

The gay community discovered Key West a long time ago. The Puritans had never made it this far south, thank God. Key West has always been a place with such a diversity of lifestyle that being gay didn't matter.

Then there were the shrimpers. Talk about a group of individuals with a reputation for bad behavior. They made rock bands look like church choirs. They, too, gathered at the end of the road because there their bad behavior was tolerated.

Into this already boiling melting pot, you add the ghosts of Ernest Hemingway, Tennessee Williams, Truman Capote, and the living presence of a host of other writers, musicians, and artists. In case that isn't *picante* enough, throw in a little hot-blooded Cuban spice: Cuban coffee, Cuban cigars, Cuban restaurants, and Cuban sandwiches. There are still *bollito* betting parlors on every street corner and cockfights on Stock Island. The Western Union telegraph line still runs under the ocean from Cable Beach to downtown Havana. Throw all of this together on a three-by-five-mile island, and you have a pretty interesting place to call home.

Enemy Airspace and the Ghost
of Ricky Ricardo

I have flown over Cuba en route to other Caribbean islands before, without incident. And on my very first instrument flight from Key West to Cancún, I was guided through Cuban airspace by Havana Center when I had to avoid an approaching storm in the Gulf. But I still can't shake that bit of apprehension at being in the airspace of the supposed enemy.

As a child of cold-war propaganda in Mobile, I watched films about what to do in case a nuclear attack occurred while I was in school. ("Get under your desk and shield your eyes from the blast." They left out the part about kissing your ass good-bye.) Then there was the Berlin Wall, and somewhere in the early sixties the newsreel accounts of the shooting down of a U-2 (what a great name for a band—I wonder if anyone's ever thought about using it?) spy plane, as Communist soldiers picked through the wreckage with bayonets and the pilot stood close by on a leash, looking like some beaten dog in a tattered flight suit. There were more television memories of tanks in Budapest and, finally, the Cuban missile crisis, which really did scare the shit out of us. Add to that pilot tales of MiG buzzings and forced landings that I had heard around South Florida airports, and the mystery and danger factor is something that you have to take into account.

But Cuba is still an island just ninety miles from my home on another island, and I have a hard time identifying what I see with what I've been taught to believe. I can see all the way across the country. Ahead of us I can make out the waves as puffs of white hitting the rocky Atlantic coast, and on the horizon lie the green waters of the Caribbean Sea. The view of the island below does not compute with what has been pro-grammed into me about communism.

Communism is dark. It is surrounded by an iron curtain. Its flag is a fearful banner with a hammer and sickle against a blood-red background. Communist countries are cold, com-posed of gray wintry landscapes, where the sun rarely shines and people live on beets and don't smile much. They are full of soldiers carrying AK-47's, who wear long, thick coats and those menacing fold-up hats with big red stars on them. Com-munism just doesn't seem suited for hot climates.

Well, that observation is obviously a bit naïve. With the Cuban Revolution, communism came charging into the Caribbean Basin like a red fox in Uncle Sam's henhouse, but it still seems like an oxymoron to me. In Caribbean countries, it is the tropical sun that cooks the culture. In Cuba people were dancing and singing long before they knew about Karl Marx—it's probably what allowed them to put up for so long with being treated like shit. It has also survived right alongside the political doctrines of the state. During my brief time in Havana on the Hemingway expedition, I remember listening to my fa-vorite radio station from Key West, and when people found out that I was American, they didn't recoil like I was some cul-tural infidel. They asked questions about baseball and Miami. Later that same day, I had a firsthand contrast-in-culture ex-hibit in an elevator in the Habana Libre Hotel. The elevator opened, and I was greeted by the ghost of Ricky Ricardo.

Actually, it was the elevator operator, who was singing "Ba-baloo." His name was Luís. I told him my name, and we began to talk in Spanish as he closed the wire door and lowered the el-evator handle. It didn't take long for me to reach the three-sentence limit of my Spanish and utter those two words of hope: *"Habla inglés?"* Luís spoke rather good English and switched immediately. When he discovered I was an American from Key West, he got very excited and began to tell me of his relatives who lived on Olivia Street and ran a Cuban bakery.

The fifth-floor light lit up, and when the door opened we were nearly stampeded to death by a group of big fat men who smelled like day-old hangovers, sweat, and strong Turkish cigarettes. These were real, by God, Communists. The kind I used to see on the newsreel, saluting the passing troops from the reviewing stand in Red Square. There was very little humor in this bunch. They looked like they should be tank drivers in Hungary. They crammed into the elevator as if Luís and I weren't even there. With the arrival of the Soviets, his mode changed instantaneously. He stopped singing and stared at the elevator handle until we reached the lobby. (As the car came to a halt, I pressed myself up against the wall so as not to be trampled by these descendants of Ivan the Terrible.) They squirted out of that elevator like a cork popping from an overfizzy bottle of champagne. Luís watched the herd rumble through the lobby, then looked back at me and shrugged. The smile returned to his face, and he was again singing the words to "Babaloo." The political doctrine of the state had not suppressed the spirit of Luís or the Caribbean, and I don't think it ever will. They will be singing and dancing in the elevators, bodegas, dance halls, and streets of Cuba long after the sun sets on the revolution.

At the Wheel of My Spaceship

Jimmy stares toward the bright Pleiades
It's so strange what his distant eye sees
Who knows why you start rediscovering your heart
But you do it again and again

—"Jimmy Dreams"

We cross the coastline of "Koo-ba" above the coastal city of Matanzas, the seat of Cuba's oil industry, and below us on the western shore of the bay the industrial sprawl is clearly visible. It doesn't take long for the fresh sea air of the Gulf Stream to be tainted with the recognizable smell of burning oil coming from the blazing burn-off pipes that glow like Roman candles in the midst of seesawing oil derricks. I check our course and log our arrival time over the island, and Pete relays our position to Radio Havana. To the west is the skyline of Havana, and I flash back briefly to my one and only visit to the city.

Out the port window of the Albatross, I could see the Cuban Keys, which begin at Varadero and stretch out of sight to the east. These were the islands where Ernest Hemingway went hunting for Nazi submarines in World War II. I started to daydream about crewing for Papa and Gregorio Fuentes, when they would load up the *Pilar* with guns, ammunition, and whiskey for the mission. Now, whether you're a kid or an adult, that's great fantasy.

My sub chase is cut short by a call from Radio Havana. We are directed down the air corridor to our next reporting point at Cayo Largo, off the southern coast. The normal afternoon land-cloud buildup, which is so common over the islands, has not materialized, and our ride at ten thousand feet is incredibly smooth. This is the skinniest part of the island, only sixty miles from ocean to ocean. With the help of our favoring winds, we quickly put the oil refinery on our tail, and the rectangular green fields of sugar stretch ahead of us to the southern shore and the Caribbean Sea.

There isn't much to do in the cockpit but keep her on course and listen to the air traffic talking to Radio Havana. All the planes are either going to or coming out of Miami from Central and South America. The sounds of the names and the accents of the pilots reporting in reconfirm my sense of adventure—Varig 231 bound for Rio; Lan Chile to Santiago; American 435 to Caracas.

We reach Cayo Largo just before sunset and report in. We are out over the open water again, and the ocean below looks rather docile, with only occasional whitecaps on the surface. We are ahead of schedule, which always feels good. Cameron has fallen asleep with his toy airplane in his lap and his head resting against the window on the starboard side of the cabin, absorbing the hypnotic and calming vibrations of the big radial engines' sixty-cycle hum. We are out of radar contact with Havana but have to report position along the way until we clear Cuban airspace and are turned over to Grand Cayman Radio. I watch the sun slip away toward Mexico and the Pacific. The sky above us is a pale pink curtain of reflective light that gives way to the darkness of night creeping up over the eastern horizon. We will soon be night flying. I flick on the instrument lights and gauge lights on the overhead panel and make the necessary transition. Oh, yes, there is a difference, a big difference.

Flying in the day is like being in the ultimate movie. On a clear day there is so much to see, and I never get tired of the vantage point that altitude allows. But at night you're living in the stars, suspended in the darkness of space with only beacons of white light from our planet below or the reflective light of distant galaxies and constellations above. When you're flying at night, you're not in an airplane. You're in a spaceship.

Since there is no view and your sense of sight is basically shut down, the other senses become more alive. There is a different feel to the plane when you hold the wheel. There is no autopilot in planes of this size. That means that you hand-fly her all the time. At night your hands become extensions of the inner ear, and you can detect the slightest changes in pitch or vibration. In the light of day, the engines and propellers rumble along with amazing mechanical efficiency. You almost take them for granted, unless one of them blows up or stops running. At night orange flames blast aft from the exhaust stacks and the engines look like mechanical dragons tearing through the air, a collection of a million moving parts producing heat and horsepower. Even my fifty-year-old, daytime, bifocal-oriented retinas seem to find an extra bit of focus at night. But to me the biggest thrill of night flying, just like night voyaging on the surface of the ocean, is steering by the stars.

The full moon had slipped behind a low cloud, and the stars above become clearer in the momentary darkness. I get a visual bearing on my old friend Orion's Belt. I have hung my hopes and triangulated lines of position on it, hoping like hell I am close to where I think I am. The Pleiades are just coming into view. Their myth and mystery has called to me since I first read about the seven sisters in an astronomy book long ago. I greet these stars with a deep affection, like long-lost friends.

We are a half hour from making our final position report to Havana and leaving Cuban airspace. I am comfortable with my ship and her position. Though there isn't much to do but enjoy the view, I take advantage of the time to run my old "what if" scenarios, which come from my days crossing oceans on sailboats and my recent experience of having to climb out of a sinking plane. What if the electrical system fails and I have to get her down? What if we have to ditch in the middle of the night? What if we lose an engine? Good pilots and boat captains are inherently aware of the precarious nature of their trade. It goes back to my old Rule of Life number 2: *Remember, it can all go to hell at any minute.* When you make the decision to take a boat out on the big ocean or fly a plane to altitude, you are moving into another world. It is a paradoxical pilgrimage, because the tools that enable us to make this journey are the results of the curious mind, which translates into technological achievements. Yet when trouble comes along, which it inevitably will in the world of weather and moving parts, it is our ancient sense of survival that gets us through. That's why I do my "what if" drills.

Once again, the gods of flight have guided us safely to our destination and the "what if" drills are just practice. We say good night to Radio Habana, and twenty-five miles from Grand Cayman the approach controller identifies us as a blip on his radar screen. Ahead and below us a small cluster of lights appears. It is a welcome sight; we hope they are the lights of Grand Cayman, but I want to be sure. Soon the lights take on a shape, like one of the puzzles where you connect all the numbers to make a picture. The bright pulsating green-and-white beams of the airport beacon reveal themselves, and then the long, thin rectangular lights of Runway 10 come into view. Landing checklist is complete, and then the giant white numbers and markings at the end of the runway fill the view of the windshield. *Squeak squeak* go the big rubber tires. We are down, and Cameron is up.

It is Christmas night in the Caribbean, and the first leg of our big adventure has come to a safe completion. I am tired but happy. I have a sense of accomplishment, as I always do at the end of a successful flight. We have left the planet and returned where we intended. That doesn't always necessarily happen. It is time for a celebration. I want a rum drink and a meal and a good night's sleep. Tomorrow I will be in Costa Rica. As we taxi to the parking area in front of the customs building, I hear the radio operator in the tower through my headset. The formal and efficient voice that instructed us toward the airport has given way to a more casual tone. "Could you tell me sometin', cap'n?"

"You bet," I respond.

"Dat be da seaplane dat got shot at in Jamaica?" I am momentarily stunned by the out-of-the-blue question about my most recent "international incident." I guess the story is now legend in the Caribbean flying community.

"Yes, this is that plane," I reply.

"Well, tell Cap'n Buffett dat we won't be shootin' at him here in Grand Cayman." A laugh comes through the radio.

"You just did," I reply.

Energy and Innocence

If you could collectively harness the energy that circulates in the body of every two-and-a-half-year-old boy in the world, you would probably produce enough power to run a small city. After three hours of confinement in a sixty-foot aluminum tube, of which half the time was spent sleeping and recharging those amazing little batteries, my son is ready to rock. He leaps from the ladder of the plane down to the tarmac and does a couple of 360's shouting and singing "Jingle Bells" as he rockets around. I leave the pilots to deal with the ramp agent and collect our overnight baggage. I take the passports and paperwork for entry and accept Cameron's challenge of a race to the customs building. We scream across our imaginary finish line, singing the last chorus of the song together, and are met by a serious pair of customs agents who sit behind a podium reading some down-island tabloid. On the front page is a picture of a most heinous-looking spider. A big, bold headline stretches across the top of the page: GIANT KILLER TARANTULA TERRORIZES TRINIDAD. Christmas music comes from a small blaster in the rear of the office. The customs agents don't seem terribly interested in the outcome of our father-son race. I try to make light conversation, but I can't compete with the killer tarantula. The larger of the two women sighs heavily and rises from her stool to deal with me.

My years of experience in Caribbean airport entries have come into play. I have done a scout's job of filling out all the paperwork for entry to the Cayman Islands. I proudly present my completed forms. But as hard as I tried to stay ahead of the paperwork game, there always seems to be at least one new form, and such is the case tonight. The customs inspector looks at the assemblage of documents, pulls out two blank forms from under the desk, and hands them to me. I go to work. Cameron hums and rummages around the empty room, and I lose sight of him for a moment. When I look up, he is hanging from a joint beam above the luggage belt. In a loud whisper I call out to him. He knows something is up and turns to face me. I point my finger at the woman, who has gone back to reading her tabloid, and I say, "Children's police." He lets go of the beam and walks quietly back to my side.

I warned him in the plane about the children's police that we might encounter, who check at airports for kids engaging in bad behavior. I now have a collection of imaginary inspectors who I traveled with in the company of Cameron. There are the restaurant police, the movie police, the playground police, and on and on. If he is bad, he has to spend quiet time in baby jail. I'm sure that there are child psychologists out there who would burn me at the stake for these tactics. I have said before that parenting is a learning experience for all of us. I happen to come from a childhood of Catholic corporal punishment, where I had my ass spanked and my knuckles whacked by nuns and priests alike, and I don't see any harm in having a few imaginary disciplinarians around. Whatever will get the attention of a fully charged child is all right by me.

Cameron clings to my leg as I present my additional forms to the agent for grading. She buries her eyes in the documents. Suddenly, Cameron's head pops out of hiding and he looks up at the woman and says, "Do you know the words to 'Jingle Bells'?"

The woman looks at Cameron and smiles for the first time. "Sure I do," she says. She stamps our passports and forms and hands them back to me. She begins to sing, and Cameron joins in. I chime in at the chorus. We walk toward the exit sign, singing together. The customs agent unlocks the door, and as we walk out, she pats Cameron on the head and says, "Merry Christmas, and welcome to the Cayman Islands."

Island Girls

Outside the customs building there isn't much going on at Grand Cayman International. The air is warm and a breeze rustles the palm trees that line the airport boulevard, but there isn't a human being in sight, much less a cab. We left most of our gear on board the plane, since we are only staying the night and will be shoving off for San José early in the morning. I start for the main terminal to find a ride and leave Randall to watch Cameron, who is playing airplane. Engine sounds come out of his mouth, and his arms are outstretched. He cruises down the sidewalk and banks left at full speed, then suddenly stops in midair. His engine goes silent.

Standing between him and the street are two pint-sized identical twins in Hawaiian shirts, shorts, and flip-flops. Down come the wings, and my macho little fighter pilot reverts to a shy two-and-a-half-year-old. He backtracks to my side and grabs hold of my leg. The little girls say hello. Cameron buries his head further in my leg. I try to get him to return their greeting and hear a muffled hello from behind my knee.

A friendly couple follows the little girls. They introduce themselves as James and Adela White, and the twins are Katie and Hallie. James is a local singer at the Hyatt, where we are booked for the night, and heard we were coming and wanted to meet me. Adela is one of those instantly likeable people. One of the greatest things about this job is meeting the people who like what I do. I love the fact that over the years many fans have become friends in my travels.

We chat while the crew unloads the bags. There are still no cabs around, and James and Adela offer us a ride to the hotel, which I accept. In the short time it takes to make our ground-transportation arrangements, Cameron has unlocked from my thigh and once again sprouted his wings, though this time he is flying in formation, with the twins. I can't figure out who's chasing whom, but I have to laugh. We haven't been on the ground more than ten minutes, and my son has already found himself not one but two island girls.

We arrive at the hotel amid the Christmas rush at the front desk. Adela has offered to baby-sit Cameron while I go to dinner. He seems perfectly happy with the idea. "I am having a party," he says as we check into our room. A chip off the old block. I order pizza for him and the island girls, who will be coming over soon. I go to the TV and find the electronic baby-sitter—the Disney Channel. Cameron is set. We settle in and watch *Winnie the Pooh*. It's a far cry from my first days down-island.

I think back to the time not that many years ago when I first ventured down here. It was in that now prehistoric time in 1976, before VHS tapes were even invented. I had bought a new boat and was headed south. I didn't know if I would be coming back. Anyway, I had rigged the boat as if I weren't. Among the improvements I'd made to the *Euphoria II* was the installation of a video deck. It was as big as a microwave oven. The half-inch tapes it played were twice as large as the eight-millimeter tapes players use today. We sailed with, I believe, five movies: *The Man Who Would Be King*, *Black Orpheus*, *The Wizard of Oz*, *Key Largo*, and *The Harder They Come*.

I remember nights being anchored up in the lower Exumas in a deserted cove, finishing off a meal of fresh lobster and conch, then setting our little TV out on the deck and watching movies under the stars like we were a floating drive-in. A month later, when we finally arrived in St. Barts, I used to bring kids on board and sit them in front of the eight-inch screen and watch their amazement at their first sight of the Wicked Witch of the West.

Pleiades Calling Me Home

The party girls arrive at around seven-thirty, with James and Adela as chaperones. They have videos and Barbie dolls. Cameron is showing them his Little Elmo. Room service arrives with the pizza, and I make my exit for dinner.

I find myself in a waterfront restaurant with one of those way-too-cute tropically descript names like the Outrigger, the Beachcomber, or the Lagoon. There I am again looking out at the heavens while me and my pilots wait for our table. It is a beautiful night, and the stars are putting on quite a show. Rum drinks arrive and toasts are made. Glasses clink and the pilot stories start to come. Before we get too caught up in the bullshit, I tip my glass to the heavens. I am a very lucky boy.

The maître d'—a Leprechaun with an Irish accent—brings us the good news that our table is ready. We find ourselves in the middle of the crowded dining room full of vacationing families. I have already sensed on my walk from the hotel that Grand Cayman is a little too American for me. There are too many fast-food restaurants and strip malls.

Dinner finished, I walk back to the hotel expecting to find Cameron sound asleep with Little Elmo tucked under his chin. Instead, I run smack-dab into a full-blown kid party. James and Adela tell me that the children stopped moving only to gobble a little pizza. Settling Cameron down takes some doing, but after we take photos of the kids and get them to come down slightly from warp drive, I thank my new friends for their wonderful hospitality, and we say our good nights, exchanging phone numbers and E-mail addresses.

As I tuck Cameron and Little Elmo in, I say my own Christmas prayer. I thank the gods that I did not come to Earth as a lobster or a rice farmer in the Mekong Delta. Nothing against either creature, but I like who I became just fine. That's the way life is. We all try to make something out of our lives, and some of us are just luckier than others.

Twenty-six Miles Across the Sea

Twenty-six miles across the sea
Santa Catalina is a'waiting for me
Santa Catalina, the island of romance
Romance, romance, romance

—THE FOUR PREPS

I wake up sometime before dawn hearing the words to this old Four Preps song in my head. I lay in bed until the song is finished, perfectly comfortable in that morning limbo. Everybody has songs that stay in their head forever. I guess some of the ones I have written do that for some people. It is an amazing thing, and I try not to figure out why certain tunes are on my lifelong play list. I just enjoy them when they come. Pardon the pun, but off the top of my head, these are a few of the selections on my internal jukebox from my early years.

"On the Back of a Crocodile." From childhood, as in "She sailed away on a bright and sunny day."
"Shaboom." From my first vacation to Miami as a kid. It played constantly on the jukebox at the Fontainebleau Hotel. We weren't staying there, I just snuck in and hung around the pool until they threw me out.
"I'll Be Home for Christmas." My mother's favorite Christmas song.

"Ain't Got No Home." Frogman Henry's classic. My cousin
and I knew all the words and mimicked Frogman's
falsetto to each other every day during the summer of
1957.

"Twenty-six Miles." It was California, the ocean, girls—hell, it
was everything I wanted to be or do.

I woke up and my gaze was met by a small pair of emerald-
green eyes inches from my own. I don't know how long
Cameron has been awake and looking at me, but there he is,
larger than life. It's a great feeling to wake up with my son
beside me, or rather in my face. "Hi, Dad! Let's get some
French toast," he says.

The Buffett boys dress quickly and head for the breakfast
buffet, where a line of early-bird Christmas tourists has already formed. The smells of breakfast have our stomachs
growling. A buffet is not supposed to be a complicated meal—
cereal, juice, coffee or tea, eggs and bacon or pancakes. But the
Christmas breakfast buffet at the Hyatt is just too much of an
opportunity for the food and beverage manager to pass by.
There are ice sculptures of swans, banana-leaf–lined food
trays, and an omelet chef. The line is backed up like the Long
Island Expressway on the Fourth of July. Suddenly the line is
brought to a halt by none other than Cameron. He has stopped
dead in his tracks just past the ice sculpture of a pelican. He is
sniffing the air like a retriever with his tiny upturned nose.
"Look at all that bacon, Dad."

In front of us is a platter larger than his red wagon, loaded
to the edges with bacon. He looks up at me with those wide
green eyes, and I connect to his conspiring thoughts. It's just
us boys. We have fled the International House of Women for a
day, where skim milk, fresh yogurt, and protein powder rule
the morning meal. All of that stuff is available here, but I load
him up with bacon, French toast, and sausage, making sure
there's plenty for the old man as well. Bacon is the quintessen-

tial representation of something that tastes so good and is so bad for you. I remember times in our sailing days when I would start the morning at sea by frying up a pound of Oscar Meyer bacon, which we would devour with hot bread, jelly, and butter as insulation against the carcinogens.

Cameron and I spot a table near the garden and sit down to our feast. At the table next to us is a friend of mine, who is a partner in a minor-league baseball team that I have an interest in. (It allows me to put "baseball team owner" as my occupation on immigration and customs forms as opposed to "musician" or "writer.") Van is here with his family for the holidays. I had been meaning to call him before the holidays and catch up on the news of a possible game in Cuba, but I hadn't bothered to call Dionne Warwick on the psychic hot line. When you travel a lot, stuff like this just happens. You're thinking about somebody you need to get in touch with, and *bam*, there they are crossing the street, in a phone booth, on a plane, or having breakfast next to you on a tropical island. We catch up on some baseball news. Cameron is kept amused by my friend's two daughters. After his big party the night before, his social skills are improving immensely; he's chatting up the girls and offering them pieces of bacon. What a guy.

We say good-bye to Van and his family and head for the airport. We have a long flight ahead of us. Knowing I'd be spending the day with my son in the plane, I diluted the syrup container at the hotel with hot water to avoid a giant sugar rush, which can turn Cameron into "whacko attacko," as we call him. Our friends at the customs office from the night before have the morning duty, and we clear in a matter of minutes. We load our bags onto the plane, and I do the walk-around preflight while Cameron and Randall kick the soccer ball on the tarmac. I go over my weather briefing with Pete and Alex. There is a ridge of high pressure over the southern Caribbean, and flying conditions are good, though we have a slight head wind. I call to the soccer team to board up, and we climb in. The soccer game continues in the rear of the plane. I head for the left seat, strap my-self in, and start down the checklist.

I don't know what it is about preflighting a plane in the early hours of morning. It's not like jumping in your car, turn-ing the ignition, and backing out of the driveway. I think it has to do with the fact that you're leaving the earth, which most people can't do, and the preparation for such a feat is almost as exciting as the event itself.

There is a slight delay with air-traffic control at George Town. They have misplaced our flight plan, but after a few minutes we are given instructions to fire up the engines. There is very little traffic at this time of the morning. The big jets full of tourists won't be arriving from the colder climates until after ten. We are cleared onto the runway and take off to the east, then turn right to pick up our course down the B767 air-way to San José, Costa Rica.

Our destination is Juan Santamaria International Airport, nearly six hundred miles to the southwest. We clear Grand Cayman airspace and radar coverage twenty-five miles south of the island at Lerol intersection. After that, it's back to basic flying, calculating time and distances to the next intersection along the route and reporting in to the radio controllers who watch over the imaginary roadways in the sky.

The system of radio checkpoints was developed back in the embryonic days of air-passenger service between North, Cen-tral, and South America. Early air carriers like Pan Am and New York, Rio, and Buenos Aires Airways (NYRBA) laid out the initial routes. They wanted to know where their planes were at all times, in case trouble developed and they had to go looking for a ditched bird or a life raft full of survivors. Ameri-can aviators are spoiled by the coast-to-coast umbrella of radar protection provided in the skies above the land of the free. But as soon as you venture down into the banana republics, it's back to the old, original, and reliable system of reporting in at checkpoints, which are usually around a hundred miles apart.

Our next checkpoint is named "Cruta," an imaginary little triangle on the chart that lays twenty miles west of the Honduran coast. The shoreline has just come into view out the right window, and the voice of the radio operator from somewhere over near the airport at Puerto Lempura asks for our estimated time to the next checkpoint. I check the handheld GPS and give him our estimate. We are a little behind schedule with the head wind but will arrive only about ten minutes late in San José, where the girls will be meeting us. Cameron has been relatively quiet for the first hour of the flight, happy in his own world, with his bear and his toy planes. There is nothing to do now but sit back, monitor the gauges, watch the clouds drift, study my little book of Spanish phrases, and enjoy the ride.

Do You Know the Way to San José?

I have been trying to get to Costa Rica for nearly twenty years. A friend of mine named Corb Donohue originally put the bug in my ear. Corb was the head of Artist Relations at ABC Records in Los Angeles. This was back in the days when record companies had active and effective Artist Relations divisions, which were involved in recording careers over the long haul. Corb was one of the best, and when I came along he had already been involved with such acts as the Mamas and the Papas, Jim Croce, Joe Walsh, and Three Dog Night, to name a few. In fact, Corb was largely responsible for me pursuing my career as a singer, as opposed to that of a Key West boat captain, and back in the seventies we all know where those boats were going. Corb may have been a great artist-relations man, but he was a surfer first. When he'd finally had too much of life in the California fast lane, he did what any good old-fart surfer would do. He quit his job, sold his house off Crescent Heights, bought a camper, loaded up his boards, his wife, and his young daughter, and with the little money he'd saved set out for Quepos, Costa Rica, in search of the perfect wave. He would send me enticing postcards and photos showing the classic tropical images that tugged at my soul. Wild parrots sat in the palm trees lining the beach and streets of the waterfront. In the shade of the trees, long-haired, barefoot men in cutoffs and women in string bikinis with long, sunbleached hair waved at me from behind a table filled with large empty beer bottles. In the library, I read everything I could on Costa Rica. I sent for travel brochures and bought those dumb books with titles like, *Latin America on a Dollar a Day*. To this day, I can't remember why I just didn't hop on a plane and head on down. That was my style at the time, but other things got in the way, and I never made it down during Corb's tenure as an expatriate. Eventually he resettled in Southern California and went back to work in the music business, but it had changed drastically in his absence. Today he works at Stuart Surfboards in Laguna Beach.

By then the Costa Rican migration bug had caught on in Key West. This was around the time when the whole mood of the dope trade on the island turned dark. Gone were the good old fun days of pot-smuggling hippies and college students, who bought and sold reefer from Rastas in the hills of Jamaica and spent their idle days between runs on the beach drinking Red Stripes, listening to "Catch a Fire," and having water-balloon fights. What followed was an invasion of greedy, coke-snorting, gun-toting macho cowboys from the barrios of Barranquilla and Bogotá, where life was cheap and money was the only thing that mattered. Pretty soon gunfire could be heard in the early-morning hours outside the all-night bars and bodies were floating up on the beaches. When this phase of the dope trade invaded Key West, a lot of my crowd began expatriating. There was rarely a thought of returning to America.

I bought a boat and headed down-island, eventually winding up in the French West Indies, where I stayed for nearly ten years. A lot of people I knew went the other way—to Costa Rica. We would run into one another occasionally on trips back to Miami or New York. They'd be showing off their newly acquired Spanish and telling stories of the beauty and peace they had found in the mountain jungles or on the Pacific coast. My compass was still pointed southeast at the time, and it wasn't until I learned to fly a plane that my interest in the other side of the Caribbean was reignited.

Lindbergh Lands at Woodstock

I didn't take up flying to just, as they say, "make turns around the patch." I wanted to fly because it is artistic. A machine in the process of defying gravity is as visually beautiful to me as any painting. And flying is the ultimate independence. I had spent too many years in tour buses and on commercial airplanes moving to somebody else's schedule. I wanted to be able to transport my own self, at my time and pace, to required destinations when I was working and to spots of my choosing when I wasn't. I wanted to fly because it was romantic. I wanted to be like Lindbergh.

Everybody dreams of being their hero, and Charles Lindbergh was certainly one of mine. As children, we need heroes. We need to think of ourselves as being part of something bigger. It helps us to become who we are. As kids, we make up games imitating the actions of those we admire. Without this drive in our nature, we probably wouldn't have made it out of the caves.

As we grow older, some people bury that wonderful ability in their toy boxes or leave it in the springs of their bunk beds. Others carry it along to adulthood as an ageless attribute. I wrote a song about my feelings on the subject called "Growing Older but Not Up." I have carried my childish ways with me from altar boy to hippie, from hippie to husband and father. More than the music and the politics of the sixties, I think what made Woodstock the legendary event that it became was the fact that a whole generation was able to act like kids again. That's what I think happens at our shows as well. They've always been known as opportunities to escape for the evening and just have fun, but you should see what happens when it rains. You would think that a driving thunderstorm would send the crowd to the parking lot or back to the warmth and shelter of their homes in droves, but not so. They yell louder. They applaud the lightning and dance in the rain. The most incredible audiences I have ever played to were there in downpours. I call it the Woodstock connection. Somehow the rain connects them to the images of that landmark event and to that thread of uninhibited, childlike celebration. They play in the mud like they did as kids, or like those lucky few grown-up children who went to Max Yasgur's farm in the summer of 1969 and never came back the same. In looking back, I see there wasn't that much difference between Jimi Hendrix playing "The Star-Spangled Banner" at dawn at Woodstock and Jimmy Stewart playing Charles Lindbergh in *The Spirit of St. Louis*.

My father took me to see that movie when I was ten years old. He had been an aviator in World War II, flying as a crew chief on C-47's over the Burma hump. It was a strange undertaking for a man who came from a long line of sailors, and it wasn't until we were both much older that I learned why he had chosen to fly. Even stranger, though, was the fact that it was my father who was taking me to the movies in the first place. You went to the movies with your friends, not your father. Most of the movies I saw growing up were matinees. There were cowboy movies, monster movies, and serials about space travelers. They had been written, produced, directed, and packaged together in double or triple features by some marketing genius in Hollywood who knew that he could make a fortune by giving mothers across America an afternoon free from raising ten-year-old boys. We were usually delivered to the air-conditioned Loop Theater at the corner of Airport Boulevard and Government Street by a rotating car pool of station wagons. We were dumped out, told to behave, and left for the afternoon. If I ever did go to the movies at night, it was with my mother. She was the one who did the Disney-movie ordeal with her children. So when my father announced to me one afternoon that he was going to take me to the movies, I didn't really know what to expect.

The images of Jimmy Stewart acting out the story of Charles Lindbergh got to both of us. By the time the movie got to the third reel my father and I were riding with Jimmy, or "Lucky Lindy," in the *Spirit of St. Louis*. We were with him as he munched on his tuna sandwich, fought off fatigue, got lost, almost crashed into the ocean, and finally found the lights at Le Bourget airport in Paris. Years later, I would fly my Citation for the first time from the field where Lindbergh had landed, and I would visit the grave of my hero in a small, quiet cemetery that looked out from the north shore of Maui over the vast Pacific. But that day at the Loop Theater in Mobile, my dad and I jumped out of our seats and cheered when the wheels touched down. Then we both sat and cried as Jimmy Stewart rode on the shoulders of the extras from central casting to the end of the movie. It was the first time I had ever seen my father cry.

J.D. and Me

One afternoon a few years ago, I touched down at the Fairhope International Airport—my name for the field where I had first started landing my planes many years ago. I passed through a layer of clouds at about three thousand feet and spotted the familiar field lying amid rectangles of fertile farmland filled with potatoes, pecan trees, and Silver Queen corn. It had been, like many other airfields that dotted the landscape between Mobile Bay and the Florida state line, a practice field for Navy pilots in training at the naval air station in Pensacola. Now it was owned and maintained by the city of Fairhope, Alabama. The runway was long enough for jets and had an instrument approach. There had been a jet charter service based there before Hurricane Frederic, but it had gone out of business. The traffic these days consisted of a few local single-engine planes, a couple of crop dusters for the potatoes, and the occasional corporate jet picking up or dropping off visitors to the Grand Hotel.

I had made it a habit of coming home whenever I bought a new plane. It had become a ritual and a good excuse to visit my folks and get the approval of my purchase from former Army Air Corps master sergeant J. D. Buffett. Dad and I had never really talked about his flying days. I was so enamored of the exploits of my grandfather that I forgot that my old man had had a few adventures of his own. All I really knew was that he had been a flight mechanic in the war and had worked on B-17's in Maine, B-25's in Africa, and C-47's in India. Now that we were both older and I had become romantically involved with airplanes, it became a wonderful opportunity to stay in touch with my dad. He had ridden with me in every airplane I had owned, and there had been a lot of them.

After I found my Grumman Widgeon in Michigan, I flew her to Nashville, where my dad came up and joined me during my flight training. The Widgeon is renowned to be a handful of airplane on water and asphalt, and it took me a while to get the feel of how she handled. One day we had come in from a grueling day of multiple takeoffs and landings on the Cumberland River and I was venting my frustration about crosswind when my dad casually said, "You should try one with a fire on board." He proceeded to tell me a flying story that made my day of training look like an afternoon at a spa.

He had been flying over the Himalayas from his base in India on a test flight in an old C-47. There was just the pilot, copilot, and my dad. They were cruising along when suddenly a fire light came on, indicating that the heater in the plane was on fire. It was located in the lower nose compartment. My father donned a gas mask, grabbed a fire extinguisher, and went down below. He found the heater ablaze and the fuel line that fed from the main fuel tank to the heater spraying aviation fuel, which immediately burst into flames. He managed to put the fire out and close the fuel valve. He picked up the headset that was connected to the flight deck to report to the pilots that the fire was indeed out. There was no reply. He climbed back out of the belly and found no one flying the plane. Out of the corner of his eye, he saw the pilot and copilot preparing to bail out. They had failed to inform my dad of their intentions. The master sergeant ordered the officers back to the controls, and when they landed he reported them to the commander of the base and they were grounded.

"You never told me that story," I muttered in disbelief.

J.D. never got to ride in the Albatross. To put it in old Army Air Corps terms, shortly before I bought it, he was ground zero for a direct hit, a hit from which he would not recover.

In early 1995 my father was diagnosed with Alzheimer's disease. He knew something had been wrong but wasn't sure what. Jane had been the one to see the writing on the wall, and we took him to a clinic in Nashville run by friends of mine who were doctors and pilots. I was in the doctor's office with him and my mother when the neurosurgeon came in and gave us the horrible news. My dad just breathed very deep, looked at us both, laughed his familiar laugh, and in a disbelieving tone said, "Goddamn."

I knew that I had to spend as much time with J.D. as I could and made frequent trips from Florida to Alabama to see him. As difficult as it was for all of my family to come to grips with the situation, I knew nothing that we were feeling could even compare to what my father was going through. J.D. had been a whiz with facts and figures. He was a draftsman and a dynamo of energy with whom few people could keep pace. Now he had to face the awful reality that he was losing his mind.

After the initial shock and once the devastating news had settled in, my father and I talked. Our conversations were more personal than they had ever been. Dad had never been a talker, and when he did talk, it was about either his work at the shipyard or his children and grandchildren. At times he was a tyrant, but nothing close to the Great Santini. Growing up, he had had to pay the price of being the oldest of four children. My grandfather was at sea for months, sometimes years at a time, and my dad became the father figure. When the war broke out, my grandfather and my uncle both joined the Navy. My father, however, joined the Army Air Corps. He had spent every day since getting back from World War II building ships and barges. First at the Ingalls Shipyard in Pascagoula and then at Alabama Drydock and Shipbuilding Company in Mobile, where both he and my mother worked until they retired.

By the time he was diagnosed with Alzheimer's, we had fortunately already made our peace. We had made it past those testosterone-produced clashes that seem to be rites of passage for fathers and sons. Now my father was scared and bewildered, and he said so. But he was a fighter and in the next breath would come out swinging, ready to "take the bull by the horns," as he put it. He never talked about licking Alzheimer's like it was some kind of opponent he was going to defeat. He knew his fate. He told me he just wanted to do a few things that he had never gotten to do. He was going to study his options and let me know.

When tragedy of such proportions occurs, the only thing you can do is hope that there have been some good times. It's hard to catch up. My parents had gotten to enjoy the fruits of my success. They went to shows, hung out backstage with my crew and band, and acted like that unique, wonderful, and very small group of people known as the parents of successful rock stars. They had traveled the world together, hoping to cruise on through the last part of their lives in the comfort of their nest, called Homeport. But that was not to be.

My father always had a great sense of humor. I think that's where mine comes from, so I think he would be most pleased if I told this little story. One day I got a call from him, asking me to come to Alabama. I flew up in a dome of high pressure that had covered the entire state of Florida. I didn't see one cloud on the entire route. I was over the Florida panhandle and had started my descent when I saw the outline of Mobile Bay, 120 miles away. I had no idea what my dad had come up with. He was mostly here in those days, but he could also go out into the cosmos. I didn't know if he would ask to go to Mars or mainland China. I started to flash on that old TV show *Run for Your Life,* starring Ben Gazzara. My father was not a big movie or television buff, but along with Jackie Gleason in *The Honeymooners* and James Arness in *Gunsmoke,* he loved Ben Gazzara. "He's a man's actor," he would say. If you don't remember or weren't born when *Run for Your Life* was a hit show, here's the basic plot. A wealthy and successful doctor finds out that he only has six months to live. What's he going to do? Give that kind of ammunition to Hollywood, and here is what they came up with. The guy buys a fancy sports car and proceeds to travel around America, falling in love with beautiful women in exotic locations. Nice work, if you can get it. As I went through my checklist on final and made the turn toward Fairhope International, I wondered if the old man was going to run for his life.

He met me at the airport and immediately threw me the keys to the car. "You didn't like the way I drove even before I got this shit," he said. It was just a small indication of his harsh reality—and his awareness that in desperate times and situations, humor is the only way out. We picked up a couple of oyster loaves and Barq's root beers at Mac's Cafe, then drove on to Homeport.

We were sitting at the end of the pier. Piers on the eastern shore of the bay were not just structures that jutted into the shallow waters. They were not just shelters from the near-tropical summer sun. They were wooden islands. Collections of creosote, two-by-fours, and tenpenny nails that connected both children and adults to the natural wonders of Mobile Bay. My father had overseen the construction of a pier that ran from the house on the bluff for the length of four footballs fields. It was his signature upon the landscape of the eastern shore. The structure cleared the marshy coastal swamp laced with wild orchids and one-hundred-and-fifty-year-old cedar trees until it reached the edge of the water, where it continued on another hundred yards. As one of his neighbors had said upon its completion, "Goddamn, J.D., I guess you wanted them astronauts to see where you lived from outer space."

Since his retirement, the pier had been his base of operation. Here he had raised his children and their children and had partied with us and his friends. He had captured alligators and awakened the neighborhood to that totally unique cry of "Jubilee," which signaled a bizarre migration of shellfish and bottom feeders into shallow water, where they would be scooped up in washtubs and Igloo coolers. Flying around the roof were signal flags and flags from every country he had visited, and Old Glory sat on the south corner of the pier on a solitary and lofty old mast. In the opposite corner stood his pride and joy, a barbecue pit and smoker that had been fabricated in a sheet-metal shop out of materials left over from the refit of the aircraft carrier *Lexington*. It looked like a small nuclear reactor and weighed about as much. It had been dragged out of the shipyard under cloak of darkness and presented to him as a surprise gift from his coworkers upon his retirement. I had eaten many a good meal that came from the nuclear barbecue. My dad called it his heirloom and the only material thing that he really loved. He was going to leave it to me in his will—that is, as he said, "if you can move the son of a bitch."

We were looking out over the shallow waters of Mobile Bay, savoring the day and the unique taste of fresh fried oysters on buttered French bread with hot sauce and tartar sauce, which made up the sandwich that's synonymous with the Gulf Coast—the oyster loaf.

"Damn, that's good," J.D. said, as he finished his root beer. "You know, when I was a kid in Pascagoula, I worked for the Barq's people. They started the root beer in Pascagoula, and then a couple of brothers had a fight and one of them took off to Biloxi and opened his own plant. The Pascagoula Barq's had red bottle tops, and the Biloxi root beer had blue ones. At the Pascagoula plant, not only did we bottle our root beer with the red caps, we sabotaged the Biloxi root beer with the blue caps."

"How did you do that?" I asked.

"We would take a rag soaked in turpentine and go to the grocery store and just wipe it over the tops of all the bottles with blue caps. It turned the root beer sour." He drained the last sip of his Barq's and stared out across the bay. "You know what I was just thinking about?"

"What?" These days that could be a loaded question.

"Remember when you got thrown out of the sailing club for leaving the race and sailing all the way across the bay?" I only had to think a moment about that major event in my misspent youth. It had been the same kind of a day as today.

"You bet I do," I said with a laugh.

"I never told you, but that was about as proud as I ever was of you. I mean, being the first Buffett to get a college degree was good, don't get me wrong, but that time you just decided to light out on your own, that was a moment."

Tears came into my eyes. I started to drift back to that incredible day, but my father's next words cut my trip short.

"I just saved you a hell of a lot of money," he said.

"What do you mean?" I asked, drying my eyes and swallowing hard.

"Well, I've decided where I want to go. I talked it over with your mom, and she thinks it's a good idea. I want to go to Salt Cay for Christmas."

"Salt Cay?" I said in disbelief. I was probably one of the very few people on the planet who had actually been to Salt Cay. It is a scruffy, parched little island to the south of Grand Turk in the Turks and Caicos Islands. Paris, it ain't.

"This disease is strange, Jim. It takes you back, you know. When it hits, I can't remember shit about what I did two minutes ago, but I can see things in the past like I was there. I had some of the best times of my life on Salt Cay when your grandfather was loading salt bound for New Orleans. I was six years old, and we were on the *Chicamauga*. She lay at anchor, and I would go watch them load the salt and then take off with a group of local kids, and we would chase flamingos and catch lobsters from the beach. I know, it ain't a place Ben Gazzara would go looking for his babes, but I want to go back." He could have asked for London, Paris, the South Pacific, or the whole world and I would have given it to him. In fitting with who he was and who he is, he chose Salt Cay.

— — —

Traditionally, my father's inspections of my planes would begin with him waiting for me at the appointed ETA (estimated time of arrival), sitting in front of the metal hangar at Fairhope International in his spotless gray Jeep Cherokee. It looked like it had just rolled off the showroom floor, but actually it had nearly 200,000 miles on it. I wouldn't dare be late. Keeping time schedules and proper maintenance were habits that he had brought home from the war and had never relinquished. If I was late, I would be greeted with a stern look as he pointed to the watch on his wrist.

Now, two months after he told me he wanted to go to Salt Cay, I was back in Alabama. My dad greeted me warmly, pointed at his watch to let me know that he was aware I was fifteen minutes late. "I had to divert for some buildups around Cross City," I explained.

"Should have figured that into your ETD [estimated time of departure]." He and Ed Grahman, the caretaker, helped me unload my stuff. I climbed into the backseat, and we headed for Homeport. He didn't say much. He looked worried. I knew from my mom that the trip to Salt Cay had not gone as he had planned. It had started off great, but then came bouts of disorientation, and he and my mom had headed home earlier than scheduled.

We picked up our oyster loaves and once again were out on the pier eating lunch together. He sat at the very end of the dock on the crabbing pier and tossed sticks to the dogs, who gallivanted into the shallow water to retrieve them. They swam back to the pier, shook the water from their fur, and dropped the sticks at our feet, waiting for the next toss. After several more throws, they sensed a change in mood and swam off toward the beach, leaving my father and me alone.

"It's getting worse, Jim," he said flatly. "It's the scariest thing I have ever been through in my life." I didn't know what to say. I was in tears but couldn't speak. Saying I was sorry just didn't feel like enough. My dad sensed this immediately and changed the topic. "You know why I chose to fly instead of go to sea?"

There it was, the question that had been nagging at me all these years. Now, on the end of the pier near the end of his lucid days, I was going to get the answer. "Why?" I asked.

"Because it was what I wasn't supposed to do. Looks like you have made a career out of that, doing what you're not supposed to do. I'm proud of you, boy."

We hugged for a long time and then walked back to the house with our arms around each other. His memory has since faded like a flare, but he still knows me when I come home. I have to look deep into his eyes and stare at his face point-blank, but I can see the light come on. In May 1996 he fell one night and broke his hip. The doctors told me to get ready for the end. Six months later he was out of bed, out of his wheelchair, and walking the grounds of Homeport again. He is almost an angel, but still with us. Today when I join him for his walks down the oyster-shelled driveway out toward old Highway 98 or down to the end of the pier, I think of the lines from a song that I wrote about a fictitious but favorite character of mine named Desdemona. "Her heart is in the kitchen, but her soul is in the stars." Change the pronoun, and you have my dad—J.D.

All Your Ducks in a Row

Date: 26 December 1996
Latitude: 15°30′0″ N
Longitude: 82°53′1″ W
Location: Approximately 225 mi. NE of San José, Costa Rica, on Air Route B757

Altitude: 10,000′
Heading: 199°
Wind: 220° @ 10 knots
Speed: 152 knots

Comments: Traffic along our route is not that heavy this morning, considering it's the day after Christmas. I listen to the conversations between other pilots on our route and the controller for the sector we're in. I have learned over the years that you can pick up a lot of information by tuning in to the transmission from planes in front of and behind you. I listen for reports of bad weather or problems with traffic, which I can then anticipate. We are on an instrument flight plan at an assigned altitude of ten thousand feet. All the other planes have their own assigned altitudes, which are, I hope, different from ours. That way we won't run into one another. The trick to instrument flying is to take care of your own business and stay ahead of the curve. The system was designed on the premise that as an instrument pilot you have the capacity to fly your ship to a specific set of instructions. There are about 600,000 pilots buzzing around the skies of America, but only a small percentage of those pilots are instrument-rated.

Flying over water alone in a single-engine plane makes some pilots nervous, especially if they're not comfortable with water in the first place. It definitely puts a few more factors into the equations of navigation and emergency survival, but it never bothered me. It may be the fact that I am a good swimmer, or that the countless hours I have spent on, under, and around the water give me a great deal of respect for but never a fear of the open ocean.

The first time I looked down behind me and saw the thin sash of mangroves that were the Florida Keys disappear over the horizon and found myself heading east out over the open ocean, I got that Lindbergh feeling and loved where I was. When I'm flying out over the water, I feel like I'm functioning at all levels of human existence, better than at any other time in my life. I have all my ducks in a row: navigational skills, engine and fuel management, local knowledge, emergency procedures, right on up to where to stop for lunch. I love the cultural transformation that took place on those early Bahamas flights, where you could jump from the hustle and bustle of South Florida to a deserted island in less than a hundred miles.

It was in those early days also that I discovered that heaven can all too quickly turn into hell. The geographic region where I was learning to fly and where I wanted to make longer flights over water was historically known for fast and dangerous weather changes. If you then throw in hocus-pocus stories of the Bermuda Triangle (which, by the way, I have never run into), you have a pretty good collection of things that could force a perfectly good-running plane, not to mention one that's in trouble, out of the sky.

I knew from what my experienced instructors had told me that if I was going to go where I wanted to explore, instrument training would inevitably get me out of some of the bad weather situations I was bound to encounter. If you keep all your ducks in a row, then even if something out of the ordinary happens, you are in shape to deal with an emergency and get yourself and your passengers or cargo back to earth. Today I am carrying precious cargo in the form of one little redheaded boy, who is now sitting with Randall in the navigator's seat with a pair of headphones on that make him look kind of like Elroy on *The Jetsons*.

Guns Are Rusting in the Jungle

Date: 26 December 1996
Latitude: 14°32'7" N
Longitude: 83°12'3" W
Location: Approximately
55 mi. NE of Puerto
Cabeza, off the coast
of Nicaragua

Altitude: 10,000'
Heading: 199°
Wind: 220° @ 12 knots
Speed: 156 knots

Comments: The view from my window to the left is of the swampy Caribbean coastline of Nicaragua. We have crossed the Caribbean Sea in a lot less time than it took Columbus or Sir Francis Drake, and we are, as the song says, "down to the banana republics." From altitude, it looks like a lot of other coastal jungles I've flown over. Meandering rivers of brown water drift through blankets of brown and green marsh grass on their way to the sea. At the mouths of these rivers, the current spills the contents of the confined tributaries in creamy patterns that resemble unfolded fans. The currents and tides of the clear blue ocean act like barricades holding the muddy water close to the shore as if to say, "That's far enough."

Though we are slicing through the atmosphere at better than 150 miles an hour, I feel the slowness and the heat of the moist land below. I come from the coastal swamps of Alabama, and humidity is in my bones. The first word that this view brings to mind is *snakes*. Second word: *mosquitoes*. Third word: *war*. The snakes and mosquitoes have called the marshes home when nobody else wanted them. War came with the conquerors in the name of God and greed. There has been a lot of blood spilled down there in the jungles of Latin

America. The tiny countries that separate North and South America have been as politically volatile as the volcanic mountains that pepper their landscape, often erupting just as unpredictably.

From the beaches of the Bahamas to the heights of Machu Picchu, history is the heartbeat of the Caribbean. When Columbus landed in Cuba for the first time, he thought he was in India. He sent a royal delegation ashore to meet the king of India but was greeted only by a tribe of naked Arawaks having a clambake on the beach. He was about fifteen thousand miles from his intended destination, but the name Indies stuck. Legend has it that the emperor of the mighty Incan empire in Peru dined every evening on fresh fish brought to him in the Andean mountain capital of Cuzco by a staff of relay runners whose lifelong job it was to run from the ocean to the dinner table. Then history marched in and changed that forever. Today history in the jungles below is doing what it has always done best—repeating itself.

As if the banana republics didn't have enough to contend with in surviving the Spanish, the pirates, slavery, and a string of homegrown dictators, there has been more than a century of American meddling in their affairs. We have an inane codependent relationship with the region that makes about as much sense as a priest counseling couples about marital problems. We rarely have a clue as to what is going on, and most of the time our policies have resulted in major fuckups.

In the dawn of October 5, 1986, a C-123 cargo plane took off from El Salvador, bound for a jungle field somewhere in Honduras. The crew was composed of former and present CIA employees. Its cargo was a cache of guns and ammo that could have been a centerfold in *Soldier of Fortune* magazine. It never made it to the jungle airstrip. The plane was shot down by Sandinistas using Soviet-made ground-to-air missiles. One lone parachute emerged from the burning plane and dropped former Marine Eugene Hasenfus into the hands of the enemy.

What enemy? Who's the enemy? Were we at war? Well, not really.

To me, our foreign policy in Latin America since the end of World War II looks like a long string of bad dope deals. You see, we weren't supposed to be there helping the contras against the Sandinistas. It was against the law, but there we were. The plane that Eugene Hasenfus jumped from may not have officially "existed," but there it was, lying in charred pieces on a hillside among the smoking banana and avocado trees, AK-47's, grenade launchers, and fifty thousand rounds of unspent ammunition. Pictures of a bewildered Hasenfus filled the front pages of newspapers around the world.

The way it was reported in *The Miami Herald* the next day confused the incident even more. "A 'friendly foreign government' acting on behalf of the United States financed the flight of a cargo plane shot down over Nicaragua." Immediately, officials at the White House, the State Department, the Pentagon, and the CIA denied that Hasenfus, the downed plane, or the other crewmen aboard it were connected to the U.S. government. As we know, that didn't turn out to be quite true. Slowly the alibis crumbled and the real story started to come out. It was better than fiction. It involved guns, hostages in Lebanon, Israeli espionage, secret armies in Alabama, secret agents in Iran, and that was just for starters. When the whole story actually emerged, there the U.S. was once again looking like a guy in the men's room caught with his pants down and a copy of *Playboy* in his hand. The whole scam had been organized by members of Ronald Reagan's cabinet. When the passing of the buck stopped, it wound up in the hands of Lieutenant Colonel Oliver North, a modern-day George Armstrong Custer. It soon became evident that everyone was into it up to their necks, except, of course, the president, who was napping during the whole ordeal.

As I cross the shore into Nicaraguan airspace, the controller in this former war zone is quite friendly. I see no missiles heading skyward. Today the country and the airspace are relatively free of gunfire. But as I look out at the whirling propellers on my plane, I can't help but wonder if the friendly controller I am talking to might have been the one who fired the missile at Eugene Hasenfus ten years ago. In broken English, he welcomed us to his country and his airspace.

These days, Nicaragua is on the back burner of world attention. For a time the Balkans regained prominence as the leading historical nightmare of the day. When the Iron Curtain was lifted and Mother Russia was revealed to be no more than an overgrown Third World country, the far-reaching tentacles that had stirred the hotbed of politics and emotion in the banana republics shriveled up as well, turning Havana into a refuge. In Nicaragua the Sandinistas were voted out of power in a democratic election. Reagan went to Santa Barbara. Hasenfus went back to Wisconsin, and Oliver North was defeated for a U.S. Senate seat in Virginia. Things are quieter in the jungle now. Ten thousand feet below me, guns are rusting in the hot sun and marsh air. I hope that time will turn them into scraps of history and the monsoon rains will wash their remains downstream and out to sea.

SECTION VI

Costa Rica

Pura Vida

Five Miles Higher and Moving Fast

The earth cooks fast in these latitudes, and the visible by-product of this cosmic bakeshop takes the form of the cumulonimbus clouds suspended just above the dark and distant horizon. Ahead, there is higher terrain. I have always been attached to the weather. From my earliest days, I was taught by the seafaring Buffetts about the forces of nature. I knew that rain was more than "liquid sunshine." It didn't appear in the sky on cue like in a movie or on a Saturday-morning cartoon show. The weather was part of a global picture, with elements like barometric pressure, air masses, convection, and Corealis effect. When you start to fly, you do not run off and charge right into the first cloud you can find. You start by learning how the cloud got there to begin with.

To me, one of the great wonders of the universe is the balance of nature. It's the reason that I became involved in trying to do something about preserving it. Flying only amplifies for me the importance of that fragile balance. As an example, we live here on the earth, and our lives are very much affected by the changes of season. Yet only five miles above the earth's surface there are no seasons and the temperatures are constantly below freezing. You can take off from Miami on a sweltering, humid, ninety-five-degree day, but just a mile above the bubbling cauldron of the Everglades, the temperature drops by 50 percent. When you look out the tiny window of the Concorde from sixty thousand feet, the sky above you is more black than blue, and the earth is small enough to show curvature. It's only twelve miles up to the threshold of space.

I check the chart. We need to climb an additional two thousand feet to give us safe clearance over the mountains ahead. Over the radio I hear a familiar voice reciting a familiar number. "Puerto Cabeza Radio, this is Citation eighty-seven Bravo Alpha, checking in at flight-level thirty-four-zero." It's the International House of Women in the jet. I listen to their report, then ask Puerto Cabeza Radio for permission to talk to them. I call out to Randall and Cameron in the back and tell them to come up front. A couple of minutes later, I spot the "con trails" at twelve o'clock. The jet is four miles higher and moving fast. I put Cameron up in my lap and point at the long streaks of frozen ice crystals that look like a pair of white ribbons moving across the sky. "That's Mommy and Delaney," I say. He looks puzzled.

"I don't see Momma," he says with common sense, seeming to question my rationality.

"They're in that plane," I tell him. I take his index finger and point up at the plane until he finds it.

"It's little," he replies. I back away from trying to complicate his simple perception that his mother is not up there in the sky, and she surely can't be in an airplane that small. I get the pilots on the radio and let them know we're chugging along below them. The girls are fine, and we'll see them on the ground in a couple of hours. In a matter of minutes, they are gone from sight. Below us the jungle disappears beneath a layer of thin clouds moving in from the ocean. The weather is changing with the terrain. We say good-bye to Puerto Cabeza and hello to Tico control. I ease back on the throttles and check my rate of descent. It's like the old joke about the thermos jug: How do it know hot from cold? Unpredictability is as much a part of human nature as it is of the weather patterns that are wrapped around our planet, and today, as we cross the imaginary line that separates Nicaragua from Costa Rica, I find myself singing the right song for the right moment:

L.A. is a great big freeway
Put a hundred down and buy a car
In a week maybe two they'll make you a star
But dreams turn into dust and quickly pass
And all the stars
That never were
Are parking cars and pumping gas
Do you know the way to San Jose?
I've got a friend up there

We break through the overcast at five thousand feet, and I get my first look at Costa Rica. We are flying in a long, beautiful valley surrounded by mountain peaks. Rays of sunlight shoot through breaks in the cloud cover like transporter beams from the *Enterprise*. A rainbow arcs in the sky to an isolated rain shower farther down the valley, and the vast Pacific peeks at us from the western horizon. It has always been a thrill to actually visit places that started out in my life as photographs in *National Geographic*. The feel and smell of salt that accompanied us across the Caribbean is gone. Now there is a sweetness in the air that signals altitude, adiabatic cooling, and fertile fields below.

Geographically, Costa Rica is a little bit of everything. It borders two large bodies of water, the Caribbean and the Pacific, and is divided by a backbone of mountains, an appendage of the Andes–Sierra Madre chain that runs along the western side of the Americas. It has rain forests and mountains, deep-water rivers, black-and-white sand beaches. It also rests on the Pacific "Rim of Fire" and has seven of the isthmus's forty-two active volcanoes, plus dozens of dormant or extinct cones. "I don't know where I'm-a gonna go when the volcano blow." Beam me down, Scotty.

The engines sense the cooling in the air as well. The cylinder-head temperature readings drop a few degrees, and the old reliable radial engines seem to add a little kick to their step. I have finally made it to Costa Rica. Two years earlier, my last attempt to come this far south was aborted when guerrillas kidnapped some diplomats in San José and the country was put under lockdown. Costa Rica is an ongoing democracy in a part of the world that's not known for such things. It maintains no standing army. It has a thriving and varied economy and a lot more, but it is still the Third World, and you have to be ready for anything.

I long ago abandoned the casual approach to country-hopping in the Caribbean. Though I have spent countless wonderful hours of solitude at altitude and on abandoned beaches of the region, I have also been detained by customs, strip-searched and bribed by various law-enforcement agencies, shot at by a SWAT team while I went to lunch, chased by Apache helicopters, and generally made to feel not very welcome.

I remember too well my first couple of trips to Belize, back in the early eighties. I would land at the airport and be treated like a giant disease-ridden mosquito that had dropped out of the sky. The problem on those first trips was that the Lake Renegade I was flying at the time was constantly being seen on the chic hit TV show *Miami Vice*. But the plane wasn't being flown by Crockett and Tubbs in their Giorgio Armani flight suits. On *Miami Vice*, the Lake was always piloted by over-dressed Colombian dope dealers. So, I was a victim of bad television writing. They thought I was a dope dealer. If I wasn't being harassed by customs, I was being offered "jobs" by slimeballs hanging out in the dark corners of the dingy little airport bar. Things are different now. Experience has been my teacher, and although it's been a sad education, I know better how to play the game.

In my mind, being a seaplane pilot connected me to a heritage that started with explorers like Antoine Saint-Exupéry, Charles Lindbergh, Ralph O'Neill, Charlie Blair, and Dean Franklin. These guys made up the rules. They went where they wanted to go, when they wanted to go. When they dropped out of the sky onto the jungle airstrips and into the backwaters of the tropics, they were looked upon with awe and admiration. Today, that's not possible in the Third World. The romantic airplanes I love to own and fly are now more connected with the dope trade than with aviation history, and I have to make adjustments due to these perceptions. These days, it's not enough to just file a flight plan and ask the control tower for permission to land. You have to cover your ass.

We are coming back to earth. The long trip from the Cayman Islands has been a breeze, but the wonderful hours of quiet now give way to the hustle and bustle of a busy international airport. As instructed by the tower, I swing the Albatross out to the west and circle back up the valley, and then the long runway comes into view. Time for the approach-to-landing checklist. Flaps emerge and the landing gear stretches itself out. The plane slows down, and the big rubber tires hang under the wing, eagerly awaiting contact with the ground. We are ready to land, and several minutes later we touch down in Costa Rica.

As we roll out to a stop in front of the general aviation terminal, there is a host of vehicles, customs and immigration people, and the welcoming committee from the International House of Women. With Cameron on my lap, I taxi the Albatross onto the ramp. He sees his life-sized mommy waving to him and he returns the gesture. Then he looks back at me with this admonishing look on his face and says, "Dad, there's Mommy. She is not up in the sky." I can't argue with that. I shut down the engines and set the parking brake. We still do not have permission to move the Albatross out of San José. Since the hijacking and crash of an American seaplane a few years ago, the rules for movement of foreign aircraft have been rigidly tightened. So, our plan B is to charter to our final destination and not get hung up in San José.

A pilot friend, with whom I had flown for years in Long Island, was in San José and helped us out now. The government officials are all very polite and extremely interested in the Albatross and ask lots of questions about engines and airspeeds.

I learned a long time ago to leave my Yankee bravado at home when I travel. The best way for an American to get around in the world is to not act like you saved it or own it. My other ace in the hole if I smell trouble brewing is to somehow relate my reason for being where I am to making a movie. Hollywood has more clout worldwide than the U.S. State Department. Very few people in the street know who Madeleine Albright or Warren Christopher are, but everybody knows Harrison Ford and Jack Nicholson.

I have a legitimate connection to moviemaking, since I am one of the producers of the forthcoming epic film, with a cast of thousands, that was to be made from my book *Where Is Joe Merchant?* My raison d'être: family vacation and "location-scouting for a tropical setting." I don't know whether it's thanks to that, the call I had made to Frank Marshall, Jim Powell's connections in San José, or the box of CD's, hats, and a dozen T-shirts that we distributed among the personnel at the airport, but whatever it was, we clear customs in a flash. It will take another day before permission to fly the Albatross around the country is granted. After a lot of handshaking and exchanges of telephone numbers with our handlers, we take off again. A half hour later we swoop in low over the slow-rolling swells of the blue Pacific and touch down on the short runway near the remote village of Tambor.

Pura Vida

I sit with Jane in the shade of the little thatched-roof hut that plays the part of the Tambor airport. Out of habit, I tried to assist in unloading the baggage but was politely told that I needn't worry. The hotel had sent out an army of bellmen and drivers, and they attacked our baggage like it was a dope drop, loading it with amazing speed into the bed of a waiting and dusty pickup. The force is led by a small, cheerful man named Javier, who smiles and laughs as he issues instructions to the baggage handlers, introducing himself to all of us and welcoming us to his country. He tells us that for the next week—though we are guests of the hotel—we are his family. Javier exemplifies the unique and wonderful nature of the Costa Rican people, or Ticos, as they call themselves. Even in these first few minutes at the remote airstrip, I feel a serenity and friendliness that I have not felt in my travels in the surrounding Central American countries. Costa Rica has been a democracy for over a hundred years, a country boasting "teachers, not soldiers." It has had no army since 1948, has one of the highest literacy rates in the world, and has a national health-care system that covers all of its citizens. There are pages of facts and figures in various travel books and brochures that further entice one to want to spend time in this country. But the Ticos sum it all up in the expression that describes their way of life: *Pura vida*, the pure life.

Where the Pavement Ends and the Dust Begins

There is salsa music coming from a radio in the guard shack by the road. Cameron and Delaney dance to the beat and run around in circles, imitating the antics of monkeys, until we are all loaded up and headed out for the Hotel Tango Mar. The narrow road winds its way west through landscape that changes at every bend. One moment we are surrounded by fenced-off pastures that remind me of my sister's ranch in Montana, then suddenly we dip down into a tropical rain forest. In the distance, beaches remind me of my proximity to the ocean, but I also feel like I'm on a continent, not a tropical island.

Javier carries on a narrative and answers our questions as we drive. The pavement runs out at the little village of Tambor, and we stop for cold drinks. Where the pavement ends and the dust begins is also the place where the time warp takes over. It has been only two days since we were opening Christmas presents in Palm Beach, but now we are bouncing along a dirt road in another world. When you are traveling on a trip like this in the right frame of mind, time and space will change. Things that seemed absolutely necessary two days ago slip from your mind. You find yourself looking out the window of the plane, boat, or car and daydreaming about going native. Time becomes something to be used, not saved. Many years ago, when I first experienced this feeling, I wrote a song about it called "Changes in Latitudes, Changes in Attitudes." It worked then, and it's working now, as we drive west to the ocean in the land of *pura vida*.

Life with a Compassionate Vulcan

It might seem as though we just arrived, like on a magic-carpet ride, on the shores of the Pacific, but that is not quite the case. In writing a book of reminiscences like this, you always hit the high points and wonderful stories that make for good reading. You tend not to delve into the boring but necessary planning that goes into such a trip. Stories about being shot at in Jamaica or hooking up with a four-hundred-pound marlin tend to hold the reader's interest more than a description of an hour's conversation with a travel agent.

Along with Jim Powell, my friend and aviation chief, we mapped out the logistics of running the airplanes around Central and South America and back again. But Jane always takes care of the rest. She's a great road manager and operates with a lot more patience and common sense than I ever could. I have had the privilege of bouncing around the world with this woman for more than twenty years. I have seen her be the center of conversation at a table in a trendy restaurant filled with celebrities at the fall collections in Milan. I have also seen her whip up a peach cobbler in the galley of a sailboat in five-foot seas for a bunch of haggard and hungry sailors, providing us with a special dessert on Easter Sunday. Jane is an amazingly adaptable woman.

Once we decided on Central and South America, one of the wiser decisions my wife made was to bring along traveling companions for each of us. Now, don't get me wrong. Jane and I truly enjoy each other's company. She is not only my wife, she is my best friend, but we still are different people with different interests. We have learned through experience that it's okay not to like some things that your spouse likes to do, and it's better to make it known rather than just go along.

Jane had met Mac a year earlier on Long Island, and they had become good friends. They exercised together, took long hikes, and had long conversations about the things girls like to talk about. Mac was one more addition to the International House of Women.

My choice for this trip was my dear old friend Kino. Kino is like one of our family. Our friendship dates back to my arrival in 1976 on St. Barts, where he was the island's doctor. Whatever those things are that work to make lasting friendships were there, and the next thing I knew, I had asked him to come along on one of our tours in the States. God knows, in those days on a rock 'n' roll tour a doctor could come in handy. Twenty years later, we are still working and traveling together, and I feel lucky to have him. In Paris for the holidays visiting his family, he would be arriving in Costa Rica around New Year's Eve and would accompany us on the rest of the trip.

Jane, the great organizer, had found an ideal place on the northwest coast from which we could explore our options in Costa Rica. After much discussion and research about what would be our second stop, Jane put Cartagena on our itinerary. It was I who wanted to go to the Amazon, but it was Jane who found the four-star hotel in the middle of the jungle. She is the best the galaxy has to offer. She is a compassionate Vulcan.

Study Your Language Tapes

It is midafternoon when our caravan finally pulls into the driveway of the house Jane had rented for us. A small white sign above the entrance reads, PRESIDEN-TIAL HOUSE. It is a sprawling complex situated atop a grassy hill facing west, commanding a panoramic view of the Pacific Ocean. The grounds are filled with tropical fruit trees and shell paths that end at a patchwork of pastures, where several contented pinto ponies stand like statues in the shade of a large, sagging tamarind tree. On the first level is a kitchen area and a patio, both open to the breeze and the pool. Across from the pool is a cluster of bedrooms where dark curtains cover the windows and a steady stream of condensation drips from the air-conditioning units above the door. The heat of the near-equatorial sun is enough to send the kids dashing immediately into the pool like salmon returning to the river. I opt for the cool confines of the air-conditioned main bedroom. Javier brings my bags in and offers to help me unpack. I politely decline but see a disturbed furrow above his brow. I try to explain as best I can that packing and unpacking is a natural process for me. He seems confused. Javier's English is excellent. My Spanish is awful.

I am in a communications vacuum that makes me feel stupid. Then I get mad. I need to blame this predicament on somebody or something. When in doubt, you can always find the culprit in religion and politics. Now I choose to blame the Catholic church, but I also throw in the public-school system and "the United States of America's role as leader of the free world syndrome" for this problem. Americans in general assume a very arrogant posture when it comes to learning other languages.

A second language is still not a mandatory part of primary public education, even today. If you want to learn to speak another language, it's basically up to you. You are not encouraged to do so in school. In my case, I was further discouraged from learning another language by the fact that the only language I was ever offered in school was Latin. Great stuff if you were going to spend the rest of your life as a Benedictine monk cloistered away behind well-worn, ivy-covered abbey walls, but pretty useless in helping you communicate with the rest of the world.

I finally took French in college, having had some ancestral stake in it due to the Cajun side of my family. It would have helped my early appreciation of the language if the teacher had looked like Brigitte Bardot, but she was a spinster with a thick southern Mississippi accent who dressed in clothes left-over from the Victorian period. She also had an affinity for Beaujolais. Our shared love of the grape was not enough to get me through the course. I got a D. My efforts at learning another language stopped there in Mississippi.

It was in France in the summer of 1974 that I came to learn the importance of language. I had been asked to write the musical score for a film on tarpon fishing that had been produced by my old friend Guy de la Valdene. It had been shot in Key West that winter. Guy and I had been introduced a few years earlier by an older friend, who is not only a great writer, but my brother-in-law, Thomas McGuane. We hit it off from the start when we met in the Chart Room bar. Guy, or "the Count," as we call him, was already a legendary figure in the sporting arena of South Florida. He had been born into a privileged world and had spent his youth crisscrossing the Atlantic between Palm Beach and France, where he had been raised in a château outside Paris, near the small village of Sainte Georges Motel. He was rich, he had a beautiful wife, and he spoke fluent French and perfect English. He was a dead-eye shot with a small-bore shotgun and a master angler with a fly rod. And he knew wine like nobody I had ever met. He had all the skills I admired and envied. So the day I got the call to go to France and write the score for the documentary, I couldn't believe my luck.

At that point in my career, I had never written anything that went beyond four minutes. I was flat broke and trying desperately to find work in the States, but I accepted the offer immediately. I would not be paid for the project, but Jane's and my expenses would be covered by the production company while we were in France. Jane had gypsied through Europe in her college days doing the dollar-a-day thing, but I had never been there. So it was with an incredible sense of wonder, two hundred bucks, and a Glad bag full of Colombian pot that I first set foot on French soil. Guy met us at Orly and drove us beyond central Paris toward Normandy and the château. I became a Francophile that day.

Since then I have made many trips to Paris, and I never consider them routine. Paris could never be that way for me. A trip to Paris is always filled with a sense of adventure, but I go now also with a sense of ease. I feel comfortable in France. I speak enough French to get by, and I am not ashamed or afraid to use it. I know the main roads through Normandy and the *arrondissements* and Metro routes of Paris; I can even drive with confidence in the City of Lights. But I will never forget that first day staring out at the French countryside. I don't know if it was genetics or romantics, but I connected.

When we arrived at the castle, Guy took us to the stable cottage, which would be home for the next month. It was right out of *The Three Musketeers*. That night we had dinner in the grand salon of the castle, with Guy's sister, Lorraine, and her boyfriend, Christian Odasseau, who directed the film. Guy was always our translator. After lots of laughter, good food, wine, and dessert from the Colombian Glad bag, I finally asked Guy when I was going to go to work, and that's when I learned that it would be a while. I had assumed my arrival had been timed so I could put the music to the finished piece of film. In fact, the editing process had gone more slowly than expected and there were still ten hours of film that had to be edited down to two. "What should I do?" I asked.

"Have fun," Guy replied. And that's exactly what we did. Jane and I spent the days on the grounds of the château, playing with Guy and Terry's kids in the pool, riding motorcycles around the property, sneaking into the cave to snitch a bottle of vintage wine. There were picnics and trips to Sainte Georges Motel and the bigger village of Dreux. It was on these trips, without Guy as my interpreter, that out of sheer necessity I started to find my French. You have to take it in small steps, and they pretty much present themselves to you. If you're hungry, you learn the words that will fill your belly. If you're lost, you learn the words that will get you home, and so on.

Finally, the film was ready for me, and I journeyed off to Antegor Studios in Paris. There I was, working on a movie in Paris, ordering my daily lunch of cucumber-and-tomato sandwiches at the brasserie on the Trocadero. I was a long way from Pascagoula.

I improved my language skills when I sailed into Gustavia Harbor on the island of St. Barts in 1976. The natives were a little more tolerant of grammatical errors than were the Parisians, and the lifestyle was the perfect blend of two cultures that I had grown to love—French and Caribbean. The islanders encouraged me to use my new words and even discovered a new variation: Drench—short for "drunk French." Inhibitions disappeared and words come a lot easier at the bottom of the wine and after a fine meal of lobster and lentil salad in an oceanfront café.

Through my own fault, Spanish unfortunately had passed me by even though I had lived in a Spanish culture for nearly two decades. From Southern California to the Southwest to Florida, it is truly the second language of America. I vowed that on this trip I would finally make a stab at Spanish. I have my books and tapes and am in the frame of mind to learn and converse, but it isn't soon enough. If I knew enough Spanish *now*, I could explain to Javier why I want to unpack myself. Now, a year after that embarrassing and inadequate moment, I am making progress. One day I plan to go back to Costa Rica and spend the whole afternoon speaking Spanish with Javier.

I Like to Pitch Camp

I lived half my life in an 8 × 5 room
Just cruisin' to the sound of the big diesel boom
It's not close quarters that would make me snap
It's just dealing with the daily unadulterated crap

—"LANDFALL"

We have wandered the airways over the Caribbean in our flying camels now for several days and have reassembled on the earth only to stretch out along a jungle road in a small procession of Third World vehicles. This vacation already has that familiar feel of a caravan looking for a campsite. It's only the latest in what seems at times like a never-ending cycle of motion. After years of traveling, I have developed a Bedouin-like ritual of settling in. Even if I am in a city for only one night, I unpack. Unpacking takes the "forced march" feeling out of the road.

I lived out of suitcases for more years than I care to remember. In the early days of touring, the road was an endless string of one-night stands. We compared it to submarine duty in the Navy. The road was our ocean, and the bus was our sub. We lived, worked, and partied in our bus; but occasionally we would need to open the hatch and let in some fresh air, which meant, on our then budget, a room at the local Holiday Inn. I would Ping-Pong between the bunk on the bus and the drab and predictable decor of my hotel room for no more than a few hours sleep. As we became more successful, we were able to trade in our bus for an airplane and actually begin to stay in hotel rooms for whole days at a time. Then the demand in certain cities had us playing multiple days in the same town. This led to my eventual transformation from a suitcase survivor to an unpacker.

One of the great joys of having crisscrossed this country so much has been the opportunity to see and know new people and places. It didn't take much to adjust my sailor's sense of wanderlust to dry land. Staying in a city for several days gave me the chance to see more than just the backstage area of the venue I was playing or the interior of the hotel-lobby bar. After years of collecting and storing information, my routine is now pretty set. I probably should write a travel guide one day. In all the major cities and most of the minor ones, I know the good places to stay and the good places to eat. I have the names and locations of the best bookstores, tackle shops, and marine-supply dealers memorized. I can find the best clay tennis courts in America without ever having to refer to a map, and then there are the museums, art galleries, and historical monuments. If I ever decide to hang up my guitar, I think I could do quite well as a contestant on *Jeopardy*, as long as I stay with American geography as a category.

Just Mention the Word Pirate

Do We Need Guns and Swords?

So, having assured Javier that I'll be okay, he goes off to see if he can help Jane. And I unpacked. As it does for almost everything else in life, music makes the task better. In the old days, I had an entire suitcase housing a sound system that could blow the doors off any midrange hotel room. Among bands on the road at the time, cool "portable" systems were status symbols. Now I just want a little background music. That, along with space-age technology, has enabled me to scale down and create a small but effective music source. My portable system is just a Sony shock-resistant CD player, a small set of waterproof speakers, a digital headset, and an adapter to wire into bigger stationary systems. The master bedroom of the house features a high-end Japanese stereo. It doesn't look like it got much use from George Bush, when he visited the hotel during his presidency. I plug it in right away. With my little adapter, soon the sounds of Bob Marley reverberate through the hills of Tango Mar.

Tapping my feet and humming along, I organize my chest of drawers and hang up my going-out clothes. After that, I set up my small writing and work area, plug in my computer and printer, and make my Internet connection. Next, I organize my toys. I assemble my fly rods, empty my gear bag, and find a small table on which to set up my fly-tying vise. Finally I find a corner for my surfboards and diving gear.

Forty minutes later, I shove my empty suitcases up on the back shelf of the closet. By the time I'm finished, Jane and Mac have taken off for the hotel and lunch; the kids are still in the pool. Armed with information from Javier, I come out on the deck. Cameron and Delaney come at me like a school of piranhas. They grab at my hands and feet, dragging me toward the pool. I tumble in with a big splash. If I didn't know better, I would swear that my children have gills. They can stay in a pool for the rest of their lives and be happy. I am basically not a pool person. I prefer salt water to chlorine. I know I'll have to come up with something really tempting to extract these two from their water world and save myself from becoming their pool toy.

"Would you guys like to go to the pirate caves?" That's all it takes. I don't even get to the waterfall. Just mentioning the word *pirate* to my kids opens onto a whole new level of curiosity. I've ignited the spark that connects to what I hope is that little bit of Jim Hawkins, Huckleberry Finn, and Becky Thatcher that's in all of us.

They spring from the pool and immediately hurl a barrage of inquiries at me. "Where are the pirate caves?" "Are there still pirates there?" "Is there treasure?" "Are there sharks and alligators guarding the cave?" "Do we need guns and swords?" Where in the world did these children get these wild ideas?

As the self-appointed leader of the expedition, I must make my authority known. Sometimes my children just think of me as a big kid. I must say that I don't discourage the idea. Thinking like a kid is a hell of a lot more fun than acting like an adult and parent. So, with the best parental tone I can muster, I say, "We are going on an expedition, and that means you have to wear clothes and shoes and bring a bathing suit." I know this last order will be questioned.

"Are we going swimming?" Delaney inquires.

"There's a waterfall right next to the pirate caves, and it drops into a big pool by the ocean." I am more excited about the waterfall, but as I expected, my enthusiasm isn't much appreciated.

Delaney furrows her brow, presses her lips together so that her mouth stretches across her face, then responds, "Okay, Dad, Cammie and I will wear clothes for the hike, but when we get to the waterfall, we can go neckie there, right?"

"Sounds like a good plan, Pud," I reply. I don't know if it's because of my lack of concern for such things or because of the island life that all my children have led, but clothes, or the lack of them, sometimes can be a problem with my youngest kids. I don't know whether it's good or bad, but with two children under the age of five, it's whatever works at the moment.

"We'll need some snacks, too," Delaney adds. Randall has finished loading in the rest of the luggage and the BSE, and I claim him for the expedition. We load up on sunblock, juice, cookies, fruit, towels, cameras, and Cameron's bear, named Bear. We pile it all on the golf cart, a luxury that Columbus had to do without, and head out, following Javier's directions.

Water Is My True Religion

We find the sign at the end of the dirt road that reads WATER-FALL and LA CASCADA, with a big white arrow pointing toward the shady green foliage of the rain forest. The kids leap from the golf cart, with Randall following in hot pursuit as I track the signs to the parking area. Yes, the parking area. I don't want you to think that I'm taking my children on a Joseph Conrad journey into the heart of darkness. We stop for a moment for photos and our daily recital of Spanish words. Today's phrase will conveniently be "*la cascada*." It takes only fifteen seconds to take a picture and repeat the word, but by the looks on their faces, you would think Cameron and Delaney are being held as hostages by Hamas.

Once released from their pose, they bolt down the path, then Cameron puts on the brakes and skids past a mimosa tree. "Bear!" he cries out. "I left Bear." This is what dads are for. I tell Randall to head out with them and I will get Bear out of the golf cart and catch up.

After rescuing Bear, I follow the path and their voices into a thick bamboo forest that blocks the sun and instantly cools the air. The earth around me is moist and covered with ferns and wild orchids. I spot Randall and the kids standing at the edge of a small stream, which I figure to be the source of the waterfall. "Come on, Dad," Cameron yells. Randall is holding them back from crossing the water until I get there. "Listen to dat," Cameron adds. There is a steady rumble coming from the direction of the ocean.

"That's the waterfall, dude."

"Sounds like an airplane."

"I know, but it's the waterfall." Randall holds Cameron, and I take Delaney as we cross the stream to the path on the other side. I don't want to get biblical here, but I have always been awed by the meeting of the waters. I am as big a sucker for a waterfall as anyone, especially one that drops down out of the mountains and winds up tumbling into the sea. Rivers meeting oceans is a powerful piece of nature and mythology. Fresh water mingling with salt water. It's the essence of life. It's baptism and redemption. It's the rivers of Babylon and the Sea of Galilee. The image of Jesus calming the waters stayed with me from childhood stories and was always the image that gave me courage when I found myself scared being caught in the jaws of a storm. Water is my real religion. But my most vivid recollections of water falling into the sea came not from the Bible but from *National Geographic.* I remember the story of Johnny Angel, a bush pilot and fortune hunter, who had crashed his plane in the jungles of Venezuela while looking for some lost treasure and came upon the longest vertical waterfall in the world, now named Angel Falls.

Next came Hollywood. I think it started with Tarzan movies and Johnny Weissmuller diving from a cliff and landing in a small lagoon with a geyserlike splash, then swimming over to Maureen O'Sullivan and Cheetah, who watched from the rocks as if grading his performance. Then there was *Mutiny on the Bounty, Donovan's Reef,* and a score of other movies and TV shows culminating with the classic *Adventures in Paradise,* starring a real sailor, Gardner McKay. It seemed that a lot of other people shared my attraction to oceanside waterfalls, but I didn't actually see one until my sailing days took me to the Windward Islands.

The Lesser Antilles run from just southeast of Puerto Rico to the northern shores of South America. They hang in an arc like a string of serrated emeralds. From St. Martin at the top to Grenada at the bottom, they cover a distance of just over four hundred miles. The islands are tropical but have enough altitude to create weather in the form of adiabatic cooling, which results in rain forests and rivers. After enduring the unpredictable but always present hardships of ocean voyaging that has to be accomplished in order to arrive in these islands either from America or Europe, sailors are amply rewarded.

In the open channels that separate the Lesser Antilles, the trade winds from Africa blow constant and hard from the east, but the altitude produces shelter and speed. Once the trade winds hit the landmasses of the islands, they become offshore breezes on the leeward side. The seas are calm and the water is deep to the shore, but the wind blows strong. Strong winds and calm seas are a rare combination in ocean voyaging. Add to that the natural beauty of the islands seen at point-blank range. You can sail in the shelter of the islands with a twenty-knot breeze blasting down the mountainside ten feet from the rocky shore. From this vantage point at maximum hull speed, you are experiencing one of the true joys of sailing.

It was on a beautiful day sailing behind the island of Dominica that I saw my first waterfall, emptying into the ocean. Dominica is the most lush of the Windward Islands. It has numerous jagged peaks that rise nearly a mile above sea level. On this tiny island there are 365 rivers—"one for each day of the year," as the locals say proudly. It was as I was racing down the shore behind the green mountains of Dominica that fantasy became reality for me. We spotted a large waterfall tumbling down the steep shore to a black volcanic beach, where it pooled up behind a natural dam of boulders, then leaked in a small stream to the sea. It was too good to be true. We had to not only see it, we had to experience it. We dropped our sails, nudged the boat near the shore, and tied ourselves off "stern-to" (a docking technique in which the bow faces away from the securing point) to a coconut tree. We launched our dinghy, swam ashore through the salt water, and went skinny dipping in the cascading fresh water of the tumbling fall. Later we unloaded lunch supplies from the boat and ate on the beach, then explored the nearby caves. Neither Tarzan, nor Fletcher Christian, nor Captain Adam Troy had anything on me that day. Their make-believe world had brought me to my own real version. I wonder where my children get some of their crazy ideas.

Everyting Gonna Be Awright

We all get very excited as the roar of the falling water grows louder. Suddenly the canopy of bamboo gives way to blue sky and ocean. Before us the Pacific stretches to the horizon in a scene right out of *National Geographic*. The little river disappears over a craggy edge of rock. Below and out of sight, a thunderous reverberation shakes the ground beneath our feet. We are enveloped in a mist, and my skin is suddenly as wet as if I just stepped out of a shower. Randall points out the swells breaking on a nearby beach, and my blood starts to race. As soon as I put in the proper amount of quality time playing pirate with my kids, he and I are taking off to go surfing, which is one of the primary things I've come to Costa Rica to do. But first things first.

There are about a hundred feet of vertical relief between the beach and us. I am suddenly overcome with a sense of parental responsibility. Would any man in his right mind take a two- and a four-year-old on this descent? This is no gently rolling hill, but a narrow switchback path carved out of the jagged cliff. There are no other children in sight. What do I fear the most? Trying to explain to Jane what happened if, God forbid, anything goes wrong on our climb, or having to listen to my kids go totally hysterical at the announcement that they cannot go to the caves and waterfall that I have so exaggerated?

As I ponder the decision, Delaney calls out, "Hey, Dad, it's Bob Marley!" Between my battle with parental responsibility and the noise generated by the waterfall, I didn't hear the music coming from across the river. There is a group of local teenagers sunbathing on the rocks, smoking joints, and grooving to Bob. Robert Nesta Marley occupies a big place in the Buffett family. Sarah Delaney grew up listening to my Marley tapes and CD's and developed an immediate affinity for the music. I used to point at the picture of Marley on the *Legend* CD and ask, "Who is that?"

"Bob," she would reply. It was her first word. Cameron Marley Buffett had been named after Bob, and the two of them are probably in a very low percentage of white children under the age of five who have been to the Bob Marley Museum in Kingston. Delaney starts to sing, and Cameron joins in. There we are, overlooking the Pacific with the ocean in the foreground, "No Woman No Cry" in the background, and the air tinted with the smell of ganja. I take it as a sign. I know we are out of harm's way. We start across the stream to the steep path all singing together. "Everyting gonna be awright, everyting gonna be awright."

Neckie in a Waterfall by the Sea

We reach the bottom of the cliff without incident, under the watchful eye of a flock of pelicans perched in a barren tree that hangs out over the edge of the cliff. I perceive the big birds to be guardian angels of the cliff, sent to watch over my children on the descent that my wife would kill me for making. Actually, the pelicans are just getting an lazy edge up on the food chain. They can see the unsuspecting school of bait fish in the shore break just as easily from the tree branches as they can by exerting the energy required to fly.

The caves are waiting. Delaney and I head right for them, but Cameron's interest in pirate caves has been sidetracked by several fiddler crabs who dash from the protection of their holes in the sand toward the edge of the water. "Here, Dad, take Bear to see the pirates," he says, handing me his bear. He dashes off in hot pursuit of the speedy little crustaceans. It takes him only five and a half seconds from the time we land on the beach to be totally soaking wet in the shallow foam of the tidal pools. Little boys who live by and love the ocean aren't really that far up the evolutionary ladder from tadpoles and minnows.

Delaney and I look around the cave. No treasure, only more questions. "Is this an island?" "What does *Costa Rica* mean?" "Was that girl up by the creek a mermaid?" I try to answer them as best I can. Javier told us that we need to get to and from the waterfall before the incoming tide covers the path. I collect my little pirates, and we make our way through the slippery rocks to the waterfall. It comes down the hillside in a series of cascades, dropping finally into a circular lagoon. Looking up from the lagoon, I can see that the Bob Marley festival is still in high gear. A few of the pelicans have launched from the tree and are dive-bombing for food just offshore. The few other tourists who are sitting on the rocks look shocked and probably a little annoyed as the pirates of the Caribbean charge, pulling off their clothes, laughing, frolicking, and dashing for the water. They have that there-goes-the-neighborhood look of serious German hikers. The expression on one woman's face needs no translation. "What in God's name was that man thinking when he let those children climb down that dangerous path?"

We splash and play, and I become the amphibian pack mule swimming with Cameron on my back and Delaney by my side to a visible rock in the middle of the pool. Once there, we spot another cave behind the waterfall. "Hey, you guys, that must be where the pirates hid the treasure," Delaney says. "I saw a place like that in a movie."

"Let's take a look," I say. Randall is busy filming us with the video camera, so I load Cameron on my back and Delaney swims in front of me. As we approach, the natural current becomes too strong for me, and we head back to the rock.

"It's protected," Delaney comments, "and there's probably dragons or monsters back there too."

"I wouldn't be surprised," I say. The tide is visibly rising on the rocks, and we gather up our clothes and packs and head back up the hill. The Marley festival has concluded and the teenagers have departed the bluff, so we sit down and have our snack. The kids wash down their cookies with juice, while Randall and I again gaze at the picture-postcard left break that's now forming up on the tide near the beach from which we ascended. We look at our watches simultaneously with the same thought—that we could take the kids back to the house and maybe catch a couple of waves at sunset—when Delaney downs the last swig of juice from the upturned bottle, wipes her mouth, and lets out a sigh. "That was delicious," she says. "Now let's go find some iguanas in the woods." Surfing will have to wait until *mañana*.

It had taken me thirty-three years to get to my first ocean-side waterfall. My kids had made it during their single-digit years. That's what it's all about. They will be moving on before we know it, headed off to adolescence and adulthood like Savannah before them. When they get there, I want them to have a sense of who they are and what the world they live in is really all about. I sit sometimes in wonder, listening to parents I know in New York talk about the proper preschool that will enable their children to be best prepared for the primo kindergarten in the city. My God, I think. Is this about what's best for the kids, or is it about what the parents missed in their childhood? The rewarding part of parenting is being able to share experiences with your children. The way I look at it, experience is still the best teacher. There's plenty of time for my kids to adapt to whatever school situation they'll eventually find themselves in. But by the time they get there, they will have ridden elephants in Thailand, experienced G-forces in an airplane, learned to bait a hook and release a fish. And they will have swum neckie in a waterfall by the sea.

SECTION VII

The Songline

"Mother, Mother Ocean"

A Shy Ex-Altar Boy from Alabama

Breakfast with Mother, Mother Ocean

Costa Rica's overabundance of natural resources includes parks, mountains, volcanoes, jungles, trails, beaches, and rivers. It's a tempting basket of goodies for bad travel-guide writers. Back in Florida, I had browsed through Jane's pile of Costa Rica books, which were full of overblown descriptions of "the Switzerland of Central America." See what I mean? There was little in those books that told me about the two things I wanted to do: fly-fish and surf. As usual, that information came from the Coconut Telegraph. I got my surfing info from my buddy Rick at the surf shop in Palm Beach and my fishing info from Guy and Charles Gaines, who had been there and done it.

After flying, clearing customs, unpacking, and exploring pirate caves, sleep came early to my band of weary travelers on our first night in Costa Rica. After the kids had gone to sleep, Randall and I readied our gear for a quick and quiet getaway next dawn. The swells that we had seen rolling in the night before gave us hope that there would be surf right on the beach of the hotel on the early incoming tide.

I awake at sunrise to the sounds of parrots squawking in the papaya trees. I am programmed by my maker not to need much sleep. I run best on six hours at night and a one-hour nap in the afternoon.

A light mist of salt air has floated in from the ocean and surrounds the house. There is very little wind, and the sun, just up, is already starting to cook the land. I listen for kid sounds coming from their bedrooms. Everyone is asleep. Randall is conveniently sleeping on the couch. I wake him up, and in a few minutes we are out the front door with our boards under our arms. We load them onto the golf cart and coast out of the driveway in neutral before turning on the little gas engine. Dudes, we are free.

We stop at the beach restaurant for some nourishment. Javier is working the morning shift and greets us warmly. I reply in Spanish, and he seems pleased by my attempt. One look out toward the beach tells the story. Warm tropical breezes, hummingbirds buzzing around the sugar bowl, hibiscus blooms on the table, and sets of perfect five-foot waves breaking around a high point just offshore to the south of the hotel. It is the old-fart surfer's dream: a four-star hotel with a perfect break all to ourselves. Remember, living well is the best revenge.

I eat my breakfast and study the waves. I can never get tired of watching a wave breaking on a shore. A wave is pure energy, its lineage connected directly to the sun, and it's born far out to sea in the belly of the wind. It is pushed and dragged across the surface of the sea not only by the wind, but also by tide and pressure fluctuations toward its predestined collision with the shore. If deep water is the birthplace of a wave, then the beach is its graveyard. I witness the spectacular death of several waves in showers of spray and blankets of white water. That's going out in style. I finish my tea just as the reverberations of a dying wave send a tremor through my body. I reach down and rub my bad knee. Today will be a test for my old wheel, which had gone out on me a few years back.

A Permanent Reminder of a Temporary Feeling

Fifty years of planetary occupation does not come without its share of bumps and bruises. Like most other survivors of the sixties, I traded my drugs and bad behavior for sleep, stretching, and physical activity. All that money I used to spend on dope now goes to surfboards, tennis rackets, and rowing gear. For my staying-in-shape activity, I had chosen basketball. I hate mindless exercise like StairMasters and rowing machines. If you want to climb stairs, go to a fucking hotel. If you want to row, buy a boat. Basketball is a great workout that's fun too, and I actually have a little skill at the sport left over from high school. I'm not tall, but I can think and shoot. My position is point guard in our band-crew pickup games in the gyms around America. Other than paddling out through the break, basketball is the only other sport that really requires and builds stamina. At my age, bouncing around like a maniac on-stage for two hours also requires a certain amount of stamina, and I get mine from basketball and surfing.

Summer tour: Chicago on an off day. A morning pickup basketball game at a downtown gym with my longtime friend and assistant, Mike Ramos. I have just tied the game at twenty apiece with a long three-pointer. The next basket wins the championship of the universe. I am back on defense. Ramos takes the ball out at half court. He is lightning fast, and I usually fall back and pick him up somewhere between the top of the key and the three-point semicircle, but this time I change my tactic. I fake like I am going to fall back but instead blast toward him. He is startled by my sudden arrival, and the ball bounces off his foot. I slap it toward the sideline and rush after it. He rushes after me. I have a breakaway layup to win the game. I hear the imaginary roar of the crowd. I dribble as fast as I can for the hoop and go up for a high-percentage layup. I watch the ball glide through the hoop. I am still in the air, but when I land something is terribly wrong. An electric pain shoots straight up my spinal cord and rings the bell in my brain like one of the strong-man machines on the boardwalk. When the dust settles, I limp from the gym with an ice bag on my knee. What the hell was I thinking? It was just a one-on-

one game at the gym, but there I was acting like it was the fi-
nals of the NBA championship. I have hurt myself. There is no
postgame interview, no Nike commercial in my future. All I
am left with is a permanent reminder of a temporary feeling.

Tests revealed that I had torn my anterior cruciate ligament,
or ACL. After consulting with my doctors back in Florida, I declined the surgical solution and tedious recovery. If I had been
an all-pro guard at the pinnacle of my career like Tim Hard-
away, I might have chosen the surgery. But as a five-foot, eight-
inch fifty-year-old singer, I reluctantly gave up basketball for a
while and chose physical therapy, a brace, and, as the doctors
described it, a wider margin of error in my athletic endeavors.
In simple language that means, don't compete with surf Nazis
for the inside lip of the wave, and don't dive for cross-court
backhands down the line. My knee was fine in the brace, but I
had been having trouble with it in the water; the simple act of
kicking could sometimes lock my kneecap. I came to Costa
Rica to test out my new brace in the water, hoping it would
hold my knee in place and let me ride. It has been a long ride
from my youthful days along the Gulf Coast to being a long-
boarder with a bad knee about to take on the mighty Pacific.

Everything but Waves

I trace my surfing roots back to the Beach Boys and the sixties. The Wilson brothers, Mike Love, David Marks, and Al
Jardine had successfully manipulated the power of music
and the speed of radio waves to transport the surf culture of
Southern California to the world stage by wrapping three
verses and two choruses in their signature vocal arrangements, the likes of which no one had ever heard before. The
"surfing sound" hit the unlikely target of coastal Alabama
with the impact of an atomic bomb. We bought it all. From
the songs and the surf magazines, we found the right look in

clothes and cars and learned the hip language of surfing. We worked at ordinary jobs as bag boys, carhops, golf caddies, and lifeguards, saved up our minimum wages, and ordered the way-too-cool Hobie surfboards from a distant and exotic-sounding place called Dana Point. We cut out color photos from surfing magazines of blond California girls in bikinis, the pier at Malibu, and the mountainous waves of Oahu's Sunset Beach and pinned them to the walls of our rooms. We dreamed of running away to Surf City. We didn't know exactly where it was, but it had to be somewhere in Southern California.

We strapped our boards to the roofs of our cars and went on surfing safaris up and down the beach roads between Gulf Shores, Alabama, and Panama City Beach, Florida. At night we would find a wino to buy us beer and then circle our beach joint, called the Hangout. We would sip cans of Pabst Blue Ribbon, camouflaged by brown paper bags. We would entice curious girls with our contraband, hoping they would join us for a sip, a ride along the beach, and—hope against hope—a midnight skinny-dip. The radio was always on, and we would sing along with the tunes from WTIX, the mighty 690 from New Orleans, erupting in collective applause at the sound of one of our surfing anthems. Yeah, we had it all—everything but the waves.

California Dreamin'

The coast of Southern California is just a tiny speck on the eastern edge of the Pacific Rim of Fire. The Pacific Ocean covers over 65 million square miles. It is six thousand miles from Tokyo to the Tressles, a famous surf spot south of San Clemente. At any given time of the day, there are said to be two thousand major storms churning up its surface from the Bering Sea to Bali. Throw in the constant tidal bulge caused by the sun and moon, high- and low-pressure fluctuations, a couple of volcanic eruptions, and the usual number of yearly earthquakes, and you've got a lot of wiggling water out there. When ocean swells finally get to California, they are further sculpted by the remnants of the ancient seabed that now takes the shape of jagged promontory points jutting out from the mountainous coast.

The shoreline of the Gulf Coast is flat and straight. We have no point breaks and very few reefs. The Gulf of Mexico is almost an inland sea. Landmasses and islands surround it. It has less than a half million square miles of surface area, and the distance across the Gulf from the beaches of Alabama to the Mayan pyramids on the Yucatán peninsula is just a little over five hundred miles. From Key West to Dauphin Island to Corpus Christi, Texas, surf in the Gulf is basically one long beach break. The only exception to the norm is the unpredictable appearance of deadly hurricanes that snake their way up into the northern Gulf.

After several years of riding the endless procession of mushburgers to the shore, I looked forward to hurricanes because they meant almost getting close to California. Against everyone's advice and, in some cases, emphatic commands from our parents, we headed for the Gulf one very gray afternoon. Gale warnings were up at the lifeguard station near the Hangout, but this was our trial by fire. We headed down the desolate beach to one of our favorite spots near the entrance to Perdido Bay, where a rock jetty provided an artificial point. I can vividly recall my thoughts that afternoon, staring out at the sea. It looked angry. The Gulf was in an agitated state. A steady procession of six-foot-high, top-to-bottom waves rolled in. They were like the poisonous tentacles of a Portuguese man-of-war stretching out from the eye of the storm, still some two hundred miles away. It didn't want us there. The sand beneath our feet reverberated from the constant pounding of the tempestuous beach break. We looked at one another—no one wanting to be the first one to express his true feelings about getting the hell out of Dodge—and we paddled out.

I banged my way through one impact zone, only to instantly be met by another. The surge and the rip tossed me back at the beach as if I had made no effort at all. Several tries later, I had made some headway to a flat spot in the watery assault where I could catch my breath and at least ride the mush in so that I could have some bragging rights about surfing a hurricane. It was as if Mother, Mother Ocean knew my cheap game. I never saw the wave that hit me. It must have been a cross rip of some kind, stirred up by the crazy water, but its body slammed me straight to the bottom. There I bounced along, end over end, and then *wham*—I was seeing stars. My board had hit me in the back of the head.

When I finally escaped the grip of the wave and broke the surface gasping for air, I saw my buds already sitting on the beach and headed their way. My ears were ringing and my mouth was full of sand. Before I could figure out whether I was hurt or not, another wave swept over me and carried me toward the beach. I tumbled over and over. I had lost my board, but in a swirl I saw the fin, grabbed it, pulled the board to me, and climbed on. I was shocked to see that it had snapped in two and was no longer than a boogie board. I spotted the other piece sliding along a tidal pool at the edge of the beach.

I was in shallow-enough water to stand. I wobbled like a drunk toward the beach and turned to look at where I had come from. There was a trail of red droplets following me. I rubbed my aching head, and my hand was red with blood.

It was only a scalp wound, and a couple of stitches closed up the gash that the fin of the board had carved into my skull. My head eventually healed, but I never ordered another board. Possibly it was my brush with Mother Nature. Maybe it was our lack of patience: Gulf surfers couldn't wait a millennium or two for the shifting shoreline of our coast to reconfig-

ure itself into a more conducive spot for swells. Or maybe it
was the approaching cultural revolution of the sixties that
would take us from our teens to our twenties and reshape our
world forever. Whatever it was, my teenage surfing days came
to a close.

Teach Me Those Three Chords

A year after we tried to surf the hurricane, I left the shore for
the first time in my life to go to college at Auburn University,
some 350 miles north of my beach. It was like going to live on
another planet. My gills dried up in the landlocked, dusty hills
of central Alabama. Auburn was a Southern college town with
all the trimmings. It was the first of many such hamlets I would
live in during my lackluster attempt at higher education. I
didn't want to be there. I had few friends from home who had
chosen Auburn, and I had no idea what I wanted to study. But
the lack of any direction and one of those wonderful chance
meetings that have steered me through my unpredictable life
happened while I was at Auburn. I found something better to
occupy my time than studying or pining for the seashore. In
the fall of 1964 I gave up surfing and took up a guitar.

Fall semester in a Southern college town has little to do
with studying and more to do with football and fraternity
rush. I didn't know much about the football team. Hell, at that
time I was really an Ole Miss fan, and to this day I still can't
figure out why I didn't enroll at the University of Mississippi.
I knew even less about fraternity rush but had heard through
the grapevine that without it and the social life it promoted,
there wasn't much to do in Auburn on the weekends. Like the
rest of the incoming freshmen, I followed down the path like a
young sheep. But I was far from being cool. For starters, I was
still a virgin, and less than a year earlier I had still been an altar
boy. I had been warped enough by my Catholic education to

lack any social skills as far as the opposite sex was concerned. I figured I could at least learn something about that in a fraternity. I went through fraternity rush week and wound up pledging the Sigma Pi fraternity. It wasn't one of the really cool frats, but Sigma Pi guys had a reputation for partying hard, and I liked a couple of those I had met during the beer-drenched days of rush week. But one of the main reasons I chose Sigma Pi was that they had rooms available in the frat house. I moved in and started to get to know some members of my pledge class and a few upperclassmen who shared my lack of concern for school. Two weeks away from home, and things were not as bad as they had first been. My life was centered around the fraternity house, and it was there one evening that I made a discovery that would change my life.

"Pledge swaps" were joint parties where the new pledges of fraternities and sororities would get together on school nights. The boys were just looking to get laid. The girls were looking for future husbands. At the pledge swap I felt every inch the shy ex–altar boy from Alabama. I watched from the sidelines, hoping to pick up some pointers from guys who seemed to have a natural ability to talk to girls, but I knew it wasn't something you just learned on the spot. I was just about to hang it up and go back to my room when I heard music coming from across the room.

A crowd of the most gorgeous girls had gathered around another pledge named Johnny Youngblood, who was playing the guitar. He had them totally enchanted. He was not six-foot-two and captain of the football team. He was a short, chubby little guy with acne scars on his face. I watched in amazement as he sang Drifters songs and songs by the Tams. Then one of the girls called out "Greenback Dollar," by the Kingston Trio, and Johnny started to sing. I moved closer. He did Sam Cook, Bobby Darin, and Maurice Williams, then finished off the set with the legendary Southern college anthem of the day, Doug Clark's "Hot Nuts," which set the whole room on fire. We all linked up arm in arm and stood around Johnny, singing the words at the top of our lungs.

> *Nuts, hot nuts*
> *You get them from the peanut man*
> *Well, see that girl all dressed in tan*
> *She don't do it but her roommate can*

It was black music sung by a bunch of drunken white college kids. On predominantly white campuses, it was black music that eventually tumbled the wall of segregation in the South. How could you hate fun? The songs were risqué but not obscene, and they provided a way of being bad without doing the big nasty. Johnny got a standing ovation and the phone numbers of several coeds. After the party was over and we had cleaned the place up, I went directly to Johnny Youngblood's room. He was a likeable guy from down around Panama City, Florida. Though he was a freshman, he was older than the rest of our pledge class, having joined the Air Force right out of high school. I didn't know if it was his age or his experience, but he had something I wanted. He was putting his guitar away when I walked in.

"That was truly amazing," I said admiringly. "How do you do that?"

"Oh, there's really nothing to it," he replied with a laugh.

"Oh, but there is. All those girls love you. You're great." I was totally entranced by what I had seen. He was like a pied piper. I didn't know much at seventeen, but I did know that that night I had seen magic performed. Johnny just laughed, went to the bed, and picked up his guitar.

"Name a song," he commanded.

"Louie Louie," I replied. He immediately sang a verse and a chorus.

"Another one," he said.

"Handy Man," I said instantly. He played it without hesitation. Halfway through the first chorus, I interrupted him. "Ballad of Davy Crockett," I shouted. He switched to that song without blinking an eye and sang the whole thing. I sat there in stunned silence. Johnny put the guitar back on his bed and reached up under the box spring. He pulled out a green pint bottle of Cutty Sark and offered me a sip. The burning whiskey going down my throat melted my frozen tongue. "You're incredible." I said. "You could be a rock star."

Johnny reached out for the pint bottle, and I passed it to him. He unscrewed the cap and took a large swig. "Lotta truth in a full bottle of whiskey, lotta lies in an empty one." He lifted the bottle to his lips and drank.

"How long have you been playin' the guitar?" I asked.

"Most of my life. My daddy taught me, but hell, I only know three chords." He shrugged. "That's all you really need."

I looked him straight in the eye and said, "Please, teach me those three chords."

By the time we reached the bottom of the pint of Scotch, I had a D chord mastered and was fumbling with the stretched-out finger position of a C. I didn't stop. I was in Johnny's room at every spare moment I could find. He taught me the three chords, and I learned a few more on my own. At future pledge swaps we played duets, and there they were, the beautiful young college girls sitting at our feet, saying, "Oh, play another one." Now I was getting the phone numbers, too. I was having so much fun playing the guitar and learning songs that I kind of forgot about what I was supposed to be doing at Auburn. By the middle of spring semester, it was apparent that I was flunking out. There was talk of making it up in summer school, but I never went back. I had learned something far more valuable than anything I had ever heard in a classroom, and I was ready to go out into the big bad world and try it out.

I kept track of Johnny and some of the guys for a couple of years after I left Auburn, but then I was off and running in a totally different direction and they slipped over the horizon. I don't know if I ever really got to thank Johnny for his inspiration and instruction, so I'll take this chance to do so, in the hope that he or someone he knows will read this book. I had traded my surfboard for a guitar. The storms of life would be even more dangerous than the rogue wave that had carved open my skull and broke my surfboard in two that day on the beach at Gulf Shores. But I was up and moving down the swell. I had no idea then how long and wonderful a ride the wave of music would be.

A Hippie in Mississippi

Mea Culpa, Mea Culpa?

My destiny took a geographic turn to the Piedmont of Mississippi and I wound up doing time in a junior college in Poplarville. I had stumbled onto the school purely by accident. I was driving back from Baton Rouge, where I had gone to try to get into Louisiana State University but had been refused. Needless to say, the thought of facing my father with the news of my academic calamity was not pleasant. Not only had I flunked out of college in April, but I hadn't told him. It was September and I had nowhere to go. I was ashamed of myself. I was a prime candidate for cannon fodder in Southeast Asia. I was going to go home, pack my bags, join the Army, and fly helicopters. I had sinned and I had to pay. Vietnam seemed as good a place as any to do penance.

On that fateful day, I took the back route from Baton Rouge to Mobile. I don't know why. I usually avoided it like the plague. It was a series of state and county roads that carved through the backwoods towns of Louisiana, Mississippi, and

Alabama that looked way too much like the hamlets I had read about in William Faulkner's books. Yet there I was sitting at a traffic light in downtown Poplarville, daydreaming about being a Vietnam War helicopter pilot, when a trucker in an eighteen-wheeler behind me sat on his horn and lifted me out of my seat like a mortar shell. I bumped my head on the roof, then stalled the car in first gear. The truck swerved around me, and the driver flipped me the bird. I managed to get the car started, but by this time the light was red again and there I sat. The only thing I knew about Poplarville, Mississippi, was that you didn't want to stay there long. This was Klan country, and there was a strange energy in the air.

That energy was dispelled by the appearance in the cross-walk at the light of several young girls carrying schoolbooks. One of the girls was attractive in that Mississippi beauty-pageant style. The others were plain-looking, simply dressed in conservative white blouses and skirts that fell below the knee. Their outfits and their manner were signposts of a Bible-belt upbringing. They were laughing and giggling, and I knew immediately that it was the first day of school, something that I was unlikely to ever see again. The cute one looked my way in the middle of the crosswalk and smiled. I waved and watched them cross the highway onto a sidewalk and disappear through a canopy of small magnolia trees that hung over a narrow asphalt road leading through a red-brick doorway. Arched above the road, the words PEARL RIVER JUNIOR COL-LEGE were etched in gold leaf on wrought iron.

Next thing I knew, I was driving through the brick gate. I couldn't figure out who or what was urging me down this strange detour, but I just went with it. It was like stepping into one of those cars on a track that takes you for a ride through an amusement-park haunted house. You are in it, but you are not in control. I watched the girls walk away down a path toward the center of a small campus. And then I was parked in front of a sign that pointed to the administration building.

I got out of my car and walked inside. I revealed my miserable grade-point average to an administrator who told me it was actually good enough to get me enrolled as a freshman on probation. There I was filling out enrollment forms and writing checks and picking up my textbooks in the small student-union building. An hour later I drove home to Mobile, packed my bags, left my parents a note telling them what had transpired, and headed off to my new school. Good-bye, Vietnam. Hello, Pearl River. Thank you once again, guardian angel.

Paris it wasn't. On my return, the reality of where I would spend the next year of my life hit me, and I started to panic. Life in a war zone suddenly didn't look that bleak, but the die had been cast. I bought a paper and searched the classifieds for a room to rent. I moved in with James, Ruby, and James Hal Breland, and Grandma. They were wonderful people and made my time in Poplarville a lot more pleasant than I had first imagined. I became part of their family.

At school, I quickly sized up the student body. There were two factions. The first was comprised of kids from the small surrounding towns of Lumberton, Picayune, Columbia, and Kiln who lacked the funds or the grades to attend the major state universities. The other faction was the flunkies. These were mainly boys from the nearby Gulf Coast and New Orleans who had spent too much time partying at the big universities and had flunked out, thereby forfeiting their student draft deferments. Guess which crowd I took up with?

School was easy, and I quickly got off probation. The dull weekday routine of class and little homework gave me plenty of time to practice my guitar and increase my repertoire of chords. Shortly after I got to Pearl River, I met a fellow guitar player, Doug Duncan from Columbia, Mississippi. He and I became instant friends and practiced together. We formed a group with Doug's beautiful teenage girlfriend, Susan Pitman, and we started playing at school functions and—this is real hard to admit—church socials.

On weekends, though, I was out of Poplarville as fast as my Ford Falcon would take me. In those days, folk music was happening and there were hot clubs on the Gulf Coast and in New Orleans. I took advantage of the geography and would take off for Biloxi or New Orleans. At Elsie & Lannie's in Biloxi mixed drinks were only a quarter during happy hour. It took about a dozen shots of the watered-down bar whiskey to catch a buzz. Once we established liftoff, we would hit the strip, stopping at Trader John's to hear real folk groups with flashy harmonies and funny stories. After that, it was dancing to the sounds of John Fred and the Playboy Band at the Vapors.

New Orleans was a different story. Unlike Biloxi or Mobile or Baton Rouge, New Orleans competed on the world stage at all levels. World-class food, world-class entertainment, world-class crime. We avoided the typical tourist places and wound up in off-the-wall bars down on the waterfront. One of these was called Las Casas de Marinos. I'll never forget the first night I walked in. It was a sailor bar packed with tattooed, drunken seamen from all over the world. There were at least three dozen conga drums chained to the wall, where you could play along with the tropical sounds coming from the jukebox. The image of the drummers lining that wall has stayed with me for three decades.

Bitten by the Bug

'Cause when that bug bites you,
You live with the sting

—"SOMETHING SO FEMININE ABOUT A MANDOLIN"

The Bayou Room was smack-dab in the heart of the Bourbon Street strip joints. It was run by a couple of junior Mafia types who had no ear for music and couldn't figure out why folksingers were outdrawing tits and ass. The people who

taught me as much about being a performer as anybody performed on that little stage at the Bayou Room. There was Brent
Webster, the consummate front man and comic; Bob Cook, the
stoic bass-playing storyteller; and Gene Marshall, the poster
boy of Southern folk musicians. I would pay my money and
sip my watered-down two-drink minimum to watch these
masters of delivery and timing work their craft.

College girls from Sophie Newcombe and Loyola packed
the tables in front of the stage. They reminded me of the girls
at the pledge swaps back at Auburn. I wanted them. I wanted
a Martin D-28 like the one Gene Marshall had strapped
around his neck, but it wasn't my time yet. I had graduated
from church socials to street corners, but that was as far up the
ladder of success as I had been able to climb. After the last
show at the Bayou Room, I would make my way to Jackson
Square with my gig bag and set up shop on the corner of
Chartres and Conti. I will never, ever forget the first time
someone actually dropped money into my cigar box and told
me I was good. I would bang away till the wee hours of the
morning, until my cuticles bled or there was no one listening.
Then I would count my money, close up shop, and relax at the
Morning Call with a cup of café au lait and an order of
beignets, those hot doughnuts covered with powdered sugar
that are a New Orleans specialty. Then I would take a stroll
along the rocks of the levee that kept the French Quarter from
being swallowed up by the mighty Mississippi. There I would
stare out over the river and watch the freighters come and go,
thinking of Huckleberry Finn in Hannibal and my surfing
buddies in Gulf Shores. Sometime around sunrise, I would
climb into my old Falcon and head north, often arriving at my
rented room just in time to run into the Breland family on their
way to church.

Two years later Brent Webster and Bob Cook had left for
Chicago, Gene Marshall had gone to California, and the girls
from Newcombe lined the front tables at the Bayou Room to

listen to a new band. They were called the Upstairs Alliance ("a sound at the top"), and they were fronted by a shy ex–altar boy from Mobile named Jimmy Buffett. It was my time.

I left Pearl River after a year but only moved thirty miles up the road to Hattiesburg and the University of Southern Mississippi. I went there not to get an education. I went there because it was close to New Orleans. That was where I was really getting the education that would prepare me for life. My weekends in New Orleans street-singing for chump change was my first paying gig. In an unpleasant meeting I had with my father after my self-exile to Poplarville, I vowed never to take another penny from him. Besides working the streets, the free-love hippie culture that was alive and well in the French Quarter did wonders for my shyness. I had joined a fraternity again at Southern. This time it was Kappa Sigma. It wasn't as much about male bonding as it was about work. Several of the guys in the fraternity played instruments and had a little band which played at the social functions. I saw an opportunity here. Doug Duncan had also transferred down to Hattiesburg and we would still get together and jam. At the fraternity house, I met a wonderful ex-fullback from Canada named Rick Bennett. His personality was as big as he was and he had a laugh that expressed his fondness for fun and mischief. It struck a familiar chord with me. We became roommates and best friends immediately. The nucleus of a dream was forming, but the economic wolf was howling at my door. While I dreamed of forming my own band, I still had to pay the rent.

Vietnam, Mississippi

During my first year at Southern Mississippi, I got a job singing in a downtown beer joint called the Pizza Pub. It was run by a big, no-nonsense woman with a ducktail haircut named Pat, who took no shit from nobody. She was tough but fair, and she truly loved music, qualities many of my future bosses lacked. (The owner of an enormously popular music club I worked for told me once after I had come off the stage to change a broken string, "If you loosened 'em up, you might not break as many.")

The local crowd at the Pizza Pub in those days made the scene at Cheers look like a family picnic. The bar had two rooms. In the front, the clientele consisted of college students, businessmen alcoholics, and a small group of gay men and women who found the confines of the pub to be the only safe haven where they could meet without fear of being beaten to death or lynched. The back was for the Army. It was in the smoky, beer-tainted air of the back room—named by the transient soldiers who drank there "Vietnam, Mississippi"—that I first experienced combat. It was in Vietnam, Mississippi, that I learned the real story of the war from the men who had been fighting it.

There was no stage in the Pizza Pub. I sat on a bar stool behind a red Naugahyde piano bar in the front room and played. When my set was through, Pat instructed me to go to the back room, where the jukebox was, and turn it back on. And before I started my next set, I would have to go back and turn it off. The first time I strolled through the groups of soldiers, most of them no older than me, huddled over tables of empty beer bottles, I felt like a yellowtail snapper suddenly surrounded by a school of hungry sharks. I made my way to the jukebox and turned it on. The rainbow-colored lights of the Wurlitzer blinked on, and the room filled with the sounds of the local R & B hits from New Orleans. Faint applause rose from the back of the room and I felt a little more at ease, then a balled-up Marlboro box hit me in the back of the head as I exited.

On my break, Pat informed me that the back-room men belonged to the 82nd Airborne, paratroopers with a history and legacy of being the meanest fighting men in the Army. They were in jungle training at nearby Camp Shelby. Some of them had already been to Vietnam and were back as instructors, but most of the soldiers were on their way over.

My break over, I nervously entered Vietnam, Mississippi, to turn off the jukebox. This action was met with a barrage of Frito bags, cigarette packs, and a couple of beer bottles. I ran the gauntlet to the taunts of the soldiers and made my way back to the sanctuary of the piano bar and the front room. Halfway through the first song of my set, the jukebox came on, and with it a wild cheer. Oh, shit. Back into the jungle I went to a chorus of boos and more debris. I made my way through the crowd, turned the jukebox off, and rushed back out to my perch. This time, before I even got my guitar strapped on, the jukebox was back on. It was now a game, and I was "it."

I didn't think of what I did next as a test of my bravery. I had a job to do. That was all. I walked back to Vietnam, Mississippi, again unplugged the Wurlitzer, and turned around to face the angry crowd. This time I didn't run through the door. I stood there and said, "Listen, I have a job to do here. I would appreciate it if you motherfuckers would let me do my fucking job." I walked back to the front room. The chorus of boos was not as loud this time, and when I got to my stool, several of the GI's followed as far as the door. Now the jukebox stayed silent, and by the time I had finished my set, the doorway was jammed.

At the end of the evening, after closing, Pat and I sat at the bar. "Most kids would have run out the door," she said. "You did real good. They asked me if tomorrow night you would play a set in the back. What do you think?"

"Fine with me," I replied.

The next night Pat rigged a P.A. system in the far corner of the back room, and the GI's began to decorate it. For the rest of the time I worked at the Pizza Pub, I alternated my set between the two bars. The GI's adopted me as if I were a war orphan, and they took to decorating the stage. I shared many beers with these brave men, but more than that, there was a generational bond. It was the veterans who had been to Vietnam who counseled me not to go. I thought for sure it would be the opposite, but they were the ones who first told me that the whole thing was a crock of shit. I don't know how many soldiers saw me play in that bar in Hattiesburg, but I hope that I was able to give them a good evening of fun. They gave me the knowledge that I needed at the time about what was really what. School looked like a far better option than dying in a rice paddy, and I honestly felt that I could do more good in the world with my guitar than with an M16.

Kumbaya, My Lord

In the spring of 1967 I got word through the Coconut Telegraph that one of the house bands that was working the Bayou Room in New Orleans had been killed in a car crash. I made a nervous phone call to the club and was told to come and audition. Doug and I had decided before going that we should have a bass player. Rick said he could play bass. The only problem was we didn't have one. What to do? There were plenty in the music building. For the week before our audition, we attempted to act like snobby music majors and "liberated" a bass from the music department. The deep tones of the big upright kicked us in the ass. We now had a sound. Rick played the bass wonderfully, or so I thought at the time. It wasn't until several years later that he admitted to me that he had never played one in his life before that week.

We drove to New Orleans for the audition. When we hit the stage at the Bayou Room, my fingers were shaking and my voice was trembling, but something happened up there. The audition was a blur, but when we finished the audience was applauding loudly. To my astonishment, we got the job and were told to report to work the first week in June.

We went out on the town and celebrated with Champale and steaks at the Buck-Forty-Nine restaurant. We had made it to the top. We would be playing the best folk club in the South, on Bourbon Street, making $150 a week apiece, and we got a 25 percent discount on all mixed drinks and beer. It just couldn't get any better than that. On the drive home that night, I knew that I was headed in the right direction.

Like a thunderstorm cloud out over the Gulf, the bottom fell out of my dreams. Two days after we had been hired, Doug was drafted. I didn't know what to do, but I knew that I damn sure wasn't going to let this opportunity slip away. I didn't care if I had to lie, cheat, or steal, but somehow we were going to play New Orleans that summer. I called the club owner and told him just that we had to replace a member. I hoped he would say, "Fine, see you in June." He did not. He wanted us to audition again with the new guy. We had no new guy. This was a Monday, and he wanted us back in New Orleans the following weekend.

To this day, I don't know how in hell we pulled this off, but in less than a week, an angel appeared in our lives. Her name was Betty Bridges. She was from Jackson, and we had met through her boyfriend, a fraternity brother. On the outside, she was a typical Southern coed with a pleasant personality, a warm smile, and an air of graciousness, but I had gotten a glimpse of her hidden passion for music. It had come at a typical frat party late at night when the beer and brotherhood made singers out of normal citizens who were sent to the bandstand, much to the chagrin of the musicians but to the pleasure of the crowd. It was on several of these occasions that I saw Betty sing. On that bandstand in the corner of the fraternity house, I saw her change from a Southern belle to a diva. With less than a week to go to judgment day for the biggest event thus far in my life, and with no other guitar players or singers in sight, I suggested to Rick that we ask Betty to join our band. We had nothing to lose. To this day, I have no idea how we convinced Betty to forsake her boyfriend, impending engagement and marriage, and a stable life to run away to the French Quarter with two relative strangers. Maybe we didn't.

Maybe, like us, she was just chasing her dream. God bless her for following her heart. On the Thursday before the audition, Betty joined the band. We went back to New Orleans, took the Sunday-night crowd by storm, and resurrected our job.

New Orleans is a whole other book that I'll write one day, but I need to try to get back to the beach in Costa Rica and end this damn chapter. Suffice it to say now that the time I spent working and living in the French Quarter in the summer of 1967 changed my entire life. I had lost my virginity and discovered dope. I smoked a little pot, but I really liked speed, especially Escatrol. Under its influence I could work until the middle of the night, party till dawn, drink Chivas, and recite the Declaration of Independence, all at the same time. It was an amazing drug. I saw a ghost, attended a clandestine gay wedding, had a high-dollar hooker as a girlfriend, met Peter O'Toole, grew a goatee, and went to the love-in in Audubon Park. In short, I made up for the lost time I had spent as an altar boy. We all know now how bad the drug part turned out to be, but it was a part of life then, and it was fun. I was young, and if anybody had told me it could kill me, I wouldn't have listened. We were bulletproof, or so we thought. It would take many years of bad behavior, the death of friends, and several close calls before I changed my wicked ways. But it was the sixties, and as our theme song of the day explained it, "Nothing could stop the duke of Earl."

Singer in a Rock 'n' Roll Band

As the soldiers at the Pizza Pub had predicted, by the time I got back to school in the fall, the war was raging. Back in Hattiesburg I felt like I was in prison. My heart had stayed behind in New Orleans though I went through the motions of being a student, but the war was the big pickle and my student deferment, that amazing little "get out of jail free" pass, was all that kept me from trading my guitar for a gun. If you flunked out or quit school, you were drafted. If you graduated, same thing. It became the game of the decade to try and figure out how to beat the selective-service process. I figured out a system by which I could stay attached to my life as a troubadour, still work, go to school, and hang on to my student deferment. I took night classes Monday through Wednesday in Hatties-burg and then raced back to the French Quarter to work for four days. No wonder one of my favorite songs of the period was "Time" by the Chambers Brothers.

Our folk group had become a folk-rock band. We grew our hair long, dropped acid, bought strobe lights and lava lamps, and learned every cut from *Beggar's Banquet* and *Sgt. Pepper's Lonely Hearts Club Band*. We toured the South playing frat dances, along with our regular gig in New Orleans. We finally ended our run at the Bayou Room and concentrated on the road. We did what every band does. First, we went into debt buying a trailer and a P.A. system. Then we fought, broke up a couple of times, changed guitar players, got back together, and finally, somewhere in the spring of '68, had the inevitable knock-down, drag-out fight, and the Upstairs Alliance was no more.

Rick graduated and went back to Canada. Betty and our drummer, Billy Kehoe, finished school and went back to the real world. Richard, our guitar player, was killed in a car crash, and I went to work again as a solo folksinger. It was the first of many full circles that I would traverse.

Needless to say, during this period of my involvement with a rock 'n' roll band playing "devil music," my schoolwork suf-fered. It is all a blur, except for my A's in Russian and Southern history, but the cultural transformation I made is still vivid. One day, though, I woke up and there I was, a semester away from graduating. This should have been cause for celebration, but I was in debt, owed the university over three hundred dol-lars in unpaid parking tickets (which I had to pay before they would give me my diploma), and I was about to get drafted.

I got my 1A notice on the day that my parents and my grandfather came to Hattiesburg to see me graduate from college. I was the first Buffett to do so. My father and I were back on speaking terms by then, and my grandfather viewed the whole spectacle and then commented, "You'll be better with a good ship beneath your feet." Like countless other young men in the late sixties, I sat at a crossroads wondering what in the hell was going to happen to me. I had not forgotten my time in Vietnam, Mississippi. I thought about running away to Canada, but I really didn't have the courage to do that. I had run under the selective-service radar for a long time and had used up all my tricks. At school, I was told by the ROTC sergeant, who knew of me and my band, that he personally would make sure that I not only got drafted, but that I would go directly to an infantry unit in Vietnam. Fuck that. I was a college graduate. If I was going, I was going as an officer, and I was going to fly Navy.

During my senior year I had started to take flying lessons and had actually soloed. My roommates were all members of Naval ROTC and were going off to become Navy pilots after graduation. As a college graduate, I could take the test for officer-candidate school, and I did. I now saw myself not as a hippie folksinger, but as a Navy flier. But my preliminary medical exam revealed that I had a peptic ulcer, which meant I was unfit for military service. Once again my guardian angel had come to bat. The next thing I knew, my draft status went from 1A to 1Y. Goddamn, I had slipped through the cracks. Thank God, because I flunked the officer-candidate school test.

Mirror, Mirror, on the Wall

I gave a speech last year at the Berklee College of Music in Boston, and one of the questions from the young inquisitive musicians who had come to hear me talk was, "Where did you get your start?" I didn't have to think about that one very long, because I knew the answer. "In front of the bathroom mirror," I replied. Pardon my *anglaise*, but there ain't a singer or actor out there today who has not sung or recited lines into a mirror when nobody's looking. If you think you want to be a singer, dancer, painter, or whatever and you do not possess a false sense of security early on, then you had better start checking out job opportunities in the lucrative computer market. The stage is not a place for the faint of heart. Where do you start? You start at the bottom.

You are your first audience, your first manager, your first agent, your first accountant, and your first road manager. Nobody else gives a shit about you at the beginning of your career except you, and of course your mother. Your mother is there in the beginning because that is what mothers do. Have you ever seen those teary-eyed moms in front of the prison walls crying to the throng of media cameras, "He was a good boy," while her axe-murderer son is being led to the gas chamber? A mother can give unconditional love. In show business, at the start of her child's career, it comes in the form of showing up at the first gig. She is usually accompanied by a bewildered group of her friends from the bridge club, who have been dragged along to the bowels of the earth to hear music they don't like or understand. But unconditional love can only take you a short distance, and soon you are back out there alone.

Viva Nash Vegas

They Looked a Lot Better as Beer Cans

I needed a break from New Orleans and the South, from school, from the dope, from the draft, and from my girlfriend. I was ready to travel, or as the therapists say, "do a geographical." The Great Plains looked like as good a place as any to get lost in for a while. I had stayed in contact with my mentor, Brent Webster, from the Bayou Room. He was working with an agent out of Minneapolis, and I contacted him. I took my paid-off sound system and went on the road as a solo act, booking my own shows, driving the car, setting up the sound system, and doing the business. The next thing I knew, I was headlining Steak 'n' Ale joints all over the Midwest, making five hundred bucks a week, with a free salad bar. At first I loved the wide-open spaces, but one afternoon in a trailer park in Brookings, South Dakota, where I was living, the siren in town sounded a tornado warning. Across the flat, open field to the west came not one but two twisters. I, of course, had been in storms at sea, but this was different. It's when Mother Nature gets so angry at man and his arrogance that she whips up a little humble pie. Well, it's no secret how God feels about trailer parks, and these storms were no different. Like heat-seeking missiles looking for a tailpipe, they smelled out the cluster of aluminum trailers on the edge of town. We hightailed it out of there and watched the whole thing from the road, as the stingraylike tail whipped along the edge of the trailers, turning several of them into chunks of aluminum the size of beer cans. That was my cue to get out of the Midwest.

I guess I went kind of crazy out there. I had been behaving rather badly for several years, and something shook my damn Catholic guilt loose again. My girlfriend, Margie, was in TWA stewardess school in Kansas City at the time, and I drove there and asked her to marry me. To this day, I don't know what made me do it, and she said yes.

I went back to Mobile and worked at a little bar in town called the Admiral's Club, where I really found my first following. I packed the joint, doing all the songs and using all I had learned in New Orleans.

I was also starting to write songs and record at a studio owned by a Mobile songwriter named Milton Brown, who had had some success in Nashville and had contacts there. I guess he liked what he heard. I made a trip to Nashville with him, and we did a set of demos with his friend Travis Turk at Spar Studios. Travis worked for a local producer named Buzz Cason, who heard the tapes and offered me a contract. I had wanted to go to California—my dream was to have a job close to the Pipeline at Malibu—but I didn't have enough money to buy the gas for the trip. So the winds of fate blew me away from the ocean, and I became a Nashville cat.

A Good Forecast from the Weatherman

When I arrived in Nashville with my new bride, we spent our wedding night at the Holiday Inn on West End Avenue, where my two keepsake guitars—I had bought a Martin twelve-string—were promptly stolen out of the trunk of the car my mother had given me. I was getting an advance from my new music publisher, Buzz, but it wasn't enough to pay the rent. Margie went to work at ASCAP, and I went looking for a day job.

The guardian angels were watching out for me, and I answered an ad in the paper for a position at *Billboard* magazine—the only "real job" I would have in my adult life.

I was hired by Bill Williams, a wonderful man who became one of many mentors to me. He was both the Southern editor for *Billboard* and the weatherman on WSM-TV. Bill came from

Nebraska and had that combination of Midwestern work ethic and charm that seems part of the heritage of the region. My first day on the job as his assistant, Bill took me on his rounds along Music Row and introduced me to his friends and contacts in the music business. I met the bigwigs and the hustlers, the famous and the not-so-famous. In twenty-four hours I had gone from just another nobody songwriter who couldn't get his foot into a music publisher's door to the assistant Southern editor of *Billboard*. Hell, people took me to lunch, I had business cards. I flew to New York for editorial meetings. I had an expense account. I had a WATTS line at work on which I called all my friends after working hours, and I got free albums from the record companies. Not bad for a real job.

My main task was to handle the overflow of work covering the country-music scene in Nashville, which was exploding at the time. I never shattered the music world with any of my reporting, but I did break the story of the Lester Flatt and Earl Scruggs breakup and got picked up as a stringer for *Rolling Stone*.

One day, sensing my restlessness and apparent boredom, Bill gave me a new title and assignment. I became the Nashville pop editor. I had been hinting at this for a long time. There was a lot of Top 40 and pop music coming out of the nearby cities of Macon, Memphis, and Muscle Shoals, and I wanted to cover it. This was mainly black music, which the powers in Nashville at the time looked upon as used Kleenex, but it was right up my alley, and Bill gave me the go-ahead. The next thing I knew I was interviewing Otis Redding and James Brown, going to lunch with Jim Stewart and Al Bell at Stax in Memphis, and hanging backstage at Allman Brothers concerts. But what I mainly saw were a lot of wonderfully talented artists and writers who let somebody else worry about "all that stuff," and I saw the trouble it got them into.

Margie and I settled into our Nashville life, though I missed the ocean terribly. Weatherwise, Nashville is the London of the Piedmont. The big cold fronts drop down from Canada, blast across the Great Lakes, and, as they lose steam, bang up against the backside of the Appalachian Mountains, then stall out over middle Tennessee. It wasn't Siberia, but to my thin-blooded soul, it might as well have been. Anyway, I was feeling way too normal. Wife, job, landlord, lawn mower. I knew I was in trouble—or that I was about to cause some.

Trouble showed itself in the form of what I wanted the most. One day in 1971 Buzz Cason called me to tell me that he had made a deal for me with Barnaby Records. It was a new label in town that had been started by Andy Williams. It was run by an ex–New Yorker named Mike Shephard, and they had made a big splash by signing Ray Stevens. I had a record deal. Oh, my God, it had happened. The first person I told was Bill Williams, who took me out for drinks to celebrate but then told me that when my record came out I would have to resign from *Billboard* because of a conflict of interest. Not a problem, I told him. Hell, I was on my way to becoming a star. It was simple: The record would come out, and I would be as big as Ray Stevens or Kris Kristofferson, who was the king of the weirdo songwriters' clique that hung around Combine Music. Bill wished me the best. Though he knew the forecast way too well, he didn't want to rain on my parade.

The record came out, and I left *Billboard*. Bill and the staff threw me a going-away party and gave me a beautiful new guitar case for my travels. One of the true joys of my later success was going back and sharing it with Bill. He was as proud as a parent when I finally broke out.

My first record, *Down to Earth*, got good reviews, and there was some noise being made out in, of all places, West Texas. Buzz contacted some musicians who were hanging out at his studio, and we put a band together. I was on my way to the big time, and, goddamn, was this exciting. We practiced and practiced and then went out for beers around the Vanderbilt campus and stayed up all night planning our careers. At the appointed time, we boarded the flight to Dallas, making sure to look like musicians, not businessmen, and headed for El Paso.

We were met by the local Columbia Records promo man who immediately took us out to lunch and then to several local radio stations, where I did interviews. We played our show at the convention of local deejays to good applause. After the show, we were taken to a famous all-night Mexican restaurant, and then we crossed the border into Juárez and did the strip joints. God, I loved my new job. I could do without the extra money from *Billboard*, the credit card, and the expense account. I was my own boss now.

We arrived back in Nashville like Roman conquerors returning from the conquest of Gaul, and then reality reared its ugly head. We had bombed in El Paso. The record was not selling, and there would be no more promo trips. I couldn't find club work around town, because in those days in Nashville, there were no clubs. Two weeks after our return from El Paso, the credit-card bill came in and I was instantly seven thousand dollars in debt.

The band went back to work for Buzz, and I started hustling my ass off as a solo act again, with not much success. To complicate matters, I was appearing locally at anti-Vietnam rallies, which did not sit well with the local moguls. Like so many other aspiring performers, I found myself looking at the fact that my career was almost over from the start.

As you might imagine, this was not helping my marriage much. Margie was working, and I was hanging out bitching about the state of the record business in Nashville to a group of out-of-work writers and performers. Somewhere along the way, I was introduced to a local manager named Don Light, who had a reputation for representing the best white gospel acts in Nashville and who also had a stable of songwriters like John D. Loudermilk and Billy Ed Wheeler. Thank God, Don took a liking to me and added me to his list of clients, helping me find the kind of work I not only wanted to do, but was best at—performing. I wasn't a songwriter or a song plugger, and I presented only passable credentials as a guitar player. My talent lay in working an audience. All the years on Bourbon Street and at Steak 'n' Ales had made me a performer, and the wisdom and advice from Bill Williams and that El Paso fiasco had sealed in my mind the charge that if I ever wanted to continue to do a show, I had to take care of the business end of things.

A Caribbean Soul

As Jesse Winchester said in his old song, "I left Tennessee in a hurry, dear."

In the winter of 1971, my marriage of two years was basically over. My career was going nowhere, and I was freezing to death, desperately missing the ocean. Jerry Jeff Walker had passed through town a few months earlier and had stayed at my house. I had first met Jerry Jeff when I was working for *Billboard* and did a story on him and a record he had made in Miami with the Dixie Flyers rhythm section at Criteria Studios. We had stayed up all night drinking and talking. He was now living in a part of Miami known as Coconut Grove. Jesus, just the sound of the words made me look south. Somewhere around dawn, Jerry Jeff had stumbled out of my house and gone back to his hotel. I had found myself alone in the laundry room of the log house we were renting, staring at a matching avocado-green Sears Kenmore washer and dryer, wondering what in the hell I was doing with my life. Jerry Jeff had given me an open invitation to come and visit him in Miami. It didn't take me long to take him up on his offer.

What work Don Light was getting me at the time was as a traveling troubador on a circuit of small folk clubs and coffeehouses throughout the South. There was the Bistro in Atlanta, The Last Resort in Athens, Georgia, the Trade Winds in St. Augustine, the Hub Pub Club in Boone, North Carolina, and several more that I can't recall. There was also a club in Miami called the Flick. It was the most difficult club to get booked into for the most obvious reason—the weather in Florida in the winter. It was also one of the coolest places to work and the home base of a very hip group of South Florida folkies. Fred Neil was the guru of this set, which included Vince Martin, Bobby Ingram, and Joni Mitchell. I had lobbied other club owners for whom I had worked to help intercede for me with the owner of the Flick. I was desperate to escape Nashville.

Driven by the vision of palm trees in a place called Coconut Grove, I lucked out and got booked in Miami. I called Jerry Jeff, and the offer to stay with him was still open. I was flat broke at the time, and left the Mercedes with Margie. I had bought it as a status symbol and then couldn't afford to fill it up with gas. It was the only thing of any value that we had, and she deserved it for putting up with my rather shallow and immature attempt at being a husband. During my "real job" period, TWA had actually given me a credit card. Though it had expired, I still kept it in my wallet thinking of it as some kind of escape device, and that is exactly what it became. I put my thumb over the expired date at the ticket counter at the Nashville airport and attempted to charm the living shit out of the cute ticket agent, hoping I could distract her enough not to check the expiration date. It worked, and on a miserable rainy afternoon in late October, I boarded a 727 bound for Miami, and I never looked back.

Jerry Jeff met me at the airport. We drove through the streets of the capital of the Caribbean in a 1947 burgundy Packard that he called the Flying Lady. I had been to Miami only twice before: once with my parents on a vacation when I was eight, and once on spring break with my roommates from college. My memories from the first trip were of the pool at the Fontainebleau Hotel, where you could see into the clear water from a giant window in the bar. The song of the summer that year was "Shaboom," and I still have the picture taken of me at Parrot Jungle with a variety of exotic birds perched on my arms. The second trip to Miami was less memorable. I had driven with my roommates from Hattiesburg, bound for John Pennekamp Coral Reef State Park in Key Largo. Miami was just a big city in the way of us getting to the Keys.

Now, the third visit was the charmer. I watched the city pass by from the open window of the Packard as we cruised down Le Jeune Road through Coral Gables toward Coconut Grove. This was the land of flip-flops, bicycles, and Hawaiian shirts. Billboards advertised typically American products in Spanish. The air smelled of garlic and salt water, with an occasional whiff of orange blossoms and frangipani. We wound through the streets of Coconut Grove under canopies of ficus trees to a small tropical one-story house on Bay Holes Drive. There was music coming from the stereo and garlic coming from the kitchen. Jerry Jeff introduced me to his girlfriend, Murphy, and her young son, Justin. Murphy, as I would later learn, was the real connection to Key West and would become a longtime friend.

When I had left Nashville that morning, it was thirty-one degrees and raining. I was broke and getting a divorce. My career was in cold storage, and I had a cracked front tooth. Four hours later, I was sitting under a cluster of royal palms with a breeze coming off Biscayne Bay. I was barefoot, in shorts and a T-shirt, eating lobster salad and drinking ice-cold beer, laughing and listening to Murphy's stories of Key West.

By nature, I am a creature of the swamps and the sea. My most vivid memories of childhood came to pass near, in, or under the water. The recurring dreams that weave their way through my subconscious are always focused on islands that may or may not exist, but if there is a heaven for me, I am sure that it has a beach attached to it. I had only been in Tennessee for two years, but during that time not a day went by that I didn't miss the ocean. The whole purpose of going there in the first place was to generate a career that would allow me to live where I wanted, which was on an island. My gills had dried up before I had been able to convince the powers that be that I was their boy. The career part had not happened, but fate had brought me back to where I belonged.

That first day with Jerry Jeff and Murphy in Coconut Grove produced a basic revelation that changed my whole way of looking at who I was and where I was going. My worries were somewhere else, and my tropical soul had finally come home to the sun. I knew from that first day in Coconut Grove that all the other shit would somehow take care of itself in due time, but more important, my tropical resurrection revealed who I was. I could not be someone else. The years in Nashville had been spent trying to fit into a system and a culture that was foreign to me. I did not come from the hills of Tennessee. I came from the bayous of the Gulf Coast. I flashed back to a time long ago when I was playing in my grandmother's backyard in Pascagoula. There was a small bayou that ran from her backyard through the marsh grass and emptied into the Gulf of Mexico about a mile away. I remembered my grandfather's stories and the pictures in *National Geographic* of faraway, exciting places. That little bayou at the end of my grandmother's backyard, I thought, could lead me there. Nashville had been a necessary detour on my songline. In Miami, that February, I was back where I belonged. I didn't know where I was going, but I knew it was the right spot to leave from.

My hosts set me up in a quiet little room at the rear of the house and gave me one of their old bicycles to use while I was there. The length of my stay was the big question. I never wanted to leave. I was in heaven, and besides, at the moment I had no money and nowhere else to go. I would just try to be a good houseguest and see how long it would take for them to throw me out. By that time, I hoped, I would have a couple of paychecks under my belt from my gig at the Flick, and I could find a place of my own. I would dazzle the club owners with my talent and work my way up the ladder to be one of the cool folkies like Fred Neil or Vince Martin. That was my plan, and I was ready to attack.

That weekend Jerry Jeff took me around to some Coconut Grove haunts, where I met many of his and Murphy's friends, who would become my friends as well. Mingling with the eccentric crowd of musicians, dope dealers, artists, and the like, I felt very comfortable. The Grove reminded me a lot of my early days in the French Quarter, and I took to fantasizing about how I would be living in a house near Biscayne Bay and working at the Flick, with scores of young college girls hanging on to the lines of my songs.

I strolled into the Flick on Monday around noon to announce my arrival. I had expected a neighborhood that looked like Greenwich Village or the cover of a Bob Dylan album, but this was Miami, and the coffeehouse was in a strip mall located between a dry-cleaner's and a pet shop. The owner, Warren Dirken, was mulling over a list of produce with a Cuban wholesaler. I eased up next to the produce man and rested my guitar on the floor. Dirken looked at me over the rim of his glasses like I had come from another planet. He said nothing. Oh, God, I thought, another hard-ass club owner. He continued to count his heads of lettuce, then came the tomatoes, then the onions, and then me. "Auditions for Hootenanny Night are tomorrow afternoon at seven. Leave your name on the list at the receptionist stand," he said in a monotone.

"No, Mr. Dirken, I'm not here for Hootenanny Night. I'm Jimmy Buffett. I spoke to you a couple of weeks ago from Nashville. I open tonight."

He stopped writing, put down his clipboard, looked at me sternly, and walked to the back of the building. I sat there among the vegetables wondering what was wrong. It didn't take me long to find out. Mr. Dirken strolled back in a few minutes, picked up his clipboard and pen, and said flatly, "Bullett, you open in two weeks. See you then."

"It's Buffett," I replied, "with two *T*'s."

He picked up a cantaloupe and studied it with his fingers. "These are not ripe," he said to the produce man. "Goddammit, how many times do I have to tell you, I want ripe melons?"

I was shocked. I knew I had not made the mistake, but I dared not question the authority of the man who was hiring me. Club owners in those days were powerful people and could make or break you on the club circuit. I dared not show any emotion, though I was on the verge of tears, thinking about what in the hell I was going to do for two weeks. I would overstay my welcome with Jerry Jeff and Murphy before I ever sang my first note in South Florida. I pondered whether or not to just drop to my knees and spill the whole can of beans about the breakup of my marriage, my floundering career in Nashville, and my financial situation, but no. I just picked up my guitar case and headed for the door.

"See you in two weeks, Bullett," Mr. Dirken called out as I opened the door to the glare of the midday Monday sun.

Several years later, after working my way up the list of nightly performers from opening act on a six-act bill to sellout headliner, Warren Dirken finally admitted to me that it had been his mistake and he had double-booked the week. By that time, he had actually learned to pronounce and spell my name correctly. I thanked him for his oversight, because if it hadn't been for the double booking, I might have never made it to Key West.

I timidly announced the news of "my mistake" to Jerry Jeff and Murphy at lunch. "Asshole club owners," was all Jerry Jeff said.

Murphy said, "Hell, Jerry Jeff, let's go to Key West."

And that is how it happened. I went from overnight folk-club sensation to assistant mechanic in one day. The Flying Lady, because of her age, was in constant need of repair, and it gave me a way to try and pay my hosts back for their hospitality. I dredged up my old shipyard mechanical skills, which I hadn't used since arriving in Nashville, and accompanied Jerry Jeff to a place called Hank & Bill's Garage, somewhere off Twenty-seventh Avenue, where we assisted the mechanics in repairing the Flying Lady. We changed a carburetor and an oil pump and waited for a brake drum to arrive. The sting of my humiliating encounter with Warren Dirken at the Flick was wearing off. The reality was that even if I never hit a guitar string again in public, I was in South Florida. Every morning since my arrival I had checked the "nation's weather" in *The Miami Herald* as I drank coffee in my bathing suit on the porch. It had been raining in Nashville since I left. It didn't take much to picture that slate-gray sky above the hills. I would rather be a suntanned mechanic in Miami than a pale, starving wannabe in Music City.

The brake drum arrived, and we finished up the repairs by the end of my first week in Miami. We drove home through the Grove with the vintage car purring like a kitten, and when we pulled into the driveway, Murphy and Justin were waiting with their bags packed. "Hell, Jerry Jeff," Murphy said, "let's take her for a real road test." An hour later we were south of Homestead, tooling down U.S. 1 toward the island at the literal end of the road that I would call home for the next twenty years.

On my one previous trip to the Keys, in a VW van on spring break, my college buddies and I made it as far as Islamorada before running out of time and money and heading back to Hattiesburg with T-shirts, conch shells, and postcards. My roommates already had their next few years of life planned out. They would graduate from college, enter Navy flight school, and eventually become fighter pilots. I remember a day at the end of the trip, sitting on a roadside table east of Islamorada, which was the turning-around point of our journey. My friends Bobby and Phil were trying to convince me to go to Navy officer-candidate school and apply for flight training. It was the days of the draft lottery, and I had been playing Ping-Pong with my local draft board for a couple of years. They were totally gung-ho about their future as Navy fliers and it all sounded quite romantic at the time, but as I have explained earlier, I had heard different tales about Vietnam from my days in that pizza joint in Hattiesburg. As we sat in the Florida sunshine eating cheeseburgers by the ocean (sounds like a familiar song title, doesn't it?), I told them that I thought I would drop out for a semester and maybe try to transfer to the University of Miami and study marine biology. "You'll be studying rice paddy 101 as a grunt in the Mekong Delta if you try and pull that shit," Bobby said. We finished our cheeseburgers and pointed our VW van north toward home. But my most vivid memory of that trip was the incredible turquoise color of the water. Silt and residue from the Mississippi and Mobile rivers tainted my bayous and bays along the Gulf Coast. Even when you journeyed offshore, the waters of the Gulf were deep and blue. The clear, shallow water of the keys left an impression on me. Like General MacArthur, I knew I would return, but I never in my wildest dreams thought it would be in the backseat of a 1946 Packard going ninety miles an hour.

It was a clear November day when I saw Florida Bay. I was remembering a TV show I had seen that had traced the route of U.S. 1 from its northern beginnings in Fort Kent, Maine, to its tropical ending in Key West. That was the first time I had ever seen pictures of Key West, and they had lingered with me. We had left U.S. 1 for a two-lane blacktop called Card Sound Road, which paralleled the main highway and rejoined it east of Key Largo, a local shortcut that had little traffic and was as straight as any road I have seen this side of West Texas, which meant you could haul ass. We were doing just that. The procession of overhanging Australian pines whizzed by the windows of the Flying Lady. Behind the trees the mangroves moved by in a blur, revealing an occasional glimpse of salt water. I was in the backseat with Justin playing my guitar, and we sang as we drove. This was Kerouac stuff and I loved it.

My first trip to Key West was like a tropical Fellini movie. Jerry Jeff knew all the funky bars and watering holes along the 147-mile route, and he felt it was his obligation to show me every last one of them. The first was a crab shack called Alabama Jack's. It was a plywood building with a tin roof that sat next to a canal where commercial crab boats lined the wharf. The arrival of the Flying Lady brought a scramble of faces to the window. From inside I heard someone yell, "Goddamn, it's Jerry Jeff." We were greeted like royalty, and Jerry Jeff introduced me to the owner, the widow of the real Alabama Jack. We moved past the reception committee on to the patio. A jukebox in the corner blared out Merle Haggard's "Mama Tried," and we immediately started to sing along. There were several locals peeling shrimp at a wooden picnic table, tossing the hulls into the ocean. A squadron of brown pelicans lay in wait atop the dock pilings. At the sight of the shrimp hulls hitting the water, they would launch a full-scale kamikaze attack. About twenty feet above the surface, they would free-fall into the water, allowing their body weight to impact the surface. "Great cannonball. I give him a nine," one of the diners said.

"Left wing was elevated too much. I give him a five," his friend replied.

"What are you? Some kind of East German fuckin' commie judge?"

The pelican high-dive continued as we ordered our food and drinks. Lunch arrived: boiled shrimp, crab cakes, and cold draft beer. It was eighty degrees, not a cloud in the sky, and a gentle breeze was out on the bay. I wondered what my friends in Nashville were doing today.

We said good-bye to Alabama Jack's and were back on the road, but not for long. The flat green vista of Key Largo stretched out before us, then where Card Sound Road rejoined U.S. 1 just north of Barnes Sound, the traffic increased and so did the number of billboards. The first one I read informed us that we were now riding on the Overseas Highway. Like everybody and everything in the Keys, the highway started out as something else. It was originally the roadbed for the steel tracks of Henry Flagler's "Railroad That Went to Sea," just one of the many stories about these islands that adds up to a rich and eccentric history. WELCOME TO KEY LARGO, THE LARGEST OF THE FLORIDA KEYS, the next sign read. Key Largo is also the title of the classic Humphrey Bogart film, directed by John Huston. As we cruised down the road, clips from the epic movie flashed in my brain. Bogart, the war hero, on a visit to the family of a dead buddy, learns the hard lesson that no good deed goes unpunished. Then there was the incredible cast of supporting characters. Lauren Bacall plays the grieving widow and dutiful daughter-in-law of the cantankerous old Lionel Barrymore. Edward G. Robinson is Johnny Rocco, the woman-abusing, cigar-champing hood from New York who likes fresh pompano. Throw into this motley gang some Seminole Indians and hurricanes, and it adds up to a classic.

I felt the car slow down, and Jerry Jeff veered to the right and into an oyster-shell parking lot in front of another bar. I had no sooner run through the imaginary film in my head than I was staring at another sign. This one read, WELCOME TO THE CARIBBEAN CLUB WHERE THE WORLD-FAMOUS MOVIE KEY LARGO WAS FILMED. From the outside, it looked like just another roadside honky-tonk, and when we walked in, we were greeted by that unmistakable barroom bouquet—Pine Sol and stale beer. It had been clamped to my chromosomes from the days of cleaning up my uncle's joint, Roy's Bar and Package Store, in Pascagoula.

It was a bar like many others, and then it wasn't. Faded stills from the movie lined the walls. I did the tourist thing and gazed at the shots while Jerry Jeff went to the bar to greet more friends. It was early afternoon, and the place was half full. They all seemed to know Jerry Jeff and Murphy. I tried to place the real location with the action of the movie, and then walked out back to the pier where Bogie thwarts the escape of the gangsters. I sat there and sipped my beer and had these strange thoughts that this was some kind of unrealized initiation into a world that on one hand I had no previous knowledge of, but on the other, I knew I would be associated with for the rest of my life.

A distant, shrill whistle sounded from the parking lot, and a wave from the Flying Lady signaled our departure. We finally put Key Largo behind us and traversed the first of the many bridges that link the islands together. It was east of Islamorada that I got that first amazing feeling that I was driving across the ocean. There were more stops at Ziggy's, the Baltimore Oyster House, and the Big Pine Inn. More friends and more beers. In those days, the normal driving time from Miami to Key West was three and a half to four hours. Eight hours from our departure, the Flying Lady cruised past the naval air station at Boca Chica. Above us there were several F-4 Phantoms in a "break" circling to land. The first one flew over the highway ahead of us no more than five hundred feet off the ground. We watched it bounce onto the runway, with the wind carrying the smell of burning rubber into the car. The second plane came right over us. As we looked out the window up at the giant fighter, I saw the pilot in the plane pointing down at our car. A decade later, I would be sitting in the copilot's seat of a Grumman F-14 as we barrel-rolled above the tower. But that day, I was new in town. We slowed down for the first traffic lights on Stock Island. "Let's go right to sunset," Murphy said. "Buffett has to see sunset." I had no idea what she was talking about. Stock Island was not what I had imagined. It looked more like the shrimping hamlet of Bayou La Batre, Alabama, than tropical Florida. Aluminum-sided buildings lined the highway, interspersed with boat-storage facilities and funky bars. When we crossed the Cow Key Channel Bridge onto the island of Key West, the scenery did not improve. The first thing that greeted us was a Holiday Inn sign. Then car dealerships, fast-food restaurants, and, oh, no—Searstown. Holy shit, I had been tricked. But then the eyesores started to melt away. The deeper we drove into the center of the island, and the closer we got to what Murphy called "Old Town," the more Key West turned into an oasis.

The fragrance of tropical flowers replaced the vision of chain hotels. I would later come to know those scents and the plants that they came from. Interlaced with the smell of frangipani, jasmine, and orange blossoms was the smell of supper being cooked. Traces of simmering garlic and onions came from kitchens of small conch houses and grand mansions alike. The heart of Key West had a French Quarter feel to it, and as good as the food and the flowers smelled, our thoughts that afternoon were not of food, but of frivolity.

Murphy was from Miami, but Key West was her old stomping grounds. She had lived there, and it was there that she had met Jerry Jeff. So we did the town according to Murphy's plan. First stop was Mallory Dock and the sunset. This was before Key West had ever seen a cruise ship, when hippies still free-danced to conga drums without looking to be paid. The music played and the sun melted into the ocean out toward the Marquesas, and when it was gone, the crowd applauded the show. Sunset has become, like many other things on the island, a tourist attraction. But on that day, the fact that there was a daily celebration of an event most people take for granted told me that this place was different. I soon came to realize that *different* is not the word for it.

The sun went to sleep, but we partied on. My old friend Tom Corcoran handed me my first beer in Key West at the Chart Room bar in the Pier House hotel. It would be the first of many beers and good times we would share. Tom became a true friend whom I could call on to help out with anything from crewing the boat to doing an album cover, and we have remained close to this day. Jerry Jeff and Murphy held court in the Chart Room; Tom orchestrated their performance and fueled it with free drinks. To the patrons of this now-famous bar, their visit was like entertaining royalty, and I was the barfly prince, Jimmy (nobody could remember my last name).

After the first of what would be many nights on the town, I found myself in a now-defunct snake pit of a bar called the Old Anchor Inn. We had done Key West, at least the wild bars up and down Duval Street. The sun was just rising in the east, and we all dug deep into our pockets for our sunglasses. Murphy said, "There's just one more place you need to see." We walked down Fleming Street on a tropical dawn. It is one of my favorite times of the day, and I was first exposed to it in New Orleans. I loved going to bed when most of the world was getting up. Now breakfasts were cooking all over the island and the smells of bacon and the remnants of night-blooming jasmine filled the air.

We took a right at William Street and wound through a series of narrow lanes until we were at the gate of the Key West cemetery. Again there was so much New Orleans about Key West, it appeared to me. The cemetery was a combination of crypts and graves that filled several acres of what some would call "prime island real estate." It was flowered with giant mahogany trees along the fence and palm trees and palmettos spread among the gravestones. I used to spend quite a bit of time in cemeteries. First, back in Mobile, I gained a reputation for being the best altar boy for funerals. I liked the work. The tips were good, it was a great way to skip class legally, and we got to eat in the priests' dining hall at Spring Hill College. In my good-boy-gone-bad days in New Orleans, tripping in the cemetery was a popular pastime among the flower children of the Crescent City, way before it was popularized by the movie *Easy Rider*. I liked the history of cemeteries, and Key West was certainly full of that.

"I just wanted you to see it," Murphy said. "There are no insane asylums on this island, only this. Just wanted you to know the rules." The early-morning November sun was already beginning to heat things up, and we moved toward the gate. Ahead of me, I spotted a very large monument with an American flag atop a pristine white flagpole. There was a gold eagle on top of the pole, and on top of the gold eagle, a real osprey sat perched with a large fish in its talons. When I got close, I saw that it was the national monument to the men who had died on the battleship *Maine.* The tombstones all bore different birthdates, but the day of departure was the same on all. These sailors had made it to Key West the hard way. I hoped I would be a little luckier.

I went back to Miami and worked my gig at the Flick, and with the money I saved from that job headed back down the Overseas Highway, stopping by myself at all the pit stops Jerry Jeff and Murphy had alerted me to. I found an apartment in Key West, got a Florida driver's license, bought a junker bicycle at the Salvation Army, and scored a huge collection of Hawaiian shirts and Navy-surplus khaki shorts at the Goodwill. My first day there, I bought a bottle of Boone's Farm apple wine and a pomegranate and bought a ticket on the Conch Train, which toured the island. (To this day, it is still the best crash course in Key West history.) For the rest of the week, I got up, rode my bike to town, and wrote down what I was seeing. These observations were the nucleus of most of my first recordings. Eventually, I would wind up on Duval Street, drinking *café con leche* at Shorty's Diner or at El Cacique, reading Richard Farina's novel *Been Down So Long, It Looks Like Up to Me,* and trying to look more like a local than a tourist.

I have spent some pretty incredible days and nights in Key West, but nothing will ever compare to that first trip down and that first night in town. I woke up the next afternoon in an unfamiliar bunk bed in the house of some hippies I didn't know on a street that I didn't recognize. I felt like I had been shipwrecked. But unlike Gulliver or Robinson Crusoe or young Jim Hawkins, I had been washed up on the shores of a friendly island, a place that I would call home for the next twenty years. Jerry Jeff and Murphy had not only given me a place to stay and a fun weekend in Key West, they had changed my life, and for that I will always be grateful. When I look back on it all now, I know that once I made that move to the ocean, I was basically there to stay, but it wasn't until I went to Australia for a tour years later and found myself on Whale Beach, outside of Sydney, that I reconnected to the umbilical pull of the waves.

SECTION VIII

Another New Year

Back to the Beach

I was in Australia for the first time in my life in 1987, but I felt as comfortable there as in anyplace I had ever been. It is a beach country and a surfing country. By chance, I found myself outside of Sydney with a weekend off. Russell Kunkel was playing drums for me at the time and had friends living outside of Sydney in, of all places, Palm Beach, Australia.

Russell had been born and raised in Southern California, and when he wasn't drumming for rock stars, he was riding waves. We captured the ever-agreeable Michael Utley and caught the seaplane out of Sydney Harbor. On the thirty-minute flight to Palm Beach, we cruised the shoreline and were given a magnificent view of the line of swells breaking at Whale Beach. Russell surveyed the conditions and announced that he didn't think the waves were big enough to kill us, so we decided that upon landing, we would have lunch, then go to the surf shop, rent some boards, and have a go at it. I would finally ride a Pacific wave. We had a great meal at a beachfront restaurant with a beachfront name like the Sand Bar or Beachcomber and, of course, some signature grog with a similarly appropriate name. I think in this case the drinks were called "wipeouts," full of powerful rum, with a splash of passionfruit juice, topped off with a slice of pineapple and a little umbrella. I believe the generic bar term for these concoctions is "fucking tikki pukki drinks." It had been our original intention to work off our dessert by surfing. In the timeworn tradition of best-laid plans being laid to waste, our original strategy was derailed by the arrival of the brandy trolley, which was rolled out to the patio by the wine steward. Paddling through the break gave way to rolling the brandy trolley out onto the beach so we could get a better look at the waves, and that was all that happened that day. We wallowed around on the beach with too good a buzz on, which seemed in our condition a better option than drowning ourselves.

A Lick of Common Sense

It took a few more years before I finally did get back into the water. I had made some significant lifestyle changes in that period after that first Australia trip. I could party with the best of them, but at some point in my late thirties, I realized I had advanced along the time line far enough for hangovers to have taken on the characteristics of recuperation from major surgery. I didn't like feeling that bad for days on end. I was blessed with, as my dad would say, "a lick of common sense" that finally got through. It came in the form of an inner voice yelling, "Hey, asshole, stop what you're doing to yourself." I had seen friends die from drugs and alcohol, and I really didn't want to do that. What would my mother say, if she read of the death of her rock-star son in the paper from the usual causes? I knew I would have to answer to her in the next world. I began to look for better ways to spend my time than doing dope and staying up all night partying.

We were on tour in Hawaii one winter when my tour manager, Charlie Fernandez, took me to see his old friend Bob Olson, or "Ole," as he was known in the surf world. I hadn't been on a board in twenty years. A lot had changed, but a lot had remained the same. The smells of resin, fiberglass, and neoprene that filled Ole's shop found their way to the surfing corner of my soul. I reconnected and bought a beautiful nine-foot nose rider that someone had ordered and not picked up. I hadn't surfed in so long that I didn't know that longboards had gone out of fashion and back in again. But the longboards of the nineties resembled their ancestors from the sixties in length alone. Like everything else these days, computers and space-age materials had enabled designers like Ole, Bill Stewart, Mickey Munoz, Phil Edwards, Donald Gakayama, and others to shape the waterline of a longboard without the weight of a small boat hull.

We put the skeg in the board, bought a leash, waxed her up, and were out the door and headed for the beach. This time there was no brandy trolley. We paddled out to a small break just south of Lahaina, and there I rode my wave. The paddle out, even through the small break, reminded me of how much arm strength is needed to surf. I banged through the foamy remnants of the expired waves and sat up to catch my breath. I had forgotten the view of the world sitting on a surfboard, just past the break. You are an ocean creature, not just a beach bum. I sat there for a while saying nothing, trying to resurrect the surf knowledge of my youth.

It took several tries and a couple of good headers, but in about ten minutes, with Charlie's help, I was up and moving down the front of the wave. When I found my balance and finally was able to relax atop the board, the yell that came out of my mouth could be heard all the way back at the Hangout in Gulf Shores. I paddled back and rode again. Things started to click again, and I wasted away the afternoon as a waterlogged longboarder. They were not the huge waves of surf-magazine centerfolds, but that wasn't the point anymore. At the end of the day, I was exhausted but exhilarated. My arms were weak and shaking, and the ends of my fingers were as shriveled as raisins. My eyes were bloodshot and my ears were ringing, but my mind was clear. Surfing did not become such an obsession that I packed up my guitar, bought a woody, and tried to recapture my youth. I slipped easily into the mold of an old-fart surfer. My frequent trips to California now included stopovers in San

Clemente, and a trip down to San Onofre with my old buddies Corb Donohue, Henry Ford, and Bill Stewart.

I eventually found myself living in Palm Beach, Florida, home of famous Worth Avenue and a lot of badly behaved trust-fund babies. I did not settle there to be a part of the social scene. I was there because the schools were good and I could run under the radar if I wanted to. Unbeknownst to me, the house I wound up buying was right across the street from a famous Florida surf break. I soon hooked up with Rick, the owner of the only surf shop on the island and an old fart long-boarder. Next thing I knew Savannah was working at the surf shop. It was in Rick's shop that I learned about the breaks on the island and first heard about the surf in the Bahamas and my old stomping grounds of the British Virgin Islands.

I took a board to St. Barts, which I left at Kino's house. I found the breaks at Flammande, and in L'Orient right next to Autour du Rocher, the infamous hotel that I had been a partner in. My many exploration flights up and down the islands looking for remote flats now also included reconnaissance for out-of-the-way surf breaks. Back at Rick's, though, there were few occasions when we would be sitting around talking that the discussion didn't somehow turn to the surfing mecca of Costa Rica.

If It's Gonna Happen, It's Gonna Happen Out There

Now, at the restaurant in Costa Rica, I take the last sip of my tea, thank Javier in Spanish, and head out to the deserted beach. Randall and his twenty-year-old torso are already paddling out through the break. I ease slowly down to the beach, do my stretches, and strap myself into my knee brace. In these situations, the years have taught me not to be afraid but to be cautious. I bounce around and twist my wounded knee in several different directions, feeling for any pain. There is none. I'm good to go.

I paddle out through the break. The water is a refreshing temperature, and the salt tastes good. As I paddle through the break, the water feels like electric energy accentuated by the roar of the surf, sending goose bumps down my spine. I spot a patch of smooth water where it looks like a deeper channel stretches from the beach to past the impact point, and I head for it. I glide through a small school of jack crevalle that bounces out of the foam. Randall passes, riding an unfolding four-foot swell. He kicks out, and we paddle out to the lineup together. We sit there bobbing on our boards and checking out the shoreline.

The thing that strikes me the most is the beauty of the coastal landscape. From the lineup in Palm Beach I can see my house as well as a thousand others. From Anse de Flammande in St. Barts I can see the arid hills. But from off the Costa Rican coast, we are looking at mountains that disappear into the clouds and emerald-green pastures that run down to the shore. Overhead the gulls and terns fly low to the waves, trolling for breakfast. It is all very pretty, but we haven't come there to birdwatch.

I paddle my board around to face the open sea, and I scan the waves. It's only a few seconds before I see the one I want. I have to paddle left to position myself to catch the unbroken peak before it spills over. Randall sees that I have the inside and paddles out of my way to wait for the next swell. I check my knee for pain—still okay. I make a sweeping left turn to line up with my spot, glance back at the approaching wave for a moment, and then paddle like hell for the shore until I feel that unmistakable acceleration that means that I am now riding the wave. The approaching wall of water lifts the board. I stop paddling. I now belong to the wave. That millisecond of transference from human resource to the energy of the ocean is a feeling akin to standing in front of forty thousand screaming fans with their hands clasped high above their heads swaying back and forth screaming "Fins to the left, fins to the right" and feeling the adrenaline rush explode in your body.

I stay prone for a second or two, flexing the tendons and muscles around my left knee, then I pop up. With my rear foot I probe for the sweet spot near the end of the board, push, make a front-side turn, and slide down the smooth mountain of water that rises up in front of me. I make out our house on the hill above the beach. I am a happy camper. I have sped down the wave and have enough room to make a slow sweeping turn to the back side. I think about kicking out and paddling back for another ride, but I am enjoying the view too much and so I ride the wave all the way to the beach. The brace has my knee in place. Thank God for technology. This is going to be a glorious morning.

I roll off my board just short of the shoreline and begin to paddle back out. The adrenaline and all the other juices that are stirred up by riding a wave have kicked in. I am running on jet fuel. I power out through the break, making S's in the water with my arms. I am just about where I want to be when suddenly the water in front of me rises steeply. It's a rogue wave, one of those weirdos that won't conform to the rhythms of the ocean. Out at sea on my sailboat, I once collided with a rogue wave that lifted the entire hull of my forty-eight-foot boat out of the water and suspended it in midair for a second before we crashed back into the trough. That impact had knocked a filling from my tooth, not to mention turning the cabin in the boat into a disaster area.

The rogue wave I am looking at now is by no means that dangerous, but there it is, hiding among the little inside waves, waiting to clobber someone—me. In the words of Captain Ron, "If it's gonna happen, it's gonna happen out there." I am in the impact zone and about to experience an overhead condition, which means that I am about to get the shit pounded out of me.

I grab the nose of my board and tilt the side underneath my body. The outboard rail heads for the bottom. I am forcing the other rail down when I hear the pop and feel the pain in my knee, but I can't let up. I continue to push, in pain, and make like a submarine. I have escaped the impact zone and feel the vibrations of the wave crashing down just past my toes. I pop up to the surface, hold on to my board with one hand, and grab for my knee with the other. I know that I am hurt and have to get out of the water. I climb back on my board, stick my sanguine limb up toward the sky, and ride the white water to the beach. I drag my board through the sand and limp over to a driftwood log, unleash myself from the board, and pry off my knee brace. I am able to pop my knee back in place, right there, and then sit on the log to catch my breath. I am done for the day after one wave.

With the logical tools in the pilot part of my brain, I try to work out what had happened out there. I think the brace worked well when I was up on the board and had my body weight to work with. That's how it was designed, but I realize that it did me no good when I was submerged in the salt water, weighing a third less than on dry land and tumbling like a spin cycle on a washing machine. The brace just dangled there, surrounding the loose sockets and ligaments of my knee.

Randall sees me on the beach and comes in to see what happened. I explain the situation and tell him I'm okay, and that he should go on back out. He shouldn't miss the day. I watch him go. I'm not mad, jealous, or pissed-off. My heart is still pounding and the memories are still wet from that one ride. Sure, I would like to have stayed out all morning, but that isn't the way it worked out.

Dragging my board, I limp up the beach. An older, obviously American couple is walking toward me. "Jeez, looks kinda' dangerous out there," the woman says.

"Right about that," her husband replies.

"You have no idea," I say, flashing a smile. "Right about that," I mutter to myself.

Maybe the fact that our brains are 85 percent salt water is what makes the cadence of human reality so easy to compare to the unpredictable cycle of the ocean. As the song says,

"There are good days and bad days and going-half-mad days." In both arenas, there are storms and there are lulls of peaceful existence. In life, as in surfing, there are waves that if you dare to ride them will kill you, and there are waves that will give you the ride of your life. From the beach break of the Gulf of Mexico to the point breaks on Tamarindo, all we are really doing in our short time on this big round ball is paddling around trying to figure out which ones are which. In my time on the water and on the beach, the most important thing I have learned is that paddling around should be as much fun as riding the wave. If it's not, you might as well trade in your human suit for a lobster costume.

The Blue-Marlin Tango

More Weenies to Roast

So it's dance with me, dance with me, nautical wheelers
Take me to stars that you know
Come on and dance with me, dance with me, nautical wheelers
I want so badly to go

—"Nautical Wheelers"

I had made the decision to go fly-fishing for sailfish long before I had encountered the rogue wave that popped my knee out of joint, and I had booked a day on a boat in Quepos. I spent the night with my kids watching *The Nightmare Before Christmas* for the thirtieth time, and then fell asleep repeating that damn chorus in my head: "Christmas Halloween, Christmas Halloween."

At dawn, I explain to Cameron and Delaney where I'm going and what I'm doing, while I make them French toast. They, of course, want to come along, but early on—in developing their fishing world—I had made the distinction between kid fishing and grown-up fishing. They bought it, and I promise to go kid fishing with them when I get back tomorrow. After breakfast, Randall and I head for the airport with rods, backpacks, and video camera in hand. I had appointed Randall the official photographer for this expedition. In case something interesting happens, I want to document the event for justification purposes later on.

The fisherman's dream would be to wander into the sleepy fishing village of Quepos at dawn, have a cup of *café con leche* at a harborside cantina, and stroll down to the dock to ask around for a boat. There he would find an agreeable and available captain for hire who looked and acted like Humphrey

Bogart in *To Have and Have Not.* Then the two of you would head out and hook up with a giant sailfish. Like a lot of dream scenarios, it only happens like that in the movies. The reality is that this kind of fishing is big business and these days requires such things as advance bookings and cash deposits.

I had set about the business of arranging my fishing trip before I left Florida. This, of course, included a mandatory trip to my local outfitter in West Palm Beach. Big fish meant big gear, and none of the fifteen or so rods or reels that I presently had in my arsenal would do the trick. I had to have a special rig for this adventure. It was also Christmas and my birthday, so the new thirteen-weight Sage rod and offshore Abel reel went right into my little stocking. Once armed, I needed to know where to go and what to do. I called my old friend Guy, who had been to Costa Rica the year before. He told me that they had truly gotten into a mess of sailfish and had a great couple of days jumping over twenty fish. Charles Gaines had put the whole thing together for them, and he suggested I give Charles a call.

I found Charles at home in Birmingham. I had last run into him in Nova Scotia with my father the year before. Besides being a fine writer and fly caster, Charles had founded and operated a very successful outfitter service that specialized in adventure fishing. He told me right off the bat that it was kind of late to be looking for a boat in Quepos. It was high season and the good captains would already be booked, but he would see what he could do. I told him I just wanted to go out on the water for a day. I wasn't on some kind of quest, and I certainly had been on a few Third World boats in my day. Charles said he would get back to me.

I also phoned another fishing buddy who was in the business of booking adventure-fishing trips. Randall Kauffman and his brother Lance run a highly successful outfitting company up in Portland, Oregon. Randall was also a writer and had penned one of the definitive books on bonefishing. We had met one day in his store while I was in Portland to play a show. These days, when I have an off day on the road, I can usually be found rummaging through tackle, hardware, and marine-supply stores from coast to coast. I had purposely taken a couple of days off to enjoy the beauty of the great Northwest, so I was delighted when Randall invited me to spend a day with him at his cabin on the world-famous Deschutes River for some steelhead fishing. We had shared our passion for finding exotic and unfished spots on remote islands, and I figured it wouldn't hurt to call him and see what he would recommend for this now-late start to finding a boat in Costa Rica. I can't remember whether it was through Charles or Randall that I came up with a last-minute boat, but just hang on to that phrase for a moment—last-minute boat.

Five-Hundred-Dollar-a-Day Fishing Habit

Okay, okay, I admit it. I am a fishing junkie with a five-hundred-dollar-a-day habit, but *it's not my fault*. Please, let me explain. The five-hundred-dollar-a-day fishing habit is a leftover need created when several million war babies figured out—through recovery, therapy, rehab, or whatever—that they couldn't get high forever. We went from fucked-up to pumped-up, but it wasn't free. (The only thing that is still free in this world is religion, which is why a lot of people "find it.") Now that we had transformed ourselves from hopheads to health nuts, several things occurred. First of all, we started getting up in the morning. We were actually thinking clearly and feeling a lot better, but we needed something to fill all this awakened consciousness. We had made huge strides in not eradicating ourselves with dope, but we now needed shit to do. That's the great thing about capitalism. If there is loose change lying around, somebody will figure out a way to get it.

The move from French-fried to fit brought with it an array of schemes, magazines, machines, and new lifestyles. The first phase of necessary products that led to a long and healthy life

ally see the fish I am chasing. But the flats are not where the sailfish like to congregate. To catch a sailfish on a fly rod, you are required to dwell in the house of billfish, and that means deep water, sportfishing boats, and trolling. I wanted to do it because I hadn't done it before, and this was the sweet spot on the planet for attempting the feat.

The waters off of Quepos hold a magical combination of natural ingredients that attract a large number of big billfish. Sailfish, white marlin, and the big kahuna, the blue marlin, cruise these waters in enough abundance to make for better-than-normal chances of tricking one into eating a large, dumb-looking fly made of chicken feathers, cork, and glue. What this translates into is money. There's a reason that boat and tackle manufacturers rarely put the prices of their products in ads. Men don't want their wives to know how much they spend on fishing junk. A trip to Costa Rica to chase big fish around the ocean ain't cheap. If you factor in the cost of airfare, hotels, food, lodging, and the purchase of all the new shit that you just have to have for the trip, you are probably shelling out a daily rate equal to that of a suite at a Four Seasons hotel. It doesn't matter. Since word got out about how good the fishing is in Quepos, anglers looking for this kind of action have come here in a steady stream. It seems that the more exotic the location and the more expensive the trip, the more attractive it is to a certain group of maniacs who look at fishing as some kind of religion. The average Tico has never seen a billfish and wouldn't think of spending five hundred U.S. dollars a day to hook one up and then let it swim away. But in Quepos they know what it means. Quepos has two natural resources— waves and billfish. Surfers, as a whole, do not have a reputation for being big spenders, so that leaves the crazy anglers who flock to the seaside village every winter to fuel the local economy.

The whole concept of hooking up a giant ocean-dwelling creature to a fly rod was considered impossible in the world of offshore fishing. Marlin and sailfish could only be hauled out of the sea by huge deep-sea reels attached to fiberglass rods as thick as a mop handle and dragged over the transoms of sport-fishing boats, Hemingway style. Using a bunch of feathers to snag a billfish bordered on the insane. So it seemed only natural that the concept came out of Key West. Nearly fifty years ago, two fly-fishing pioneers, Dr. Webster Robinson and his captain, Lefty Reagan, came up with the "bait and switch" technique on Atlantic sailfish and then exported the idea to the billfishing hot spots down through the Caribbean to the Pacific. Dr. Robinson was the first person to fish Quepos with a fly for billfish. Once Dr. Robinson landed the first one, the race was on. We fly rodders from the seventies have been aided much in this concept by technology. Once we started to put men on the moon, the by-products of that technology found their way into rod and reel construction and created a whole new scenario for fly fishermen. Fishermen love this kind of practical application of their tax dollars at work.

Once the gear was invented that would enable a fly fisherman to hang on to a jumping billfish without shattering his rod into a thousand pieces, the race was on. I don't know who landed the first billfish on a fly rod in the Pacific waters off of Quepos, but I can tell you that it didn't take long for the word to spread. There is no harder secret to keep than a fishing hole or a surfing spot. However the word got out, it opened a whole new venue for those smart enough to see that there were a lot of people out there who were willing to indulge. Have fly rod, will travel.

When in Rome

In all my years of fishing, I had never even seen a sailfish or a marlin rise to take a bait, much less a fly. I had of course read about catching sailfish and marlin in Hemingway and Zane Grey. I had actually heard a tale or two from the lips of Grego-

rio Fuentes, the man on whom Hemingway based the fisherman in *The Old Man and the Sea,* but the experience had totally
eluded me. This was pretty amazing, because I had worked
part-time as a deckhand on a sportfishing boat in Key West for
a good number of years. The boat was named *Petticoat III* and
was owned and run by an old friend named Norman Wood.
Back in the eighties, Norman had single-handedly played a
hunch and had discovered a run of marlin off Key West that
sprouted its own cottage industry. He had caught dozens of
big blue marlin, started a tag-and-release tournament, and
held several world records. I had accompanied him on many a
trip out to the Gulf Stream, and I would see the pictures and
hear the stories of the big blues, but I was never there when
they were landed. But that is just what big-game fishing is:
endless hours of boredom speckled with moments of complete hysteria. I had spent enough days trolling with Norman
to know that it was not my cup of tea, especially after I fished
the flats off Key West for the first time. I preferred silence, shallow water, and push poles to loud engines, heavy rods, and
deep water. I didn't relish the idea of pounding out to sea for
two hours out and then trolling in the equatorial sun for six
hours more. But that was where the big fish were, and I had
heard from a lot of my fishing buds who had made the trip to
Costa Rica that it was well worth the money and the effort.
Hell, I had jumped out of a plane when I was nineteen, and
I've never thought of doing it again, but at least I had done it
once. If I was ever to get a billfish to eat a fly, it would be more
likely to happen in the magical waters off Quepos.

Abducted by Alien Fishermen

This is not a dream, or maybe it is. Wherever you may be
reading this book—on the beach, on a plane, or at home—*we
now have your mind.* Don't fight it. We will not harm you, but

you are going with us to Quepos. It's okay, I'm paying. Just remember, you could be at work or having to sit through a Tony Roberts seminar on personal power. You are better off here. And remember that at the end of the day, all it cost you was the price of this book, while I had to shell out for the plane, the boat, the beer, and the ice. Climb on board, 'cause here we go.

Date: 28 December 1996
Time: 1442 Z
Latitude: 09°43'4" N
Longitude: 85°00'05" W
Location: Tambor Airport, aboard N7622R (Cessna 208 Caravan on amphibian floats)

Altitude: 2,000'
Skies: Clear
Wind: Calm
Temperature: Already way too hot

Comments: We are on our way to Quepos with a friend. The Albatross couldn't make the trip and sits in San José, the victim of more Third World complications. As many times as I have been in and out of airports, filling out paperwork, and begging permission, I think I have seen it all. That will never happen. We have all our paperwork in order for the Albatross to fly around the country and even land in the water. This in itself is quite a feat. We are officially engaged in location scouting for the *Joe Merchant* movie, thanks to Frank Marshall and Kathleen Kennedy, and have access to all the coastal waters for landing. Even so, we still cannot fly the Albatross to Quepos because the runway will not hold the weight of the plane. It seems that the asphalt in the equatorial sun has a tendency to take on the consistency of saltwater taffy, and the Albatross might wind up like Brer Rabbit and the tarbaby.

The kids are happy as clams on the beach at Tambor, and Kino has just arrived after a fourteen-hour flight from Paris and is jet-lagging. Jane and Mac are going to Quepos to have a look around. Javier has arranged for a friend of his to meet them at the airport.

We are at an altitude of just two thousand feet, a perfect vantage point from which to view the natural beauty of the Pacific coast. The ocean is docile. There is no chop, just the pulsating swells moving toward the beach. The lush landscape can't help but get our attention. There's an emerald-green blanket that falls from the mountains to the shore. A narrow coastal road traces a path south between the foothills and the beach. We pass over several spots where a jungle river empties into the ocean. Talk about beachfront property. This must have been what California looked like once upon a time. Surf breaks stretch to the horizon. Ribbons of waves line the straight shoreline and wrap around the points. We fly directly over a small beach cottage barely visible, hidden in the necessary shade of countless overhanging palms. There are a lot of places to get lost, which is what many people have done in the hills below us. I have heard lots of conversations that went something like this:

"What ever happened to him?"

"Oh, he took off for Costa Rica, and nobody has heard from him since."

A large lagoon comes into view. It has a tiny tributary feeding it from the ocean and is surrounded by cane fields. There is a small dock on the south end. My first thought is to check the depth for landing the Albatross. We pass over the harbor. From the air, it really does resemble a quiet fishing village stuck like a postage stamp to the shore. We turn back for the airport over rows and rows of perfectly planted small palm trees that surround the lone landing strip. Gear is down and locked. Flaps to landing position. We are returning to Earth.

They Paved Paradise

Don't it always seem to go
You don't know what you've got till it's gone
They paved paradise and put up a parking lot
                    —JONI MITCHELL, "BIG YELLOW TAXI"

Date: 29 December 1997   **Elevation:** 85′
Time: 1517 Z   **Skies:** Clear
Latitude: 09°27′02″ N   **Wind:** Calm
Longitude: 84°08′05″ W   **Temperature:** Asphalt still
Location: Quepos Interna-   solid
    tional Airport

Comments: We touch down at Quepos International. As we taxi toward the end of the runway, I look below the pontoon of the plane just to make sure we're not melting. The terminal is what I wanted to see. It is an old, military-green Quonset hut that houses a snack bar, gift shop, and two small counters for the shuttle flights to San José. There is an old red and yellow biplane parked off to the right. Our plane is the only other one on the field, though it appears that a shuttle must be arriving soon from San José, as there are tourists waiting in the terminal.

Quepos International has held on to its character and its simple charm. It reminds me of my old home field on St. Barts, before they paved paradise and put up a fancy airport. The old St. Barts terminal was just a square concrete building with a giant tamarind tree in front that held two closet-sized offices for Air Guadeloupe and Windward Air, but it was one of the truly unique gathering places in the Caribbean. There was no customs. The plane parking area was a grass field surrounded by hibiscus blooms and tea-oil trees. The show was to watch the unsuspecting passengers spill out of the plane after experiencing one the closest things to a carrier landing in commercial aviation. The little airport bistro was more than just an air-port snack bar that served a great *petite punch* and *croque mon-sieur*. It was a local hangout, and the heart of the St. Barts Coconut Telegraph. But sadly, in the name of progress, it was all taken away. The new terminal in St. Barts is all concrete, filled with modern counters, boutiques, and ATM machines. Gone are the characters, the sandwiches, and the charm. Hang on to your past, Quepos. It's worth it. I am thinking to myself that if we ever get to make a movie of *Where Is Joe Merchant?* this is what the airport at Boomtown should look like.

Been There, Done That, Got That T-Shirt

Tryin' to tell myself that my condition is improvin'
And if I don't die by Thursday, I'll be roarin' Friday night
  —"My Head Hurts, My Feet Stink, and I Don't Love Jesus"

Time: 1522Z

Location: Quepos International

Comments: We are waiting for our ride, and I shoot some video of the quaint little spot. For a moment, a horrible picture appears in my mind of the Albatross bogged down in the syrupy asphalt. Jane and Mac are met by Javier's friend, and after we set a time to meet back at the airport, they depart with *Vanity Fair* and travel guide in hand.

Our pickup arrives. A nice fellow, obviously American, greets us. His name is Hal, just like the computer in *2001: A Space Odyssey*. But, this Hal has a very Southern accent. He welcomes us to town and tells us that our boat is waiting at the dock. He is accompanied by a man named Tex. I pray to God that Tex is not the captain. Fortunately, it turns out that Tex is just another client from where else—Texas—and he is a *huge* fan. Hal has brought him along to meet me. My mentor Gam-

ble Rogers gave me a piece of advice many years ago. In refer-
ring to over-zealous fans, he said, "They still love you despite
their bad manners. Just remember patience, Jimmy. It takes no
more time to be a nice guy then it does to be an asshole." I
smile, shake Tex's hand, and sign an autograph.

Tex rides with us to town in the backseat of Hal's island
clunker truck. It reminds me of my old truck that I used to
prowl the neighborhoods of Key West in.

Tex's eyes are hidden behind oversized, polarized fishing
glasses straight out of Neiman Marcus, but he still has clear
signs of that "been up all night for the first time" look etched
on the visible part of his face. He smells like alcohol and appears to still be drunk but not that far from the approaching
tequila hangover. Under his breath I hear him mumbling the
lyrics to "My Head Hurts, My Feet Stink, and I Don't Love
Jesus." Oh, God, my own words are coming back to haunt me.
I have given Tex an anthem. He talks with a twang about all
the fish he and his buddies from Lubbock caught, then rattles
on about the big beach fiesta. I don't see any stitches or fresh
tattoos, so it couldn't have been all that wild a night. Tex in-
vites me to come along tonight. I politely decline the invitation. Been there, done that, got that T-shirt.

We drive into town with Hal, who gives us the two-minute
tour. I ask him how he ended up here. He tells me he has been
in Costa Rica for twenty-three years and has no desire to return
to his home state of North Carolina. I know not to go any further. One thing about Americans in the banana republics: They
usually have a past. I only knew Quepos from what I read in
the travel guides and from an envelope of pictures that Corb
Donohue had sent me twenty years ago, but in a sense, I have
been here before. It has the look of the typical beach town. I
have spent time in many. There isn't much to look at in the way
of colonial architecture or fortresses. This is a simple fishing
village done in the motif of late-twentieth-century construction. Wood had given way to concrete, and small buildings of
both kinds line the narrow streets. Bougainvillea vines and co-

conut palms grow wild in the tiny alleys, and a smell of wood smoke hangs in the morning air. The church steeple towers above everything in town. This is a very Catholic country.

We wind through a labyrinth of sharp turns, finally emerging on the main drag, which is lined with restaurants, shops, and bars named after clichéd ocean terms or fish. Quepos has all the elements of being another Margaritaville. There is the smell of bacon and bread coming from the kitchen of one of the *cocinas*, and music blares from some distant radio playing battle of the bands with the well-hidden but always boisterous roosters crowing at the top of their lungs. We stop at a little bodega and Hal quickly grabs our lunch. Here, thankfully, we say good-bye to Tex. It is obvious that his hangover has set in, and he mumbles something and holds out a pen and a piece of paper. I sign an autograph, and he stumbles happily back toward his hotel.

The aromas of the hot sandwiches and grilled onions make my stomach growl. We drive south down the main drag toward the pier at the end of town. I ask the inevitable question, "How's the fishing?" One thing you can absolutely count on is that no guide or captain will ever answer, "Not good," or "We didn't catch shit." The response is always filled with Chamber of Commerce descriptions of lots of action and lots of fish. Hal tells us that somebody here had set a world record a few days earlier.

Time: 1552Z

Location: Quepos town pier

Comments: The town pier is as big as a bridge, jutting out into the water a good thousand feet and standing three stories above sea level. It houses an old rusty tin storage warehouse surrounded by empty cable drums, container vessels, and an assortment of other cargo and fish traps. This is no marina, where pristine yachts line up, each in its own berth, creating a city of boats with all the expected amenities. The pier is Quepos's artery to the rest of the world and serves the shipping industry as well as the fishing fleet. Our ride down the creaking timbers is halted by a sizable señorita in a uniform who holds up her hand and pokes her large face out the window of the booth.

Though Columbus had come to the New World as Admiral of the Ocean, he named every single island for one of the saints. But what he was after was gold. That history has held steady more than five hundred years later. God may have created the giant fish that dwell in the waters off of Quepos, but the government now controls them. Remember that basic rule: Nothing is free. On this day on this dock, it is fifty bucks apiece to drop your hook into God's great ocean. Hal chatters away in perfect machine-gun Spanish with the woman in the booth. I am envious.

"There's your boat," Hal says, pointing to a small blue sportfishing vessel that I recognized as a Bertram 28-foot. From a distance, she looks fine. She lays at anchor among a fleet of boats that rolls gently in the continuous swell of the Pacific. A whistle and a wave brings the boat to the dock. The captain, a young, dark Tico, spins her around stern-to, and I jump aboard the *Numero Uno*. Randall and I transfer our gear with the help of the mate, whom Hal introduces as Bobalou. I like that name. The captain is just El Jefe. Hal and El Jefe get into a rapid-fire conversation. I may not speak much Spanish, but I know right away that something isn't kosher. El Jefe throws his hands up in the air and signals for Bobalou to cast off. This is not a good sign, but I figure Hal will take care of things. Not to worry.

Suddenly the engines roar to life and thick black smoke belches from the exhausts. Hal is still on the dock. I yell at him through the smoke, "You're not coming?"

He is coughing and clearing the air with his right hand. "No, but Bobalou speaks good English. See you at four, and don't forget to try the hot sauce on the sandwiches. It's great." He climbs back up the stairs through the lingering smoke. I am beginning to get a bad feeling about this trip. I have neither time nor desire to pursue the issue of Hal's absence on the boat. I know it has something to do with gringo politics, and I don't even want to get into it. I wave up to the captain. He stares at me long and hard, nods slightly, and guns the engines. Not a good sign. I begin to whistle the theme song from *Gilligan's Island*.

Ready, Set, Fish

Time: 1548Z
Latitude: 09°25′48.0″ N
Longitude: 84°10′25.8″ W
Location: Aboard the
    Numero Uno

Seas: Calm
Wind: Light
Temperature: 92° F. in the
    shade
Course: 090°

Comments: Fishing with strangers is something I rarely do. I have been fishing long enough to know the guides in the spots where I go, but in Quepos I am winging it.

The Boat. I know my vessels like the back of my hand, how they are rigged and how they operate. Charter boats are a different story. I don't care where you go in the world, no boat you charter will ever be as good to an angler as his own, even if it is. The old *Numero Uno* looked a lot better from the distance and height of the pier than she does at close range. On the old 1-to-10 scale, she gets about a 2. I know I'm a bit spoiled, but for what I'm paying, I'd think that at least I'd get a boat in which the head wasn't filled with buckets of engine parts and mildewing foul-weather gear. Then there's the basic bunk—a nest of old fishing tackle, tangled lures, and artificial baits, hardly a spot where I might grab a nap. I don't even think about going all the way forward to the V-berth. God knows what's living in there, but thoughts of the Creature from the Black Lagoon come to mind. Well, there isn't much I can do about it now. I find a spot out on the aft deck above the engine box where I can work on my gear and rest if I want.

The Crew. After checking the boat, the next thing to do is establish a good working relationship with the crew. Normally, this is not a problem. Fishermen speak a basic similar language, and all it usually takes is an easygoing conversation about the sport with the captain or mate. It's like the first couple of pitches of a game or the first few rounds of a fight. You feel each other out and establish a mutual purpose. This being my first time fly-fishing in Costa Rica, I'm looking for help as well. The only problem here is the language barrier. Goddam, why hadn't I learned my Spanish?

El Jefe is perched like a pillar of salt on the bridge, staring straight ahead at the open ocean. He has no English phrase book in his hand.

Well, Hal said that Bobalou, the mate, speaks good English. He is busy setting poles into the rod holders when I approach him to talk about the plan. It takes about two seconds to discover that his English is about as good as my very bad Spanish. It is going to be an interesting day on the water.

As we headed offshore, I boned up on fishing terms in my Spanish-survival paperback. I must say, there is no better way to learn a language quickly than to have to. I manage to put together a few sentences and am able to comprehend some of what Bobalou is saying. I show him the flies I've brought with me. *"Está rojo? Está azul?"* I feel like I'm on *Sesame Street,* but it works.

"Rojo, rojo," he replies. Now we're getting somewhere, but soon it's time to end Spanish class and get ready to fish. We retreat to our respective corners. He goes back to rigging his teasers, and I climb to my perch in the corner of the cockpit and begin to rig up.

As we make our way further east, the mountains disappear so that only the faint patches of cumulus clouds on the western horizon hint at land. One of the factors that makes getting to the fishing grounds off Quepos unique is that the ocean in these latitudes is nearly always calm, which enables small boats to go long distances without taking a pounding. If I had walked out on that dock to an ocean panorama of whitecaps and short, steep waves like I was accustomed to from sportfishing days in the Atlantic and the Gulf of Mexico, I would have been back in town having breakfast in a flash. The rolling deck of a twenty-eight-foot boat, especially this one, in any kind of sea can be duplicated only by wedging yourself into a jumbo tumble dryer at the Laundromat and dropping twenty-four quarters into the slot. Hang on. Thank God we are in the Pacific.

Ride, Captain, Ride

Time: 1650 Z
Latitude: 09°19′21″ N
Longitude: 84°21′4″ W
Location: 14 mi. W of
   Quepos

Wind: Hot
Seas: Calm
Temperature: Don't even
   ask

Comments: We leave the green water of shore behind us. There is a clear line that divides this warmer, shallower water from the dark blue, deep ocean ahead. It is nearly nine in the morning, and the temperature is already in the midnineties. One thing we do have on board is plenty of cold water. I have recovered from my initial trepidation about the condition of the boat. I have grown comfortable in my spot atop the engine box, and I am feeling the groove of the ocean. Sunscreen alone is not an option in these latitudes, and I lather up and try to squeeze myself into the sliver of shade that cuts across the engine box. I check my GPS and mark our position. By the time the information in my little Garmin handheld spits out, I know where I am and how far I have come. What an amazing big-boy toy this little machine is. I even carry it on the road and mark the latitudes of cool bookstores and barbecue restaurants I discover. I wonder if constantly knowing your latitude and longitude is the equivalent of what psychobabble would call "being grounded"? Out of the blue I start to sing one of my old-favorite ocean songs.

> Seventy-three men sailed out
> From that San Francisco Bay
> Callin' everyone on board to come
> Sail away

I am tempted to yell up at El Jefe, "Are we there yet, Daddy?" but it is a joke that only I will laugh at. Being able to entertain yourself in boring situations is an essential part of survival. Humor is the antitoxin for terror. I have been practicing my Spanish for a while, concentrating on phrases I might need in the next hour or so. "Donde está el pescado?" "Está izquierda o derecho?" I am watching the flying fish skipping across the surface, daydreaming about the famous flying-fish sandwiches on sugar bread with Matouk's hot sauce found only in Bridgetown Barbados. I did learn one new trick from Bobalou. As soon as we boarded the boat that morning, he had taken the sandwiches from Hal and stowed them in a small metal container that was attached to a stringer above the engine. He then sealed the engine box, grinned at me, and said, "My microwave."

I am brought out of my trance by a sudden change in temperature. A high cloud cover has momentarily blocked the burning sun, and there is immediate relief from the heat. The clouds are spread over a wide patch of the sky. I don't know what effect it might have on the fishing, but right now I don't care.

> Ride, captain, ride,
> Upon your mystery ship
> You have seen the simple things
> That others might have missed

Time: 1700Z

Comments: El Jefe slows down, and I watch Bobalou set his baits. Chatter from the marine radio now filters down from the bridge. We are not alone. There are about six other boats in the vicinity, already rigged up and trolling. I think I now know what pissed him off. He was leaving late and having to come back early. Not a lot of time to catch a big fish and earn a big tip.

Bobalou wants me to try a few practice casts. I strip out my line, crank out a couple of false casts, then lay the long red fly inches behind the starboard-trailing teaser. He pats me on the shoulder. The most frustrating thing for any guide is to put people on fish who can't reach them. Out of the corner of my eye, I spy El Jefe on the bridge watching me cast. I turn my head up, and my eyes meet his. At least I can cast. He nods in approval. It's time to do what we have come so far to do.

Randall stands by with the camera, and El Jefe motions for him to come up to the bridge to shoot. I scan my fly line on the deck for tangles, make a few more practice casts at the teaser, then check my fly. The boat swings in a wide arc back to the east. It is exciting. With this kind of fishing, you hope like hell you get a fish up in the first thirty minutes, or it can turn into a long, boring day.

The Blue-Marlin Tango

Time: 1705Z

Comments: I am leaning against the gunwale studying the bubbling wake behind the boat for the telltale sign of a bill rising out of the water. Though I have never actually seen one in the wake of a boat before, I know exactly what to look for. I run my old "what if" scenario. What if I actually get to cast at a sailfish today? What am I going to do? Since I really haven't gotten any inside info from Bobalou, I start with something that I know—tarpon. I have hooked and released more than I can remember. They are bigger than sailfish, and they jump as well. Set the hook and bow to the fish. I am as ready as I can be under the circumstances. I hear a shrill whistle from El Jefe above, and Bobalou springs to the transom like a coiled snake. *"Qué pasa?"* I ask. He's too busy to answer. The air is filled with electricity, but half a minute later nothing has happened, though I am sure El Jefe saw something. I relax slightly.

Time: 1735Z

Comments: I sit for a moment on the gunwale keeping my eyes glued to the small wakes of the baits skipping along at ten knots behind us. I am still highly energized. The doldrums of trolling have not set in yet. We make another big arc to starboard, heading back to the west. I spot a gull coming in from starboard just above the surface moving from right to left. Any good fisherman knows that where there are birds there are fish. "Jesus Christ! There it is!" I yell as I see the long pointed bill pop up in the wake behind us like a periscope. Bobalou is again on the rods.

"Marlin azul," El Jefe yells out. Holy shit, it's no sailfish. It's a blue marlin. I see it turn. It's not only a blue marlin, it is a big fucking blue marlin.

"You getting this?" I yell to Randall, as I brace myself in the port corner of the cockpit for the cast.

Make Way for the Big Enchilada

Time: 1736Z   Longitude: 83°34′1″ W
Latitude: 09°13′4″ N   Location: 26.1 mi. WSW of
                               Quepos, Costa Rica

Comments: I see the giant fish moving in the wake on the port side. It turns suddenly to the right and heads for the closest teaser. I don't have time to comprehend what's happening. What the fuck do I do with a marlin? I guess the same thing I was gonna do for a sailfish. No time to reevaluate. He is at least four hundred pounds, and his body is pulsating like a neon sign. If I hook him, it won't be for long. I make my cast, and my red fly falls right behind the red teaser. He is on it. "You got it! You got it!" Bobalou calls out as I strip the fly. All of a sudden the marlin hurls himself out of the water horizontally to the wake of the boat. Make way for the big enchilada. Here he comes: bill, fin, tail, and all. He crashes the fly and the line goes tight. My God, I have him on. I go to set the hook. A momentary tug and then nothing.

"Aw, shit!" I scream. But he hasn't fled the scene. He doubles back to the port side, and I make several more casts at him, but all in vain.

"Push it, push it, push it!" Bobalou calls out. I take that to mean cast. "No, no!" he calls out. He manages to get the marlin to chase the far teaser and frantically begins to reel it into casting range, with the big fish following close behind. I see him coming back to the boat and begin to cast. "Move it, move it!" Bobalou calls out. My instincts tell me the fish is in range and I can make the cast. I start to go and Bobalou yells, "No, no!" I stop casting. The fish disappears.

Time: 1737Z

Comments: It's all over that fast. I don't know how I feel. Pissed-off that I didn't set the hook and get at least a couple of jumps, or elated that I actually had a take. My heart is banging against my rib cage, and adrenaline has the hairs on my arm on edge. I am stunned. Bobalou is more excited than the fish, and is still running around, working the reels. I just stand there with my limp line trailing in the water behind the boat and a big shit-eating grin on my face. Randall and I are laughing and jabbering away about the amazing thing we have just witnessed. He got the whole thing on video, and I will have a constant digital reminder of the big one that got away.

It seems, though, that our crew does not share our joy. I can feel the vibe. These guys have come to catch fish. I attempt a conversation with Bobalou. Speaking English this way is almost like learning another language. I ask his advice. "More slow to bite next time," he replies. I think I comprehend. In my world we call pulling the hook out of a fish's mouth a premature extrapolation. I don't dare try that Scrabble winner on Bobalou.

Time: 1750Z

Comments: The cloud cover has moved on, and the sun is back full strength. I am again lodged atop the engine box in the tiniest piece of shade. Going below is out of the question. I hear the whistle from above. Another fish is up. I spring from the box, determined to correct my initial mistake of not waiting to set the hook. This time it is a sail stabbing at the farthermost bait, but the fish is way too far out of casting range. Bobalou plays with the bait and bounces it across the water like a flat stone, but this fish isn't interested and disappears beneath the wake. We make a circle, but there's no sign of him.

Time: 1806Z

Comments: We spend nearly an hour circling the area where the first two fish came up. The rest of the fleet has moved in around us. With my arms folded, I watch in silence from the gunwale. Bobalou sits on the other side of the cockpit, quietly scanning the wake. I know that if a fish pops up, he will let me know. The action has long since stopped, and the trolling blues are beginning to set in.

I pass the time watching a huge boat off to our right. Holy mackerel, this is some rig I am looking at. It has a tuna tower that is as high off the water as a small oil derrick. There are several spotters in matching uniform shirts clinging to the aluminum ladders, scouting for fish. The helmsman is aloft in the small steering station atop the tower. I can hear music coming over the water. Oh, God, they're playing Donna Summer.

I move down to the deck and a more interesting view. There are two very attractive women in string bikinis serving the two fishermen drinks as they dance around the cockpit with a video camera. My binoculars allow me to observe that the breasts behind the little patches of material that cover them look way too perfect to be God's work. The men are dressed in the latest offshore, sun-repellent polyester-cotton-blend fishing outfits. The shirts have some kind of fishing-team insignia on them. I look back at my boat and crew for a second, then at Randall and me. Hell, we look like we're the crew. I conclude that it is only a mirage, but it is the only show on the ocean today.

I return to my binoculars and continue my surveillance. There must be a dozen fly rods resting in some special kind of rod holder around the fighting chair. The tips of the rods fan out from the base. To top it all off, not only do these guys have a hot boat, chicks, and tunes, they have hooked up in the time I was away from my binoculars. There is a good-size sailfish jumping repeatedly behind the boat, and an angler leaning into him with his rod bent in two as the captain backs down and sends a wall of water up and over the transom. The girls are wet now and squealing. It's a floating "Hooters." This must be some kind of test sent by the fishing gods to tempt us.

Meanwhile, back on the old *Numero Uno,* sweat is dripping from every pore of my body onto the camera, and I'm afraid I might short-circuit. Over on the disco boat, I can see that the main saloon doors are closed. That means it's air-conditioned. I can't take it anymore. I have to ask. They must be shooting a beer commercial. No boat and crew look that perfect. Bobalou tells me that the guy is a champion fisherman, and that it's his private boat. He has come from California and has fished for twenty days in a row. He is out to set world records for sail-fish on three different weights of line.

It's time for lunch. Bobalou breaks out our hot sand-wiches from the "microwave," and we chow down. At least we're eating well. Hal's lunch spot has produced an amazing shredded-chicken sandwich on a fresh Cuban-style bun. There is a bag of shredded lettuce and sliced tomatoes. I look for the killer hot sauce that Hal told me about but don't see it anywhere. I look across the boat and I see Bobalou putting some on his sandwich. When he is finished, he tosses the unfinished pouch of sauce overboard and digs into his sandwich. Before I launch into a Mr. Rogers dissertation on sharing, I catch myself and just laugh. In my mind I conjure up an imaginary vision of the brochure for *Numero Uno*. "Billfish on fly rod, excellent boat, expert crew, speaks perfect English, gourmet lunch, and all the ice-cold agua you can drink (hot sauce not included)."

Time: 1815Z

Comments: Still no action. Bobalou changes to a new teaser. The sailing disco is starting to move away. The rest of the fleet is south of our position. The sun is directly overhead, and my shade is gone. I have resorted to towels soaked in seawater to cool off. Boring.

Time: 2010Z
Latitude: 09°13′55″ N
Longitude: 84°34′32″ W

Comments: The heat is working on me. I am daydreaming about jumping ship and swimming for the "Hooters" boat, but they would probably throw me back into the ocean. The now familiar whistle from the bridge brings me back to my boat. A second marlin has come up in the wake. He's just behind the far bait. I can't believe that I am actually getting to do this again. He's not as big as the first fish, but he's much more active. This guy sashays up the wake darting back and forth like a mad Argentinian tango dancer.

Bobalou hauls the line closer to the boat, and the fish follows. He finally attacks the new teaser with a vengeance. I can see his big eye locked on the teaser; it's the size of my fist. I can't help but admire this amazing fish, but I am ready for him. This time I will not make the same mistake. I need to let the fish have the fly longer, and then set it. Just one jump, God. You can smash my rod into a thousand pieces. Just one jump. This time I don't wait for Bobalou's command. I wait for the fish to get into range and trust my fishing sense to tell me when. He's still locked on the teaser. The windup and the pitch. Strike two. The fly lands where it should, and the fish is on it. I feel him tug, and I fight the inclination to set the hook. I count. One thousand one, one thousand two. *Wham*, here we go.

I yank back the rod in my right hand and at the same time pull tight on the line in my left. There is no resistance. The fish is there no more. I see him still dancing in the wake and make several more casts, but I will not get my dance card signed today.

It's time to go home. I take off my sunglasses, look up to El Jefe, point to the west, and say, "*La playa.*" He nods his head in agreement and turns the bow towards the distant beach. On the long ride home, I admit to myself that I am glad the fish got away. If we had caught one, it would only have meant a lot of hoopla back at the dock. This way, I had experienced the thrill and could slip back into town unnoticed. I looked down at my notebook, quickly jotted down my final thoughts of the day, and realized that I had, in fact, landed that fish in the most perfect way. His brief appearance in our lives was now the best trophy I could want—a story.

That's What Living Is to Me

Time: 2241Z

Comments: I am awakened from my nap by the sudden drop in engine RPM's and the smell of land. The water is green again, and the pier at Quepos is but half a mile away, according to trusty GPS. The afternoon buildup of clouds and the offshore breeze is like a welcome-home gift. The earth has rotated and the sun is heading for the next morning on the other side of the International Dateline over the Pacific horizon.

Hal is standing on the dock, cigarette in one hand and a marine radio in the other. El Jefe backs down toward the barnacle-laden pilings:

"How'd it go?" he calls down from the pier.

"It was fun," I call out. "We got a couple of shots, but no takers."

"How'd you like that hot sauce on them sandwiches?"

For a moment, I almost want to tell him the truth, but opt instead for a politician answer. "Great sandwiches," I reply.

"Tough way to fish, you know," Hal adds. "Well, there's always tomorrow. Can I buy you guys a beer before you gotta go?"

"You bet," I reply. I say good-bye to El Jefe and Bobalou and leave them a piece of swag we had brought with us.

El Jefe reaches down and shakes my hand. "*Hasta luega,*" he says. Though it is the furthermost thing from my mind at the moment, he knows I will be back.

Return to Land, Return to Earth

Time: 2300Z

Location: Quepos International Airport, Costa Rica

Comments: After a short stop in town at the local watering hole for a couple of beers and a few more autographs, Hal drops us off at the airport. The girls are waiting with tales of their explorations and seem very cheerful. Perhaps they ran into Antonio Banderas taking a shower in a waterfall. In any event, they had come up with a plan for coming back to Quepos for New Year's Eve. I launch right into my fishing tale, trying not to rattle on too long. They feign interest but change the subject back to New Year's Eve. It seems Javier's friend works at a local hotel in Manuel Antonio called Si Como No. Jane looked at other hotels with him but spent the afternoon at Si Como No by the pool and said it was a very cool place. It was owned by an American who happened to be a big fan of mine. On a hunch, Jane figured that a trip back for New Year's seemed a little more exciting than spending it at our hotel in Tambor. They had booked a room. The owner, Jim Damalas, was out of town but due back on New Year's Eve. He had faxed the hotel when he learned we were around and had offered us his house. I like the idea and the owner already and am game for a return to Quepos. I have never been one to miss a good party, but there is an ulterior motive. As we climb aboard the plane to head back to Tambor, I am already thinking about an encore performance of the blue-marlin tango.

This is not a dream, or maybe it is. Have you been abducted by alien fishermen, or haven't you? If so, we'll see you in the tabloids. We are now returning you to your regularly scheduled program, already in progress.

Island in My Dream

That night, exhausted by the sun and all the excitement, I dream of the recurring island that seems to be suspended in my subconscious. It is an island that I visit often, but even though I am there, I know it isn't real and keep telling myself so in my dreams. Sometimes it is out past the Marquesas at the end of the Florida Keys. Other times it sits in the middle of the Gulf of Mexico, and still other times it is off the coast of the Yucatán and I can see the ancient Mayan pyramids on the distant horizon. If there is a heaven, I hope this is my corner.

On this visit, I am in a beach house on an island right next to Fort Jefferson. It is the beach house from the movie version of Hemingway's *Islands in the Stream,* the one that is home to the weird painter Thomas Hudson, played by George C. Scott. I know it is the house from the movie, and I am wondering what it is doing in my dream. All of a sudden, a huge blue marlin floats through the window and hovers over my bed. He is as big as a ship, but I am not afraid. He pokes around the mosquito net with his big beak and finally locates the separation on the fabric, and the bill comes toward me in bed. I watch it as it comes slowly toward my shoulder, where I see a tattoo of a sinking ship. The end of the bill is as sharp and pointed as an ice pick, and I wonder if this is it. I start to get a little frightened and move across the bed. The fish follows me, and when I'm at the edge of the bed, he pokes me ever so slightly with the point of his bill and then speaks. "Missed me," he says, and then breaks out into a huge laugh and floats back out the window.

I follow him from the bed, scratching at the spot on my arm where he touched me. I look out the window, and there is the disco boat. There is a huge party on the deck, but the crew is all fish and mermaids. The big marlin sees me looking and urges me to come on to the party. A gorgeous mermaid urges me to come through the window. Then they start to chant in unison, "We want pancakes, we want pancakes." I crack open one eye. It isn't the big blue marlin or the bare-breasted mermaid ordering breakfast. I am back.

While I mix the pancake batter and wait for the skillet to get hot, I peek several times out the window of Presidential House just to see if the disco boat is sitting offshore, but the sea is empty. The news of our decision to return to Quepos for New Year's Eve was met with mixed emotion back in Tambor. The kids seemed happy to stay put, but Javier and the hotel staff seemed sad that we wouldn't be joining them for the big event.

We spend the rest of the day on an island excursion in a small open boat that we rented in Tambor. We cruise the shoreline of the Nicoya Peninsula, stopping at several beaches along the way for swimming, snacks, and cave explorations. I honored my commitment to go kid fishing, but there isn't much biting. I already know that when I get back to the hotel I am going to call Hal back and book a boat for the day of our return to Quepos. When I reach him later that night, he tells me El Jefe is booked, but he could put Bobalou on his other boat. I laugh at my sudden image of the "other boat" but say yes and tell him I want my own hot sauce with the sandwiches. What a glutton for punishment I am.

Night of the Iguana Meets the Jitterbug Champ

Amateur Night

I have always thought of New Year's Eve as amateur night. It comes from the fact that for so many years I viewed the celebrations from a bandstand. New Year's Eve was always a gig, and I always felt more comfortable working than playing. The first time I found myself out in the crowd, as opposed to up on the stage, I was uncomfortable. I really didn't know what to do, and there were too many people "trying" to have a good time. I might be a little jaded as well, because I see what amounts to a full-blown New Year's bash at least thirty to forty times a year at our road shows.

As a celebration, New Year's Eve is too predictable. Everybody knows exactly when it's going to happen. Take, for example, this hysteria surrounding the upcoming turn of the century. Here we are two years away from the millennium and the whole world is booked this far in advance. Well, actually we don't even really know if it is the millennium or not. Recorded history seems to be a little out of whack by one to four years, but don't tell that to the majority of the civilized world. They are getting prepared for something to happen on the last day of December in 1999. All the Concordes are booked for a bunch of idiots who want to fly at supersonic speed east from the international date line to experience the event more than once. Every cruise ship in the world is booked solid. Forget about a hotel room in any place cool. Hell, you can't even hire a llama in Machu Picchu. What people are going to be doing on New Year's Eve 1999 is now a frequent topic of conversation at dinner parties and get-togethers. As for me, I'm going to wait until the very last moment and see what happens. If I know anything about parties, I know that the best ones are pretty spontaneous (with the exception of Don Henley's wedding, which so far gets my vote as the party of the century).

That is what I liked about the idea of going to Quepos on the spur of the moment. We have no idea what to expect, but we know it will be more interesting than the celebration in the hotel restaurant. We are going to celebrate this New Year's *pura vida* style. We make our Groundhog Day return to Quepos International on New Year's Eve morning. Kino has surfaced from the cloud of jet lag and joined the party. Everything is the same as we left it. The planes at the airport haven't moved, and the funky little terminal hasn't been replaced by a new one. Hal is there to take me fishing (thank God, minus Tex), and Jane and Mac's guide has returned with another cute college-aged Tico bellboy from Si Como No. They tell us Jim sent them down to help us. The girls seem happy with that plan. Kino passes on the fishing trip and wisely goes to the hotel, while Randall and I return to the pier to fish another day.

Jerry Lee Has Seen the Pacific

There is a classic old road story about Jerry Lee Lewis that sums up my last day of fishing in the year of my fiftieth birthday better than I can. It seems that Jerry Lee Lewis and his band were on tour, and the route to the next gig took them close to Niagara Falls. The band got all excited and nagged Jerry Lee to take them to see the falls. He consented. When the bus arrived in the parking area near the tourist attraction, Jerry Lee told them all to wait inside. He climbed out of the bus, crossed the road to the viewing area behind the iron rail, and stared down. A few moments later he came back to the bus, got on board, took his seat up front, and announced,

"Jerry Lee has seen Niagara Falls." Then he told the driver to proceed to their original destination.

My day on the water prompted the same kind of reaction. We had spent six and a half hours at five knots on a boat that looked like Fidel Castro's *Grandma*. We carved an endless procession of circles into the surface of the ocean without seeing a single species of fish, and after staring at miles of churning wake, we called it a day. Hell, we didn't even get our sandwiches, much less the hot sauce.

Upon our return to port, I climb the ladder to the top of the pier, sling my fly-rod case over my shoulder, cinch up the contents of my backpack, shake Hal's hand, walk to the end of the pier, and hail a cab for Si Como No. Jimmy B. has seen the Pacific.

We head up the hill toward the state park at Manuel Antonio, where we hoped we'll run into the hotel. I am ready for a swim and a drink. A few miles out of Quepos, the road starts to gain altitude and we are surrounded by the thick green coastal rain forest. The temperature drops, and a cool breeze moves up from the ocean through the hills. I stick my head out the cab window to soak it in. Birds sing and a few monkeys screech and holler from the tops of the trees. I guess they are getting ready for the party too. We wind through a corridor of shops and small hotels looking for our destination. Many of them have signs out front advertising Spanish-immersion centers. The very wise idea of teaching Spanish in a tropical setting has caught on as a business, and Costa Rica is full of these schools. This is not a bad place to be going to school. It sure beats the hell out of Hattiesburg, Mississippi. I make myself a New Year's resolution: 1997 will be the year that Jimmy learns Spanish. Little do I know that I would get a lasting lesson later that night.

We pull into the entrance to Si Como No. It is the biggest of the hotels we have seen. The office is at street level, the hotel itself follows the vertical relief of the hill behind it. I spot Jane and Kino at the desk talking to a tall middle-aged man with curly dark hair. Jane introduces me to Jim Damalas. I shake his hand and thank him for his hospitality, feeling an instant ease and familiarity. Jim takes care of business first. He tells us that we have our room at the hotel to crash in for the night, and then offers Jane and I a bedroom at his house across the street. We go to take a look.

Jim's house is one of the coolest tropical residences I have ever seen. It reminds me of Hugh Kelly's mountain hideout on Moorea where I wrote "One Particular Harbour." . . . It reminds me of the favorite fictional island home that appeared in my marlin dream. It is like a giant tree house, and it's very obvious that it had been a labor of love and time. There had been no master plan, architect, or contractor. Yet there couldn't be a more perfect structure in a more perfect surrounding. My only regret is that we are spending only one night here. We drop our gear and make camp. This is going to be a long and a late-starting night. Costa Rica certainly has that Spanish tradition of siestas and late nights. Dinner at the hotel will be served beginning at ten o'clock. This gives me time to have a snack, a boat drink, a swim, and a nap and then get up and have dinner, dance, and ring in the New Year. So like the monkeys in the trees, I've got myself on rain-forest time.

Jane, Mac, and Kino continue with Jim on a tour of the hotel, while Randall and I head for the pool. We follow a stream down the hill as it meanders through the quaint rooms and cottages of the hotel and finally cascades over a ledge into the pool. There is a natural diving platform next to the waterfall. No, it isn't the cliffs at Acapulco, but it is a point from which everyone can play Tarzan safely for a moment. I wait for a group of kids to make their collective leap and follow them into the pool. I surface and enjoy the cleansing moment, then swim toward the submerged bar stools, where I climb up and order a conch quesadilla and a very large margarita on the rocks—no umbrellas. Bob Marley comes from the speakers hanging over the bar. The bartenders, all Ticos, are young, friendly, and speak American, not English. It doesn't take me long to learn that they have all gone to school in the States and have come back home because they love their country.

Jim comes over and we chat while he fields a series of interruptions from employees and a mixture of Tico and American hotel guests. He possesses that magic ability to operate calmly in the middle of turmoil, and he switches from Spanish to English as easily as changing a channel on a remote control. It doesn't take long for expatriates to either connect or not connect. The basic premise of leaving all the bells and whistles of mainland America behind is an easy starting place. There are really only two types of expats. Those who embrace the local culture and those who fight it.

Blame It on Norman Paperman

The conversation goes quickly to how Jim wound up in Costa Rica and the hotel business. We both had entertained the absolutely insane idea of running a hotel in a Third World country, following the lead of the legendary Herman Wouk character Norman Paperman. My path to being a part-owner of a Caribbean hotel was a comedy of errors, starting with Wouk's classic tale *Don't Stop the Carnival*. I had given up a few years back, but Jim had persevered. For that alone, I have tremendous respect for him. Before I even get a chance to ask him if he's ever read the book, he is already asking me how my plans to produce a musical based on *Carnival* are going. Like just about any off-islanders I have ever run into who had been in the hotel business in the Caribbean, Jim treated *Don't Stop the Carnival* like a tropical version of the Bible.

Jim had been an art director in the film business in Southern California. We soon discovered a number of mutual friends from the old days in L.A. During the midseventies, he had been a regular at the infamous Pear Garden on La Cienega, a very in watering hole for record-company execs on expense accounts, film types, rock 'n' rollers who wanted to act, and actors who wanted to be rock stars. This was way back when artists actually used to like to hang out with people who worked for the record companies and get a free meal as well. It was quite a time and quite a mix. Jim had lasted about as long as he could in the world of Hollywood, but it finally drove him south. He wound up in Costa Rica twenty years ago, camping out in the nearby rain forest that would eventually become Manuel Antonio State Park. He was surfing, partying, and running away—a familiar scenario. Jim had gone to Quepos. I had gone to Key West. We had only been a few degrees of latitude apart. Now he is the proprietor of a thriving world-class hotel only a mile and half from where he had pitched a tent in the rain forest on his first visit. For a moment, I look at him and think that it could have been me, if fate and Corb Donohue hadn't sent me to New York to play Max's Kansas City.

God Save Me from the Lilliputians

I am awakened by the sound of heavy rain pounding on the tin roof. Wait, I don't have a tin roof on my house. What time is it? Where am I? Talk about a nap. After a couple of margaritas by the pool and a day in the sun, I feel kind of like Rip Van Winkle. Or is it Gulliver? God save me from the Lilliputians. They have me strapped to this unfamiliar bed. I can't move my arms. Actually, I slept so heavily on my arm that it's lost all feeling and seems to want to float away from my body. Now I know how Igor must have felt dragging a lifeless arm around. I spring up in the bed and start to beat my arm against the mattress. Oh, God, it's my fingering side. The right arm and fingers are for strumming, not a big loss, but the left arm needs to move, if I am to continue to be a troubadour. While I am in the throes of this fit, Jane walks in dressed to kill. I tell her my problem. She tells me we are late for dinner. Dinner, my God, I have no sense on earth of what time it is. I look at my watch. It reads nine forty-five. I'm thinking about breakfast. What's all this talk about dinner? It starts to make sense to me. Costa Rica, New Year's Eve. It's all coming back now.

Boogie Nights

It isn't until about halfway through dinner that I clear the cobwebs from my mind, the Lilliputians from my arm, and get enough oxygen to my brain to get me back on the current time line. The restaurant at Si Como No is hopping. I opt for a shot of tequila and a glass of champagne to jump-start myself for the big boogie night ahead, and I am soon right in there again with the rest of the revelers at the table. After dinner we commandeer a van from a line of taxis in front of the hotel and head for town, with a local character called Merlin and his girlfriend as our guides. Merlin has a mental list of places to go and tells us that the parties will carry on until dawn. Dawn coming from this way around is something I have not seen in a while. First stop is a big beach club called La Marina or something like that. It is still raining when we arrive, and our cabdriver is trying to do us the courtesy of getting us to the entrance dry. The only problem is that if we stay in the van, it will be dawn before we arrive. So we bolt and run through the rain toward the entrance, and Merlin deals with the doorman. Soon we are inside.

This is a Tico evening. The only gringos I see in the crowd are a few surfers, obviously underdressed for the occasion. The locals, on the other hand, are dressed to kill. There are about three or four hundred people packed onto a concrete dance floor in front of a large bandstand where a ten-piece Tico orchestra blasts away. The sound is basic Central American salsa, with lots of horns and percussion, and the beat is molded for the merengue. The songs are as familiar to the crowd as my songs would be to Parrotheads, and the locals sing along on the chorus with the band's tall lead singer, who prances around like Mick Jagger, waving a long red scarf around his head. There is no inoculation, and the infection is immediate. We all break out dancing, blending into the mass of gyrating humanity, getting into the merengue.

No Movement Below the Belt

Growing up a Southern Catholic white boy, I wasn't introduced to movement below the belt until I got to New Orleans, and movement below the waist is what the merengue is all about. But my mother did send my sister and me to ballroom-dance classes, for which I am extremely grateful to this day. I loved the tango and the cha-cha, but the jitterbug was our thing. Hell, Laurie and I won the jitterbug contest at the Bit and Spur Riding Club dances for weekends on end. Thinking back on just where in the hell I developed my ability to perform and be comfortable onstage, I have to say that it started at the Bit and Spur. I passed on my limited talent as a hoofer to Savannah, and she became my jitterbug partner. Jane is from South Carolina and is firmly entrenched in the Piedmont tradition of the shag, which I cannot do. The shag and the jitterbug do not mix. They're the oil and water of the dance world, so we just stick to slow dancing with a little merengue thrown in.

Happy Asshole

Tonight I see some very cool couples doing the merengue. The best pairs press their bodies close together and move as one, occupying a tiny area of the dance floor. It is the closest thing to sex with your clothes on. It's moving without moving. In the Caribbean it is called "renting a tile." The band plays on, and we dance the night away. An hour later they finally take a break. Kino has scouted the whole place, and comes back with news that there is a patio area with a large pool and tables overlooking the ocean, and a mariachi band is playing there. Boy, are we in the right mood for mariachi music. We head toward the party within the party. The crowd is making the most of the night, and there is a great feeling in the air. Costa Rica is a much more Castillian culture than its neighbors, Nicaragua and Guatemala. The patio reminds me more of the Rambla in Barcelona or the Born in Mallorca.

We luckily find a table in the corner and pitch camp. We order shots of the volatile Tico cane whiskey, and I start to speak a little Spanish with the band and fellow revelers. For the moment, we have the band's attention, and they surround our table and play our requests as we attempt to sing along. We are feeling the *pura vida*. The band suddenly stops in mid-song, as if someone pulled the plug, and then I realize it is time. The countdown comes from the giant P.A. system out on the dance floor. We all hug and kiss, and I added merengue lessons to my list of New Year's resolutions. *"Feliz Año Nuevo, feliz Año Nuevo,"* the crowd roars. The mariachi band breaks into "La Cucaracha," and champagne flows. From the far corner of the patio, bottle rockets whiz out over the ocean and die their quick death like falling stars.

"Feliz annus!" I repeat with the crowd, over and over. The next thing I know, I am locked arm in arm with Merlin and a

string of revelers who have joined this impromptu chorus line and start to move to the music. The Rockettes we aren't but there are no critics in the house. *"Feliz annus!"* I shout at the top of my lungs. With the moves of a career diplomat, Merlin slides in next to me in the chorus line. He is dancing and singing along with the crowd, and when he sees the perfect moment, he subtly whispers in my ear, "Jimmy, it's *año, feliz Año Neuvo.* You are wishing them all happy asshole."

My asshole puckers and my mind screams, "You idiot!" But I am a semiprofessional entertainer, and I know how to hide my feelings. Dancing on, I make the vocabulary correction without missing a beat, but I can promise you that there are two words that I will never again get confused in the Spanish language for as long as I live.

No Plane on Sunday

No plane on Sunday
Maybe be one come Monday
Just a hopeless situation
Make the best of it's all you can do
　　　　— "No Plane on Sunday"

They're Playing My Favorite Songline

 I do not stay up until dawn. There is enough party going on at La Marina to last me until all my fun tickets have been punched, which was around three-fifteen. The next morning we have breakfast with Jim, and then he drives us to the airport, where we exchange numbers and E-mail addresses. Quepos is now another place, and Jim Damalas another name to add to my songline. We have made contact with fellow travelers out on the songlines, those imaginary threads that stitch together the lives of the wanderers. I might return to Quepos next year and study Spanish, or it could be ten years before I see Quepos International again, but it won't really matter, for time on the songline just picks up wherever it left off.

We arrive back at the hotel and spend New Year's Day on the beach with the kids. From Angela's and Aileen's reports it seems that they all had a very good time bringing in the new year at the hotel party.

I can't believe that we have been a week in Costa Rica and it's time to start packing again. We are about to split up for a while. The little kids are heading north toward home with Randall. The big kids are continuing south toward the equator. We will meet up with them again if and when we emerge from the

Amazon jungle. In the words of George Clinton, "I got ants in my pants, and I feel like I want to dance." It is terrible that I'm like this. Ten days ago I was desperately in love with the idea of Costa Rica, and now I feel I have been here too long. That damn gypsy soul strikes again, but hey, just think, if wandering weren't part of the human spirit, the apes would have just stayed in the trees in Africa, and Columbus would have taken a look at the Bahamas and headed back to Spain. Captain Cook would have stopped at Madeira, and I would never have left Mobile Bay.

The next morning, we check out and head for the airport at Tambor. We are bound for San José, where the kids will head home and we will spend the night. Kino and the girls will explore the cultural and gastronomic offerings of the capital city, while I will curl up in a suite at the Holiday Inn to watch the Florida–Florida State football game for the national championship on satellite TV.

Sitting in Limbo

The flying station wagon will drop the kids off in Florida, return to pick us up in San José, then head south to Cartagena, Colombia. The Albatross will be flown east to Trinidad, where she will wait in limbo, like a deposed dictator looking for a country that would tolerate him, until our return north from Brazil. My dreams of flying through Central and South America at treetop level have been held hostage. I never planned to take the *Hemisphere Dancer* to Colombia, for the most obvious reasons. In the number-one cocaine-producing-and-exporting country in the world, a plane like the Albatross would be looked upon as a prize. She wouldn't stand a snowball's chance in hell of being left alone by one of a dozen cocaine cartels, who would be licking their chops at the sight of her enormous fuselage and load capacity. I did not want to get a phone call from the U.S. Embassy telling me my plane had been located, crashed on a remote airfield somewhere in the Turks and Caicos Islands. But now our request to operate her on and off the Amazon has been turned down by the authorities in Manaus. The times have changed. In a land where these planes had once been welcomed like chariots of the gods, they are now looked upon as the property of people up to no good. The view is that they can only be hauling dope or guns, not the dreams of a flier who is hopelessly romantic.

Back to Basics

We are all assembled at the Tambor airport once again, awaiting the arrival of the plane that will take us back to San José. Javier and the staff are standing around waiting for the inevitable time to say *adios*. This is not going to be an easy good-bye. Oh, God, how I hate good-byes. I can feel that there are tears waiting to be shed, and I know some of them are mine, but as Saint-Expuéry said, "Tears are a kind of wealth."

Our somber departure is suddenly interrupted by a call on the two-way radio from the office at the hotel. Javier tells me there is a problem with the plane. It hasn't left San José yet. According to Paul Simon's song, there might be lasers in the jungle somewhere, but that technology hasn't made it to Tambor. There are no cell phones in the jungle—yet. I might be a slave to my toys, but I have never forgotten how to survive without them. In this case, the memory of many nights standing in line outside a funky phone-company office on a remote island trying to contact family, friends, or the engine-parts guy in Miami have not been erased from the survival menu in my brain. It is almost an hour back to the hotel, and the two-way radios present more problems than they solve in relaying messages. I spot a phone line going to the guard shack across the parking lot. God knows what the lone sentry occupying this building is guarding against. He is asleep in his chair when Javier and I reach the shack. Awaking from his siesta in a foul mood, he wants nothing to do with us. Javier manages to convince him that we are dealing with an emergency. The guard watches us cautiously through one eye for a few minutes, but by the time I get San José on the line, he is back to guarding his dreams.

I reach Alex and he starts to explain that the plane that is supposed to pick us up has some kind of mechanical problem. I interrupt his explanation and ask if the Albatross still has permission to land in the water. He says he'll check and call right back. "Do not hang up that phone!" I shout. The guard is getting restless and keeps checking his watch while I wait with the receiver in my hand. Finally Alex comes back on and says we still have permission. "Then come and get us," I say. "We'll meet you in the harbor." I don't know who sounds happier about the fact that we'll finally be getting the *Hemisphere Dancer* wet. By God, the old girl is going to get to make one splash in Costa Rica.

Freed Bird

The Albatross has been freed to do what she was built to do—water rescue. Granted, we have not been shot down in combat, nor are any of us dying of exposure, but at this moment, the only way to get us all back on course is to pluck us from the sea. Miracles do happen. We have turned what had the potential of being a Third World transportation disaster into a triumph. I put our army of bellboys to the task, and we race to the town dock, hoping to get there in time to see the *Hemisphere Dancer* do her thing.

The dock is similar to the one in Quepos. It sits a good twenty feet above the surface of the water to allow for the tidal fluctuation. This morning there is little activity there. A few fishing boats are huddled up near the rusty ladder at the end of the dock, and business of some sort is being transacted. The men in the boat glance up briefly at our arrival. Obviously they are not used to seeing gringos on the commercial dock. They go back to their fish business in silence.

I hear the identifiable rumble of those big old radial engines before I ever spot the plane. It is music to my ears. She comes in from the northeast, makes a low pass over the bay, circles around, and lands into the wind. This gets the fishermen's attention, and they stop counting fish and watch the air show. I view the landing and, as always, marvel at the transformation of a twelve-ton piece of aluminum from a flying machine to a boat. When you are actually landing or taking off, you're too damn busy to appreciate the beauty of that basic maneuver. The Albatross is a handful to fly, and I can assure you, you are not thinking aesthetically when you bring in takeoff power. The real beauty of this old bird can only be seen from a dock, a boat, or a beach, and she is already having that effect on the few people who are in the right place at the right time to witness her landing.

Cameron and I arrived at the dock with the first wave of luggage, and I secured a boat to take us out to the plane. Now I try to point out to him the plane on the water, which is usually exciting to him, but at this moment he is more interested in watching a young local boy clean a bloody *bonito* at the end of the dock. The *Hemisphere Dancer* skims across the water and comes off the step in a cloud of spray as she bangs into a few swells that curl around the headland to the east. She makes a slow 180-degree turn and idles toward the beach. I can't resist the Kodak moment and pillage through the piles of bags on the dock for my camera.

I scan the shoreline with my binoculars. It is humming with activity and excitement at the arrival of the seaplane. The road leading down to the beach is already lined with cars stopping to take a look. In a matter of moments the sleepy little harbor town has come alive. I sit on my big pile of luggage and feel

goose pimples run up and down my arm. This is the way of
the Caribbean way back when. If there ever was a time and
place where the beauty of nature and the accomplishments of
aeronautical engineering come together, it is the occasion of a
flying boat arriving on a tropical shore. As I watch the plane, I
find myself thinking like a pilot. I know what Pete and Alex
are doing as they ease her carefully toward the shore. They are
setting up, planning their departure while at the same time
preparing to anchor. Water landings carry with them a different box of tools, and once you get down, you have to be able to
get back up. I see a head pop out of the forward hatch and
lower the anchor over the side. There is a sudden increase in
engine noise as they back down on the anchor to secure the
plane and then cut the throttles. From across the bay on the
beach, I hear the faint sound of applause.

Oh, No, Not Again

"Dad, look at dat boat," Cameron says from behind me. I am
still watching the plane and don't really respond, as there are
numerous small boats in the harbor. "Dad, look at dat big
boat," he says again. I look back at Cameron and follow his little finger to where he is pointing.

"Oh, shit," I blurt out.

"Dad, you said a bad word." Boy, had I. I can't believe what
I am seeing. From around the point on the west side of the harbor, the sharp bow of a warship slices through the swells. It is
steaming at high speed right for the plane. Because of my recent experiences at dodging bullets in Jamaica, I can only assume the worst. I try to reach the plane on the handheld radio,
but they aren't answering. The gray gunboat pulls in behind
the plane, then eases up alongside it. I have no idea what's
going on, since the aft hatch is obscured from view in my
binoculars, but I can see several men standing on the boat. The
good news is that they aren't carrying guns. Then I see one of

them catch something thrown from the plane. We are safe. Several more items follow. T-shirts and tapes are as good as money in the Third World, and the crew has gone right to the old swag bag. The gunboat eases away from the plane and takes up a position just astern. I try the radio again, and this time I get Pete. "What's going on?" I ask.

"Oh, they came to make sure we're okay," Pete says. He speaks perfect Spanish, so I know nothing has been lost in interpretation.

"Who sent them?" I ask.

"The captain of the boat is the brother of the guy who cleared us into San José. They were patrolling the area and just wanted to make sure that nobody bothered us. They had also seen the shirts we had given to the guys at the airport."

"A little different from Jamaica," I added.

Much relieved that we are not about to face another SWAT-team attack, I head out to the plane with my son and a small boat full of luggage. I love it. Here we are, Cameron and I riding atop our possessions, being transferred out to our waiting plane, which had come to rescue us. I wish it was 1929 and we were heading south on the NYRBA, puddle-jumping the coastline of South America to Rio or departing the lagoon at Bora Bora, bound for New Caledonia. But as much as I want to, I can't push the time-machine button and go back there. I will take what I can get, a twenty-minute flight to San José. From my recent experiences in bouncing the *Hemisphere Dancer* around the customs offices and waters of the Caribbean, I know that I'll never know when I might get to do this again. Lust for the future, I reminded myself, but treasure the past.

Back in the Left Seat

By the time I get back to the dock, Kino is there supervising the loading of the remaining luggage. Javier and his troops stack the gear into the boat, and then Jane, Mac, and Delaney emerge from a shoreline cantina, eating carved mangoes on a stick as they stroll down the dock. In all the confusion, there isn't much time for good-byes. Javier's tears start first, and ours follow. We exchange big hugs and kisses and promise to write. Javier looks me in the eye and says, "More than that, you must promise to come back." I promise. We load everything, tie down our baggage, strap in the passengers, and fire up the engines.

I am back in the left seat, no longer a tourist, but a flying-boat captain. We run our pretaxi and takeoff checklists, and I move the plane farther back into the corner of the bay, watching the depth gauge. I want as much calm water in front of me as I can get for the takeoff. When it reads five feet, I apply differential power to the engines and she swings around into the wind. The breeze has picked up a bit and it is apparent that we will still hit a few swells at the end of the takeoff run. I do a final check of the flight controls and pause for a brief moment, wave to the people watching from the shore, and slide the side-vent window to the closed position. It is time to fly. I scan our takeoff path for anything unusual. We look good to go. "Follow me up with the power," I say to Pete. I push the throttles forward. The big engine roars to life, and the indicators on the manifold pressure gauges hold steady at takeoff power. Pete gives me a thumbs-up on the instruments at sixty knots. "Sixty knots of flaps," I say. A second or two later, the plane responds and I can feel her start to rise. Ahead of us are the swells. I adjust my attitude. As my favorite Florida folksinger, Fred Neil, so aptly put it, we are "skipping over the ocean like a stone." The deep *V* of the Albatross's nose takes the frontal assault of the swells, and then they are gone. We lift up, and I feel the hull escape the grasp of the water. I level out to gain some speed, then make a slow turn back to the beach and put her down on the deck. We whiz by the gunboat no more than five feet off the water. I glance briefly out the window to a

SECTION IX

Colombia

Send Lawyers, Guns, and Money

The Worst Club Sandwich in the World

Colombia? Are You Nuts?

Colombia was not our first choice for this trip. Do I have to tell you why? I didn't think so. Here is a brief description of Colombia, courtesy of your U.S. State Department.

The security situation in Colombia is volatile. Violence by criminal and guerrilla organizations is widespread. Travel by road outside the major cities is particularly dangerous because of guerrilla activities in the countryside. Guerrilla activity is increasing, particularly in rural areas as the rebels attempt to sabotage upcoming local, state and national elections. Violence by narcotraffickers, paramilitary groups and other criminal elements may also increase as elections take place in 1998. Some terrorist groups have targeted foreigners, multinational companies, and U.S. interests and the pattern is expected to continue in the future. Public facilities and modes of transportation may be targeted.

Kidnapping for ransom occurs throughout Colombia. Since 1980, the Embassy has learned of 85 U.S. citizen kidnap victims; of these, 11 were murdered, one died from malnutrition during captivity and the whereabouts of several others remains unknown. Americans of all age groups and occupations have been kidnapped, and kidnappings have occurred in all major regions of Colombia. Because of widespread guerrilla activity and U.S. policy that opposes concessions to terrorists, including payment of ransom in kidnapping cases, the U.S. government can provide only limited assistance in these cases.

In other words, you are on your own and you better watch your ass.

Colombia? Are we nuts? Well, yes, a little bit, but some things in life you just have to let happen. Here is a brief tale of how we chose to go to Colombia.

The world is a big place, and picking vacation spots can sometimes get confusing. There are so many things to see and so many things to do, and so little time to fit it all in. Then there is the reward system, in which I am a firm believer. Look for anything that is cause for celebration and compensation. Things like being a good dad, visiting your parents, going to social functions with your wife when you would really rather be watching a basketball game. Then there are the usual celebrations, like the end of the summer tour, the completion of a book or album, and, of course, your birthday—especially your fiftieth birthday.

This trip is one of my rewards. I might be able to give it to myself, but I needed Jane to plan it. This woman can organize. Hell, two years ago, she decided to remodel our house in Florida and build one in New York. Both places turned out incredible, and we stay married through the process. So when it came to trying to figure out a trip grand enough to be the reward for half a century of existence, I went to Jane for help.

We had always spoken of our desire to go to the Orient, and that was our first idea. Jane set about putting the trip together, but it wasn't long before I was already having second thoughts, and instead of just saying I didn't want to go, I whined a lot. "Too many miles and too many scheduled things to do." "It's really nothing more to me than a glorified tour."

Finally, she'd had enough. She lifted herself out of an array of maps, travel guides, and magazines, and said matter-of-factly, "Jimmy, where the hell do you really want to go?" My immediate response was "Machu Picchu." But because of the hostage situation at the Japanese Embassy in Lima, our visit to Peru was not to be.

Blame It on the Bong

For those of you who are not familiar with South America, Incas, or Peru, once upon a time, long before soccer was invented and long before Columbus brought the first cruise ship to the Caribbean, there was a vast empire. The Incas had the Andes to themselves until the Spanish came. In 1532 Francisco Pizarro arrived with 180 men, unopposed by the Incas, who assumed that the fair-skinned Spaniards were returning Incan demigods. Pizarro gained control of the Incan state by making Atahualpa a prisoner in his own house. Atahualpa offered the Spaniards a roomful of gold as his ransom. Even as an extensive store of gold ornaments was being amassed from all parts of the empire, Pizarro had Atahualpa strangled to death in 1533. After witnessing Castillian hospitality, it dawned on a faction of the leaders of the Incan empire to get the hell out of Dodge, and that is exactly what they did. The result was the citadel of Machu Picchu. It was never discovered by the Spanish conquerors and remained a mystery to the entire world for nearly five centuries until 1911, when an explorer named Hiram Bingham peeled back the green foliage of the mountain jungle to reveal the Lost City of the Incas. This was a mysterious place inhabited by a mysterious people who eventually melted away into the jungle, leaving behind the world's greatest hideout.

I was introduced to this fascinating enigma by a percussion player named Carlos, who I shared the bill with in my early days at the Bistro coffeehouse in Atlanta. I don't know why I was so taken with the Incas and their culture. It could have been Carlos's stories, or maybe the first-rate gold bud that he had access to. Carlos was not only a great drummer, he was also the ganja Amway man in Atlanta in those days. Many a night after work we would circle the bong in the musician's apartment above the club, suck away at the sweet smoke, and connect ourselves to "the children of the sun." I don't know if it was the bong or maybe the buzz-on belief and early-morning rationalizations that planted a seed in my mind that I was actually descended from the Incas. Talk about altered states. Whatever the origin, my sense of connection to the Incas was strong. Carlos faded from the scene, eventually heading off to New York and then back to Peru. I thought maybe I saw him briefly one night on the *NBC Nightly News* with Tom Brokaw, when a story about the Shining Path guerrillas was featured, but I couldn't be sure. What I did know was that my good pot connection was gone, but my tether to the Incas was still intact.

"See, that wasn't so hard," Jane replied to my answer. So we were going to Machu Picchu. I checked with the State Department and was told that the Shining Path movement was on the run in the mountains and their leaders were in jail. Peru was prospering under its dynamic president, Alberto Fujimori, and it was the perfect time to visit.

Three Days and Two Nights in a Pirate Town

A week before Christmas, I was making French toast for my kids and watching Katie Couric, when Ann Compton led the hour with a story I didn't want to hear. It seemed a group of uninvited guests, armed and dangerous members of the Tupac Amaru revolutionary movement, sporting guns and alibis, crashed a Christmas party at the Japanese Embassy in Lima. The attackers were holding hostage an international array of diplomats and people who had obviously made a bad choice of which party to attend that night. Over the next few days the story filled the airtime left vacant by the O.J. trial. As I watched the grainy nightscope images of the siege on TV, I knew that my dream of ascending to Machu Picchu was also being held hostage behind the embassy walls. Once things cooled down, we would try again, but I knew from experience that now would not be a good time to be traveling in Peru. Safety wasn't the issue. My God, it was probably the safest place on earth at the moment. The problem would be the security fascism that seems to crop up after these international terrorist incidents. In my years of touring and playing shows, I have had more problems with overreacting security people than with rowdy fans. The world stage is no different.

So, it was back to the map and travel books. What caught our eye were the photos of the walled city of Cartagena. Like Habana, it was a crossroads on the Spanish Main, a strategic port where provisions sent out from Spain were warehoused and treasure pillaged from the mines of the Americas was dispatched back to the coffers of the Spanish court. Cartagena had been a hot spot for a long time. Put all of that on a peninsula almost completely surrounded by the Caribbean Sea, and you had the makings for larceny. It didn't take long for the pirates to arrive. I liked what I was reading. My favorite pirate, Sir Francis Drake, looted Cartagena in 1586, and many more buccaneers followed. Three days and two nights in a pirate town on the way to the Amazon sounded fine with me—just another unscheduled pit stop on the road of life.

Latitudes and Altitudes

Date: 3 January 1997
Time: 1930Z
Latitude: 09°32'3" N
Longitude: 82°52'2" W

Location: Airway G440 at
ISEBA intersection
Altitude: 29,000'
Weather: Fair

Comments: I am in the left seat of the Citation II somewhere near the border of Costa Rica and Panama bound for the banana republics. The Albatross is on its way to Trinidad, and we'll see her in a week when we emerge from the jungle. The kids made it home with no problem. It is a perfectly clear day up here, and I can see the San Blas Islands off to the east. Soon we will be crossing the Panama Canal. I have a saphead vision of the Albatross crossing from ocean to ocean above the lakes and locks of the famous artery, but the whole canal is a no-fly zone, like the airspace around the White House and southern Iraq. That means they shoot first and ask questions later. I want no more to do with that. I am perfectly happy to be sitting up here with the autopilot on, monitoring the gauges and cruising along at 450 miles per hour. We will be in Cartagena in an hour and a half and having lunch in a café in the heart of the walled city. Since we are basically flying into a combat zone, Jim Powell has had the hot wires humming. We have alerted embassy security and the best handlers in Colombia of our impending arrival. Nothing to do but sit back, relax, and enjoy the view.

Date: 3 January 1997
Time: 2007Z
Latitude: 09°25'6" N
Longitude: 82°31'4" W

Location: Airway G440
over Enrique Adolfo Jim
Airport, Overhead
Colon
Altitude: 33,000'
Weather: Fair

Comments: Hugging the Caribbean shore of Panama below us are the San Blas Islands, formerly known by the more exotic name Archipelago de las Mulatas. If Dominica has a river for every day of the year, the Archipelago de las Mulatas has an island for every day and some say even more.

The islands begin near Colón, the Caribbean entrance to the Panama Canal, and stretch to the border of Colombia. They have a history of persistent and sullen unfriendliness in an effort to repel invasion by foreigners. Though the San Blas Islands have been unfortunately dragged somewhat into the modern world, the biggest protection they still enjoy is not the poison arrows of the blowguns that used to pierce the throats of white men who stayed after dark, but the jagged coral reefs that surround these tiny islands like a natural minefield and prevent the invasion of the cruise-ship armadas.

My attention is turned from the reef below to the radio in my panel, where I just overheard the air-traffic controller in Panama telling the pilot of a plane up ahead of us to expect a thirty-minute delay at Cartagena. I am very fond of pilot reports, information that comes over the radio from people in the area. Down here in the banana republics, pilot reports on weather and flying conditions are usually the only real sources of current information. One of the things you pick up after a while is to always listen to the radio. It's amazing what you learn from a voice. For example, the voice on the radio has no local accent. The guy sounds like he's from Kansas and very military in his calls and responses. I know, therefore, that he is a U.S. Air Force controller working from Howard Air Force Base in the Canal Zone.

I call him myself. News is obviously coming in from Cartagena, and at least no one has blown up a plane or the airport. The controller elaborates, telling me that a private plane experienced a nose-gear collapse and is still on the only runway at Cartagena. This is not good. Back in America, a disabled aircraft is not an everyday occurrence, but it happens often enough so that most airport crews respond quickly, trying not to delay landings and takeoffs for very long. But we are not in Kansas anymore.

Time: 2022Z   Location: Ponpo intersec-
Latitude: 09°16′1″ N   tion—approximately 183
Longitude: 78°11′9″ W   mi. E of Cartagena

Comments: We are directed to intercept the A574 airway at
the Ponpo intersection and report in at Bogal. We also get
more bad news. The controller in Panama informs us that the
plane is still on the runway in Cartagena and they are estimat-
ing an additional forty-minute delay. The airways are lighting
up with traffic. Seems everybody's going to Cartagena today.
Our estimated time of arrival is still just over an hour away.
The optimist in me says that should be plenty of time to take
care of the problem on the ground. My small but often accurate pessimistic nature reminds me that we are deep in a Latin
country. I flash back to that State Department bulletin and
start to hum the melody and mouth the words to Warren
Zevon's classic song: "Send lawyers, guns and money. The
shit has hit the fan."

Date: 3 January 1997   Location: Bogal intersec-
Time: 2029Z   tion—133 mi. SSW of
Latitude: 09°58′7″ N   Cartagena International
Longitude: 77°37′7″ W   Airport
                                  Altitude: 36,000′
                                  Weather: Fair

Comments: We start our descent and say good-bye to the
controller with the Midwestern accent as he turns us over to
Barranquilla control. The new voice on the other end is certainly not from Kansas. English is supposed to be the universal
language of air-traffic control, but my mind's eye sees this guy

in Barranquilla manning the radio with an English phrase-book. To make matters worse, he now has to talk to about six planes that are heading toward Cartagena and still can't land. Half are speaking English, half are speaking Spanish, and he sometimes gets confused as to which plane he's talking to. He is issuing instructions to hold at the Cartagena beacon. We are a half hour from the Colombian coast, and like everybody else up there, we start looking at our fuel situation to figure out how long we can really hold and where we can go if we can't land in Cartagena. I look at Randy and he looks at me. It's obvious that the guy in Barranquilla has little experience in stacking up airplanes to circle around a beacon on the ground. We start to study our options.

Date: 3 January 1997   Location: A574–Detok in-
Time: 2042Z   tersection
Latitude: 10°1'4" N   Altitude: 5,000'
Longitude: 76°3'0" W   Weather: Partly cloudy

Comments: A glimmer of hope. I hear a private plane in front of us talking to Barranquilla, and he is told that the plane on the runway at Cartagena is only about two thousand feet down the ten-thousand-foot runway. He explains to Barran-quilla that he needs only five thousand feet of runway to land. He can overfly the disabled plane by two thousand feet and still have enough room to land. I chime in right behind him and tell Barranquilla that we can land in three thousand feet. There is silence on the radio. Finally I hear "Victor Oscar Romeo"; we are both directed to the VOR (very high frequency omnidirec-tional radio) at Cartagena and cleared for a visual approach to Runway 36, where we are to land on the last five thousand feet. My God, we have found a way down. Yankee ingenuity is alive and well in the skies above Colombia.

Date: 3 January 1997   Location: Cartagena VOR
Time: 2047Z   Altitude: 5,000'
Latitude: 10°12'6" N   Weather: Partly cloudy
Longitude: 75°30'5" W

Comments: We turn at the VOR on the course that will take us through the miracle of instrument navigation right to Cartagena. The plane in front of us is down with room to spare. We are in a cloud layer at 5,000 feet but break out at 3,500 and can see the ground. We run the landing checklist. I am an hour from a rum drink.

Not so fast, gringo. Suddenly Barranquilla tells us to abort the landing. I am instructed to climb to 5,000 feet, return to the VOR, and continue holding. The airport will be closed for another hour. I don't believe them anymore. We have two hours' worth of fuel on board. When it comes down to it, the crew is responsible for the ship, not the guy with the phrase book in the tower in Barranquilla. Out of the corner of my left eye, I see a big plane pop out of a cloud. It is not close enough for me to have to maneuver to miss it, but the sight of it and the machine-gun chatter in Spanish and English on the radio tell me that it is time for us to be the captains of our own fate. These guys are not trained to handle this much traffic at once.

I look at Randy, and we don't even have to say a word. He calls Barranquilla and cancels our instrument flight rules (IFR) flight plan, and we get off of this potentially dangerous merry-go-round. I aim for the coast. I can see the city below and the airport. I can also see the plane on the runway. If I wanted to, from my present altitude, I could slip down, tuck in, and land in about a minute. There are no planes going into Cartagena, so there would be no traffic. If this were the Bahamas, I wouldn't think twice. I would have landed and, as they say, "beg forgiveness, not permission." But we are strangers in a strange airspace where guns still outnumber cell phones, and my instincts tell me to play by their rules. We set a course for Barranquilla fifty miles east. I don't even attempt to ask the controller to relay a message to the ground handler who is meeting us in Cartagena. I just hope to God the people in Barranquilla will have the foresight to prepare for the diverted traffic coming their way. Nothing like landing a private jet full of people wearing sundresses, shorts, and T-shirts at an international airport in the middle of the largest cocaine-exporting area in the world. I rub my Saint Christopher medal and start down again.

Welcome to Hell

Date: 3 January 1997　　　　Location: Ernesto Cortissoz
Time: 2107Z　　　　　　　　　International Airport—
Latitude: 10°53'6" N　　　　　Barranquilla, Colombia
Longitude: 74°47'0" W　　　　Elevation: 94'
　　　　　　　　　　　　　　Weather: Partly cloudy

Comments: Tim Drummond, one of the many ex–Coral Reefers, is one of the most traveled road-dog musicians I've ever met, and he has the tattoos and stories to prove it. He's been in bands with everyone from Conway Twitty to James Brown to Crosby, Stills, Nash and Young. His years on the road have earned him a treasury of one-liners and expressions based on his experiences with the inevitable struggles that road life presents. When on occasion we would find ourselves in some fleabag hotel, or playing a "chicken-wire" gig,* Drumbo, as we called Tim, would just scan the situation, roll his eyes, smile, and say, "Welcome to hell, boys."

---

* A show played in a place where fights among the crowd are so likely that the bandstand is enclosed in chicken wire to keep the flying beer bottles from hitting the people onstage.

Tim's words are what come to mind when I hear the squeak of the Citation's tires on the runway at Barranquilla International Airport. From the air, it just looks like another long runway. The land around it is flat and pocked with tin roofs and small houses with large satellite dishes aimed skyward. A modern terminal sits off to the right of the runway, with several commercial airliners parked at the gates, but there is definitely something wrong with this picture. As I taxi the plane closer and we follow instructions to parking from the ground controller, I notice a squad of soldiers, all shouldering machine guns, surrounding an American Airlines 727 parked at the gate. I don't know if they are protecting it or attacking it. I have a sudden impulse to apply full power and take off from the taxiway to head back to the land of *pura vida,* but I follow the instructions from the tower. I am quick to point out in my two-way transmissions to ground control that we have been forced to land here because of the situation in Cartagena. More soldiers by the fire trucks. This is weird.

I park near a fence that separates the taxiway from the taxi stand. There is not a soul around. I figure that the soldiers are all hiding, waiting for a signal before they surround the plane. We get out and look around. Still nobody approaches the plane. Suddenly, I hear the roar of an engine. The trap has been sprung. They must be arriving in a convoy of troop transports like the Germans did to Steve McQueen in *The Great Escape.*

I have never in my life been happier to see a fuel truck. The men who climb down hold fuel nozzles, not automatic weapons. Even in this strange place, the guy who sells the fuel is the first one to the plane. Kino asks the fuel-truck operator for directions to customs. Kino and I go in and leave Randy and the girls at the plane. About halfway to the door, a lone soldier emerges and heads toward us. Like everyone else I have seen so far in Colombia, he is not smiling and wears mirrored sunglasses and a dark green, perfectly pressed uniform with a big gun hanging from his shoulder. Kino again explains our situation. The soldier seems unconcerned, pointing us to the door and saying something about civil aviation. Little did I know that the pandemonium that lay behind that door would severely test my fascination with the tropics. "Welcome to hell," indeed.

Time: 2120Z

Comments: Kino explains the problem for the third time to a fat man in civilian clothes sitting behind a desk watching soap operas. We ask to use the phone to contact our handler in Cartagena. Permission denied, but we are told to go to the airport business office. We head back to the plane to let everyone know what we're doing, and to make sure the plane and my wife and pilots are actually still there. They are. "If we're not back in an hour, call the U.S. Embassy in Bogotá," I shout back, and we set out in search of the airport business office.

Time: 2140Z

Comments: At the business office, we run into two of the meanest-looking, most bored civil servants I have ever seen. They won't even discuss letting us use the phone. We realize that we are there to pay our landing fees, not to get any help in getting out of town. Or even to let one of the hundreds of people walking around the airport with guns and badges know that we are *in* fucking town. It takes almost a half hour for them to prepare our receipt. I am tempted to reach through the tiny window and seize this asshole by the tie, but that would surely mean instant death by firing squad. We just wait for the receipt.

Time: 2240Z

Comments: We are now in the meteorological office, where they actually know about the runway in Cartagena being closed, but that's about it. Use the phone? No way. They do tell us there is one in the terminal but that we need to file a flight plan first. I do that, while Kino learns from another pilot who enters the office that there are now six Cartagena-bound planes that have been diverted to Barranquilla. I go back to the fence to assure our crew that we have not been captured or sold into slavery. My wife is not happy. "To hell with this," she says, and leads a procession toward door number one, the civil aviation office, which is at least air-conditioned.

Beg Forgiveness, Not Permission

Time: 2300Z

Comments: Kino and I go off to the main terminal to find the telephone office. He asks me if we should really be wandering around like this. We still haven't cleared customs or immigration. Tim Drummond is not the only old road dog with a pocket full of well-worn expressions. My favorite one for the situation we are in now is "Beg forgiveness, not permission."

We eventually wind up at the main entrance to the airport terminal. Ahead of us is a security rampart that resembles the now defunct Checkpoint Charlie at the Berlin Wall, complete with German shepherds and a nest of cops and gun-toting soldiers. It finally hits me what Kino is talking about. We are running around in an international airport in a country that has more kidnappings, shootings, and explosions than in all Bruce Willis's films combined, and nobody is asking questions. I am dressed in a T-shirt, shorts, and deck shoes, wearing pilot sunglasses, a Nantucket Nectar baseball cap, and carrying a green backpack, and I have yet to see another gringo in the airport. Now what in the hell do I look like to the security guards? Correct, the answer is—a gringo dope dealer. Line 'em up and shoot 'em on the spot. I panic. I tell Kino to make the call while I wait outside.

I pace up and down the sidewalk, sweating like a pig, wondering what in the hell I'm doing in this place. This is the kind of shit that happens to Hunter—my old friend and sometime fellow traveler Dr. Hunter S. Thompson—not to Jimmy Buffett. I walk over to the end of the building, and I can see the plane. I don't wait long. I now feel as if I'm sticking out like a sore thumb and everyone who passes me must be after my money or my life. I conclude that I'm safer inside the building. I get up my courage to run the gauntlet, hoping that if I get stopped, I can explain my predicament, or just fall to the ground weeping and praying that they don't shoot. I take a deep breath and try to look casual. The giant pit stains under my arms nullify that attempted disguise. Beg forgiveness, not permission. Keep breathing, and smile, asshole, smile. I am in. No sirens. No barking dogs. Boy, am I having fun now.

Time: 2314Z

Comments: I find Kino at the *telecommunicado* office. He's waiting in a long line behind twenty people. There are only four phone booths. There is an operator behind a desk shouting out names and taking money. Oh, shit, we have no Colombian money. I run back out to the terminal and find the change booth. In survival Spanish, I am able to change my money. When I return, Kino is waving desperately. He is at the front of the line, and the crowd behind him is getting angry because he won't go into the booth. We make the call to Bogotá to a number that Jim Powell has given us. It's the main office of the handler. I pick up a little of the conversation and decipher the fact that whoever Kino is talking to is in Bogotá, not Cartagena. The good news is that the office in Bogotá has actually heard of us. They tell us the handler is coming phone number. We try the cell number and get a message in Spanish that basically says we cannot call cell numbers from the phone we are using. FFFFFFUUUUUUUCCCCCCCCKKKKKKK!!!!!!!!!

Time: 2332Z

Comments: We go back to the weather office, for now that
we have paid our landing fee, we will be allowed to file a
flight plan to leave. If that fucking airport in Cartagena doesn't
open soon, we are leaving. Caracas is looking awfully good to
me right now. We are now looked upon as regulars at the
weather office, and everyone says hello when we pile back
through the door. I hear from another pilot that Cartagena still
hasn't opened up. My God, there is a message for me at the
weather office. It's from our handler. We are to go to the civil
aviation office and call him.

Time: 2350Z

Comments: Back to square one, where Jane, Mac, and the
pilots are sitting reading books and munching on snacks from
the plane. I haven't eaten since we left San José, what seems
now like days ago, and I am starving. I devour a pack of
peanut-butter crackers while Randy reports that a guy wearing a badge told him that the authorities are aware of our presence. I have no idea what that means. Cartagena still hasn't
opened up. I don't even want to contemplate the thought of
spending the night here.

Time: 2359Z

Comments: We are just getting adjusted to the *mañana* element of life in the civil aviation office when the door flies open
and the angel of our salvation enters the building. Her name is
Barbarella. I am not kidding. It says so on one of the dozen or
so photo ID's that hang from lanyards around her neck and
rest on her artificial cleavage. The Wonder Bra has made it to
Barranquilla. Barbarella is a cross between Jane Fonda and
Janet Jackson, with a little Jodie Foster attitude thrown in. She
is about five-foot-three, dressed in a lime-green see-through
blouse and a white miniskirt that barely covers her ass. She
expertly balances like a high-wire artist atop a pair of at least

eight-inch stiletto heels that click like tap shoes when she moves across the floor. There is no doubt that she has the run of the place. The phone and a two-way radio stuffed in her shoulder bag are going off simultaneously. She rattles something to the unintelligible voice coming from her radio and then tells us to follow her. I don't know who she is, but I get in line.

We follow almost single-file behind Barbarella as she sways through the corridors and back rooms of the airport, talking to everyone we pass. She is obviously taken with Kino and his God-saving Spanish. We finally emerge back into the main terminal, which for Kino and me is old familiar territory by now. Barbarella points us toward the entrance to the airport restaurant, tells us to wait there, and that the agent from Cartagena will be here soon. We all thank her and wave goodbye. She is back on the radio shouting orders as she disappears around the corner with the echo of the stiletto heels trailing off behind her.

Time: 0010Z

Comments: The restaurant is open to the hot afternoon sun, and the aroma of jet exhaust lingers in the sticky air. We are all starving. The menu contains some odd-sounding items. We try to stay simple. Chicken sandwich? *No tiene.* Turkey sandwich? *No tiene.* Finally I see a recognizable item. Club sandwich? *Sí. Siete club sandwich y agua mineral y quatros Coca-Colas.* Not only are we happy to actually be ordering food, so are the seven jillion flies that are circling our table. We move to a booth by the window, and so do the flies. They are not stupid. These just might be reincarnated Nazis, and they are mean and hungry. They remind me of the flies in Australia. Those bastards had no shame. They would fly right up your nostrils. These guys are just waiting. Thirty minutes later, the food arrives, or whatever it is the waitress puts down on the table in front of us. It is not like any club sandwich I have ever seen. The bread is crumbly and stale and there seems to be some kind of egg thing in there, with some form of meat that resembles the Spam-like product that used to appear on my high school–cafeteria lunch tray. We used to call it mystery meat. It definitely ain't turkey or ham. If I am going to sample it, I have to hurry, for the flies have picked up the scent. I take a bite. Ladies and gentlemen, let me tell you, it was the worst club sandwich in the world. We collectively look at each other and then at the sandwiches and start to laugh. Small chuckles at first, which quickly turn into belly laughs. As the Joni Mitchell song says, "Laughing and crying, you know it's the same release." We move the sandwiches to another table in hopes that the flies will follow, and they do. Then came the jokes of the day's experiences, and we're laughing uncontrollably.

Time: 0040Z

Comments: We are watching the air bombardment and betting on individual flies when a man walks up to us and says, "Hi, I'm Dario." We have been rescued. Dario is the agent from Cartagena. He is tall and thin and dressed in the uniform of the tropics, a white guayabera shirt. He speaks perfect English and looks like he has dealt with this airport before. He tells us to take our time and finish our lunch. We collectively answer, "We have," and break out laughing. Dario laughs along with us, but I don't think he gets the joke. What he tells us brings a cheer from our small crowd: Cartagena has just opened up and we will be on our way shortly. He tells us he'll be right back. Halfway to the door, he turns around and says, "Oh, yes, and whatever you do, under no circumstances do you leave this restaurant." How close had Kino and I come to getting shot or kidnapped? The stern warning in Dario's voice more than hinted at danger in the air, and he moves and talks with a sense of urgency, as if he wants to get us the hell out of Barranquilla as soon as he can.

Time: 0100Z

Comments: True to his word, Dario returns in a few minutes and herds us off back to the weather office. Of course, the original flight plan we had filled out earlier is now expired and we have to do another one. No problem, we're damn near locals now.

Time: 0130Z

Comments: We file through the gate back to the plane that afternoon feeling like we are getting out of prison. We thank everyone and pay off the soldier who has "watched" the plane during this whole ordeal. He makes a lame inspection of the plane, looks at our passports, and we give him twenty bucks for his time. He looks at it and then demands more. At this point, what's another twenty bucks?

Time: 0145Z

Comments: We are out of here. Randy calls out the engine-start checklist, and we fire her up, waiting for permission to taxi, when Dario comes back out to the plane accompanied by a not-so-happy-looking bureaucrat. I open the small window in the cockpit, and through it he screams to me above the noise of the engine that we need to clear customs. Uh-oh, they got us. I shut down, and we all climb out and are escorted to the customs office, where another group of grim-faced men smoking cigarettes waits for us. They are all sitting around and watching the Spanish version of the Sally Jessy Raphael show, which is playing on a small TV set situated on top of cargo beneath a giant poster of the Madonna. No, not the one that played Evita, the real one, the mother of God. This could be bad.

Time: 0155Z

Comments: All I can say is that it could have been worse. There were lots of questions about why we didn't do this when we first arrived, now more than five hours ago. I am thinking that we could probably have driven the Pan American Highway from San José to Cartagena in less time. Finally, we catch a break, and we are only detained there for about ten minutes. We say good-bye to Dario, and I get all of his numbers. You never know when they might come in handy. I tell him if he ever gets to Key West, he can have a cheeseburger and margarita on me. We climb back into the plane, and as the sun sets over the western Caribbean, we make our second takeoff of the day bound for Cartagena.

Time: 0230Z

Comments: I don't know if it was because Barranquilla was so bleak or if my instincts about Cartagena moving to its own rhythms are true, but the mood of the day changes instantly upon our arrival at the airport. We have already cleared customs, so that was out of the way. The handler at the airport whizzes us and our baggage to waiting cabs, and we are on our way to town.

Time: 0250Z

Comments: Out of the twilight, a glow appears ahead of us. The cabdriver is delivering his well-rehearsed cabdriver version of the history of the West Indies, but I am not listening. I am looking. We turn onto Avenida Santander, and there we are, cruising down the boulevard in traffic between the Caribbean Sea and the ancient walled city of Cartagena. I have seen my share of Spanish colonial architecture in San Juan and St. Augustine, but nothing compares to my first look at Cartagena. I tune back into the cabdriver when his speech comes to current conditions. He tells us that today Cartagena is full of Colombians who come here because they can walk the streets in safety. "Here, people make love, not crime." The approaching darkness hides most of the city from us, but the unmistakable silhouettes of cannons run out through tiny slits atop the towering ramparts speak of another time. And besides, this is not some theme-park interpretation of history made out of Bondo and chicken wire. This is the real thing.

The Hour of Mysterious Flourishing

Déjà, déjà, déjà vu
Believe it and it will come true
Veja, veja, veja du
What works for me might work for you
—"OFF TO SEE THE LIZARD"

Spanish Time

I had first run into the idea of partying all night and sleeping all day when I became a nightclub singer on Bourbon Street in my misspent youth. So on my first trip to Spain, when I discovered an entire country that shared this unconventional nocturnal lifestyle, I just fell happily and easily into the tempo of Spanish time. Not only did Spanish time make it to the New World with Columbus, it flourished like bacteria in a petri dish in the tropical latitudes of Central and South America. It didn't take long for the conquistadors to tire of tromping around in the heat wearing chain plate, armor, and steel helmets, battling Indians, bugs, snakes, and disease until they were all looking for the shade of a palm tree where they could get a little rest. In their insatiable appetite for gold and glory, fostered by the Hapsburg king, Charles V, the Spanish spread their empire through the Caribbean and down the coast of South America toward the bottom of the world. Towns and even cities sprang up along the trade routes. It was called the Spanish Main, and at the heart of that infamous string of settlements at the southern edge of the Caribbean Sea on the northern edge of the South American continent, the city of Cartagena came into being in 1533.

When we finally pass under the ramparts at Baluarte do San Francisco Javier, I feel like I'm entering another era. There is electricity in this place. I can feel it. It's as if the walls of this old city keep its vibrant lifestyle contained and protected from the mundane blue meanies on the outside. If the impact of history were measured on a Richter scale, Cartagena would be off the charts.

From its origins in 1533, Cartagena was a supposedly well-protected garrison in the heart of the Spanish Main where few intruders dared to tread. That was until 1576, when Sir Francis Drake, the single most influential sailor of his time, snuck up the peninsula of Boca Grande, took Cartagena, and held it for ransom. Even to this day there are hard feelings among the locals for old El Draqui, as he was scornfully referred to by the Spanish. He was a thorn in the side of Spain for nearly fifty years, plundering and burning the outposts along the Spanish Main, literally at will. It is said that when Drake finally died, King Philip II uttered these words: "This should cure my sickness."

After Drake's attack on Cartagena, work was begun on the wall. It took two hundred years to construct, and worked pretty well in keeping most of the thieves and predators at bay. Most of it remains intact today: Seven miles in length and in some places sixty feet thick, it surrounds a hundred square blocks. As English historian Arnold Toynbee said when seeing the completed fortifications, "South America does not speak English because of this."

The physical protection the wall offered also molded the city into a truly unique place. For lack of a better term, I knew I was in a pirate town. In Key West, the pirates were so thick at the beginning of the nineteenth century that the U.S. Navy sent a full-fledged expedition there to drive them out. The pirates fled, but the Navy is still there. Yes, I know a little about pirate towns. "When in Rome" seems to apply, and after our horrifying day, we certainly have a good enough excuse to go

out on the town. It has been a while since I abandoned my pi-
ratelike behavior for a more conventional "rise with the sun
and go to bed when it's dark" sleep pattern, but if there ever
was a place and a time to revert for a night to my former
lifestyle, I sense it is Cartagena. And now that I am fifty, it's
even more important to throw a few curveballs at my meta-
bolic clock and ward off the horrifying thought, God forbid, of
a routine life.

The scorching heat and nerve-racking day have worn us all
a bit thin, and the night is still young. The pace of the Cartagena night has meshed with what we thought to be our tardy
arrival. All I need is to check in, get a snack and a drink, grab a
combat nap, and have a shower, and we can still be fashionably
late for dinner at ten. At the check-in desk of the Santa Theresa
Hotel, we are met by not one, but two smiling, well-mannered
young managers, a far cry from our earlier greeting in hell. Hu-
bert is from the home office of the hotel chain in France, and he
and Kino immediately make that Franco-world connection.
Roberto is from Cartagena but went to school at the University
of Florida and is a Parrothead. God, I love it when that happens. I have been lucky enough to run into fans like that in faraway places, and it seems to happen, amazingly, right when
you need them. Roberto is beaming with pride and talking
about the University of Florida football team, which has just
won the national championship the night before. He graciously
offers us a drink and a tour of the hotel, but we opt to settle in
first. He recommends for dinner a restaurant within walking
distance of the hotel called La Vitrola, a very popular local spot,
but it's Friday night. He knows the owner, he says, and he'll see
what he can do.

The hotel was originally a convent, and though it has obviously been recently renovated, the musty smell of the ancient
walls is still in the air. Our spacious room surely must have
been built for a long-departed mother superior. As we settle in,
I wonder what the nuns who occupied the old convent would

have thought of the Frette sheets, the minibar, and the satellite TV. Maybe if they had been allowed such accoutrements, they wouldn't have collectively been so goddamn mean.

We are the only gringos in the lobby. Everybody else speaks Spanish or some other Latin-based tongue. Even in the fine hotels of Europe a good deal of the clientele is American, and Americans can stand out in a crowd like a sore thumb. I guess that if you want to get away from the crowd, you should really consider taking your vacation in a country that constantly makes the top-ten-most-dangerous-places-to-travel-in-the-world list.

Roberto succeeded in getting us in at La Vitrola, so we head out into the night. He has assured us that it's perfectly safe to walk the streets of Cartagena and suggests a route along the west wall.

Old Walls Never Die

I don't know what it is about the walls of old forts. On the surface they're just cracked reminders of long-ago days, but to me the stories that surround them are as active as any volcano and reach back to the shores of Mobile Bay. As a kid I used to relish trips to old Fort Morgan on the Gulf Coast, a famous Civil War citadel that guarded the entrance to Mobile Bay. It had been the scene of the famous battle where Admiral Farragut uttered his infamous phrase, "Damn the torpedoes, full speed ahead." I had first gone there on a Cub Scout field trip, and the experience had awakened some connection to the past. On every family trip to the beaches at Gulf Shores, my behavior was like that of a saint, because I knew my reward for not fighting with my sister would be an excursion with my dad to Fort Morgan. He would read the paper with one eye, keeping the other one focused on me climbing over old cannons and mortars and manning my imaginary post to do battle with the ghosts of

Admiral Farragut's fleet. Finally, he would reach into my made-up world and bring me reluctantly back to reality.

On my first voyages through the Caribbean on my own boat, I made a point of finding and discovering the old forts left over from the era when the islands and the waters that surround them were a stage for the colonial powers, who were constantly warring for world domination. Among my favorite haunts were the Royal Navy docks at English Harbor; Brimstone Hill—the "Gibraltar of the West Indies" on the western shore of St. Kitts; and the voodoo-shrouded ramparts of Henri Christophe's amazing Citadel Laferrière atop the jungle mountains of northern Haiti.

Earlier in the day, we had flown over the remains of the fortifications at Porto Bello, and the surrounding waters where the bones of Sir Francis Drake rest in a lead coffin at the bottom of the Caribbean Sea. In my recent travels to Alaska to do research on *Where Is Joe Merchant?* I found myself again manning imaginary gun batteries in the pillboxes above Dutch Harbor wondering what it must have been like to be filling the air with hot lead in the path of the attacking Japanese Zeroes. Now here on the ramparts above Cartagena, I have discovered another stop on my magical songline.

The Déjà Vu Congregation of Ex-Catholic, Geo-Natural, Afro-Oceanic, Aboriginal Gypsies

There are certain places on this Earth where I just feel that I belong, or have visited before, or just have some kind of unexplained connection to. This sense of place is rooted for me in an appreciation of history, which has always fascinated me. I grew up in a town that had a great history from the time of the French explorers to the battles of the Civil War. I was not only infected by the history, I was connected to it as well.

There are towns and streets and seashores that are not just dots on a map. They are a part of what the aboriginal tribes in Australia call songlines. When I first read about the concept in Bruce Chatwin's book *Songlines*, I knew that they existed. The simple and beautiful idea of a songline is that music is the way to measure time. Life is a journey that's measured not in miles or years but in experiences, and the route your life takes is built not of roads but of songs. How far is it from Key West to Miami? To some it is 147 miles. To me, it is about eleven songs.

I don't possess the misguided fervor that seems to be a part of all organized religions. I just hope that there is actually somebody in charge. If I had to have a name for the church I would belong to, it would be something like this: the Déjà Vu Congregation of Ex-Catholic, Geo-Natural, Afro-Oceanic, Aboriginal Gypsies. I truly believe in the thread that connects this planet and this galaxy and so, it stands to reason, the universe. I guess it starts with gravity and the moon. If the physical relationship between the Earth and moon can move mountains of water up and down every day, then it only stands to reason that the water in our bodies has to be affected as well. I have seen too many beautiful and terrifying things on the ocean and in the sky that make me feel mortal, but at the same time I can feel the interdependency of fear and fun.

Lost Words from Hole in the Pants Pocket of García Márquez

What I am feeling at the wall is the relationship of Cartagena to my songline. Gabriel García Márquez worked in Cartagena as a reporter in the forties. I have read just about everything he's written. There are times when you get lost in one of his passages, and when you finish, you go, "Where in the hell did he come up with that?" As we stroll atop the walls toward our dinner, I can sense that I'm in the land of magical realism. A guitar melody carries through the narrow streets and echoes off the ancient ramparts. The balmy breeze coming off the Caribbean is warm and salty and carries a perfume of night-blooming jasmine with an underlying aroma of garlic being sautéed in olive oil. Somewhere this night, fine meals will be served and a beautiful Creole woman with a gardenia in her hair will be made love to by the guitar player under a mosquito net and a slowly turning ceiling fan. I don't know how, but I just know it.

I stop for a last moment at the top of the stairs leading down to the restaurant. I pick a dark angle through the line of streetlights and headlights along Avenida Santander and block out the sound of horns and mufflers from weekend traffic whizzing by. I eventually find an unobstructed sight line out to the western edge of the Caribbean Sea, where the last faint slice of orange sky clings to the horizon. Above me, I see the stars popping out. Venus first, and then back over the city toward Laguna de San Lazaro, my old friend Orion's Belt. The descriptions in the books that had aroused my curiosity about coming to this place can't compare with what I am experiencing now. I now have a clue as to where García Márquez found some of his inspirations. I feel his shadow. I would like to think that the words and sentences I jot down have been spilled like coins from a hole is his pocket and have come to rest in the hidden cracks between the ancient carvings, waiting to be found and put back on the page. As I descend the stairs I find myself muttering the words to one of my favorite lyrical hook lines: "All and all, I'm just another brick in the wall."

Another Snowy Day in Paradise

Date: 5 January 1997
Time: 1600Z
Latitude: 10°26'7" N
Longitude: 75°31'0' W

Location: Cartagena International Airport
Heading: 092°
Weather: Partly cloudy

Comments: I am awakened earlier than I want to be by the pilots. Spanish time is no longer in effect. We are back on Greenwich mean time. The good news is that the pilots haven't been shanghaied and the plane is still at the airport. The not-so-good news is the weather at our destination in Manaus. None of us have been to the heart of the Amazon before, but the same rule applies there as does over the open waters of the Caribbean—be a fuel hog. From our weather connections in Houston, Randy received word that there is considerable thunderstorm activity from the equator south toward Manaus. Normally that's not a big problem. You load on all the fuel you can and head out. More often than not, the weather will improve and you will land where you want to, but you can't always count on it. If the weather stays foul, you just have plenty of fuel and your flight plan to an alternative airport, and land there where it is safe. South of the equator the rules change. Once we pass Bogotá, there will be nothing but eight hundred miles of green jungle, crocodiles, Indians, and anacondas until we hit Manaus. None of the pilots on board cherish the thought of being down there dodging thunderstorms with the fuel gauge dropping and nowhere to go. Randy figured the "what if" factor, and if we go from Cartagena to Caracas and take on fuel, we will have enough to get to Manaus and back to Caracas if we have to. This is no big decision. It just takes us an extra hour to go to Caracas, and, hell, Jerry Lee has never seen Caracas. We settle on a departure time of 1600 Zulu (GMT or International Coordinated Time).

There is no need to go back to sleep. I roust the troops and tell them of our change in plans. Fortunately, even after our big night out on the town, I stuck to the cardinal rule of the road and packed last night. I close my suitcases and head out for breakfast on the roof. Kino follows me and tells me he'll take care of checking us out. I set out for town and a final walk along the walls. When I arrive at Plaza Santo Domingo, it is as deserted as if an alien spaceship had come down and taken every person, chair, and marble-topped table to some distant planet. It is now just a parking lot with a few cars sitting by the curb. The night before there were a thousand revelers crammed into this space. I am trying to figure out what caused this sudden transformation when an old reminder clues me in. The giant bells of the cathedral of Saint Peter Claver sound, and I realize it is Sunday. It is the first time in a long time that I actually thought about what day of the week it is.

My final mission of the morning is to find a local record store where I can pick up a few CD's of *vallenatos* bands. This accomplished, we assemble in front of the hotel a little after ten-thirty and say *adiós* to Cartagena, but as we drive under the old walls at the main gate of the city, I know I will be back someday.

At the airport, our handler, Theresa, who had met us upon our late arrival a few days earlier, was there to deal with the mound of paperwork that's required to move a private plane around the skies of South America. She is the picture of efficiency and has us all through passport control and customs in a matter of minutes. All that is left is the final customs inspector. We wait at the plane in the building heat of the day, and finally a van pulls up, filled with Colombian soldiers and a dope-sniffing dog. Our luggage is piled on the baggage cart next to the plane, and the customs agent says not a word. He has the "presumed guilty until proven innocent" attitude as he pokes around inside the plane. Then he comes back out and lets the dog loose. The dog jumps on top of our luggage and starts walking back and forth. He looks more like he was searching out a place to pee than like a drug-sniffing dog in action. I am not comfortable. The last two days in Cartagena drain from my thoughts like a ruptured hydraulic line. We are back in the land of armies and airports. The knot in my stomach that had just subsided when we left Barranquilla is back. What if this dog has a bad day, or suppose a chromosome dislodged at this particular moment and his nose is reprogrammed to sniff dirty socks or Cuban cigars. What then? Finally, the goddamn dog jumps off the cart. The conquistador just motions with his finger that we can depart, jumps in his van, and is driven back toward the main terminal. We all breathe a sigh of relief.

Date: 5 January 1997
Time: 1658Z
Latitude: 10°34'6" N
Longitude: 72°58'8" W

Location: Colombian-Venezuelan border on JA552
Altitude: 33,000'
Weather: Clear

Comments: We are heading east to Caracas with the Caribbean Sea on our left and mountains to the right. There is an amazing sight ahead of us. We are flying in perfectly clear weather with little cotton puffs of cumulus clouds below us at around 25,000 feet. Off the right side of the plane are the snow-covered peaks of the Sierra Nevada de Santa Marta, the northernmost reaches of the Andes. Off the left side is the southernmost coast of the Caribbean and the town of Santa Marta, and I can see the white-sand beach running along the shore. In all my travels, I can't think of any other place where I have witnessed such a panorama of beaches and snow. I love the irony and make a mental note to try and come back here one day and fulfill my dream of swimming in the Caribbean while staring at snow-covered peaks.

Date: 5 January 1997   Location: Lake Maracaibo,
Time: 1718Z   NW Venezuela
Latitude: 10°43'2" N   Heading: 095°
Longitude: 71°37'3" W   Altitude: 33,000'
                                                        Weather: Clear

Comments: We are crossing over the Gulf of Venezuela. The city of Maracaibo and the old fort are clearly visible, even from six and a half miles up. So are the thousands of oil rigs in the lake. This is about the best place to see Maracaibo, because down there it is hot. The gulf is encircled by the mountains that cut off the ocean breezes, creating one of the most torrid spots in the tropics. If that isn't enough, the industrialization that came with the discovery of oil here has left the lake a mess, some say worse than the Great Lakes twenty years ago, when the Cuyahoga River in Ohio actually caught fire. The number of oil rigs, drilling platforms, and leaky underwater pipes dwarfs that of the Gulf of Mexico south of the Mississippi's mouth. I have read about efforts by the people who brought back Lake Erie to help the Venezuelans address these problems. One of the interesting things about traveling is the perspective it gives you. When I leave America and go abroad to other, less developed regions, I fully appreciate our attempt to try and correct our mistakes. We are not by any means perfect. My God, we have made some mistakes, but at least we are trying to get better and are sometimes willing to help. It would have been enough for the saviors of Lake Erie to pat themselves on the back, get a plaque from the city of Cleveland, and be done with it. Instead, they used what they had learned to help others. They won't get their pictures on any cereal boxes, but they are heroes just as well.

Date: 5 January 1997   Location: Caracas,
Time: 1828Z   Venezuela
Latitude: 10°36'4" N   Elevation: 235'
Longitude: 66°59'3" W   Weather: Clear

Comments: Pit stop in Caracas at Simón Bolívar International. Of course we have come for fuel, but we also find frozen cookies 'n' cream ice-cream bars at the airport snack shop—a little taste of America before heading south. The weather on our route has improved a little, which is good. All we see of Venezuela are tourist posters on the walls of the airport. Our plans now are to come back through Venezuela and land at Angel Falls, the highest waterfall in South America, and, I think, another stop on my songline. But we are hearing tales at the airport about landing restrictions and 727's full of German tourists who have overrun Angel Falls. I make a note to call Jim Powell and tell him what I've heard. He'll be back to me by the time I reach Manaus with a fifteen-page memo about the situation.

When I bought the Citation, I was in France and the plane was in Germany. I was allowed to make the trip across the Atlantic as the copilot. We left Paris, stopped in Iceland, then flew to Goose Bay, Labrador. We were moving so fast that we hadn't had time to talk to anybody. When I ran from the plane in the subzero January chill to the waiting room at Goose Bay International, I had no sooner walked through the door of the terminal than a man in a uniform came up to me and said,

"Mr. Buffett, you have a phone call." It was Jim Powell. He had tracked us to Iceland, gotten our departure time, estimated our Atlantic crossing time, and placed his call. I have never met a more thorough pilot.

We are fueled and we have our clearance. We're off to the Amazon.

Date: 5 January 1997	**Location:** Crossing the
Time: 2101Z	equator at Madko inter-
Latitude: 00°24'7" N	section on UA315
Longitude: 61°29'8" W	**Heading:** 169°
	Altitude: 35,000'
	Weather: Partly cloudy

Comments: Greetings from the equator, where down is up and up is down. When we land in Manaus, the toilets will flush backward and the seasons will be opposite. We are now in the bottom half of the world. Up here at 35,000 feet, the only way we know we're on the equator is to read out the numbers on the GPS, but we are going so fast that by the time I reach down for my GPS unit to photograph this record of our passage, we have passed it. My passengers in the back are sleeping or reading and don't seem to be sharing my enthusiasm in the moment. I can't help it.

We haven't run into the storms yet, and we have good contact with the ground. There is nothing down there but green jungle. Several minutes back, we crossed a road that went from horizon to horizon. If I didn't know better, I would have thought someone had actually carved out a line around the world, but satellites don't lie and the GPS verified that it was just a long dirt road, a man-made intrusion into the rain forest.

I had first heard about Macapá, the village where the Amazon River meets the equator, from a Tampa pilot named Tom

Ferguson, whom I met in George Town, in the Exumas. I was coming back up the islands from St. Barts, and he was headed to São Paulo in an AgCat crop duster. He made his living transporting the crop dusters south, and over drinks he told me stories about his ordeals along his flight route. Macapá was one of his favorite places. That was enough of an endorsement for me. I read about it, and then Tom sent some photos. In one of the shots he was standing in a jungle clearing next to a giant marble sculpture. At the base of the statue read the words, LATITUDE 00°00′0 — MARCO DE ZERO. I wanted to go there, but time and circumstances ruled it out. I will have to take a rain check on my shot at standing on the Amazon equator.

I did straddle the equator on another spot. It was in a bar in the mountains of Kenya that sits smack-dab on the *marco de zero*. The enterprising owner of the Hemisphere had imbedded a six-inch-wide brass rail into the wooden floor with a giant 0° carved above it. The bar is a mirror image of itself, one for each hemisphere, allowing the patrons to have a drink in both sides of the world. It may seem like nonsense to some people, but so what? There's more to celebrate in life than birthdays, anniversaries, and deaths. The significance of an equatorial crossing comes from sailors. After repeated days at sea on the north-south routes from Europe to South America, things got a little boring, and crossing the *marco de zero* was more than anything else an excuse for a party. I like to think that crossing the equator, whether it's dancing over a brass line in Africa or whizzing over the green jungle of South America, still means something. A poem pops to mind.

> *Where life becomes a spasm*
> *And history a whiz*
> *If that is not sensation*
> *Then I don't know what is*
>
> —LEWIS CARROLL, "POETA FIT, NON NASCITUR"

Date: 5 January 1997 **Location:** Curi intersec-
Time: 2120Z tion—54.2 mi. N of
Latitude: 002°12′4″ N Manaus, Brazil
Longitude: 060°29′1″ W **Heading:** 169°
 Altitude: 25,000′
 Weather: Overcast

Comments: We dodge thunderstorms as we start our descent for Manaus. We are at the core of tropical moisture, so these babies are climbing upward to fifty and sixty thousand feet today. That's a whole lot of mean energy in the form of giant anvil clouds out ahead of us. They are called anvil clouds for a good reason. When they decide to release all that energy, they put the hammer down. Though they are beautiful to look at, you don't want anything to do with what's inside them. They are scattered enough this time for us to pick our way around them with the radar.

Flying through the clouds puts the fun of flying back at my fingertips, as I corkscrew around the storms and dive slowly back to earth. I remember stories I have read about how fighter pilots in World War II used the clouds as camouflage for their daring raids, hiding out above their targets down upon the sea until the time was right to strike. We spiral down and break out of the weather at about seventeen thousand feet, and my God, there it is—the Amazon jungle.

We are still thirty miles from the confluence of the Amazon and the Río Negro, and the landscape, or should I say waterscape, stretches before us. Flat, wide sheets of water. You can smell it in the air. I have heard that during the rainy season on the Amazon there are days when the air's water content nearly matches that of the river. We ask permission from Manaus Control to descend to a lower altitude, and they oblige.

Date: 5 January 1997   Location: NW Brazil
Time: 2142Z   Heading: 093°
Latitude: 03°01′2″ N   Altitude: 1500′
Longitude: 60°13′3″ W   Weather: Overcast

Comments: We're cruising down the Río Negro. It is rare to fly this low in a jet, and it's certainly fun. I still can't get over how much water there is. My image of the Amazon was of a big river cutting through green jungle, but the area around the river looks like one of those shots of floods in the Midwest, with sheets of water extending to the horizon. And this is the dry season! God knows what it looks like when the monsoons come. I pull the throttles back, and we drift along at 140 knots. There is a large sand beach ahead, something I didn't anticipate seeing, and beyond that the skyline of Manaus pops up out of the gray backdrop of a thunderstorm to the north. How this city got here and what it became is what drew me here in the first place, and what I hope to find out over the next few days. We check the radar and see that the thunderstorm is moving away from the airport. I would like to just fly around for a while, but it's getting late and there are people waiting for us on the ground. Time to put the rubber on the asphalt.

Date: 5 January 1997   Location: Manaus
Time: 2206Z   Elevation: 275′
Latitude: 03°02′4″ N   Weather: Cloudy
Longitude: 60°03′1″ W

Comments: My last memory of Colombia was a dope-sniffing dog. My first impression as we open the cabin door in Manaus is of smiles and music. Music is at the heart of Brazil, as I had learned on my first and only previous trip to this country. We climb out of the plane to what has to be one of the most incredible sunsets I have ever seen. The scattered storms of the day, the heavy humidity, and probably the fact that we are sitting on the middle of the Earth have something to do with it. The sky to the west shines bright gold, doubly illuminated by the curtain of darkness coming from the east. We are met not by soldiers but by a pixie of a woman in a bright orange skirt. Ponce smiles, welcomes us to Manaus, and guides us through the customs area and out to our waiting cabs. As I have read, darkness comes quickly in the Amazon, and the golden sky has picked up its tent and is gone. As we drive down the dark road, I recognize the familiar smells of diesel fuel and wood smoke that I have come to know so well in my travels. I recite the only three words of Portuguese that I learned on my other visit to Brazil. It's been fourteen years, and I'm glad to be back. *"Tu ta bien."*

SECTION X

The Amazon

A Second Look

Fun Tickets in My Pocket

Fun tickets in my pocket
Visions in my brain
Grandfather always told me
If I went down
I might never come back again

I studied the language tapes
And I read all the books
Still nothing prepared me for my
Very first look

—"First Look"

My Brazilian history starts about four hundred years after the colony was established. It was in the winter of 1981. Jane and I had split up. She had gone to New York, and I had limped back to Key West on the knees of my heart. I rented an apartment in the same block I had lived in back in the heyday of Club Mandible, and all-day lunches at Louie's Backyard, and all-night romps down Duval Street. I was working on an album, a very melancholy record, because I was brokenhearted. I had lost the girl I really loved. I didn't even bother to redecorate the apartment. I sat around in a room full of furniture that had obviously come from Goodwill or the Navy-surplus store and poured my heart out in songs with titles like, "If the Phone Doesn't Ring, It's Me," "She's Going Out of My Mind," and "Bigger Than the Both of Us." Key West was the only place I really felt I could go live with my blues.

I think you really do create your own aura, and as if the depression and hangovers weren't enough, I was lying in bed one afternoon feeling sorry for myself and reading Ambrose Bierce when the plaster ceiling in the apartment fell on top of me like a bad vaudeville gag. In an utter panic, I called Sunshine, my partner, confidante, and friend, and told her the sky had literally just fallen on my head. When I think back to it now, I laugh. At the time, I did not. With her wonderful simplicity, Sunshine said to me, "Jimmy, you're rich. What are you doing living in that dump? Get yourself a nice apartment, stop whining about Jane, and go have some fun."

While I was sitting there in the plaster dust contemplating Sunshine's evaluation of my situation, the phone rang again. It was an old friend of mine from St. Barts who just happened to be calling me from Rio. The more he talked, the more I listened. I left the plaster where it had landed and drove to Miami, where I took a suite at the Coconut Grove Hotel and went shopping for something other than cutoffs. A day later I heard through the grapevine that my friends Bob Rafelson and Lou Adler were down in Rio location scouting for a film. Something or someone was pointing me toward Rio town. Three days later, I was in the office of the Brazilian consulate in Miami, and at the stroke of midnight on Mardi Gras Saturday, I was on a Pan Am Clipper to Rio.

The weekend went by like a Fellini dream. I found Rafelson at the hotel, then ran into a bunch of Brazilian friends whom I knew from St. Barts. There were parties, hoodlum drinks, dancing in the streets, and, to cap it all off, I found myself on Ash Wednesday at sunrise singing in bad Portuguese to my friends on a hang-gliding launchpad above the city. Hello, Brazil. With Carnival done and Lent in full swing, I wasn't ready to go home and wound up staying with friends near Cucumber Beach and then taking off to Buzios, a hip little coastal town north of Rio. I rented a seaside villa, complete with maids and beach boys and plaster that stayed glued to the ceiling. There were, of course, thoughts of moving there. I don't think I have ever been anywhere that I liked without fantasizing about living there. Nevertheless, in a couple of weeks I came home. But something about Brazil's devil-may-care culture had spoken to me.

Back in Key West, in my new apartment with my new attitude and my new Portuguese phrases, I ran into a talented Brazilian painter named Dalva Duarte, who listened with amusement to my stories. Dalva and I remain good friends to this day, and it was at her studio in Fort Lauderdale, a week before my departure, that I reconnected to that affection for Brazil I had locked away in a corner of my heart.

Without Geography, You're Nowhere

Last year I received a most complimentary letter from Dr. William V. Davidson, chairman of the Department of Geography and Anthropology at Louisiana State University in Baton Rouge. The letter described his efforts in creating a fully credited geography course called "Geography, based on Jimmy Buffett's Songs." I was thrilled and honored. One of my pet peeves is the indifference educators and students feel toward geography. It is small minds and small thinkers who don't consider anything outside of their neighborhood important. We are all citizens of the world. You'd better come to terms with that concept or get ready to spend your life behind a fast-food counter.

I wrote Dr. Davidson back to thank him and accepted his invitation to give a lecture. "Oh, my God," some of you parents may gasp, "what has the world come to?" Well, before you start asking for your child's tuition refund, let me try to win you over to the fact that such a course just may be all right. I have always used a few good rules of a few well-traveled writers when I sit down to compose. Hemingway said, "Never forget the weather." Mark Twain said, "Write what you know about." A bumper sticker I bought in a map store on Farragut Square in Washington, D.C., says, WITHOUT GEOGRAPHY, YOU'RE NOWHERE. All of these precepts are contained in my work, even though I had no idea there was enough there to be the basis of a college course. So, before we dive into the fun and adventure of our days in Amazonia, let's start with a little geography lesson. And, oh yes, there will be a quiz.

Facts About the Amazon

The Amazon system is four thousand miles long but only rises from sea level at the Atlantic to three hundred feet on the eastern Peruvian border.

The Amazon drains one sixth of the world's total freshwater runoff into the oceans. One day's runoff at the mouth of the river, 4.5 trillion gallons, could supply all the drinking water for the entire United States for five months.

Belém is the port city at the mouth of the Amazon.

The Amazon at its mouth is 160 miles wide.

In volume of water, the Amazon is twelve times as large as the Mississippi.

There are pink dolphins in the Amazon.

In the late thirties, Henry Ford bought a seven-thousand-acre plantation near Santarém and named it "Belterra." In his attempt to capitalize on the rubber resources and bring the American Midwest to the heart of the jungle, he constructed a picture-perfect replica of a Michigan town to house ten thousand rubber workers. It came complete with roads, electric streetlights, hospitals, and town squares. It didn't catch on and today lies in ruins, having been reclaimed by the jungle.

The floating docks at Manaus were completed in 1902 and are still fully functional today. They were designed by a Scottish engineer to cope with the incredible rise in water level during the flood season.

There is a Kentucky Fried Chicken in Manaus.

Doing the Amazon

I have a terrible habit of listening to conversations at other tables when I'm dining out. I justify this by saying that I am a writer looking for material and the best fiction is still the truth. Somewhere in Florida, back when this trip was idle conversation, I was having dinner with friends and overheard someone at the next table to me commenting on what she had overheard of our discussion at our table. "Oh, we did the Amazon," she said nonchalantly. "Not much there but a bunch of dirty people, dirty towns, and dirty water." Doing the Amazon to this woman probably amounted to a cabin on a cruise ship and a roll in the hay with a Captain Stubing look-alike. She may have *been* to the Amazon, but she had not *done* the Amazon.

The Amazon was first "done" by a Spaniard named Francisco de Orellana. A lieutenant of Francisco Pizarro, he led an expedition out of Quito, Ecuador to explore the then unknown territory to the east. In April 1541, he reached the junction of the Napo and Marañón rivers, where his group persuaded him of the impossibility of returning to Pizarro. Instead, he began an exploration of the Amazon system. Drifting with the current, he reached the mouth of the river in August 1542. Proceeding to Trinidad, he finally returned to Spain, where he told of hordes of gold and cinnamon and of encounters with tribes led by women resembling the Amazons of Greek mythology—a comparison that is presumed to have led him to name the river the Amazon.

The Jesuits did the Amazon. Founded by Saint Ignatius of Loyola in 1534 and confirmed by Pope Paul III in 1540, carrying a banner inscribed with their motto, "To the greater glory of God," the Society of Jesus, under Father Manuel Nóbrega, arrived in Brazil in 1549.

Alexander Von Humboldt and Aimé Bonpland did the Amazon for five years, from 1799 to 1804, in Central and

South America, covering more than six thousand miles on foot, on horseback, and in canoes. Starting from Caracas, the naturalist-botanist team traveled south through grasslands and scrublands until they reached the banks of the Apure, a tributary of the Orinoco River. They continued their journey by canoe as far as the Orinoco. Following its course and that of the Casiquiare, they proved that the Casiquiare River formed a connection between the vast river systems of the Amazon and the Orinoco. For three months Humboldt and Bonpland moved through dense tropical forests, tormented by clouds of mosquitoes and stifled by the humid heat. Their provisions were soon destroyed by insects and rain; the lack of food finally drove them to subsist on ground-up wild cacao beans and river water. This was no jungle cruise.

Jere Van Dyk and Alex Web did the Amazon in 1994 and wrote about it in an amazing feature for *National Geographic*. Moving upriver from Belém, they covered life on the river from its mouth to its source, which Lorne McIntyre, a writer who had been part of a 1971 *Geographic* expediton to locate the great river's source, referred to as "the trickle of the Amazon."

Buffett had not done the Amazon and didn't want to. I just came to have a look around.

I have been up on the Internet and downloaded information about trips to the interior, where you live off the land and put yourself up to some tremendous challenge. If that is what you need to make yourself happy, then go ahead. My first visit to the Amazon was going to be more like a field trip back in grammar school. I wanted a base camp to work from. I wanted to go out and spend the day on the river in a boat. I wanted to fly above the river system in a small plane. I wanted to see the incredible opera house in Manaus, and anything else that happened to be interesting was fine with me, as long as I could return to my air-conditioned hotel room, have a shower, dinner, a bottle of wine, and a good night's sleep.

Fifty is not the age to try and start a new life. Begin your adventures as early as you can. I promise you, you will not get burned out. It actually becomes the most enjoyable way to spend time on Earth as opposed to just pacing the cage. Oh, hell, I am a compulsive individual and I admit to having wanted to do it all. Even five years ago when I went up to Alaska with my friend, the artist John Alexander, we were flying between the jagged peaks of the Alaska Mountains and landing on skis in the snow at the base camp for climbers attempting to ascend Mount McKinley. Doug Getting, our pilot, had given us the big ticket ride to the top of the continent. Having taken the shortcut to the peak, I was convinced I should go back and climb the mountain. It didn't look all that difficult. I asked Doug what he thought of the idea. With the same pilot stoicism that Dean Franklin had used when thwarting my idea to circle the world in a flying boat, he said, "It's a lot longer to the top of the continent than it looks." His words of experience were confirmed almost instantly when we took off and circled the majestic peak. That is, until I looked down on the antlike balls of lint coming and going up the side of Denali and realized they were people, not bugs on the windshield. I thought about them that night when I was eating a perfectly cooked filet of salmon and sipping a fine glass of French white burgundy by a warm fire in Talkeetna. Those folks crammed into their Mountain Hardware sleeping bags curled up inside their North Face one-man tents in subzero temperatures were doing what they wanted to do, and so was I. I couldn't be them any more than they could be me.

Now, that is not to say that I don't have walkabout time left in me. I know I do, and I know the places I would go, but I won't put them in this book, because then I might set out on my journey and find you at the end, waiting for me with a margarita and a hundred questions. That's not how it works. Fun is about as good a habit as there is, especially when your search for it becomes tempered with the wisdom of time on the water. The destination is not that rewarding if you have not had the experience of the journey. My walkabout place cannot be yours. Your walkabout place cannot be somebody else's. You have to find your own.

Fourteen years ago I got my first look at Brazil in Rio. Now I am here for my second.

Manaus: Day One

A Very Special Price

After landing, we parked ourselves at the Tropical Hotel, a suitable base camp for our next three days. The Tropical is a mammoth structure owned and operated by Varig, the national Brazilian airline. It caters to tourists who come to get a look at the jungle and take back souvenirs ranging from trinkets to emeralds.

Crossing the equator had taken it out of me, and after dinner we went to bed. Now I am awakened from my "Heart of Darkness" dream not by the sound of the jungle creatures stirring to consciousness along the banks of the Río Negro. No, it's a telephone ringing loudly in short, unfamiliar blasts, more like a bell signaling a jail break.

"Hello, Mr. Jamie Toofay, please. Dis is Conrado Farias from Amazon Jungle Tourism, but my friends call me Conrad." Of course his name would be Conrad. "I speaken at da concierge to da hotel in last night about a boat for Mr. Jamie Toofay. We do very, very Jungle Amazon Trip for to see meeting of waters, on fine, fine boat at very special price to include jungle trip to see giant lily pads and rain forest, and we finish off da day with alligator hunting, all for very special price. I call early for you to be first on boat for seating. Get good seats."

Oh, my God. Tourism is alive and well in the Amazon. I look at my watch. It is five-thirty in the morning. I tell Conrad to hold on, and I slip out of bed and go to the other room to talk so as to not wake up Jane. "Conrad, we are five people, and we just want our own boat."

"Dat can be arranged, dat can be arranged, and for a verry special price," he replies.

"I am sure it can," I say, knowing from the change in his speech pattern that the phrase "private boat" signaled to him that he had a big fish on the line.

I have never been a bargainer, especially in foreign countries. It is not in my nature. I know basic fair prices, and I know rip-offs. I take it or I leave it. I don't like to argue about money. I did enough of that in the old days of working clubs when my counter total would differ from that of the club owner, night after night. Bargaining should not be a part of life after fifty. By that time you know whether you can afford something or not. We're a bunch of white people coming to look at the jungle, and we're not on a shoestring budget or looking for bargains. Yet I have the feeling that though this is the real Amazon, it is almost being marketed as a packaged, theme-park version. So after dinner I asked the concierge if he knew of a company from which I could charter a private boat to go where we wanted to go, when we wanted to go. That's how Conrad came into our lives.

"We would like to leave the hotel at nine and spend the day on the river."

"Yes, yes, yes, dat is not a problem. I arrange dat for you right now. I give to you my cellular number, and you can to call me back in half hour, Mr. Jamie."

"It's Jimmy," I say, interrupting him.

"Okay, Mr. Yimmie, Amazon Jungle Tour take care of everything for you. Have a good day. Ciao." Before Conrad's call, I had planned to rise early but not this early, have a look at the river in the morning light, eat breakfast, find us a boat, and buy a new camera. The boat is in the works, and by some amazing stroke of good luck I had spotted a camera store in the hotel lobby. My amazing new digital video camera went on the blink in Cartagena. I had picked it up at Sharper Image over the summer, but I have never been kind to high-tech gear. It could have been the filming on the beach, the swim in the waterfall, the banging around inside the seaplane, or a dozen other things, but to put it in sailor talk, "the fucking fucker was fucked." It would only shoot five seconds of video at a time.

The trip from the front desk of the hotel to our room the night before had been an adventure all its own, sorting through a confusing system of floor and room numbers that was a vintage page out of the hotel-from-hell scenario that I had seen too many times on the road. This morning my return trip isn't much better. As I wind through the long, deserted corridors, the place kind of reminds me of that hotel in the movie *The Shining*. Goose pimples roll down my arms: "Red rum, red rum." Yikes, let's get that unpleasant little thought out of the old skull. I manage to navigate through the maze to a signpost that points me toward the lobby. I pass the restaurant, which hasn't yet opened, so breakfast will have to wait. The sign on the door of the camera store says it opens at seven. All that is left is the river.

What the Hell Would Tom and Huck Think?

I find the marked trail that leads out into the shadowy light of the morning. Finally I can hear the birds in the trees and feel the heat of the jungle already brewing up. My first day on the Amazon is being orchestrated in an impressionistic veil of gray and pink and green. I have seen it before in the amazing landscapes of Frederic Edwin Church from the series of South American paintings that he had created on his trips to the jungle in the 1860s. I am not a painter, but I know inspiration when I see it. I start singing the chorus to Al Green's classic "Take Me to the River."

I continue swaying to the beat and reach a set of roughed-out steps carved from the rocks that lead to the dock on the dark waters of the Río Negro. The low clouds are gone now, and a breeze has sprung up with the sun as it makes its pres-

ence known with long shimmering reflections of light across
the dark water. There are several tourist boats tied up to the
dock. They look like a cross between shrimp boats and old
paddle wheelers, with double decks and rows of benches. I
wondered what kind of craft Conrad is out trying to hustle up
for us. I could hear him on that cell phone now. Work that big
fish, Conrad, work that big fish, don't let him slip off the hook.
There is already a steady parade of boats moving up and
down the river. The Amazon system is the water world's version of I-95, and while the tourists pop their flashbulbs and
point their video cameras, commerce moves along the river
like it has since the beginning of time. The Amazon is not just
there to be looked at and photographed. It is the river of life.

I sit on the end of the dock watching the boats and thinking
that this must have been what the Mississippi was like before
the Civil War, when it, too, was the transportation artery that
dissected and connected the interior of America. But this is the
Amazon, not the Mississippi. It's the land of endless green jungle snakes forty feet long, Indians with poison darts and blowguns, shrunken heads and man-eating fish from here to the
Andes Mountains. South to the ocean are lost civilizations,
gold mines, spiders as round as umbrellas, and boats, thousands of boats steaming up and down the river carrying the
wayward adventurers, the jungle farmers, the missionaries,
and the lost souls, and contraband of all sizes, shapes, and descriptions, the gossip of the day, whiskey and card games,
guns and ammo, love affairs in the bathrooms and hammocks.
It's all out there. What the hell would Tom and Huck think of
this place?

I am already breaking a sweat. The humidity hangs in the
air like an invisible curtain on the clothesline of the morning.
You cannot escape the moisture. There is as much water in the
air as there is in the river. The earth is spongy beneath my feet,
but I like it. Something about this environment speaks to the
ancient spots in my body where my gills used to be attached. I

come from the swamps, and by God, here I am in the mother of all swamps, about ready to go rolling on the river into the heart of darkness to catch alligators and God knows what else with a tour guide named Conrad, all at a very special price.

The Food Room

I walk back to the hotel and check in with Conrad at my appointed time. He answers amid a cackle of voices and static, but I get the message that we have a boat for nine o'clock and he will meet us at the hotel. I call the girls to let them know our schedule, and Jane tells me Kino is already in the restaurant. *Restaurant* is not quite the term to describe the place where I find him. There are tables and chairs, but it looks more like a cafeteria in a hospital. There is no hostess, no maître d', just a nest of waiters in white jackets walking around with coffeepots in their hands. In the center of the room, a long table is adorned with a breakfast buffet that contains an array of recognizable and unrecognizable items. Kino sits alone at a table by the window with a view of the adjacent shopping plaza. He is reading a brochure when I arrive and looks up and says, "Welcome to the food room." I crack up. We have spent too much time together on the road not to make the same observations. I pass on the buffet and stick with the things that look familiar, then I tell Kino of my arrangements with Conrad. The clientele in the food room are all headed for the river in one fashion or another. Some are obviously dressed for the jungle. Very few of them are speaking English, but they all have cameras. Oh, God, my camera, I've almost forgotten. I gobble up the rest of my tiny croissant and leave Kino in the food room to pay the bill and wait for the girls, then dash off to the camera store.

There on the door is a big sign in Portuguese and English that reads CLOSED FOR INVENTORY. Behind it, I can see several people laughing and walking around. There is my camera on display on the counter, but when I knock on the door, they give me a look like I'm Jack the Ripper and just keep counting. I knock again and only get the attention of one of the girls behind the counter. She is young and thin with a long braid that hangs all the way down her back. She smiles at me and waves her head and finger. I fold my hands altar-boy style and give her my best lost-puppy look. I hate to do it, I really hate to act American, but I have no choice. I pull a wad of Brazilian cruzeiros out of my pocket and wave the money in front of the window. The girl with the braid opens the door slightly. She asks me in English what I need and why I look so crazy. I tell her about my broken camera and my immediate need for a new one. She tells me to wait at the door and goes back in and picks up the phone. Now, we're not talking about one of those instant cardboard things—this was a real camera with a stiff price. I still can't believe they even have one. As she talks, I stand at the slightly opened door listening to the wonderful sound of Portuguese being spoken. It's a language that is sung more than spoken, with a flow and a softness that's unique among the Romance languages. As with most Americans, the first Portuguese I ever heard spoken was by Astrud Gilberto, singing "The Girl from Ipanema." If in my time left on this planet I can get my French to a more adequate level and learn enough Spanish to get me through South America, then I will be happy to go out knowing I can tell a joke or sing a song in Portuguese.

The girl hangs up the phone and signals for me to enter the store. A few minutes later I depart with my new camera, new batteries, and a fresh supply of film. I spot Kino, Jane, and Mac in front of the hotel waiting for me. Near them, a large, dark-skinned man dressed in a T-shirt and shorts holds a cellular phone stuck to his ear with one hand while the other hand orchestrates his conversation. There is no doubt that this is the one and only Conrad.

Conrad introduces himself and then takes me aside to do the money deal. He needs the price of the boat in cash and an advance for the lunch as well. He adds my money to an extremely large roll of bills that he pulls from a pouch that circles his large, round stomach. "Okay, we go now." I start to walk down the trail that leads to the river where I saw the other boats depart. "No, no, no, boss. We meet da boat in town." I think it kind of odd that we have to drive twenty minutes into Manaus when the hotel boat dock is right here.

"He couldn't meet us here?" I ask.

"It's better to go to Manaus for da boat. Your first trip to Manaus, no? Need I show you all da sights." That is not the explanation I'm looking for, really, but we have no choice. Conrad has locked in on us tighter than the target radar on an F-14, so we just go with the flow. As we pile into a taxi and head to town, I realize it's better in a way because I do want to see the famous floating docks of Manaus.

We drive at the usual wild pace of a Third World cabdriver through the roadside sprawl that I have seen from Africa to Mexico. You rarely see a roller coaster in these parts because driving to town is the ultimate thrill ride and it doesn't cost anything. As we swerve in and out of traffic and dodge everything from city buses to donkey carts, Conrad is still trying to pitch the nighttime excursion to catch "live Amazon crocodiles." He proudly shows us his picture book. Shots of pale tourists with headlamps on, looking at an eleven-inch-long crocodile held by Conrad do nothing to change my mind. I flash to one of those serpentariums that used to dot the Tamiami Trail west of Miami to prey upon the tourists heading south. I have the feeling that this day trip out of Manaus will be as predictable as the tide, and that factors like fuel cost and insurance premiums will be attached to the "adventure."

"What do you think, boss? Da crocodile hunt is verry verry good."

"No, Conrad, I think we just want to cruise on the river."

"Not a problem, boss. It's your boat for da whole day."

If Conrad resembles anybody he's a Brazilian version of Captain Ron. He's a hustler, but I like him. I've worked for too many rock 'n' roll promoters whose games were the same as Conrad's. I am a sucker for the entrepreneurial spirit.

There are nearly a million people living in Manaus now, and it looks like they've all decided to drive to town this morning. An hour after leaving the hotel, we arrive at the floating docks. It's a beehive of activity, with people, animals, trucks, and cars coming and going between the artificial mountains of cargo containers that are stacked ten stories high at odd intervals along the waterfront. The port still maintains the functional yet romantic feel of an exotic waterfront. Boats of every size, color, shape, and description pack the docks. At the end, the cargo booms of several freighters stacked with containers loom above the decks of the tour boats and river ferries that connect the towns along the Amazon from Belém to the Peruvian border.

We make our way through the crowd out to the end of the dock, past several boats that have satellite antennas sprouting from their top decks. These must be the first-class boats from Rio and São Paulo, which cruise the river with running water and soap operas, which the entire country is addicted to. After climbing over several other boats, we find our Amazon yacht for the day, the *Arrau Santos II*. She is just what I hoped she would be. About thirty-five feet long, she looks like the *African Queen.* She has two decks, the lower painted bright red. There is a long wooden table with chairs. The top deck is bright blue, as are the awning and the wooden deck chairs. What a yacht. I feel the river about to take us away. Conrad introduces us to the captain and his wife and daughter, who will accompany us on the trip, and Mowgli, his assistant, who climbs on board at the last minute. He is a young Indian boy who speaks better English than Conrad. Conrad introduces him as his top guide. Conrad will be going with us to the market and then getting off. He'll be busy working things up for us for the rest of our time in Manaus.

Shortly after we board, the captain fires up the old two-stroke diesel and we slip away from the busy dock and head south down the river. I have picked my music for the day— Brazilian, of course. We have Antônio Carlos Jobim, Milton Nascimento, a collection of songs from Bahia, Caesario Evora (Evora is actually from the Cape Verde Islands, but because her native tongue is African Portuguese, she is very popular in Brazil), and a tape I had made of Dalva's friend Claude Duarte Sa. The music will be part of the experience. The headphones may be plugged into the CD player, but the music is plugged into the big artery of life that flows through northern Brazil. One of my prerequisites for travel is to go to countries where music is more than entertainment, where it is almost religion.

We have only been under way a few minutes when the roof of the *mercado* in its entire unique splendor comes into full view. It, along with the amazing Teatro Amazonia, are the landmarks of the city. Manaus is basically a three-trick tourist town. There is the opera house, the market, and the river. Like everything else in Manaus, the roof of the *mercado* speaks of better days, the days at the last turn of the century when rubber made multimillionaires out of those daring and/or foolish enough to trek to the Amazon in search of their fortune. We pass the distinctive landmark of the roof of the *mercado* that resembles the metal components of another structure built by Alexandre-Gustave Eiffel. When the rubber planters were living like potentates out here in the heart of the jungle and they needed a roof for their marketplace, they called the man who built the Eiffel Tower for the job. The *mercado* was built in 1902 as a miniature version of the old Parisian Les Halles. Much of the ironwork was imported from Europe.

I notice that we're not pulling in for supplies. I ask Conrad about it, and he says we're going to the town market farther down the river. I sit back and enjoy the view as we pass by one of the many floating gas stations with long lines of watercraft waiting for their turn at the pump.

We are part of the flow now, the artery of the river pumping through the heart of the city on its banks. We flew over this spot yesterday, but the view from fifteen hundred feet at 140 knots was not the same as the one from our little riverboat at 10 knots. Manaus has to be seen from the river to really be appreciated, for it is from the surface of the river that you see how intertwined river life and city life are here in the heart of the Amazon. The floating dock is the core of the water activity, but for miles above and below the city an almost endless procession of boats lines the waterfront. Some are just tied up for the night, while others have made their last trip and are tied up for good, their engines rusting away and their hulls full of worms.

Just south of town we pass a string of marine railways that lead from the high ground to the water's edge. Here are more boats in various states of repair. Conrad tells me that there are no mechanical lifting devices used on these railways. The river provides all the muscle. You haul your boat when the flood waters come in the spring, do the work, and wait until the next rise of the water the following year to refloat it. Little speedy pirogues with big Japanese motors zip between the large riverboats up and down the Río Negro, and we just putt along. I am happy as a clam. I tap my feet to the sounds in my head and pull out my little palm-top computer and begin to take notes. This immediately arouses Mowgli's curiosity, and he leans over my shoulder for a closer look as I show him the amazing little machine. I fired off several pages of images and notes and hit the magical button of our time, SAVE. I thought of my saved notes as little pan nuggets that, when the time was right, would hopefully lead me back to the rich vein of the story of my first day on the Amazon.

A half hour after we left the main dock, the captain eases the *Arrau Santos II* to a small wooden dock near the town market. Conrad charges from the boat and motions us ashore. Why do I get the notion in my head that he has done this routine before? There isn't really much to keep us on the boat. The show on the dock consists of a couple of skinny dogs stretched out amid several passed-out humans, so we all disembark from the *Arrau Santos II* and follow Conrad along wooden planks that have been laid over the smelly ooze along the shore. This is not the trip to the market that the girls envisioned. We make our way through the crowd of men lounging around the dock who lock onto the girls with that testosterone radar. The town market does not look like a place on the tourist trail. This is not Fisherman's Wharf, the French Market in New Orleans, or the Fulton Fish Market in New York. There are no disposable rubber gloves here, or ornamental roofs designed by Eiffel, and it certainly is no 7-Eleven. It's just rows and rows of tin roofs and plastic tarpaulins, which cover an array of vending booths and wet cement floors that showcase everything from peacock bass that hang from hooks still flexing their gills to fresh iguana meat being sliced off the carcass with surgical precision. These sights and, in particular, the smells send the girls back to the boat. I ramble on through the carnage with my video camera, taking in the piles of green bananas and huge stacks of red wooden cases holding six-ounce Cokes. What distribution those people from Atlanta have. The unlikely sound of Mike and the Mechanics blares overhead, perfect background music for the pace of activity in the market. Saws rip, hammers pound, and cleavers carve out the staples for the customers of the day. Conrad's giant face appears in the viewfinder of my camera and scares the shit out of me for a minute. He just laughs at my reaction. "Boss, it's all set now, lunch for us is to the boat. All fresh and nice. Dey cook it up for you when you wants. Lunch by the river. Better to get going now." I pocket my camera and head back to the boat but notice that Conrad is off in another direction.

"Mowgli my best guide. He plenty good for you. I work on airplane trip and other things. I call you tonight. Ciao." And he disappears into the market.

Mowgli is waiting when I get back to the boat. He is a lot calmer than Conrad and seems to have things under control. When I get out my little palm-top computer to make a few more notes, he sits beside me and watches me work. If the computer isn't enough to get his attention, the GPS makes him laugh. I try to explain the concept of the signals from satellites, but he just keeps laughing. He has heard of such things but has never seen one.

We do the tourist rounds at the meeting of the waters where the black Río Negro and the muddy brown Río Solimões come together and form the Amazon. We look for pink dolphins but find none, then head up a small tributary toward the game preserve. When it's time to savor our lunch, the captain just eases off the power and runs the boat up into the tall grass on the edge of a little bayou. We share our lunch with Mowgli, the captain, and his family. Over a bowl of fish stew and some unrecognizable yams, Mowgli levels with us. He tells me that the game preserve we are going to today is just for the tourist boats from Manaus. The real adventure lies at least a five-day boat ride up the river.

Mowgli comes from an Indian village near the town of Tefé, halfway between Manaus and the Colombian border. He came to Manaus like so many other young people of the region because it is the only thing happening. The simple life of the Amazon still has its devotees, but more and more young people take off for the city. Mowgli was a jungle fighter in the army, or so he said, and what the hell, even if he wasn't, I like the idea. I ask him what he had thought of Manaus when he saw it for the first time. "Big," he replies. He tells me he came down in a dugout canoe from his village and made contact with Conrad through friends in the army. Like everywhere else in the world, even in the jungle it is who you know.

It starts to get hot, real hot. The boat is making enough apparent wind to generate a little breeze, but it is now, under the equatorial sun, that the red deck doesn't seem like such a cool idea. If you stand for more than five seconds in any one spot, the bottoms of your feet start to blister. The little blue awning overhead offers some relief from the heat, and we find ourselves playing musical chairs with the sun and the shadows. We see more people than animals, as boatload after boatload of tourists move back and forth between Manaus and the little nature preserve on Lago de Janaurino. We arrive at a main building situated beside the river where you can buy an array of Indian crafts and, if you're lucky, a cold Polar beer. There is a hiking trail through the tall trees where we spot a few monkeys and parrots, but it's obvious from the start that the heat will make this a short trip. We leave the breeze at the dock and trek toward the interior. There is a well-worn footpath through the tall trees, and Mowgli leads us along. The jaguars and the forty-foot anacondas that you see in all the coffee-table books have left the world of man a long time before we arrived, hightailing it to safer and less traveled territory. God knows how many mosquito and sand-fly stings it took for some dedicated photographer to get those shots, but I'm damn sure they were not within a day trip of the Tropical Hotel.

The river around Manaus is very civilized by jungle standards, and the day trips are not so bad. At least they keep the curious intruders concentrated on one small part of the river, and it is good for the local economy. There is a lot of money to be made in giving tourists a safe and easy look at the Amazon, and our tour is not much different in presentation from the alligator wrestling at the Seminole village in the Everglades or the Conch Train tour of Key West. And yet, as tacky as this kind of tourism might be, there is a huge underlying change in attitude toward it since Teddy Roosevelt blasted his way up the Amazon at the turn of the century. Eco-tourism makes money without destroying the natural surroundings. This is a big change in these parts and one that can have a major lasting effect on the way the children of these Amazonians view their world and the world that comes to visit them.

We do not stay long at the preserve. It's still the river that's the big attraction to me, and we're in need of the man-made breeze. I restring my hammock in a patch of shade and prepare to cruise home. Despite the heat and the tourist trap, I am a contented fellow, just moving with the motion of the boat through the relatively calm river water, staring out at endless miles of nothing. It is exactly what I came to do. I haven't a care in the world. I have spent relaxing days out on the ocean, but there are always sails to trim and sun lines to advance and your mind is not really free to disengage. But on the *Arrau Santos*, I am not in charge, nor do I even have the slightest urge to be. I make like a native, curl up in my hammock, and just watch the world go by, letting the motion of the boat and the thump of the diesel do their jobs, while for one whole day I put my life into neutral.

I Want to Fly

It is late afternoon as the *Arrau Santos* slides back up the river toward the hotel dock beneath another amazing backdrop of sunlight reflecting on water and the clouds. The hot air has been blown away by a stiff breeze that came with the sunset, and the temperature is comfortable. As we near the dock, I am treated to one of my favorite sights in the world, one that complements perfectly the end of our first day on the Amazon. A small seaplane circles above the river just beyond the hotel dock, then descends and makes a perfect landing on the water's glassy surface. I rest my chin on the top rail of the boat, take my binoculars from my bag, and focus in on the plane. It is a two-seater ultralight amphibian, probably built in the pilot's backyard or garage. The pilot looks like one of those guys in the Levi's ads—young, handsome, with that water-flier style. He taxis the little plane to the beach, cuts the power at the perfect time, and the plane glides gently forward, the nose kissing the shore. He jumps from the tiny cockpit with a bowline in his hand, holds the plane like an obedient horse, and waves toward the dock. When I move my glasses along his line of sight, a beautiful Brazilian woman with long hair, dressed right out of a Banana Republic display window, runs toward the pilot. She throws her arms around him, and our boy manages to hold on to the plane and get his other arm around the woman at the same time. They kiss one of those long movie kisses, and then he takes the small backpack she is carrying and stows it in the bow compartment. He effortlessly picks her up and eases her into the rear seat, unfastens the bowline with a flick of the wrist, and then shoves off from the beach. With a perfectly timed jump, he climbs aboard his craft and immediately begins to work the rudder pedal so that the wind will turn the plane toward the opposite shore. He closes the canopy, fires up the little engine, and starts his takeoff run. The ultralight seems to jump from the water like a bait fish running from a barracuda and climbs slowly to an altitude of no more than a hundred feet, then levels off and turns west. I watch through my binoculars until they are absorbed by the brilliant Amazon sunset. Who are they, and where are they headed? It's the universal question of all pilots who find themselves on the ground looking up at someone else's fun.

Manaus: Day Two

Rainy-Day Manaus

I have always enjoyed being sent into or brought out of sleep by the sound of a rainstorm in the morning, or napping through those late-afternoon squalls that pop up from the humid sectors of the Everglades and are pulled by the steering winds toward the Gulf Stream offshore. There are some smart people out there who have recorded these sounds of gentle rain and subdued thunder claps to sell to the insomniac market; Sominex on tape is a big business.

I am awakened at dawn on my second day in Amazonas by what I think is one of those comforting rainstorms, but it takes only a few seconds of lounging in limbo before my foggy mind catches on to the fact that this is a different kind of storm outside my window. The thunder booms sound like a B-52 strike and shake the floor. It is as if the low gray overcast that enveloped the morning has been unraveled at the seams by spilling sheets of water from the sky. The rain sounds like a roaring waterfall, and the visibility is nonexistent. From my window I can't even make out the pool below, fifty feet away. There is no sign that this is a passing storm, no hint of hidden sunlight or cloud formation. This is monsoon weather, which comes in December and January and initiates the tremendous volume of water that eventually reveals itself in the flood season.

No, this does not look like a day to be out on the river. If it rains this hard the rest of the day, we will have to leave our rooms because the river will probably be in them. I call Jim Powell in Florida to try and find a pilot contact in Manaus to check the weather in the region. The forecast is not as bad as it looks. This is not the beginning of the long monsoon rains, just a pocket of low pressure moving through. The bad news involves our planned trip to Angel Falls. The weather was moving in that direction, and even worse, Jim has gotten word that there isn't a room to be had at the small hotel near the airstrip at Katima. A German tour group has the entire place booked for the week. We are on stand-by for a room. I tell him, as always, we'll just play it by ear. If we don't go to Angel Falls, then we'll just fly straight to the island of Tobago. As soon as I hang up, the phone rings again. It's Conrad. "Looks like we are washed out today," I say.

"Oh, no, boss, just a little rain, nothing to worry 'bout. I got speedboat with good canvas, no leak roof. Not a problem. He meet you to the hotel dock in one hour." I just laugh. I love his tenacity.

"I don't think so, Conrad. We'll try again tomorrow morning. How are you coming with the flying trip?"

"Almost all done. Tonight I know. You want to do a bus trip to Indian village or market? Got big air-conditioned bus."

I cut him off. "No, Conrad, we'll just take it easy today." I lied. I know we're headed for the opera house. With the river enveloped in a deluge, we will seek a few minutes of solitude in the Teatro Amazonas, at our own pace, not Conrad's.

All Dressed Up and Nowhere to Go

There's nothing quite as dangerous as having a whole lot of money and being stuck in a place where you can't spend it. That was the problem that befell the adventurous rubber-plantation owners of Amazonas in the late nineteenth century. Life in the jungle was still hard and void of European culture, which had taken two thousand years to cultivate. The Amazon planters didn't have that kind of time, but they did have a hell of a lot of money, so they sped up the process. They used their immense profits to bring the first electric lights and automobiles ever seen on the entire continent of South America to Manaus. But lights and cars weren't enough, and there were no mail-order catalogues or Internet shopping guides in those days. Next came the engineering equivalent of painting a masterpiece when a Scottish engineer designed the floating dock to harness the flood-prone waters of the Río Negro. Great engineering, but not a lot of fun. It is said that the more affluent citizens of Manaus couldn't find a decent neighborhood laundry, so they sent their clothes to Paris to be cleaned. With that kind of decadence, it didn't take long for the bored rubber barons to come up with a project that would satisfy their taste for the extravagant and at the same time bring them some fun. They were all dressed up with no place to go, so they created a place to put on a show.

The Little Rascal Put on a Show in the Jungle

Again, it was a damn movie that had stirred up in me the idea of seeing the Amazon. This time it was Werner Herzog's *Fitzcarraldo*, the story of a man who fails in his grand scheme to construct a railroad across South America but instead decides to build an opera house in the middle of the Amazon jungle. It's one of those love-it-or-hate-it movies, but if you can get past the German dialogue and English subtitles, the sight of Claudia Cardinale as the operator of the whorehouse is enough to hold you until the incredible scene where Fitzcarraldo, played by Klaus Kinski, gets a tribe of Indians to haul a three-hundred-ton riverboat up and over a mountain to a river on the other side.

Truth is a whole lot stranger than fiction in the jungle, and *Fitzcarraldo* certainly depicts that part of Amazon history accurately. In the late 1800s there was a lot of money being made in wild and unsettled parts of the world. From the jungles of Manaus to the silver and gold mines of the Colorado Rockies, there were big fortunes in the hands of people who had never had them before. The men who pursued their dreams in such places were as wild as their chosen surroundings. It was not unlike the smugglers I knew in the Caribbean in the seventies and eighties who lived on million-dollar yachts with beautiful women, duffel bags of cash, and the best dope in the world. It was boom or bust, and everybody knew it. Every era has its pirates, and the rubber boom in the Amazon had its share. Opera was the popular music of the day, and these guys could afford to build a lavish opera house that competed in size and grandiosity with the fine halls of Europe, and they could hire the best singers and pay them what amounted to fortunes to come to the frontier and entertain. It was nice work, if you could get it.

The rain has emptied the streets of Manaus and cooled the air to a pleasant temperature. We creep along in our cab toward downtown. Everything about the cab ride reeks of twentieth-century life. Too much traffic, too much exhaust, potholes in the road, really bad drivers. But halfway to town, the rain stops completely as if God has just decided to close the overflow valve. The pedestrian population begins to emerge from the temporary shelter of porches, overhangs, umbrellas, and sheets of blue plastic and rejoins the mainstream of people in a hurry to get somewhere. The cabdriver deposits us alongside the square of São Sebastião. The air still holds the cooling effect of the overcast, and the din that is the soundtrack to the afternoon activity of downtown Manaus seems to have been abruptly muffled as we stand staring across the dressed-stone access that leads to the entrance of Teatro Amazonas. We walk in the comfort of this sudden silence, through statues and rose gardens.

Early photographs of the Teatro Amazonas under construction give you an idea of the wonderful absurdity of the times. You see this immense structure that looks like it belongs in the capitals of Europe, but instead it sits among palm trees and thatched-roof huts that lead down to the river. Today the neighborhood around the the giant pink structure has evolved into squares, churches, and more permanent housing. But just the presence of such a shape in such a place sets the mind reeling. Photographs do not do it justice. You have to experience it yourself.

At first sight, the pink façade of the building reminds me of one of those giant, sugarcoated, hard-candy Easter eggs, which were the prize finds of my family egg hunt, at my crazy old uncle and aunt's house on a bayou just south of the creosote plant in Gautier, Mississippi. The egg was the envy of all the cousins who had gathered for the family weekend. I found it only once, and I can remember that discovery to this day. It was hidden in the ribbon grass down along the bayou far from the main house, tucked away in a blackberry thicket. The egg was as big as a cantaloupe, pink, with little roses all over it. At one end there was a small glass window. I held it up to the sun and looked through the opening like I would a spyglass, and there inside was a tiny country scene, with Peter Rabbit sitting at a table having tea.

We hire a young, English-speaking guide in the lobby, and he shows us around. The first interesting thing that he explains is the silence that we all felt in the square. The stone road that surrounds the opera house has latex in its composition to reduce the noise caused by the wooden wheels of the carriages passing by. Those rubber barons had thought of everything.

"The builders of the Manaus Opera House spared no expense," the guide says as we enter the main auditorium. Along with the sound quality, the decor of the building is a whole separate box of eccentricities. There is the painting on the ceiling of the auditorium by the Brazilian artist Crispim do Amaral, which produces the vision of standing under the Eiffel Tower and looking up. The chandelier brought from Paris was made of the finest French bronze and Italian crystal. Twenty-two Greek tragedy masks, attached to a column of the auditorium, represent such famous artists, writers, painters, and musicians as Shakespeare, Molière, Goethe, Mozart, Beethoven, and Wagner. The Noble Room ceiling features paintings by Domenico de Angelis, and a drop cloth by Crispim do Amaral, which rises entirely to the dome to prevent damage to the painting, represents the "Meeting of the Waters" of the Negro and the Solimões rivers, forming the Amazon. I just keep thinking about what it must have been like for Caruso to step from the boat onto the streets of Manaus and see the town and the opera house for the first time.

When we have seen all there is to see, we walk back through the tiny square to meet our cab. I feel like I did after coming out of art exhibits of Winslow Homer and Frederick Edwin Church at the National Gallery in Washington. I can't put the feelings into words; the closest I can come is to say that the sights and sounds of such things may enter the body through the senses but they find their way to the heart, and that is what art is really about. And for me, the only true way to feel the wonder of this wonder of the world would be on that stage with my guitar in my hand. I know as we leave the rubber street and head back to the clamor of town that before I am through, I will play the Teatro Amazonas.

Manaus: Day Three

Da Plane, Boss, Da Plane

It was our third and last day in the Amazon, and we make the most of it. "Boss, we have a plane," Conrad announces to me on his daily morning call. "I also have speedboat back to da dock. Short trip to you swim da river with Mowgli and den we go for da fly. What you tink, boss?" Well, the morning is pretty much open. The weather is good, and we packed last night. It looks as if Angel Falls has been scratched; the pilots called to tell me the weather wasn't good over Venezuela. We are bound for Tobago and a rendezvous with the kids. We miss them. My old friend Charlie Hergrueter managed to slip away from the Harvard Medical Center for a week and is bound for Grenada, where I will pick him up in a couple of days and we will explore the region's fly-fishing possibilities. We have heard tales of remote tarpon spots hidden in the Grenadines.

After a quick visit to the food room, we go down to the dock to meet the speedboat. Mowgli gives us our options, and we settle on a hike in the jungle and possibly a swim in the river. We cruise in the funky little boat across the wide span of the Río Negro about five miles upstream of the hotel, then follow a smaller tributary through some amazing scenery. The bayou snakes through a microcosm of Indian and river culture, as we pass houseboats and repair yards that remind me of the Gulf Coast. Finally, the captain slows the boat as we enter a lagoon filled with giant cedar and cypress trees that rise out of the water to a height of a hundred feet. I think about my fly rod and the stories of the famous peacock bass. This smells like a spot, but I have no gear and the jungle waits.

Mowgli has picked up another guide, and when we settle on a landing spot, the two of them jump out and lead us to the interior, swinging machetes. The canopy of trees overhead is so thick that it blocks the sun and alters the light to a strange hue. The breeze ceases to blow, and the humidity is almost thick enough to cut with one of the machetes. Now I know what the steamy jungle feels like. As we wind through thick foliage, I flash back to a grammar-school science project for which I had made a terrarium depicting a miniature jungle-life scene. I had combed the creeks near my house for ferns and moss, then caught a few tadpoles and a water snake. I am identifying with those tadpoles now. I am just a tadpole myself, checking my trusty GPS to make sure we can get out if our guides decide to strike or play a real nasty trick on us, but the cover is so thick that it blocks out the satellite signal. After about a half hour of hiking, we are hot, sweaty, and have seen enough. We know it's time to end our excursion when we meet a spider the size of a pie plate hanging across our path. That's the icing on the cake, especially for the girls.

On the way back to the hotel, we stop at a deserted beach. Kino and Mac stroll the shore, while Jane and I frolic around in the dark water. This is, of course, before the release of that attention-getting movie *Anaconda*. We aren't attacked by piranhas or crocodiles, and we climb back into our canoe with all limbs attached and head back to civilization.

The green of the jungle is soon replaced by the green hue of a tray full of emeralds at the jewelry store in the hotel. I buy a few to toss into my treasure box back in Palm Beach. At lunch I run into the largest group of Americans we've seen since leaving the States. It's one of those safari-fishing expeditions, just returned from a week up the Río Negro, where they have been jungle-fishing for peacock bass. There are Southern accents everywhere, and a few Parrotheads among the anglers ask for autographs, happily showing me pictures of their catch. God knows how the stories will wind up once they get back to Atlanta and tell their buddies about running into Jimmy Buffett in the middle of the Amazon. Take it from one who knows. Fishermen have been known to stretch the truth.

Conrad is here to meet us right after lunch. Our transportation to the Ponta Pelada airport is a beat-up Plymouth Barracuda, with no muffler but plenty of pink upholstery. The driver is a thin man with a few teeth missing who just sits behind the wheel, revving the engine as if he's at the start of a stock-car race. We all cram into the backseat and head out into the exciting world of Manaus driving. I get the feeling that Conrad doesn't quite know how to get to the small airport. Finally I see a little Cessna on a final approach and point it out to Conrad, who seems to get his bearings and finds a familiar street that leads us to the office of the charter company.

The little field has the look of a hundred small airports I have been in and out of. Like everything else in Manaus, it has the feel of having seen better days. This had been the original airport for all traffic flying into Manaus, but when the new modern terminal was built twenty miles outside the city, Pelada airport was relegated to just handling private airplanes and small charter companies, making it just the kind of place I like to browse around. Conrad goes in search of his connections, and the rest of the gang plops down in the shade. I snoop through the hangars until I come upon a familiar sight. Parked among a gaggle of small Pipers and Cessnas I spot a shiny Lake 250 amphibian, the same type of plane I had bought over ten years ago, the one in which I learned to fly and land in the water. This means that there are seaplanes operating on the Amazon, which is not what we had been told back in Florida.

While I'm looking at the plane, a voice from behind me tells me in English that my pilot has arrived. I turn to see a small lady in a flight suit. I ask if she knows who owns the Lake. It is hers. Her name is Eva, and as we walk back to the terminal, she tells me she also works in the tower. I can't believe what I'm hearing. I tell her about my Lake and about my Albatross and the problems that we ran into before leaving the States. She looks puzzled. She says she knows of no restrictions on flying or landing in the water. The only restrictions she knows of have to do with debris in the river during the flood season, when driftwood the size of full-grown trees comes downstream and presents big problems for water landings. But now, in the dry season, it is no problem. As usual, time is not on our side. Our pilot is at the plane ready to go. I tell Eva I will drop in on her when we return.

We exchange our seats in the Barracuda for the safer surroundings of a Cessna 210. The pilot, Alberto, is a very nice fellow and has the bearing of a good pilot. He does a quick preflight check and then asks us what we want to see. We have paid for forty minutes, and since we have traveled south of Manaus by boat, we choose to head north up the Río Negro. There was an extra seat, and I invite Conrad to come along for the ride. He tries to act cool about the whole thing, but if I were a betting man, I would say that it is his first time in a plane.

We leave the Amazon with the same view that we had upon arrival—the bird's-eye view. With our forty minutes' worth of fun tickets used up, we land back at the small airport. I stopped by Eva's, get her name, phone and fax numbers, and leave her a copy of my album, several T-shirts, and a picture of the Albatross. She looks at the photo for a moment, then shows it to her coworkers like it was a photo of my children. She thanks me and tells me to call her if I ever want to bring the plane back.

Yesterday, on the way back to the hotel from the Teatro Amazonas, we stopped briefly at the Indian museum, run by Salesian missionaries, for a quick tour. The small building more resembled a convent than a museum, and the displays were an amateur presentation of handicrafts, ceramics, clothing, utensils, ritual objects, and primitive paintings that depicted the life of the Indians in the upper regions of the Río Negro. But in one room hung a huge painting that stopped me in my tracks. It was a jungle scene showing some Indians gathered beside the river. They are in a state of excitement, some pointing their spears toward the sky, others pointing their fingers. The children in the background are bouncing up and down with their heads turned up. The focus of their attention is a Grumman flying boat passing overhead near treetop level. For me it said everything about why I had come here and what I was looking for. I felt a connection to all those crazy men and women who had preceded me. I don't know how or why, but it is there. As the song says, "There's a cowboy in the jungle."

We make Conrad get us a cab for the ride to the big airport. One death-defying road rally a day is about all I can stand. We say good-bye, and I give Conrad a big bundle of swag for him and Mowgli. The T-shirts will get plenty of wear, and I like the idea of the myth taking hold in these parts. Who knows, when I come back to play the opera house in Manaus, I might even draw a crowd. Conrad hugs us all and doesn't miss the opportunity to pass out his cards. He will definitely find a page in my address book. I will certainly recommend to anyone visiting Manaus, "You have got to call Conrad."

Randy is waiting, the bags are packed, and customs has been taken care of. There are no dope-sniffing dogs or guns in view, just smiles and waves from the ground crew as we taxi out, take off, and turn on our course back to the Northern Hemisphere and to the islands.

Three days is by no means anywhere near enough time to "do the Amazon." And then again it is. The river, and the life it generates, certainly has seen its share of adventure in the past, and I am sure there is still some waiting for unsuspecting intruders in the future. Somewhere far from Manaus up in the icy heights of the Peruvian Andes, the sun melts the snow into pools of clear water that are already feeling the tug of gravity. It comes together at the Carhuasant River and becomes the longest water slide in the world on a four-thousand-mile journey to the mouth of the Amazon. It is joined downstream by the

icy runoff from Ecuador. The moving water carries its past into
the present. The ghosts of the Incas and the conquistadors ride
on the ripples with the dust from the charcoal sketches of the
Andes by Frederic Edwin Church. They travel a predestined
course toward the eventual meeting with the salt of the ocean.
Along the path where the water laps against the shore, the
lonely jaguar sneaks out of the jungle for a cool drink. It touches
the lives of the villages and cities ripe with the sweet and sour
fruit of life in the hinterland between modernization and isolation. It will nurture, flood, and kill, and carry the commerce of
ships and dugout canoes up and downstream. It will pass beneath the hand-laid timbers of a little red riverboat named the
Arrau Santos II and its load of curious English-speaking passengers, who will spend a minuscule amount of time on a small dot
of the entire surface of the river. Amazonas is not the outpost it
once was, but nothing is. But the river, like the Oscar Hammerstein lyrics, just keeps rolling along, simply playing its part in
the puzzle known as life on Earth. And in January 1997, it became a part of the experiences of this child of the swamp who
had come to have a look around and fly out of the jungle with a
little Amazon river water flowing in his veins.

SECTION
XI

The Islands

The Spicy Kind of Life

Back to the Islands

Over the Jungle

It takes a mere two hours and eighteen minutes to get us out of Manaus, back into the Northern Hemisphere, and on to the Caribbean. Our path of flight is straight north to Port of Spain, Trinidad, with a slight jog to Crown Point Airport on the small and still unspoiled island of Tobago.

The exploration phase of my trip is over. I haven't succeeded in finding even a goddamn postage stamp of water on the continent of South America where I could land my flying boat. The islands, I hope, will be a different story. I have the name of a guide in Tobago, Captain Frothy, given to me at a bar in Manhattan, along with stories of big tarpon and permit in the waters around the Bucco Reef. Those are all the clues I have, but searching is half the fun. Life is much more manageable when thought of as a scavenger hunt as opposed to a surprise party. The Albatross will be waiting in Trinidad after her trip from San José across the southern islands of the Caribbean. The kids will arrive from Florida in a day, and all seems fine in my little world. I want a boat drink, and I am looking for Captain Frothy, who will take me to tarpon in Tobago.

There is weather ahead—big thunderstorms right down our course to Port of Spain, so we have to fly east of the airway to get around the buildups. Between the moisture content, the heat, and the lifting index, the northern portion of

South America is a weather-making machine of enormous proportions. All you have to do is add water. The storms stretch out along a hundred-mile line that takes us damn near to the coast before we find a break. As we carve around the weather, I think about the mysterious terrain that occupies the northeast corner of this continent. From our altitude, it all just looks like green jungle, but I know from my books and the stories I've heard that the geography and politics of French Guyana, Surinam, and Guyana are anything but mundane.

As recently as last year, gold hunters massacred an entire Indian village along the northern Brazilian border in their insanely greedy quest. They fled to Venezuela, where they were caught and sentenced to hang. In Cayenne, the capital, French colonial life still goes on. Populated by Creoles, Lebanese, Laotians, Haitians, Vietnamese, and the descendants of Devil's Island, it is the elephant burial ground of the French colonial empire where today soldiers of the victorious and defeated armies of the mother country cohabitate with the once oppressed and now liberated subjects of the French colonial system. It is a strange world, where ex-legionnaires and refugees from Southeast Asia sip coffee at the Café des Palmistres in Cayenne. Snake hunters and soldiers of fortune crowd into the Eldo Grille with stories of their attempts at the golden ring of reptile raconteurs. They are still looking for the ten-meter anaconda. If taken alive, it will net them the fifty-thousand-dollar bounty offered by Theodore Roosevelt at the turn of the century. Rocket ships tear through the dense tropical sky near the newly created town of Kourou and send European satellites into orbit, lighting up the dark and macabre remnants of Devil's Island just offshore.

There is a lot of bizarre history down there on the other side of these pressurized windows, and it passes quickly with a 60-knot tailwind and a ground speed of 420 knots. Before I know it, I am looking down at the wide delta of the

Orinoco River that marks our passage into Venezuela. I turn back for one last look at the green and hear the drums from this exotic coast calling me back to what I know is another undiscovered spot on my songline. I guess that's why God invented turbine engines and kerosene and gave us a magnetic field and stars to steer by, so that we can always get to where we want to go.

Trini Jimmy

Spicy Kind of Life

It's in the mood, it's in the blood
It's in the food, it's in the mud
It's the spicy kind of life
Creola

—"CREOLA"

Our arrival over Trinidad is marked by big flames shooting skyward like signal flares guiding us home. No, it's not another SWAT team after us, it's the burn-off of the offshore oil wells. We are descending for our landing on Tobago, and I can feel the islands now. The flames accentuate the legacy of the land below as hot, hot, hot. We have drawn away from the continent to the south and are now at the bottom of the island chain that I have come to know so well. Trinidad occupies a strange and wonderful part of my history. Today my children are in the care of Angela Washington and Aileen Hippolyte, two wonderful women from Trinidad who are a part of our family. Cameron Marley and Sarah Delaney have expressions and certain words in their vocabularies that are coated with a distinct Trinidadian accent. The staff kitchen in our house is called the "Trini Kitchen," sporting flags and photos of Trinidad.

My first taste of Trinidad and Tobago was in the form of a hot sauce called Matouk's, which you will not find in most grocery stores in America. I first ran into it years ago in Key West. Like the other condiments and flavors of the islands, it had surely been brought there by sailors. Matouk's comes in what looks like a ketchup bottle, but don't be fooled. It is the real thing, and just a little dab will do ya. It is Trinidad in a bottle, and like the island and the culture itself, it has to be taken in small doses before you can finally just pour it on.

My second and more important connection to Trini is its music. Trinidad is the birthplace of calypso. And the music of Trinidad is the steel drum, or "da pan, mon." I first heard steel drums on records by the Roaring Lion, Lord Invader, Kitchener, and the likes that belonged to my grandfather. His favorite was "Rum and Coca-Cola," not by the Andrews Sisters, but the original, by Lord Invader. He was a lover of Caribbean music, long before it gained worldwide popularity through migration and technology. He would return from his trips south with boxes of seventy-eights, which I would play on my grandmother's Victrola.

The next step in the Trinification of Jimmy came from my friend Glenn Frey. I was on the road opening for the Eagles on the *Hotel California* tour in 1977, and one night in some unholy hotel room, he put on what he said was his favorite tape. It was *The Path*, by Ralph MacDonald, an instrumental calypso symphony that traces the roots of Trinidadian music back to Africa, via the Caribbean and the island of Manhattan. Ralph was born in New York, but his father was a famous bandleader in Trini in the forties who had migrated to the Big Apple. Ralph grew up in Harlem and went to work as a drummer for Harry Belafonte when he was seventeen. From there, his talents became legendary in the world of drummers and percussionists. *The Path* became one of my favorite albums as well. I had been living in the islands on and off for a good number of years, and the sounds I heard were finding their way into my music. I believe that one of the reasons I've been able to survive this long in the music business is the fact that I have no rules to go by when it comes to developing a sound. As in the great stew of Trinidad, *calaloo,* the mixing of a wide variety of ingredients and spices is what makes it taste so good. Ralph's music was something I wanted to put into the pot of whatever was to become my identifiable sound. In my

way of thinking, steel drums and congas could blend perfectly
well with steel guitar and blues harmonica.

I was finally introduced to Ralph by Elliot Sheiner in New
York. Later, when Elliot was producing my *One Particular Harbour*, at Village Recorders in Los Angeles, he contacted a steel
drummer named Robert Greenidge to play on the session. I
had come back from Tahiti with tapes of the title song that I
had recorded in a small studio above a coconut-soap factory in
downtown Papeete. As a part of this wild recording experience, I had somehow convinced a Mormon Tahitian choir
to re-create the vocal style of a Polynesian chorus that had
haunted me from the day I had heard it in the soundtrack of
the movie *Donovan's Reef*. My idea was to blend the culture of
the Pacific, represented by the unique vocal style of the choir,
with the steel drum from Trinidad. That little burst of creativ-
ity sent me down a road that, I am happy to report, I still travel
on today. "One Particular Harbour" is still one of my favorite
songs and comes with a lot of history. Both Ralph and Robert
still have very successful careers and have also been a part of
the sound of the Coral Reefer Band for more than ten years.

Up, Up, Up on the Hill

The lights of Port of Spain are just beginning to dot the shore
of the island as nighttime approaches. I can see the ships and
cranes along the waterfront section of Queen's Wharf. Trinidad is a working country, not a tourist island. It has the most
culturally diversified population in the West Indies chain,
rooted in a twisted concoction of French and English colonial-
ists, African slaves, and indentured servants from India, all
brought together long ago by fate and history. Trinidad has an
identity. It is not just another island clamoring for the lucrative
dollars of the tourist trade. Trinidad has oil, manufacturing
plants, and abundant produce exports, and somewhere back

around World War II some genius got the idea to carve drums out of oil barrels and a new musical instrument became the musical voice of the island.

I can follow the terrain as it rises from the sea. The sun is behind the far side of the island and lights up the shore like a giant backdrop of purples and soft blues. It has been nearly ten years since I was last in Trinidad, but it doesn't take me long to trace the peculiar hill crowded with shotgun shacks and houses that look like they are stacked up on one another. It is called Laventille, and it occupies a most special place in the heart of my music. It was a dark night in February 1989 that I was climbing up the winding road to the top of the hill. This was a tough neighborhood and one that doesn't see a lot of white people. But my driver was Ralph MacDonald, and on Laventille, that was like traveling with God. We waved and the locals waved back. The smell of fried yardbird and garlic permeated the night air, and from every window music could be heard. On that night, I was afforded the unique opportunity to experience the magic of Trinidadian music that had affected me for so many years, in the very womb of its existence.

The King of Somewhere Hot

The journey up the hill had started a year earlier. We had recorded the *Hot Water* album, which Ralph coproduced with Russell Kunkel. As part of the promotional tour, we scheduled two benefit concerts in Florida, one in Key West at the old baseball field and one at the Marine Stadium on Key Biscayne in Miami. I had written several songs with Ralph and Bill Salter for the album. One song, "The King of Somewhere Hot," contained an incredible steel-drum arrangement that Robert had written. Robert divided most of his time between Los Angeles, New York, and Laventille. He had grown up on the hill and

had been a member of one of the premier pan bands that compete annually as part of the Trinidadian Carnival.

The WITCO Desperados were as famous in Trinidad as
those four lads from Liverpool were in England. They had
formed as a band in 1941 and had been a musical force in
Trinidad ever since. Robert Greenidge joined the band in 1965
and is now its leader. These international ambassadors of pan
music have played in Europe, Africa, Royal Albert Hall in
London, and Carnegie Hall. It was time they came to the
island of Key West, or so I thought. Somewhere out on the
proud highway one night after a show, we came up with this
idea to bring the Despos up for the shows in Florida. If I had
known then what it meant to bring a sixty-piece steel-drum
band with all the trappings to the good old U.S. of A., feed
them, pay them, house them, and get them out of Key West
again, I probably would have jumped out of the plane that
night, but it sounded like a good idea at the time.

The Miami and Key West appearances were the last shows
we would do for the season. The plan was to have the Desperados open the shows with a selection of classical and calypso
pieces, then I would hit the stage with my guitar and do a couple of special numbers with the entire steel band. I couldn't
wait to see how it would work out. It was the kind of excitement that you need to come up with every now and then, just
to keep things interesting. I had been in St. Barts for a couple
of weeks before the shows. Our plan was for Robert and Ralph
to go to Trinidad and rehearse the songs "Creola" and "The
King of Somewhere Hot" with the band. Then they would call
me when they were ready, and I would fly down and do a
rough rehearsal. The truth of the matter is that I wasn't really
needed at the rehearsal. In fact, we have a policy of not re-
hearsing very much anyway, but hell, I just wanted to go to
Trinidad and hear the band live.

The call came, and Kino and I boarded the island hopper to
St. Martin to catch the BIWI flight to Port of Spain. In true "No

Plane on Sunday" mode of Caribbean transportation, for a trip of just over five hundred miles, we made three plane changes on three different islands that took a total of just over eight flying hours before we landed at the Port of Spain International Airport. Then there was customs—a line about a New York City block long. Kino and I were contemplating whether to start drinking heavily when a gentleman in a blue Pan Am blazer identified me and told me to follow him. He was moving past the customs line with an air of authority, and we just joined in his cadences. Words were exchanged with the women in the booth, and the next thing we knew we were curbside and there was Ralph and his girlfriend (now wife), Gracie. In the car Ralph told us that the Pan Am agent was a big fan of his, not mine, and he had run into him at the airport. Thank God for faithful fans. When we checked in at the Trinidad Hilton, there was a message from Robert that they were running a little late. No problem, mon, we were on island time. There was a rum and coconut water in my immediate future, the perfect appetizer to what lay ahead of me that night.

It was just before midnight when we started up the narrow road to Laventille. Laventille was always a hotbed for Carnival from early stick fighters to calypso tents to the pan yards. If you are a Christian or a Jew, then Bethlehem is your place. If the steel drum is your baby, then Laventille is the cradle, and let me tell you, it rocks. The history of Carnival in Trinidad is full of confrontations with the colonials, who banned the fiesta on numerous occasions. But it still went on in Laventille in open defiance of the oppression of fun. The people on the hill could trace their roots back to Yoruba and Nigeria. It was around Laventille that the biscuit-tin bands found a whole new vein of music in the street scene after World War II, when the steel drum was invented and perfected.

I might be a navigator on most days, but on this night I had no idea where I was. I asked Ralph where we were headed. "The pan yard, brother," he answered. Where does a sixty-

piece band rehearse? I figured it would be in a school gym or
a church or something of that size. Ralph was grinning with
excitement, which infected me. And, of course, there was the
rum now cruising through my bloodstream. We waved at the
neighbors who were going about their lives up on the hill, and
though it was near midnight, the place showed no signs of
shutting down. There was something in the air, and that something was the music of the Desperados.

Up, up, up on the hill we went, and then I heard it. The
music flowed down from above us like a stream of lava, and
on the streets everyone was dancing or moving to the music.
The higher we climbed, the louder it got. The bass pans were
now clearly audible in their low register. My body was humming with the electricity of the moment. I didn't want to touch
anything because I was so charged I thought I might arc a
spark and explode right on the spot. The song was "The King
of Somewhere Hot," and as we came to the top of the hill,
there was the whole band gathered in the pan yard, an un-
painted frame building with open windows and a tin roof. Inside, Robert was directing the movement, and outside there
must have been a couple of hundred people just listening and
moving to the groove. I sat in the car with goose pimples on
top of goose pimples and a grin from one edge of my face to
the other. It was the musical equivalent of being launched in
an F-14 off the deck of an aircraft carrier.

My joy quickly turned to a wave of nervous fear, for I
wasn't there to listen. I had to play. Thank God for the Vat 19,
rum, the great Caribbean equalizer. I got out of the car,
grabbed my guitar case, and went inside like I knew what I
was doing. Robert stopped the practice. I figured that the band
knew of Robert's work with our band, but nobody ever
thought they would see Jimmy Buffett up on Laventille.
Robert introduced me to the musicians. I was scared shitless,
but I was the only one who knew that (another trick of the
trade). We chatted for a moment, but I was too excited not to

just want to get in there. I fired up my little portable amp, gave the old Gibson F-hole a quick tune, and then we were off.

The song starts softly, with just a guitar and one drum, but about twelve bars into it, when the Desperados came in, the goddamn thing exploded like a nuclear bomb. I was singing and listening and laughing inside, all at the same time. There is something about the sound of the steel drum that connects like a jumper cable to the musical fiber that I believe is in us all. Some people are more in touch with it than others, and in Trinidad, music is as much nourishment as food and water. Most people know of pan music only as the recognizable handful of island classics played poolside at island resorts, but in Trinidad the drum is not cocktail-hour background music. It is a way of life.

There I was, this white boy on top of one of the toughest hills in Port of Spain, being picked up and flown by the power of the music and the place. I thought of my grandfather and wondered if in his travels he had done something similar to this and parked the experience on some gene for me to cough up in my forties. Just like a jet ride in the F-14, it was over too quickly. We went through both songs, and then the band had to pack the drums for the flight to Miami the next day. The crowd that had watched the rehearsal all joined in to help the band put the gear away. These drums would not go to Miami in the black shockproof Anvil cases that I knew so well from my years on the road. They were being put into plywood boxes that only a few days before carried salt cod to the island from Newfoundland. The smell of the codfish, familiar from my childhood, was still fresh in the wood. The fish had come to Trinidad as a staple of the islanders' traditional diet. Now the music of the island was leaving in the boxes that had brought the fish.

A week later I stood on the stage of the Marine Stadium in Miami, the capital of the Caribbean. The skyline of the city and about a thousand boats filled with revelers were behind us. In front, a grandstand was packed with an additional four thousand fans. The Desperados had opened the show with a performance that earned them a standing and yelling ovation from the crowd.

I walked out onto the floating stage and plugged in my guitar. The crowd noise settled, and I began to sing. I would have never felt the same way about the song, or the performance, if I had just gone to a rehearsal hall and played through the songs with the band. No, on that stage in Miami that night came the whole experience of my trip up the hill. I could still smell the codfish odor from the drums riding on the evening breeze that blew in from the Gulf Stream. The night was ripe with the convergence of all its factions. I didn't play the song, I just climbed on board the groove that the Despos laid down and took a ride. Halfway through the song, I turned to glance at Ralph and Robert, and they were laughing their heads off. When the song ended, there was a split second of silence, like the vacuum that sucks the oxygen out of the air right before a lightning strike, and then they let loose. The crowd went nuts. The band went nuts. I went nuts and jumped into the bay after the show to the shock of the crowd and the horror of my road crew. Those lucky enough to have been at the show will tell you that they saw something special that night, and I felt exactly the same way. Because for just ten minutes of one night, I really knew what it felt like to be the king of somewhere hot.

Looking for Captain Frothy

Tobago is a meeting point for all of us—plane, family, and friends. I am sure that when Angela and Aileen arrive with the kids tomorrow there will be some kind of family reunion for them either in Tobago or in Trini. Charlie will be in Grenada, ready to come over if the fishing report is good, and as we touch down on Tobago just before dark, there on the tarmac, parked to the east side of the tower waiting like an obedient retriever, is the Albatross. I pull the Citation in alongside it, and while the pilots busy themselves with unloading and customs formalities, I go over to the Albatross, do an informal walk-around, and give her a pat on the nose. I feel a bit of a cold shoulder coming from the *Hemisphere Dancer* and almost break out into some kind of an explanation about the legal hassles that had kept her from making the trip to the jungle. But I figure that if the customs officials see this, they'll probably take me to the nuthouse. "We'll go up tomorrow," I whisper under my breath, giving her another pat on the nose.

At customs when I am asked the questions about my occupation, I don't hesitate to list what I consider to be my true profession. In some countries you have to be careful. I sometimes put down my occupation as writer, journalist, pilot, and even baseball-team owner, depending on what I think will cause me the least hassle. In Tobago I just answer "musician," because here I know it is considered a very honorable profession. The conversation with the customs man immediately loses its formal tone and we talk music. I know that Tobago is not exactly the hotbed of Parrothead activity in the Leeward Islands, so I tell him I play with Robert Greenidge and Ralph MacDonald. *Bang* goes the big rubber stamp into my passport, and we are in.

Tobago is about as far from the hustle and bustle of Port of Spain as you can get. It is a very laid-back island, blending a little tourism with a still vibrant local lifestyle. The beaches are anything but crowded. There is a central area for the small tourist trade, which allows the majority of the island to be West Indian. Goats and cows still roam the streets. This is a good sign. You can tell an island that still had a grasp on its roots by the fact that the livestock still takes precedence over the tourists. At the hotel, we settle in and I start to make my calls to the number I have for Captain Frothy. No answer.

The next morning I go flying. The weather is beautiful, a perfect flying day. I want to get my hands back on the stick. But again we are denied permission to land in the water.

We take off and buzz around the island several times at low altitude. If we can't land, we can certainly fly low and look for fish. I head up the northeast coast, and in about fifteen minutes I'm at the northern tip of the island. The windward side of Tobago is just that, rocky shores and lots of wind, beautiful scenery but nothing fishable for us. I roll around the point and head south toward Bucco Reef. This big broad reef is the heart of the tourist trade on Tobago and has everything from glass-bottom boats to jet skis blasting around. If there are tarpon and permit in Tobago, this is where we will find them, but from the air that day I see no fish, only a lot of white-skinned tourists wading in low tide. I return to the airport and try to make contact again with Captain Frothy, with no luck. Charlie calls from Boston, wondering where he should go, and we stick to the original plan of him flying to Grenada. If the fish or Captain Frothy show up, we can just fly back to Tobago and fish for the day.

Captain Frothy never surfaces, but my kids come in as scheduled. They hug and kiss us for about two minutes at the airport, then want to go straight to the beach. Angela and Aileen catch a late flight to Port of Spain, the kids stay with Jane, Kino, and Mac, and I head off in the Albatross to pick up my fishing buddy. If the winds blow right, we will all meet up tomorrow on the tiny island of Bequia in the Grenadines.

As I taxi out to take the runway for takeoff the next morning, the radio operator in the control tower asks if Mr. Buffett is on board. "Oh, God, what now?" I think. I tell him he's talking to Mr. Buffett. He says he has a message from Captain Frothy. Nice timing. The message is, "Sorry I missed you, but was fishing. Good tuna and sailfishing offshore, no tarpon yet on the reef. Will be better in the spring. Call me then." That is the way of the Caribbean. Here it is the second week in January, and Captain Frothy is perfectly willing to wait until the spring as if it were next week.

I feel the quadriceps in both my legs start to ache from the amount of pressure I have to exert with them to guide the heavy steering system on the Albatross. It's like the old girl is telling me that I've been in that damn easy-flying, candy-ass jet for too long. "You think you're a pilot, big boy? Well, we're gonna find out." The weather this morning as we lift off from Crown Point is overcast with a thin gray layer of clouds at about five thousand feet. We make our takeoff run and are airborne halfway down the runway. I make a right turn out, climb to five hundred feet, run the after-takeoff checklist, and slide the window open. I glance down at the flat below me. "Goddamn!" I shout. Pete jumps as if something is wrong with the plane. "A school of bonefish just spooked off that flat when the shadow of the plane went across." I look at Pete, and the panic in his eyes tells me that he thinks me quite capable of landing the plane, jumping out on the wing with my fly rod, and having him drive me in pursuit of the fish. "Next time," I say, just to reassure him, and I take up the course for the only group of islands in the West Indies I have yet to visit.

New Territory

Beethoven and Blue Skies

Date: 10 January 1997
Time: 1530Z
Latitude: 12°0′2″ N
Longitude: 061°47′3″ W

Location: Point Salines
  International Airport,
  St. George's, Grenada
Elevation: 40′
Weather: Partly cloudy

Comments: The airspace above the Grenadines is new flying territory to me. My travels to this point have taken me as far south as St. Lucia, but I have never seen the island chain of the Grenadines or St. Vincent or our final destination today—Bequia. That's one of the reasons we're here. There's not much air traffic in these parts, compared with the busier air corridors of the more populated islands to the north. We have signed off with Crown Point and headed out into uncontrolled airspace, where we don't have to talk to anyone. This is another one of the great things about island flying. Today, in the busy airways above the U.S. of A., you are required by law to stay in radio contact in a vast majority of the airspace, and the reality is that even if you are not required to talk to air-traffic control, due to the volume of traffic and the number of people in the air who really don't know where they actually are, it is best to stay in touch. In the islands, especially in the Albatross, I avoid flying using Instrument Meteorological Conditions as much as possible, unless the weather is a problem. I don't want to talk if I don't have to.

It's Friday morning, a great day to be alive and back at the wheel of the *Hemisphere Dancer.* There is a very particular feel to flying this big bird, and it takes a little while to get used to being back in the saddle. Unlike the more modern planes I have flown, it has no autopilot. In a way it's good, because it means you have to pay attention and you are constantly in touch with your ship, not just sitting back and checking the gauges. We may not have an autopilot, but by God, we do have music.

I have to weave through a layer of thin cloud cover and a few showers about twenty-five miles out of Tobago. We break into the clear about thirty miles out of Crown Point, and I jot down our position on my notepad. With clear blue sky above us and the green Caribbean below, I pop in my CD of Beethoven's *Pastoral* symphony, conducted by Sir Georg Solti and the Chicago Symphony, trim the rudder a little, crack the window open a little more on my side, and just bask in the moment.

It doesn't take long to get back into the cockpit routine of the *Hemisphere Dancer*. As part of the usual safety scan, I glance back at the left engine to make sure we're not leaking any fluids or, God forbid, trailing smoke. The pure beauty of watching the big prop rotate and checking the leading edge of the long wing that stretches out to the float on the wingtip gives me a thrill. With my legs and hands I am controlling this big and wonderful machine.

Ten miles out of Point Salines, we have to check in on the radio with the tower, which we do, giving our departure point and all the other info they need. A few minutes later we say good-bye to Sir George and Ludwig, put out the flaps for our initial approach to landing, and start to look for the runway. It isn't very hard to spot because it's damn near as long as the shuttle strip at Cape Canaveral. There may not be a logical reason for a lot of strange things in this part of the world, but there is always a story, and the runway at Grenada certainly is a story.

Hey, Mr. Spaceman

One of the remarkable paradoxes of life in the islands is that such an Eden-like area has historically been a constant scene of war and death. This cycle did not end with the close of the colonial period. Manifest destiny is alive and well as the ultimate excuse for America to still police the region as it applies, as a State Department spokesperson might say, "to ensure our best interests." Grenada is only the most recent in a long history of places that have been willing or unwilling participants in old-fashioned gunboat diplomacy by Uncle Sam.

Grenada became an independent nation on February 7, 1974, under the premiership of a former trade unionist named Eric Gairy. His rise to power was marked by violence, strikes, and a lot of controversy surrounding his views about UFO's. In March 1979, Prime Minister Gairy went up to New York to deliver a speech before the United Nations on how his country wanted to be the world leader in reaching out to UFO's and recognizing the existence of the aliens already on Earth. Meanwhile, back home on Grenada, it wasn't the aliens who were causing trouble. A more pragmatic bunch of revolutionaries, called the New Jewel Movement, led by one Maurice Bishop, who believed more in Che Guevara than in ET, staged a bloodless coup and proclaimed a people's revolutionary government on the island. Mr. Gairy was lost in space, the Cubans arrived from Havana, and up in Washington the movie-star president, Ronald Reagan, was pissed off. It didn't help Mr. Bishop's cause when engineers from Havana began to construct a nine-thousand-foot-long runway on the island. Now, this was no Cuban missile crisis, but there hadn't been much happening in the Caribbean since the invasion of Panama and the capture of Manuel Noriega, with the help of modern-day weapons and very loud, bad rock 'n' roll. So on October 25, a U.S.–led invasion of paratroopers, air cavalry, and Navy SEALS defeated a contingent of Cuban construction workers at the now infamous airport. Maurice Bishop was killed, order was restored, the hotels reopened, and the sun rose again on a free and happy Grenada with a brand-new airport inspired by aliens, built by Communists, and captured by capitalists.

Any Lead at All

There is no evidence of the battle visible when we land, just freshly painted signs welcoming everyone back to Grenada. I find Charlie surrounded by his fishing gear, sitting in the terminal next to the duty-free pearl shop. He has that pale "been in the operating room too long and I need to go fishing" look about him, and we waste no time in getting cleared through customs and back on the plane. I can't help but try again to get permission to land in the water. Maybe with the all-new, welcome-back-tourists posture of Grenada these days, I could talk somebody into it. All I get is more questions than answers.

So once again our only option this day is to look for spots in the Grenadines that might be conducive to the kind of fishing we want to do. Charlie and I have put a lot of lines in the water since our first meeting on Shelter Island, and we know what to look for. He tells me that he has information on a guide in Bequia. He starts laughing. "His name is Fabio," he says.

"You have got to be kidding. A bonefish guide named Fabio?" I can only see that Italian hunk who poses for the covers of romance novels in a banana-sling bikini that barely contains his balls, posing on the deck of a flats skiff with a fly rod in his hand.

"He's an Italian Rasta," Charlie says. "A buddy of mine ran into him in St. Vincent last year at the hospital." One thing about a die-hard fisherman is that he will follow any lead at all if the end result is a fishing hole that no one else knows about. Once I was gassing up at the airport in George Town, Exumas, when a tourist couple came up to me and asked innocently,

"Do you land that thing in the water?" I replied, "Sir, I'll drop into sulfuric acid if there are fish there."

That Maniac Is Me

I watch the islands below on the left, and Charlie sits in the navigator's seat on the starboard side, his nose pressed against the round porthole. We are looking for flats and mangroves, which become sparser the further down-island you move. If you travel all the way down the chain from Miami to Trinidad, you first pass through the flat terrain of the Bahamas and the Turks and Caicos Islands, which are prime spots for bonefish, some permit, and scattered schools of tarpon. There is not a lot of vertical relief until you hit Hispaniola and Puerto Rico, but the heights of these islands are nothing compared with what lies further south. The Leeward Islands, starting with St. Kitts, are the peaks of ancient mountains that still rise over a mile in the air. The earthquakes and volcanoes still erupt. Waterfalls, rain forests, and black-sand beaches are the by-products of prehistoric catastrophes that shaped the geography of the entire region. There are spots of reef, but overall the water is deep to the rocky shore. From St. Kitts down to St. Vincent, the pattern repeats itself on Martinique, Guadeloupe, and St. Lucia, and then the scenery changes.

The Grenadines are like a cluster of small oases, a collection of marble-cake swirls of turquoise water, white sand, protected lagoons, and Eden-like small islands that are the essence of escapism, surrounded by the blue depths of the southern Atlantic. On my first view of these islands from altitude they remind me of the Bahamas, but I can feel that I am deeper into the tropics. We fly at five hundred feet above the inviting water, waving to fishermen, looking at topless women stretched out on the foredeck of chartered sailboats, and sneaking up on a couple of beachcombers from behind, all of whom wave back as we pass by.

There I sit with my left arm hanging out the window of this giant airplane, skimming the whitecaps, rocking the eighty-foot wings back and forth, looking at the earthlings below. It's one of those moments that I am lucky to experience on a pretty regular basis; I am thankful for the life I have carved out of the pie. The faces looking back say it all. The best part of this old bird is the role she plays as a kind of a prop to Caribbean life. A flying boat in these surroundings just can't help but conjure up dreams and visions of romance and adventure, but like our show on tour, it's more work than one might expect to keep it looking fun.

Near the tiny island of Carriacou, Charlie blasts my eardrum on the headset. "Look at those flats!" he shouts.

"Pull that mike back a few inches from your mouth, doc, or I'll be checking into Harvard Medical with hearing loss." I swing the plane out to the right and see what Charlie is seeing. Below us a beautiful little harbor is tucked into the leeward side of the island. A two-lane dirt road, lined with palm trees, runs parallel to the sand beach of the harbor. Off to the north of the channel a series of flats and mangroves stretch to land's end. I glance briefly at the chart and make a mental note of the contour of the island, and sure enough, I see this little peninsula that shows a bayou surrounded by hills. We drop down to three hundred feet, make a couple of circles around the island, and check the spot closer.

"There are fish back there on that wreck floating on top," Charlie says. "I think they're tarpon." I immediately mash the SAVE button on the GPS in the panel of the Albatross, and the latitude and longitude appear in the display window. I give the stick to Pete and rename the file, spelling out my hopes in the naming: T-A-R-P-O-N.

A half hour later, we line up for the approach to the runway at Bequia. It looks hairy. The runway has only recently been built, and it's one of those places like Telluride, Saba, and St. Barts, where God never planned for a runway to be but man in his infinite wisdom decided to put one. The approach to the numbers takes us over a jagged peninsula stretching out west from the main island, and I can see that the trade winds that are being praised by the sailors aboard the boats below us are a curse to the Albatross today. A belt of whitecaps wraps around Bequia, and dust devils bounce around the peaks to our left. A challenging landing is never a thing to take lightly but at the same time it's nothing to fear. I have a lot of experience. Bequia will be interesting but a piece of cake compared with St. Barts, where you pretty much have to go to school to learn how to land. "If you can do St. Barts, you can do anything," the pilots in the islands say. I have on my game face and am connected mentally and physically to the throttles. As expected, I get hit with a couple of good wind shears just above the ground, but we stay level and bleed off the speed, as we should have passed over the seawall touching down on the numbers. I immediately put the props in reverse and lean on the throttles. They teach you short-field landings when you learn to fly, but that's in a small plane. In the Albatross it's more like a carrier landing, but we are down and nothing is broken and we have a thousand feet of runway left on a three-thousand-foot field.

We taxi back to the terminal. The props hadn't stopped turning before the crowd starts gathering. There are customs officials and airplane admirers and passengers waiting for the small commuter flights that connect them back to the real world. They all come to look at the Albatross and probably wonder what kind of maniac would fly such a big plane into such a small field. The maniac is me.

Bequia Sketches

If It's Good Enough for Zimmerman,
It's Good Enough for Me

I first heard of Bequia from sailors in Le Select in St. Barts. They all talked of it as if it were a piece of the past that somehow had not rushed full speed ahead into modern Caribbean history. Bequia had held on to its traditions. The local fishermen still hunted whales in longboats with handmade harpoons.* The people of Bequia were known as the finest boat builders in the islands. Until just a few years ago, Bequia had no airport, which meant you had to get there on a boat. It all translated into Bequia being a piece of the maritime past that every sailor in the Le Select wished he or she had experienced firsthand.

One afternoon I was walking down Rue Victor Hugo in Gustavia to my morning vantage point at the corner table of the Bar D Double, where I could watch the pedestrian traffic and check with anyone who happened to roll around the corner in their car about any business I had with the island for the day. I hadn't even put the honey in my tea when I overheard the talk at the next table. *Water Pearl* was in the harbor, and everyone was talking about whether or not the owner was on board. She was a beautiful traditional Bequia schooner that had been built on the island and was a home away from home to a Minnesota boy named Zimmerman, or to those who don't

---

* Bequia was granted a dispensation from the International Whaling Commission to hunt a certain number per year as part of the food supply for the island population for a limited time. Today no whales are killed in Bequia.

know, Bob Dylan. As I was scanning the front page of the *Herald Tribune*, a fellow walked to my table and introduced himself as Chris, the captain of *Water Pearl*. He told me that "the boss" was on board and heard I was in town as well and asked if I wanted to come out and see the boat and have lunch. I checked my busy schedule and immediately said yes. What, are you kidding? Ironically, I had heard through the grapevine back in the States that at an antinuke rally in California, Dylan and Joan Baez had performed a duet of my song "A Pirate Looks at Forty." I was amazed and honored. Here, a couple of weeks later, I was going to lunch with Mr. Tambourine Man.

We didn't talk music. We talked boats over lunch and enjoyed the afternoon on the hook in Gustavia Harbor. He gave me a tour of *Water Pearl*, and I can still smell that unique combination of pitch, canvas, and wood that is the essence of a traditional sailing rig. Today in St. Barts, Jimmy Buffett couldn't have lunch with Bob Dylan and spend a quiet afternoon on the hook without it making Page 6 in the *New York Post* or being interrupted by paparazzi in wetsuits on jet skis circling the boat with waterproof Nikons. Such is the way of the world, and I am just glad our meeting happened when it did. I watched from the hill under the religious statue on the hairpin turn above Gustavia as *Water Pearl* glided out of the ship channel, raised her sails, and took up a course to the north. It was a gentle reminder that I needed to visit the island where she was built. I have seen Bob on a number of occasions since then, but that was the last time I saw *Water Pearl*. She foundered on a reef off Panama a few years later and went down.

It's All School to Me

Bequia reminds me of St. Barts before it turned into the St. Tropez of the French Antilles. Though the tourist-oriented business interests on the island carved an airport out of the rocks and the seabed, Bequia still exudes a firm connection to its nautical roots. Cruise ships are not allowed to visit the port. Only a few smaller boats, with sails, are allowed to drop anchor off Port Elizabeth. The ride down the hill to the center of town reveals a harbor that identifies this island as still being a "boat place." We pitch camp for our brief visit in a quaint little harbor hotel called the Plantation House. It is run by a nice French couple, which gives me a chance to brush up on my Français before we head on to St. Barts in a couple of days.

On the way in from the airport, we stop to pick up a local hitchhiker. I spot his easel and get an idea. Sarah Delaney has shown a keen interest in drawing and painting since she first figured out that crayons were not for consumption. Bequia, being a real island, has no Sea World, water slides, dolphin shows, or video arcades, which leaves just the beach to entertain the kids. Cameron is at home anywhere there might be the chance of finding a lizard, a hermit crab, a spider, or a coconut. He is a very good self-entertainer, which is a skill we all need. Delaney, on the other hand, is a little higher-maintenance. My idea is to see if the hitchhiking painter might be interested in making a few extra bucks teaching Delaney to paint. It turns out that the painter, whose name was Malcolm, teaches art in the Bequia public school. He and Delaney hit it off right away, and we schedule art lessons. Cameron will be close by, immersed in the pool trying to regrow gills. Jane and Mac have books to read and hiking to do, and Kino will be visiting friends on a boat. The decks are cleared for Charlie and me to escape to the water in search of whatever.

As if on cue, before dinner, a thin, tan man of about forty, dressed in shorts and a khaki shirt, appears at our table and says he heard we were looking for him. The good old Coconut Telegraph is still working. It can't be anyone other than Fabio.

The Fishin' Expedition

I am awakened early this morning by the telltale signs of a very windy day. The rustling of the coconut palms that surround our cottage is constant, and every now and then I hear a thud as a coconut hits the ground. There is some kind of amazing statistic that I can't remember about the number of people in the tropics who are killed or maimed for life by falling coconuts. From the harbor comes the sounds of the wind gusts rattling the rigging of the dozens of boats that lie at anchor. The wind has not let up since my battle with the breeze upon landing at the airport yesterday. The port of Bequia was chosen as a safe harbor centuries ago because of its natural protection against the prevailing trade winds. The winds from the east are blowing twenty-five to thirty knots and wrapping around the island, leaving very little in the way of calm water, which is what we need for the type of fishing we do. Heavy wind doesn't make for a pleasant day of casting. You're more likely to wind up hooking yourself than a fish, but we are there, and we are going fishing.

We are going "exploring fishing," and this approach is always a crapshoot. If we happen to luck out and find some incredible spot where a lost tribe of tarpon has been secretly holed up, undiscovered since the time of the Arawaks and Caribs, then that will be the great payoff. If we never wet a line but have a great time exploring, then that's just as good.

Fabio meets us at the dock. I like him immediately. He is a far cry from his Hollywood namesake, to be sure. Tall, thin, and with graying beard and dreadlocks falling down his back, he is unmistakably Italian but wrapped in a layer of Caribbean "soon come" that speaks of years in the islands. His boat is a beautiful little handmade Bequia skiff, with a knifelike bow for slicing through the waves and a very narrow beam. It's a far cry from my old Maverick flats skiff, but such things do not exist in these parts. We are in the world of exploring fishing, in which you take what you can get, knock on wood, and set out.

We cruise the south shore of Admiralty Bay, staying as close as we can to the rocks to avoid the large swells that are wrapping around the headland. Fabio is not that familiar with fly-fishing, but he's very interested. We show him our limits as far as casting range goes, and I explain that these aren't ideal conditions. In fact, we are in the worst conditions, and I'm not as interested in catching a fish as I am in not hurling myself into the water from the tiny bow of the skiff while casting. The boat is pitching, which makes casting comparable to fly-fishing from the roof of a monster truck as it bounces over a line of junked cars. Fabio tells us there are no flats at all around Bequia, which I have already surmised from our flyby yesterday. But he has seen tarpon moving around the rocks at the end of the airport, although it was in the summer. *Summer*—that's the magic word of the day. Even though we are deep in the heart of the Caribbean, it is still winter. Yes, Virginia, the Caribbean *does* have a winter. It may not be quite as noticeable to snowbirds flocking to the warmer latitudes from the great white north just to thaw out, but on the hemispheric scale, we above the equator do share the same seasons. I know from my Florida and Bahamas experiences that fishing in the winter is a lot different from fishing in the summer, and I suspect the same thing applies in the Grenadines.

Still, we idle on in Fabio's little boat, banging our way around the point, with Fabio pointing out the huge section of rock that was sheared off by the recent earthquake. We head toward the rocks at the end of the airport, but we see no tarpon, just more choppy water. Now we are in the teeth of the obviously stirred-up trade winds and getting the shit kicked out of us. I tell Fabio I don't care where we go or whether we even see a fish, but we need to look in the lee of some kind of land, or else it's back to the hotel for French toast. He gets the picture.

We plow through the open waters and cross the channel to the group of small islands called Isle Quatre that lies between Bequia and Mustique. We stop behind one island, which, Fabio tells us, is where the locals used to bring the whales from the annual hunt to butcher. We work our way along the rocky edge of another island, and Fabio moves the little boat into shallower water where we can see the bottom and hopefully attract something out for a look at our fly. We finally get out of the wind but never out of the swell. If the waves aren't coming from the direction of the open water, they ricochet off the rocky coastline.

Charlie is braced in the bow section, blindly casting toward the rocks, when his pole bends in two. This is always a good sign. It's not the kind of bend that signals a big fish, but it is a fish. A minute later, Charlie boats his scorpion fish, and at the site of the mean face and sharp teeth I suggest that Fabio remove the hook so that the good doctor can keep all those highly trained appendages intact. As the fisherman say, "The skunk is out of the boat."

It's my turn, and I crawl to the bow, wedge my feet in so that I won't launch like a depth charge, and begin to cast. I already know that we're not in the fish. The wind, the winter, whatever it is tells me that this is not the place. A few minutes later Charlie and I look at each other and know it's time to reel 'em in. Fortunately, we're upwind and the ride home will be a little more tolerable than the one out. Since we're not clinging to the boat for dear life, we talk fishing. Fabio tells us that he's heard about tarpon and bonefish down in the Grenadines on the little island of Carriacou. A smile comes across my face. "I knew they were there," I say to Charlie.

Fabio drops us at the dock just before lunch and, as I expected, there is Cameron thrashing in the pool and Delaney sitting close by with Malcolm next to her, working on her brush strokes. I am spotted, and immediately Cameron calls out, "Dad, when are you going to take me fishing?"

"Right after lunch, dude." That's the price we grown-up fisherman pay for running away in the wee hours. The little fishermen are waiting when you get back. After lunch, though I just want to escape to one of the hammocks hanging from the coconut trees by the beach, I keep my promise to my kids and we hike along the rocky path above the hotel, counting the lizards that cross our path and working our way around the point to a little beach on the other side. The high-dollar fly rods are resting in their designer cases back in the cottage. We're back to hand lining with cut bait for little jacks cruising up and down the clear shallow water just beyond the shore. We fish for several hours and catch a few jacks, but to my kids they all fight like Monstro the whale. As I bait hooks, unhook fish, and toss the little yearlings back into the water with good-luck wishes out there in the food chain, I am as happy as if we've found the lost tribe of tarpon. Hell, maybe tomorrow we actually will.

Flattop Tarpon

Still no luck with the poor Albatross. I so hoped we could take her to Carriacou, landing in the picturesque little harbor and just jumping off and going fishing like in one of those well-orchestrated fishing shows on ESPN. But Carriacou is part of Grenada, not St. Vincent. To even attempt to obtain permission to land in its water, we would have to fly back to St. George's and immerse ourselves in a nightmare of red tape. It's like in Monopoly when you get that "Go directly to jail: Do not pass Go, do not collect $200" card. I was beginning to expect that purgatory for me would be comparable to two things on Earth: 1) being in a room full of all the socks you have ever lost in your life and having to match them, and 2) trying to get permission to land a seaplane south of the twentieth parallel. All that lovely seaplane water, and we still can't get her wet. But

I'm not ready for another bureaucratic adventure. I just want to go fishing in Carriacou.

I call the airport and find a charter. The next morning Charlie and I board a little Twin Commander for the thirty-minute ride to Carriacou. I got hold of a contact on the island. Steven Gay, better known in these parts as Scraper, owns a bar and restaurant in Tyrrel Bay where we can charter a boat. The lady who answered the phone seemed a little perplexed when I explained that we were flying in for the day to fish and needed a boat. She told me to hold on. After a very long wait, a male voice came on the line. I imagined her walking across the road to the harbor and telling one of the guys hanging around the dock that some white guy on the phone wanted to go fishing. The man on the other end of the phone announced himself as Ja. Thank you, Robert Nesta Marley.

In my years in the islands, I have observed that there have really been only three things that have drastically altered the pattern of life as a whole in the Caribbean: cruise ships, satellite dishes, and Bob Marley. Vaughn ran the local water-taxi service on Carriacou. I didn't try to explain to him that two maniac fly fishermen were invading his island to launch an assault on the lost tribe of tarpon that had been reported in his area by an Italian Rasta fishing guide in Bequia. I just told him we would like to hire him and his boat to take us fishing for the afternoon. He told us to meet him at the dock across from Scraper's.

The pilot is named Tony, and he is based out of St. Vincent. He has heard I am on the island and asks if he can take a look at the Albatross before we take off. I guide him on a quick tour, and he is like all the other pilots who come aboard. His eyes fill with wonder as he marvels at the amount of space inside the plane and then examines the flight deck, imagining what it must be like to take her around the patch. After the tour, we climb aboard Tony's Commander and take off, heading south. I fly in the copilot's seat, and Charlie catches a combat nap in the rear. Tony and I talk on the headsets about the two things that matter most to me, after, of course, my wife and kids: planes and fishing.

According to Tony, the Albatross problem can be handled in two days, but it will take two different trips to two different capitals. He knows the aviation chief for Grenada, but as I figured, it will take a day of schmoozing in St. George's. As for St. Vincent, his boss is a good friend of the prime minister there. I tell him that we can use the story that we're scouting locations for the *Joe Merchant* movie. He tells me that he worked on a movie just shot in St. Vincent called *White Squall*, with Jeff Bridges, and that they used seaplanes on that film. He tells us he'll set it all up for us if we want. I thank him but tell him we're heading north the next day, but if I get back with the Albatross, I at least now know who to call.

I still can't get over the beauty of these islands from the air and just stare out the window at all the boats below us. Whoever named these places gave any writer worth his salt the means to an end, as far as a story is concerned. Who wouldn't want to run away to places with names like Sail Rock, Palm Island, or Petit Martinique and write to tell about it?

Date: 11 January 1997
Time: 1900Z
Latitude: 12°29'3" N
Longitude: 61°28'6" W

Location: Laurriston
    Airport, Carriacou,
    Grenadines
Elevation: 16'
Weather: Clear

Comments: The now familiar shape of Carriacou appears on the horizon, and we use up the last few minutes of the flight to fill out the ever-present paperwork that comes with changing countries. We grab a cab from the tiny little hut that serves as the Carriacou airport and tell the driver we are meeting Vaughn at Scraper's. That's all it takes. Compared with Carriacou, Bequia, with its four thousand residents, is like Manhattan. This island is not only in another country, it's in another time. We drive through the main town of Hillsborough, creeping along the main road, which is packed with children in uniforms going to or coming from school.

As we round the north end of Tyrrel Bay, I see an old rusty tramp steamer at anchor in the sleepy half-moon harbor. We move close enough to read the name through the rust: *Seaview.* It lights up my dreams of one day owning a tramp steamer and running cargo among the islands. Along the shore, a small fleet of local fishing boats sits at anchor or just nudged up to the beach. No windsurfs, no jet skis, no parasails. This is still a quiet little fishing village. The only hint of an intrusion from the modern world is a shiny fiberglass sportfishing boat with outriggers and a raked tuna tower. It makes quite a contrast to the old tramp steamer. The steamer echoes the simpler days when she probably plied these waters on a routine basis bringing passengers, livestock, dry goods, and mail to the locals. The sportfishing rig stands out like a sore thumb and immediately elicits a "what's wrong with this picture?" reaction. I pray it isn't a vision of things to come for Carriacou. Unfortunately, the sportfishing boat in the harbor too often means that marinas and condos are not far behind. V. S. Naipaul once wrote that tourism is the "slavery of the twentieth century." On too many islands, a few profit-driven individuals can erode an entire culture. Carriacou has somehow avoided the attack so far, but there is always the threat of the wolf in sheep's clothing, scavengers from the corporate world.

The cabdriver wishes us good luck and drops us off in front of a path leading to a wooden dock, where a thin young black man with a not-too-drastic set of dreads and an infectious smile is waving at us. His boat is an extension of his admiration for Bob Marley. In design, it's a very traditional down-island fishing vessel with a long snout of a bow and about twenty feet of waterline. She was been built for the needs of a down-island fisherman who had to make his living in the off-shore waters, but she is our only bird in the hand and we are taking her to the bush. Like a colorful icing on a Rastafarian cake, the boat looks like a cross between a Mardi Gras float and the royal barge of Haile Selassie. The hull is black with yellow cap rails, and the interior is bright red, which will be very interesting for the bottoms of our bare feet once the sun gets high in the sky. The wooden seats are painted yellow and green, and the name written across the gunwale in yellow hand lettering is *Selassie.*

We quickly load our gear into the boat and head across the harbor for the mangroves I spotted from the air. There are two flats at the entrance of the bayou that extend out to the north-east end of the harbor. I have Vaughn slow the boat to a halt as we approach it so that I can check the direction and the stage of the tidal flow. There are no tide tables or weather stations for Carriacou, so it's back to the old ways. All indications are that we are on the mid-outgoing tide. In my familiar fishing haunts, that's good news. The fish would be riding the high water into the bayou to feed and would drift back out to the safety of the open water. The harbor of Carriacou and the little bayou are tucked way in from the headlands of the bay, and though the wind is still howling out there, there is just a slight breeze in the bay. The sun is hot and the sky is blue, and we are fly-fishing in Carriacou.

The narrow entrance to the bayou opens up once we're in-side to a broad lagoon lined with mangroves on both sides. In-stead of trying to explain fly-fishing to Vaughn, I just show him how it's done. I ask him to stop the boat in the middle of the lagoon, strip sixty feet or so of line off my reel, and make several casts at the bank to show him where we would like the boat to be. I ask about tarpon in the waters, and he says he thinks he has seen some. I explain what they look like. Many of the same fish are called by a whole variety of names in the different oceans of the world, so it's always better to draw a picture. The good news is that I know we're probably the first guys to ever come in here with fly rods. The bad news is that Vaughn doesn't have a clue what kind of fish I'm talking about.

All our conversation ends when Charlie calls out, "Bubba, there's nervous water at your three o'clock." I spin around in a second and do not see the fish, but I do see the unmistakable rings of water moving away from the center, where a few seconds before something moved.

I climb up on the sharp bow of the *Selassie* to get a better look and see the shadow of the fish ahead cruising away from us. I ask Vaughn to just idle with the boat to get some speed, and then cut the engine and let us drift up on the fish. He is on the money and has us up and near the swimming fish with the skill of a professional guide. A couple more rolls ahead. This is it. We are chasing that lost tribe of tarpon. Charlie is already manning the video camera, and I am locked on the nervous water ahead. Then as suddenly as the signs appeared, they are gone. I've been here before. Stalking fish like this is no guarantee that you will even get close enough for a shot, but that too is the thrill of this kind of fishing.

"There they are!" Charlie calls out. "Up ahead at two, about a hundred yards." This is kind of weird. The water is emptying out of the lagoon, but the fish are heading upstream. I think about it for a minute but then just say to hell with it. I'm a fisherman in strange waters, and it's better to throw out all the rules and just go with the flow. Vaughn stays right on the school. Eventually the lagoon ends and they'll have to turn around, and that is where we'll ambush them.

As we sneak up on the moving fish, I start humming the melody to that old Crosby, Stills, Nash, and Young song "Déjà Vu." It's hard to tell that I'm fifteen hundred miles down in the Windward Islands tucked back into the tiny and, as far as I can see, only mangrove system in the Grenadines. The smells of

the low tide and the underwater bramble of mangrove roots
are all too familiar. I might be back in the middle of Hell's Bay
in the Everglades or in the Snipe Keys, just north of Sugarloaf
Key. The slender outline of the fish comes into view as it floats
to the surface. He's not big, maybe three feet long, but he is
real and he is within casting distance. I check the wind and the
overhanging branches that might snag my back cast, then I
crank it up. The fly lands softly at the end of the loop, long and
to the left of the fish. He doesn't spook. I strip the fly and the
fish turns for it. Here we go. To me, the take is the most exciting part of fly-fishing: fooling a creature who lives by his
senses in the daily survival world of the aquatic food chain
into attacking a hook disguised with a few globs of glue,
thread, and feathers that he thinks is a snack.

The fish pushes toward the moving fly, and just when I am
ready to set the hook, he makes a sharp turn away from the fly
toward the boat and I finally get a look at his profile. "Son of a
bitch," I mutter as the line slips from my fingers and the rod
tip slumps to the rail of the boat.

"What is it?" Charlie asks. He is still looking through the
viewfinder of the camera like he's tracking Marlin Perkins. I
start laughing. Vaughn looks completely confused. I turn
toward the camera, still laughing.

"What it is is a flattop tarpon."

"What the hell is that?" Charlie asks.

"The biggest goddamn mullet I have ever seen."

An hour later we are back at Scraper's having lunch and
talking about, what else? Fishing. The beer is cold and the flying fish is fresh. Scraper finally shows up and introduces himself, offering us rum punches that we have to turn down if we
don't want to turn into iguanas. The fishing story we came for
is not the one we go home with, but you have to admit, it is
original. After the first giant mullet was exposed, we saw
many more. They jumped and splashed in the water in what
looked like mockery. With every jump, I thought how much

better these fish would look as smoked mullet, but they had us figured out all the way.

Still, we fished right up until the time we had to get back to the dock, grab a sandwich, and catch our plane at the appointed hour. There was one other small piece of fishing excitement that crossed our path. What looked to be a snook darted from under the mangroves and made a tentative lunge at Charlie's fly while he was roll casting along the bank. The lost tribe of tarpon was still lost. I have this picture of them wandering from island to island, always careful to avoid contact with two-legged creatures carrying long poles. Still, this place has all the makings of a potential hot spot. The flats are healthy, the water clean, and there is plenty of food-chain activity in the area. But as in Bequia, I know it is the season. My sense is that the fish are around but offshore in the channels and deep pockets of the surrounding islands. "Johnny Too Bad" plays on the radio in the bar, and the deejay from the local station ad-libs along with Jimmy Cliff.

Vaughn has loosened up a bit after spending six hours in a boat with us, and now he's asking questions about the rod and how to cast. Halfway through lunch, he tells us about talk around that there are plans to fill in the lagoon and make some kind of a Coast Guard or Army base. I almost choke on my flying-fish sandwich. Oh, God, I think. Another expensive, useless idea in the "war on drugs." What politicians in Washington and the capitals of too many islands don't understand is that in a region where contraband has been one of the main natural resources for several centuries, it isn't just going to go away. I don't do dope anymore, but if I wanted to, it would take me maybe fifteen minutes in any major city to score anything I want. That is what all the millions of dollars spent on the war on drugs has gotten us. Nothing is going to change until you take the military approach out of any possible solution. Programs like AA and rehab and counseling have much more of an impact on solving the drug problem than turning wetlands into helicopter pads, and besides, fishing is the logical alternative to smuggling. I have certainly seen it happen in the Bahamas, where guides can make more money taking people fishing than they could when they ran dope. They also then realize that protecting their source of income, mainly the fishing grounds, is as important as being able to cast a fly rod. Politicians can make all the speeches they want and governments can do all the public-service ads money can buy, but in the islands the reality is this: If you want people to stop selling dope, they have to be able to make a living doing something else. As we sit eating our sandwiches with Vaughn, that wonderful slogan that I bought on a T-shirt comes to mind: "Give a man a fish and you feed him for a day. Teach a man to fish and you feed him for a lifetime."

Vaughn rides with us to the airport, and I get his address. I plan to send him a book and a starter fly rod as part of the payment for his services. He has that spark that just might ignite the passion for this crazy sport, the by-product of which just might be protection of this great little fishing spot. Teach a man to fly-fish, and you just might show a young Rasta that a mangrove swamp is a better place to work than a military base, and better than running from the law like Johnny Too Bad.

The plane makes a low pass over the rusty old freighter as we say so long to Carriacou and head back to Bequia. Charlie is due back in the real world tomorrow and goes to town to buy souvenirs for his wife and kids. I drop all my fishing gear at the hotel and take Cameron to the beach for a quick swim. I ask where Delaney is, and he tells me she has a surprise for me.

When we walk to the cottage, I am treated to a one-woman art show, laid out around the steps of the porch. The artist arrives with a hibiscus in her hair that definitely compliments her basic uniform of a jeans skirt and T-shirt. She proceeds to explain the show to me. Her drawings are full of color and imagination. Lots of flowers and palm trees, seahorses and starfish, which tells me that Delaney is seeing the world around her. Traveling is the best education, and I want her to develop her own love for the people and these islands. I heap praise on all of her work until I get to a drawing that stops me in my tracks. Delaney and Cameron start that almost uncontrollable childish giggling as I study the drawing. There I am on the paper, my head the size of a basketball, with two strands of hair sticking straight up like Alfalfa's. My body looks like a stretched pear, and my feet are webbed. I am straddling an airplane, and there are sharks chasing me. Charlie comes back from his trip to town and hears all the laughter. He looks at the drawing and with that well-developed bedside manner says, "Spitting image of your dad, Delaney." He joins the children in their mocking laughter and leaves me staring at the portrait, wondering if this really is the way children view their parents.

Island Hopping

Date: 13 January 1997
Time: 1700Z
Latitude: 12°59'2" N
Longitude: 61°15'8" W

Location: J. F. Mitchell
Field, Bequia
Elevation: 14'
Weather: Clear

Comments: We depart Bequia in separate planes for separate locations. The girls and kids are going directly to St. Barts. The boys are headed to Guadeloupe, after dropping Charlie at the St. Vincent airport, and we will be in St. Barts in a few days.

Date: 13 January 1997
Time: 1730Z
Latitude: 13°08'6" N
Longitude: 61°12'8" W

Location: E. T. Joshua International Airport,
St. Vincent
Elevation: 66'
Weather: Partly cloudy

Comments: We drop Charlie at the airport, sending him home with a couple of fish stories, nothing more. On his way back from town yesterday, Charlie told me that as he was walking along the waterfront path back to the hotel, he happened to look down into the shallow water that was lapping against the seawall and to his shock saw a school of about a dozen big-tailing bonefish. They were as casual as could be, feeding in six inches of water, moving slowly between the legs of the children playing in the shallow water. After two days of bashing our brains out offshore and chasing mullet around Carriacou, the bastards have been right under our noses the whole time. Well, at least we know they're there. If we had known, we could have fished from the bar with a boat drink in one hand and our fly rods in the other, but then that would have been way too easy and a totally unbelievable fish story. No, that's not for me yet. The fun is still in the process of discovering something that nobody else knows.

Martinique: Put Your Lips Together and Blow

> *Well now if I ever live to be an old man*
> *I'm gonna sail my boat to Martinique*
> *I'm gonna buy me a sweat-stained Bogart suit*
> *And an African parakeet*
>
> —"MIGRATION"

Date: 13 January 1997
Time: 1900Z
Latitude: 14°36'3" N
Longitude: 61°16'5" W

Location: 10 mi. W of
Lamentin International
Airport, Fort-de-France,
Martinique
Heading: 340°
Altitude: 3,500'
Weather: Cloudy

Comments: We are dodging some afternoon buildups off the coast of Fort-de-France. This is where my love affair with the Caribbean reached a pinnacle. It all started with those calypso records of my grandfather's, but it came to life in the magic of one word: Martinique. I had never even heard of Martinique until it appeared like a vision at the beginning of the movie *To Have and Have Not*. Based very loosely on the novel by Ernest Hemingway, the movie made more of an impact on the world than the book did, thanks to one memorable scene, in a funky hotel room atop a waterfront bar in Fort-de-France, Martinique. There, a gorgeous nineteen-year-old Lauren Bacall uttered those memorable words, written for the screen by William Faulkner, to Humphrey Bogart: "You know how to whistle, don't you, Steve? You just put your lips together and blow." That's a sentence full of innuendo as far as I am concerned. Yet, by today's standards such a line isn't even controversial. All the taboos are down, and the screen is filled with "motherfucker this, motherfucker that" (I think Joe Pesci leads the world in the category of "Actor Who Says *Fuck* in a Movie the Most). But in 1944, Lauren Bacall's line caught the world's attention. People might not have known what the double entendre meant, but they knew it was something dirty.

It was more than Bacall's lines that caught my attention, it was the whole experience. A good movie is supposed to suspend your disbelief and take you away from reality. My taste in films hasn't changed at all over the years. I go for escape or a thrill. I am not into films that portray real life. Hell, I see enough of that. It doesn't matter that the story and the location were drastically changed, or that Bogie mispronounces *conch* (it's "conk," not "konch"), or that Lauren Bacall doesn't really sing (the song was dubbed in by a teenage Andy Williams), or that Harry Morgan was a rumrunner, not a patriot. The Martinique of the movie was the vision of the Caribbean that I wanted it to be.

There is a scene in the beginning of the film where Bogie comes back in from a hard day of fishing with his asshole client, and they are at this bar in this hotel. Palm trees, ceiling fans, exotic clientele, and to top it off, Hoagy Carmichael is at the piano leading the band and singing "Hong Kong Blues." Django Reinhardt is hidden in the background, playing his legendary style of guitar, and Bacall is the beauty marooned in this waterfront bar, who after a couple of rum drinks jams with the band while she is waiting to roll the asshole fisherman and get enough money for a plane ticket to the States. When she finishes the song, all hell breaks loose; cops are chasing people, and the asshole fisherman gets shot accidentally in the crossfire. Well, that was it for me. I just wanted to go to Martinique.

My initial fantasy was supplemented by facts as I read everything I could about the island. I was particularly enthralled with its being a magnet to artists and writers, and I, of course, saw myself there. The dream became reality when in the spring of 1977 I sailed into the harbor at Fort-de-France under a full moon. We found a slip at the small marina near Bakoua beach on the south side of Bahie Fort-de-France. It wasn't exactly the waterfront in the movie, but it was close enough for me. We spent days exploring the city and eating meals of the local spicy crayfish (*ousouss*) and beer, but it was on a tour of the whole island in a rented mini Moke that I discovered a place where I knew I could be comfortable living out the last years of my life.

We were winding down the main road on the windward side of the island, through endless stretches of tall sugarcane, when the scenery suddenly changed. The cane fields ended, and to the left the Atlantic reappeared, bashing into a small group of barrier islands off the coast. There was a dirt road leading up from the sea lined on both sides by tall palm trees. It crossed the main highway and ended to our right in front of a two-story colonial house, surrounded by red and yellow hibiscus bushes. It had 360 degrees of porches and ceiling fans on both levels and faced the ocean at a perfect angle. I stopped the car and stared at it for the longest time, wanting to make sure that I memorized every detail. This was where I would grow old. Sitting on the porch of this big house, sipping *petite punch* and telling stories of the incredible life that I had led to anyone who cared to listen.

> *I'm gonna sit him on my shoulder*
> *And open up my crusty old mind*
> *I'm gonna teach him how to cuss,*
> *Teach him how to fuss,*
> *And pull the cork out of a bottle of wine*

Several years later, when Jane was pregnant with Savannah, we decided to move to Martinique and have our baby there.

We headed back down to Fort-de-France and started looking for places to rent. Unfortunately, Jane had complications and we wisely abandoned our romantic notions. Savannah was born by caesarian section in the high-tech hospital in Aspen, Colorado, but the myth of Martinique remained with me.

I don't get to Martinique that much anymore, but my visits are always memorable, and now as we pass by St. Pierre, the clouds have dissipated and I can see the town and its black beaches and daydream again about what it must have looked like back in its heyday, when it was called the "Paris of the Indies," before the volcano blew it off the face of the Earth. Whatever the reason, I have some kind of tie to this place.

Kino comes up to the cockpit and points to a big house on the hill. It is Pecoul, a plantation that belonged to his uncle Andre DePaz, which sits on a hill above the town and below Mount Pelée. I once spent an incredible weekend there with the DePaz branch of Kino's family. I was taught about cockfighting, hot-pepper planting, and rum distilling, three things I will need to know about if my songline does end on the windward shore of the island. I promise myself that I will take my children there, especially Savannah, since there but for fortune she would have been born a Creole girl.

The clouds move in again almost like a curtain, folding over the top of Mount Pelée and rolling down toward the sea. Martinique disappears as we continue north, but I always know she is there, at her physical latitude on the face of the planet, and in that special part of my Caribbean soul.

Dominica—There's Absinthe in Them Thar Hills

Date: 13 January 1997   **Location:** Over Plymouth,
Time: 1930Z   Dominica
Latitude: 15°32'7" N   **Heading:** 350°
Longitude: 61°29'3" W   **Altitude:** 500'
                                                    Weather: Cloudy

Comments: Legend has it that when Columbus returned to the court of Spain after his second voyage of discovery and was explaining the islands to Queen Isabella, when it came to describing the topography of Dominica, he just crumpled up a piece of paper and set it on the table. Dominica probably doesn't look much different today than when Columbus so aptly represented it to Her Royal Highness. There are a couple of towns on the west coast where most of the population lives, but on the north end it is still largely uninhabited. The last remaining faction of Carib Indians, those fearsome cannibals of the past, live there on the edge of the rain forest.

I stopped in the tiny town of Plymouth on the northwest coast on my trip down to Martinique on the *Euphoria II* but I only went ashore for provisions and then moved on south. Several years later, I returned to Dominica by air with an old friend of mine named Jacques, a charter pilot from Paris who had flown all over the world before settling in St. Barts. He was the first person I had ever met who had flown a small plane across the Atlantic via Iceland, Greenland, and Labrador, something I wouldn't do for another twenty years. Jacques knew the islands as well as anyone and had invited Jane and me and some other friends to Dominica to go hiking in the rain forest. One of the things that makes the Caribbean so unique still is the proximity of such varying cultures and topographies in such a small number of square miles.

We landed at the little airport on the leeward coast near Roseau and trekked up into the mountains in a beat-up minivan to a destination known only to Jacques. It was my first time in a real rain forest, and I was fascinated, taking in its sounds, smells, and feel. As the altitude increased, the temperature went down. At sea level it was in the nineties. In the rain forest we were putting on jackets. Wild parrots flew overhead, squawking out their special language above the damp, rich smell of life being generated, a combination of moss, tropical blooms, and a hint of orange blossom from the hundreds of trees that grew in the wild.

Finally we arrived at a small mountain inn, where Jacques greeted the proprietor, a very suspicious-looking German character, and his wife. They had names like Hans and Helga, and they were straight out of central casting. One thing you never do in old Caribe is ask what somebody used to do, but I couldn't help but wonder. Their presence in this outback inn on one of the least populated islands in the Caribbean immediately aroused my curiosity, and as Hans expounded on the marvels of nature on the island, I wanted to ask, "What did you do during the war, Hans?" It wasn't the manners that my mother tried to instill in me that kept me from doing so, it was the fact that I had to sleep in his inn that night.

We were shown to our cottages, which were no more than tepees with plywood floors, and pointed to the stream that ran through a small avocado orchard. That was where we could bathe. The bath was its own adventure, between the freezing water, the chill of the mountain air, and the crayfish nipping at my toes while I tried to get the soap out of my eyes. After that experience, I couldn't wait for cocktail hour. Dinner conversation was mainly in French, and I picked up what I could and just smiled and listened. Somewhere toward the end of the evening, as we were sitting around the fire in the bar puffing on Cuban cigars, Hans disappeared for a moment and came back to the table with a very old, dusty bottle in his hand. "Absinthe, anyone?" he asked. I had, of course, read about the wretched and forbidden drink but had never tasted it. It seemed the perfect place to try it, and as Lord Buckley would put it, "I took a slash." I can't really remember any dramatic change in my behavior. After all, dinner had started with rum punch, followed by several bottles of wine, but I can tell you that I dreamed incredible dreams that night—waterfalls, naked girls who smelled and tasted like orange blossoms, and giant crayfish that chased me down the road shouting out that they only wanted to eat my toes.

Those toes are now well in touch with the gray matter upstairs and are sensing the rudder of the Albatross. We have descended to the perfect flying-boat altitude of five hundred feet and are buzzing the harbor at Plymouth. The good thing about Dominica is that since there aren't many people here, we are in uncontrolled airspace, on nobody's radar, under clear blue skies. I take her over the tops of the few masts that are anchored in the harbor and then through a wide opening between two hills that sit on a small peninsula to the west of the island. I make a turn around the point and come back.

Thoughts of a touch-and-go landing flash through my mind, but I am still a little gun-shy, pardon the pun, from my Jamaica experiences, so I opt for just a very low pass. I catch a glimpse of a few black figures on the beach running along and waving as if they want to be swept up by the plane and taken along for the ride. We aren't exactly visitors from another planet, but I know that as I gain altitude and head for Guadeloupe we are the next best thing, and the few seconds of our appearance over Falmouth Bay will be talked about in the bars and on the beaches for a few more days.

Wonder Why We Ever Go Home

Date: 14 January 1997
Time: 2000Z
Latitude: 16°16′ N
Longitude: 61°31′5″ W

Location: Raizet Interna-
tional Airport, Pointe-à-
Pitre, Guadeloupe
Elevation: 36′
Weather: Partly cloudy

Comments: The field at Pointe-à-Pitre is way too familiar to me. During the years that I lived in St. Barts, going to town meant traveling to one of two places: St. Martin or Guadeloupe. St. Martin is the Los Angeles of the Caribbean. Its unique political roots go back to some treaty that split the island into a Dutch portion and a French portion, and today there is still evidence of the original colonial culture. The real culture today is based on cruise ships and jumbo jets. Some people still cling to their native tongues, but the language of the island is English, because most of the tourists that drive the economy come from America. Guadeloupe, on the other hand, is an appendage of the French colonial system. In the streets of Pointe-à-Pitre, you rarely hear English spoken. I preferred going to town in Pointe-à-Pitre, because it has a Creole link that I connected to. I get the same feeling in Fort-de-France and in Cap Haitien and Jacmel in Haiti. That French West Indian culture moved through these islands as a result of "wars and beheadin's, funerals and weddin's" and wound up on the shores of the northern Gulf of Mexico, where I was born into it. My grandmother spoke a patois in Pascagoula that was not much different from what I heard in the streets of Pointe-à-Pitre.

Most people I knew hated going to Guadeloupe. It had that much-ado-about-nothing feeling that hung in the air of all the island cities of the Caribbean: lots of noise, talk, hustle, and confusion, with not much really getting done. Pointe-à-Pitre

felt foreign and strange, exactly what I thought the French
West Indies were supposed to feel like.

Guadeloupe was also Kino's home and where a lot of his
family still lived. He, of course, spoke French and patois. On
my visits to the island, I inevitably tagged along with him. I
was welcomed with open arms into the homes of his aunts
and uncles, cousins and *cousines*. In a way, his island family
became my island family. Now, after landing and surviving
customs at the all-new airport, we drive out of the hustle and
bustle of rush-hour traffic and soon are cruising through the
cane fields toward his old family estate. We stay the evening at
Kino's uncle's house. It is one of several old Creole homes of
the family, who had carved up the original boundaries of the
plantation run by his eccentric grandfather.

Over dinner with Kino's cousin Mati and her husband,
Charlie, I listen to the recollections of life on the plantation,
from the visit of Pope Pius XII to the stories of Grandpère, who
tried to pass on to the workers in the cane fields his love of
opera by the introduction of outdoor speakers. I have this
bizarre vision of black field hands doing the backbreaking
work of cutting cane by hand as Puccini filled the humid air.
What in the hell must they have thought? But those days are
long gone. Guadeloupe is now an outpost of a socialist government in Paris that has no idea what its future will be. It sits
in limbo, a microcosm of the problems ailing the mother country across the ocean. Jobs are scarce and crime is high. A series
of hurricanes damaged the banana crops, and sugar prices are
not holding. There have been revolutionaries in the mountains
for years, who occasionally come down and blow up a car or a
power transformer.

As we drive to the airport the next morning, we talk about
the sentimentality we both seem to hold about the places we
came from. Kino is a world traveler, but he is still attached to
his roots in Guadeloupe. That kind of connection to the land is
also a very Southern trait. I too move around the globe in an al-

most constant state of motion, but when I think of home, I think about Pascagoula and the eastern shore of Mobile Bay, not Long Island or Florida. Home is where you come from. It is not where you live at the present time, and though I doubt I will ever live in Alabama again, I will always think of it as home.

> *Years grow shorter, not longer*
> *The more you've been on your own*
> *Feelin's for movin' grow stronger*
> *So you wonder why you ever go home*
> —"WONDER WHY WE EVER GO HOME"

Montserrat: Da Volcano Blow

Date: 14 January 1997
Time: 1500Z
Latitude: 16°43'7" N
Longitude: 62°07'8" W

Location: 2 mi. E of
Montserrat
Heading: 004°
Altitude: 3,500'
Weather: Overcast

Comments: I hear from another plane this morning as we are crossing the northern shore of Guadeloupe that the volcano on Montserrat is blowing its top again. It has already made the international news, when after one eruption the town of Plymouth was covered in ash and soon afterward the islanders had to be evacuated. There have been rumors of tidal waves and all kinds of other things that were being blamed on the volcano on Montserrat. The ash cloud is being blown to the west by the trade winds, and there are caution alerts for planes flying in that direction. A cloud full of volcanic ash could choke off the air supply to the best of engines and ruin a pilot's day. As I listen, though, traffic moving along the windward side of the island reports no problems and there is an excellent view of the steaming crater. I check my chart and pick up a new heading for the coast of Montserrat.

I have a personal attachment to this particular volcano. I went to Montserrat one winter to record an album at Air Studios. For the duration of recording camp I lived in the shadow of this dormant jungle peak and wrote a tongue-in-cheek song about it and its effect on island life. In terms of volcanoes, the Soufrière on Montserrat was considered a pipsqueak compared with nearby Mount Pelée on Martinique and Mount Misery on St. Kitts. I made several hikes up the mountain, where we would take mud baths in the hot sulfuric stream and feed mangoes to the giant iguanas that would appear out of the bush. When the recording was finished and we needed a name and a photo, we settled on *Volcano,* and hiked back up the hill. There I stood, right next to the vent of the volcano, and had my picture taken.

Now there is a layer of clouds at about ten thousand feet, which casts a gray shadow across the flat sea, but under it the weather is clear and the visibility is good. As we approach Montserrat, there is an eerie feeling in the air. It reminds me not of the lush tropical little piece of paradise where I lived, worked, and made lifelong friends one winter, but of Skull Island in the movie *King Kong.* I can't even recognize the coastline from the last time I had flown by it, nearly two years earlier. For starters, the top of the mountain where I stood to have my picture taken is gone, blown to smithereens, as is one whole side. Montserrat is known as the Emerald Isle, but the closer we get, the more I see that it has been singed almost beyond recognition. The landscape looks like a cross between pictures of Iwo Jima from World War II and the La Brea tar pits in downtown Los Angeles. Random steam vents pop through the lifeless valley that now runs to the sea, where a new peninsula is being formed by the lava and mud flow.

We make a radio report to the tower at the V. C. Bird Airport in Antigua, giving our location and the conditions. I think about all my friends here and hope that they made it out.

There has been talk of some kind of concert or benefit to aid the island people, and I am glad I am seeing the destruction firsthand. If the call comes asking me to do something for the survivors of the Emerald Isle, I will be there.

Nevis: Strange Bird Flying Low

Strange bird flying low
'Cross the Gulf of Mexico . . .
God only knows where the strange bird goes
When he's flying

—"STRANGE BIRD"

Date: 14 January 1997
Time: 1700Z
Latitude: 17°09'0" N
Longitude: 62°38'8"

Location: Nevis, West Indies, 1 mi. W of the Four Seasons Hotel
Heading: 349°
Altitude: 50'
Weather: Clear

Comments: We are flying along the coast of Nevis along one of my favorite stretches of beach in the Caribbean. Now there is a Four Seasons resort at one end and a lot more activity than when I used to pull my boat right up to the shore and take four-year-old Savannah Jane to the beach to watch the fishermen empty their nets in the morning. I am flying very low over the blue water when ahead of me and above me I see something that presents a problem—a parasail hanging in the sky. I have to dodge a lot of them up in Florida along the beach from West Palm to Miami, but I haven't seen one down here in a while. The biggest thrill on Nevis used to be riding Ira Dor's horses through the shallow salt water and up the hill to the old plantations. Well, we are about to invent a new ride. I make a 360-degree turn, dropped down till we are fifty feet above the ocean. The parasailer is drifting along dangling from the chute at an altitude of around two hundred feet. He never hears us coming, but when we go by and the noise of the exhaust and props stuns him, I see him hanging there with his mouth dropped open. I tip the wings, and the people on the boat pulling him are all waving, but he still just hangs there. I don't know who he is, or where he is from, but I do know we leave him with a lasting and unexpected memory of his Caribbean holiday.

St. Barts: Return to the Quiet Little Fishing Village

Like New Orleans, Key West, and Aspen, St. Barts is one of those places I have dwelled where I can pick up the thread of my life in an instant, whether I've been absent for two months or two years. It's like plugging a lamp back into the wall socket and illuminating the bulb of your life. For me as a pilot, the instant reentry to this particular kind of island life starts on the approach to the tiny runway behind the mountain. You don't routinely land in St. Barts. You make what amounts to a carrier landing. In the old days, watching planes land and, yes, watching some of them crash was the only real form of entertainment on the island. There were few Americans here, and the place was still just a quiet little fishing village. That, of course, has all changed. There are about as many rental cars as people, and the airport has ATM machines, parking lots, and a new terminal where the expatriates used to play softball on Sunday afternoon, with the rules being that each team had to have at least two Frenchmen in the outfield.

I know I can't land in the harbor of Gustavia because I attempted it long ago in my old Lake 250. The French, of course, have some very strange rules about seaplanes, and on this island, where both I and my planes are well known, I can't fake unawareness. Unfortunately, I know the rules in St. Barts. Still, I make an approach to landing and bring the *Hemisphere Dancer* in over the hill, then fly down the length of the runway and out over Bay St. Jean before turning for the Grand Casse Airport on the French side of St. Martin. I might not be able to land, but at least my family knows I'm in the area. Below us on the sand beach in front of Chez Francine I see people ducking as we roar overhead. That is always the sign of a good flyover. An hour later I'm in the same position above the runway, but this time my old friend Larry Gray, chief pilot, ticket taker, and tire kicker for Air Mango and former captain of the *Euphoria II*, was guiding his old trusty Aztec to a smooth landing. Waiting at the airport snack bar are my barefoot children, clad in bathing suits and ready to take off for the beach at Saline. It looks like adaptability to island life is a family trait with the Buffetts.

A Graveyard by the Sea

The day I first laid eyes on St. Barts, Larry "Groovy" Gray, Jane, Tom Corcoran, and I had sailed over from Marigot in St. Martin. It was near dark when we arrived, and after consulting our guidebook, we decided to just anchor off for the night and come into the harbor and clear in the next day. It was a perfectly calm night on the water with little breeze, a slightly rolling sea, and a full moon rising to the east. By the light of the moon, we sailed south past the harbor and rounded up in a small cove called Gouverneur. Here we anchored up, went ashore, cooked out on the beach, and slept the night. Early the next morning as we were getting under way to head back to the harbor, a school of pilot whales surrounded the boat and swam with us all the way. It was only after being in St. Barts for quite a while that I realized what an amazing first night that had been. First of all, Gouverneur lies on the edge of the windward side of the island, and there is usually a heavy beach break and swirling winds ricocheting off the surrounding hills, making it a most unpleasant anchorage. I have never seen the ocean as calm as it was that night. I took it as an undeniable sign that this was a magical place.

That morning, as we sailed into the picturesque harbor of Gustavia for the first time, I thought I was starring in my own version of *Adventures in Paradise,* replacing Gardner McKay as Captain Adam Troy. I stood behind the wheel of the *Euphoria II,* the early-morning light framing the teardrop-shaped harbor and the buildings that composed the waterfront. Again I saw those ironwork balconies that marked the port as French. There was a religious statue on the hill above us to the left, and below the hill across the sand path that bordered the beach was the prettiest little cemetery that I had ever seen. If there was ever a place to rest in peace, that looked like the spot, and I told myself right at that moment that it looked like the perfect place to spend eternity. Years later, however, as St. Barts got more popular, a fence was erected around the graveyard and a rent-a-car storage lot was constructed across the street. I have now decided not to spend eternity there. I am still looking for the right spot on the right beach.

Captain, My Captain

Captain Groovy had been my sailing partner since I rented a small catamaran from his stand at the Pier House when I first moved to Key West. Groovy and Jane had been friends since they were roommates at the University of South Carolina in Columbia back in the sixties. We were drinking buddies at the Chart Room, and it was Groovy who had invited Jane down to Key West, where I met her through him.

I actually didn't know I had met her, because she and two other friends were crashing at Groovy's apartment and living out of the same backpack. Jane's two friends looked very much like her. We had met briefly in a phone booth outside the Chart Room, where Groovy introduced us. The next time I saw her was at Louie's Backyard, where she was dining with

her parents and wearing a tight, long, pink dress that made a
lasting impression on me. For the next couple of nights I was
moving around the bars and restaurants pursuing the knock-
out friend of Groovy's in the pink dress. What I didn't know
at the time was that all the girls were sharing the same dress
and I was actually making my move on several women at the
same time. Jane cleared that one up, and I happily found myself having dinner with the right girl in the pink dress.

Groovy and I shared a love of nonsense, staying up late,
and, more important, of the ocean. He was a natural waterman
and the kind of guy you want around when the shit hits the
fan. The shit did hit the fan a few times later on when he became the captain of the *Euphoria*, my first sailboat, and I was
glad he was along. Groovy was the only other sailor I knew
from Key West who had taught himself celestial navigation.
After several years of skippering my boat, he bought his own
boat and then singlehandedly sailed the Atlantic. I remember
asking him when he finally arrived safely on this side of the big
pond whether he had seen God. He just said flatly, "Bubba, believe me, I looked for him out there, but I never found him, at
least not on the piece of ocean I traveled. Maybe he lives in
Bermuda in the winter."

When I decided to take up flying, Groovy wasn't far behind. My sailing buddy became my flying buddy. When I
decided to move home from the islands, Groovy came back
for a while and tried to fit in, but it wasn't in his nature.
Today he lives happily in St. Barts and runs his own little
charter company called Air Mango. He is a great pilot,
though I get on his ass about how bald his tires are. He tells
me I worry too much. I always look forward to visiting St.
Barts and hearing his stories. It takes a storyteller to know
a storyteller, and I find myself today living vicariously
through his island exploits. But back in the winter of 1976,
neither of us had any idea of the part St. Barts would play in
both our lives.

The Children of the Moon

The morning of my first arrival in the harbor, I was busy cleaning up the boat when a small dinghy full of young kids approached. It was driven by a tanned young girl with long blond hair. She was about eight years old, but her skills with a dinghy told me that she had been raised on a boat. The young helmswoman eased the throttle and pulled alongside us. I could smell that wonderful aroma of fresh baked dough coming across the water from the port, and my stomach began to growl. "You're Jimmy Buffett, aren't you?" one of the little boys said.

"Yes, I am," I replied.

"We are the children of the moon," they chimed in.

"Welcome to Earth," I said.

"No, not the real moon. That's the name of our boat," a younger girl said with a laugh.

"Oh, I'm relieved. I thought I was being boarded by aliens," I called back. "Come aboard, if you like."

"Thank you, but we have to get back to the boat and do our school work." One of the tow-haired, tanned little boys lifted up a brown paper bag that had a little grease smudge leaking through, and I knew where that bakery aroma had come from. "We brought you a little present to welcome you to the island," he said.

"We hope you stay a long time," the helmswoman said. "You have lots of fans here. If you want to know what's going on, just go to Le Select. They already know you're here." She cranked the little British Seagull engine, and they putted off in the direction of a double-ended ketch anchored across the harbor.

The children of the *Moon* were Mishka, Magnus, Heather, and Suzanne. I would meet their parents that evening, who in turn introduced me to their friends, who happened to be the right people to know on the island. It only took about twenty minutes for me to know that St. Barts would be home for a while. By dinner that evening, I knew I had found another spot. It was that same kind of feeling that I had about Key West the first night I set foot in the Chart Room bar. I wrote a song about my little friends a few years later called "Chanson Pour Les Petits Enfants." They are all grown up now and have gone on to become not lawyers, thieves, or bankers, but hot-dog windsurfers and folksingers. To me they will always be the children of the *Moon*.

Stopping by the Office

It has been twenty-one years since I walked into Le Select the first time after the children of the *Moon* had brought me my *petit déjeuner*. The courtyard now sports a brand-new brick patio that has replaced the shell and hard-packed-dirt floor, but other than that, things haven't changed that much. The pictures of Bob Marley and the king and queen of Sweden still adorn the beams, along with photos, flags, and other memorabilia that have been left by patrons through the years. The stuffed bee still hangs precariously by a worn piece of waxed sail thread above the bar, though the fur on his ass is worn thin from the many shots it has taken with champagne corks. Le Select is shoe-box–sized compared with the new hotels and beach bistros that have recently come on the scene, but it still possesses that unique sense of place that can serve as the heart of the local social hub as well as being an oasis for travelers and a photo opportunity for tourists. And like a shoe box, for me it holds a lot of island memories.

Since I'm only going to be on the island for a couple of days on this trip, all I really need to do is see the people I want to see and stop by the "office" in the afternoon for a *petite punch*. It is there that I met Kino, Maya, Randy and Nicole Maurius, Eddie, Lucien, Maxi Taxi, Maurice, and the rest of the local crowd. It's where I picked up my mail in the old days, and it was the switchboard of the Coconut Telegraph, where the bartenders knew who was on the island and who was not. It is where we went to celebrate the purchase of our dream hotel, Autour du Rocher. After that fateful purchase, it is where I danced with Joni Mitchell on the dirt floor and then took her to our hotel to play "Carey" for Groovy on his birthday. It was our version of day care, where we would leave our rug rats with Maxi or Maurius or Helena while we buzzed about town doing our chores. It is where I wrote "Little Miss Magic" for Savannah Jane. Le Select was part of her growing up as well, and now I hear her on occasion tell stories of her own recollections. Like how she learned her first French words from the firemen, whom she would beat constantly on the pinball machine in the corner of the bar. It is where she returned one afternoon with tears in her eyes and blood running from her little ears after we had decided that she should get her ears pierced at the local leather shop. It was in the bar that I had to clear myself with Maurius and the local population after the fiasco of events, including my arrest, after the infamous *Rolling Stone*–cover affair. It is where I sold the *Euphoria II,* and it is where, seated at the little table by the front door, I almost bought *Ticonderoga,* the boat of my dreams, from Ken MacKenzie for an amazingly low price. It is where on different occasions I ran into Mick Fleetwood and John McVie, Bobby Short, Lauren Hutton, Mikhail Baryshnikov, Steve Martin, Lorne Michaels, Paul Simon, and a host of other celebrity gypsies who came and went from the island. It is where I played to some of the wildest crowds I have ever seen from the corner of a sardine-packed bar where they splashed the floor with champagne so that it was more slippery to dance on. And it is where we toasted the end of an era when Autour du Rocher burned to the ground.

Now, the day before our departure for the final leg of our trip back home, I sit at a corner table on the patio sipping my punch, listening to Bob Marley, like I have done a thousand times before. I'm trying to get used to the new floor under my tapping feet when the mayor strolls into the bar with some friends. He is also a pilot and worked in the tower at the airport before being elected. I know he appreciates airplanes, and if anyone can get me permission to land in French waters, it's Bruno. We say our hellos, and then I bring up the subject. He says he'll see what he can do. Well, it isn't no. I'm making progress. The bar quickly fills up, and the smell of grilled onions coming from the Cheeseburger in Paradise Grill fills the air. Many years ago, I gave Eddie Skatelborough permission to use my song title as the name of the hamburger stand in exchange for a lifetime tab. I saw pictures once in an old hotel of Nazi submarines anchored in the harbor of nearby Isle de Fourche, where Bartians were loading diesel fuel from their fishing boats onto the decks of the subs. Barter is the only true economics of the island.

My kids arrive with Angela and Aileen from the beach for supper. Like Savannah before them, they take to the surroundings like little birds in a familiar nest. The pinball machine is now a video game with bells and whistles and audio chips that go off regularly. It attracts them like a magnet. The patio begins to fill but with more unfamiliar faces than familiar ones. The bar crowd from my era has been hit hard by the pitfalls of island living. Some are dead. Some are in jail. Many, like me, have moved back to the mainland, but some are still here, stuck like glue to the worn-out barstools. The era of pirates and vagabonds who called St. Barts their favorite port of call in the seventies and eighties has given way to cruise ships and castles in the hills. But Le Select keeps the pulse of the island alive and kicking, and I can come back and plug in anytime.

Around the Rock, One Last Time

Follow in my wake
You've not that much at stake
For I have plowed the seas
And smoothed the troubled waters
Come along, let's have some fun.
The hard work has been done
We'll barrel roll into the sun
Just for starters

—"BAROMETER SOUP"

The ruins of my old hotel sit atop the promontory hill that borders the beautiful bay of Lorient. As ruins go, it looks sadly like only the latest monument to Folly chasing Death's ass around through these islands. The place is now just a heap of burned-out remnants that somehow survived the back-to-back hurricanes that ravaged the rest of the island. Owning a hotel in the Caribbean requires a lot of misguided reasoning. Just ask Norman Paperman. But I wouldn't trade the experiences that came my way as a result of owning a small part of Autour for the world, which is what I told my accountant the day I invested in the place. It was a five-room hotel, a restaurant, and a big open bar. In its heyday, the place was the staging ground for some of the worst behavior I have ever seen. It was the only hotel I ever heard of that had a jewelry store that opened at midnight and closed at five in the morning.

The drill went something like this: It would be empty until about one in the morning, when the restaurants emptied out and the masses would arrive. There was no parking lot, just an open field where the Mokes and Gurgels* would stack up like cordwood at the bottom of the steps that led to the bar.

* Cheap Brazilian cars made of fiberglass

We had no idea how to run a hotel, and we certainly didn't make any money, but we made our mark. The French hated us until the very end, just for being American and for being smart enough to buy the property in the first place. When I heard the news that the hotel had burned down, my suspicions were immediately aroused and I started putting together a list of the opportunistic sharks who I thought could have been arsonists, but as fate would have it, the fire started in the deejay booth of the disco.

One of the great tales of St. Barts will always be the party after the fire. The fire occurred before Christmas, so there was nowhere to go for New Year's Eve. Somehow, someone got permission from the mayor to let us have one last fling. And so out of the woodwork they all came. Waiters, carpenters, tycoons, fashion models, and one aging singer to scrape up the makings of one last New Year's Eve bash from the ashes of the disco meltdown.

I had not seen that kind of celebration since my Carnival-in-Rio days, but up the hill they came, and friends, did we have a party. All I am allowed to tell you is that after having a total blast, I left the premises at about three in the morning and went home. When I awoke on New Year's Day and walked out onto my balcony, in the distance I could still see a nearly full field of cars below the ruins. I dressed quickly and drove over to the hotel, and they were still going strong. No one wanted Autour to die. They were sitting around drunk and crying, telling me how we couldn't sell the place, that it had to live. It reminded me of film clips of people trying to rescue beached whales and send them out to sea, when in fact the whales already know they're dead and turn around and head back to shore.

It's all just another chapter in the history of the once-quiet little fishing village now. One last time around the rock, and then I am headed for the airport and will be home in Palm Beach in a day. The smell of the olive trees rides on the trade winds and there is a nice left break out over the reef in the bay. As if it were a sign to move on, our old neighbor and partner in the bizarre, Jean Marie Rivere, had just died and the Caribbean version of the Folies-Bergère that he put on every night at La Banane was gone with him. We sold the property a few years ago. It was more than just a real estate sale. It was the end of an era. Out past Cock Rock, a small sailboat rode the African rollers on a broad reach with her bow pointed in my direction. Were they travelers like we had been, leaving a boring or volatile past behind them on the way to making up a new life? Hell, I hope so. It had worked for me, and I hoped it worked for them.

St. Barts has such a place in Caribbean history that it could be a whole book, which I am sure some younger, more inquisitive, and commercially driven writer than myself will attempt to write someday. I can see it on the counter at Borders now, with a title like *St. Barts: From Cannibals to Haute Couture.* My small portion of that history has been a lovely, exciting, and sometimes dangerous cruise. It was from my base in St. Barts that I set off hell-bent for excitement in boats and planes and explored the Leeward Islands, where I found my stories, my songs, and my life. And though I have moved on in terms of a roosting place, like a predictable comet I am bound by the laws of physics, nature, and romanticism to revisit this place as I follow my predestined orbit with a little less fire in my tail than there used to be.

Back on the Triple Nickel

Date: 17 January 1997   Location: Gustavia Airport,
Time: 1500Z   St. Barts
Latitude: 17°54′7″ N   Elevation: 20′
Longitude: 62°40′1″ W   Weather: Clear

Comments: After a couple of days of seeing friends, lounging on the beach, sailing aboard *Ticonderoga*, and eating dinner
at Maya's restaurant, I unplug myself and we load the caravan
up for our hopscotch flight from St. Barts to Grand Casse. We
manage to sidestep the now constant hustle and bustle at the St.
Barts terminal, and with Groovy's influence we ease our way
through the cargo area to our waiting plane. The usual suspects
show up to bid us farewell. Maurice brings me a picture, and
my old friend Jerome Lefort is there to help with the gear. At
Grand Casse, Randy is waiting with the jet for Jane and the kids.
They will be in Palm Beach in about three hours, the time it will
take us to get to our first stop on the old familiar slow road up
Amber 555, the air artery from the Caribbean to the States, better known among those who fly it as the Triple Nickel.

There is the usual cloud cover over Puerto Rico, but we stay
well to the north and ride a slight tailwind out over the open
water. A couple of hours later, the green shallow water of the
Mooches Bank appears below us, and shortly after that the
thin lip of land to the northwest that I know to be Grand Turk.
Just before dark we drop down to pattern altitude and come
back to the earth. I taxi past the spot where I first laid eyes on
an Albatross. I have come full circle from the then-burning desire to own one, and now I have come back, almost as if to a
shrine to give thanks.

There is no one here to cover the event. In fact, it is just another one of those shitty days in paradise. Some charter plane
from the Dominican Republic can't get an engine started, and
they're ferrying passengers back to Santo Domingo in single-

engine Cessnas. The crew of the *Hemisphere Dancer,* with all of their paperwork properly filled out and with passports in hand are a welcome sight. We are cleared through in a matter of minutes and are in a cab on the way to the hotel.

The next morning Kino and I ride out to the hotel with a wonderful old cabdriver named Lawrence, who rules his world from behind the steering wheel of his 1982 Chevy wagon. He has a cell phone, a VHF marine radio, and a walkie-talkie lined up on his dashboard. A pine-tree air freshener hangs from the rearview mirror, and he greets us with a warm smile. "Dat's a fine airplane you got out dere. You know, dere was one of dose parked here for de longest time. I think it was a dope plane, and den one day it be gone." He snaps his fingers and adds, "Just like dat. Dat ain't da same plane, is it?"

"No, but I remember that old plane, too," I reply.

"Where you fellas been?" he asks.

"All over," Kino says.

"Don't say. I been all around myself. I left dis rock back when I was a teenager. Not enough to keep me here, had to see da world. Got a job on a boat in Miami cooking. I didn't know much about cooking, but den I kind of got into it, and a good chef could always get a job on a ship. Worked on freighters, worked on cruise ships. Cooked my way around de whole world from Europe to Japan and South America. Spent nearly tirty years on ships."

"What made you quit?" I ask.

"Dey ran out of ketchup," Lawrence replies, and laughs, as do we. "No, I don't know, I guess it was because I had seen it all. Deez days most travelin' anybody wants to do is to Disney World. I come from a different time. I was dat black sheep dat da Bible talked about, and I ain't talkin' 'bout my skin. I wanted to see it all. When I finally did, dat's when I came home. I just said dat it was time."

We pull up in front of the airport, and Lawrence helps us with our bags and walks out to the plane with us. I toss the last bags up the ladder to Alex, pay Lawrence, and tell Alex to hand me a CD from the swag box, which I hand to the driver. We shake hands, and he gives me one of his cards and tells us if we are ever back on the island to give him a call. I walk up to the flight deck and strap myself in. Lawrence is standing in front of the plane looking up at me. He lets out a little whistle, shakes his head, and laughs. "I bet you could cover some territory wif dis machine. It kind of gets dat old adventure blood goin', don't it?"

I poke my head out the window and shout back to him, "It certainly does."

Epilogue

The next day, in the completely comfortable and homey waters of Staniel Cay in the Exumas Islands, I finally land in the water. It has been so long since I have made a water landing that I just want to see if I can still do it. There are a few bumps and a power change or two right before touchdown, but I set her down on the water with a wings-level attitude, savoring that wonderfully strange sensation as we bump across over the small waves until I finally pull her off the step. We haven't had a wet hull since that one rescue in Costa Rica, but I have learned a lot. Some of the places we visited I will certainly return to, while others I may never see again. But my knowledge about how and where to fly has increased tremendously. I have the information I can only get by going out there and finding it.

By the time the sun sets on January 18, I am back on the balcony of my house, staring out at the sea in the direction from which I have just come. We followed a 4,700-mile ellipse around the shores of the Caribbean Sea in about three weeks. It wasn't Concorde speed, but that wasn't the point of the trip. The world spun away from the sun, and the darkness moved in. A dying star dropped from space, falling brightly against the backdrop of time in motion, but unlike most falling stars that I have wished upon in this life, it kept going down into the last rays of daylight before it disappeared from sight. We have made it home. The plane is in one piece, and all crew and passengers are accounted for. It should be a time for reflection and satisfaction at completing such a circle, and thoughts of that nature certainly run through my mind. But as I stand on this balcony, I see the lights of a ship heading east toward the night, and I can't help but wonder where it's going and what its passengers are up to. I've been home barely an hour, and I'm thinking of where to go next. What is that all about?

Now, sitting in the same room, a year to the day after that homecoming, I am drawing this journal to a close. I take a moment to quietly move about the room and check in with a few old friends for some parting words. I scan my favorite books: Beryl Markham, Don Sheldon, Mark Twain, and then I pick up an old copy of Don Blanding, and there they are, the words I need to close out this section of the book and this chapter of my life.

The Double Life

by

Don Blanding

How very simple life would be
If only there were two of me
A Restless Me to drift and roam
A Quiet Me to stay at home.
A Searching One to find his fill
Of varied skies and newfound thrill
While sane and homely things are done
By the domestic Other One.

And that's just where the trouble lies;
There is a Restless Me that cries
For chancy risks and changing scene,
For arctic blue and tropic green,
For deserts with their mystic spell,
For lusty fun and raising Hell

But shackled to that Restless Me
My Other Self rebelliously
Resists the frantic urge to move.
It seeks the old familiar groove
That habits make. It finds content
With hearth and home—dear prisonment,
With candlelight and well-loved books
And treasured loot in dusty nooks,

With puttering and garden things
And dreaming while a cricket sings
And all the while the Restless One
Insists on more exciting fun,
It wants to go with every tide,
No matter where . . . just for the ride.
Like yowling cats the two selves brawl
Until I have no peace at all.

One eye turns to the forward track,
The other eye looks sadly back.
I'm getting wall-eyed from the strain,
(It's tough to have an idle brain)
But One says "Stay" and One says "Go"
And One says "Yes," and One says "no,"
And One Self wants a home and wife
And One Self craves the drifter's life.

The Restless Fellow always wins
I wish my folks had made me twins.

Unlike the rest of my attempts at completing a journal, this one will not have to live out its life on paper stuffed in one of those cedar boxes filled with unfinished business. No, it will make its way to the bookshelf above my fly-tying desk and rest with copies of my other books in a far corner near my research books, just past the saltwater-fishing section. As the song says, "The stories from my favorite books, take on many different looks and I'm home again gone again."

Jimmy Buffett
Palm Beach, Florida
January 17, 1998

Singer-songwriter JIMMY BUFFETT has recorded over thirty albums, which include the two hit singles "Margaritaville" and "Come Monday." He is also the author of two bestselling books—*Tales from Margaritaville* and *Where Is Joe Merchant?* He plays to sold-out stadiums across America every summer, and his "parrothead" followers are known to be among the most devoted fans in the music industry. Currently, Buffett is collaborating with Herman Wouk on a musical, *Don't Stop the Carnival*. He resides in Florida, summers on Long Island, and has managed to keep the same summer job for thirty-four years.

ABOUT THE TYPE

The text of this book was set in Palatino, designed by the German ty-
pographer Herman Zapf. It was named after the Renaissance calligra-
pher Giovanbattista Palatino. Zapf designed it between 1948–52, and it
was his first typeface to be introduced in America. It is a face of unusual
elegance.